SPECTRAL ANALYSIS
OF ECONOMIC TIME SERIES

PRINCETON STUDIES IN MATHEMATICAL ECONOMICS

NUMBER I

SPECTRAL ANALYSIS OF ECONOMIC TIME SERIES

BY C. W. J. GRANGER

IN ASSOCIATION WITH

M. HATANAKA

1964

PRINCETON UNIVERSITY PRESS

PRINCETON, NEW JERSEY

Dedicated To

All Those Whose Work Provided Both

Insight and Encouragement

FOREWORD

Considering the long time that economists have been occupied with time series, it is striking that the evolution of advanced notions and correspondingly sophisticated methods for their analysis has progressed as slowly as has been the case. Only quite recently has the analysis of economic time series reached a level commensurate with the inherent difficulties. The development of spectral analysis, of which this book gives one of the first comprehensive accounts and to which it makes significant contributions, is an event of great importance. There can be no doubt that the powerful new methods now available are going to transform completely the study of economic time series. These methods will be developed further; but even in their present state they yield new insights into economic relationships which were not expected, and they have put on a firmer basis others which heretofore could not be sufficiently justified.

It was natural that economists should try to distinguish several "components" of a time series, to compute and eliminate each one in order to study them separately. But the methods available for their separation were too simple for the inherent difficulties; and it was not until 1936 that A. Wald presented ideas that were a match for the tasks involved. His work on seasonal variations has unfortunately remained unknown, at least in the Anglo-American literature. In addition, it is clear that any attempt restricted to merely those components for which a plausibility argument could be developed, mostly based on subjective, common sense ideas, was inadequate given the complexity of the phenomenon.

Thus it would have been logical to look at methods developed in the sciences and astronomy. Fourier analysis had established itself firmly in the natural sciences and further methods were derived from it. Yet economists paid hardly any attention to these developments, repelled by the idea that rather irregular "cyclical" movements should be rooted in notions of "periodicities." Furthermore they were unfamiliar with computing tasks which were commonplace, for instance, in astronomy. The few attempts to apply Fourier analysis were rejected, since inconclusive use was made of the method and perhaps also because too few coefficients were calculated. Thus the subjective approach prevailed, extremely simple direct "observation" of alleged peaks and troughs was made and, consequently, very little information was obtained from time series thus analyzed. This procedure is contrary to the spirit of statistical analysis where every effort is made to extract the last amount of information from data that are difficult to obtain.

When I confronted him with the issues involved, it was not difficult to arouse the interest of John von Neumann in these matters. Soon the plan arose for us to attempt a large scale application of Fourier analysis to economic series and to make such modifications of this theory as would conform to the properties of the series and be in accordance with better formulated analytical goals. Since this was prior to the advent of high speed digital electronic computers, we considered building analogue computers, modeled after those used by some neurologists at that time. However, since the digital computers would have been so vastly superior to such devices and von Neumann already was building his own (later to become a model for so many other developments in this field), our work was postponed time and again. When the computer finally became available it had to be devoted at first to other, more pressing work in atomic physics. The untimely death of von Neumann in 1957 destroyed our plans, but to the last he urged that I not give up in the endeavour.

In the meantime great strides had been made in spectral analysis and the entire field of prediction theory had been in active development. Some of the finest results in modern mathematics were obtained in these areas. So it was gratifying that John Tukey, one of the key figures in this splendid movement, took an enduring interest in the efforts to put economic time series analysis on a modern basis. Clive W. J. Granger undertook the work of which this book is one of the first fruits.

The economist will find much in this volume that is unfamiliar to him and he will be required to re-think many of his usual concepts as well as to learn new ones that do not easily fit into accepted patterns. Yet this is to be expected whenever powerful new mathematical methods, germane to the subject matter, are being introduced. Such progress always requires new concepts and new techniques and, now, these are coupled with the intricacies and enormous power of present day digital electronic computers. Without the latter there would be little application. Even more, these modern facilities offer possibilities of experimental exploration which can serve to guide theoretical work. The present book makes ingenious use of these new possibilities and thereby advances our understanding in critical areas (such as the role of non-stationarity of economic time series). It is now clear that whatever validity there may have been in rejecting conventional techniques of Fourier analysis for economic time series, such considerations no longer apply. Spectral analysis rests on solid ground and its development and application to economics is an event of first-order importance. The study of economic fluctuations, in the large as well as for individual markets such as the stock market, is put on a new, firmer basis with results that even in this early stage foreshadow the need for substantial revisions of some of our notions about the dynamics of the economy. The two chapters contributed by Michio Hatanaka give an idea of what is in store in that respect. These results reveal that we are confronted with far more complicated relationships than are normally recognized and that there are many notions which, though widely believed, are spurious.

Firmly convinced, therefore, of the significance of spectral analysis and anticipating further developments of the method, I believe that this book will have a profound and lasting influence. It will contribute toward moving economics from an often intuitively oriented and severely limited approach to a germane penetration by proven modern concepts and methods. The book is written in the same spirit in which during the last two or three decades a number of notable contributions have been made to economic science.

This present work will be followed by other studies sponsored by the Econometric Research Program of Princeton University in the area of time series analysis. These will deal more specifically with applications of the new methods, but it is in the nature of things that these too can be expected to undergo further development as they manifest the fact that economics and economic statistics are jointly in a phase of vital growth.

Oskar Morgenstern

Econometric Research Program
Princeton University

PREFACE

A time series is a sequence of data, almost certainly intercorrelated, each of which is associated with a moment of time. As the majority of data in economics is found in the form of time series it has long been recognized that the development of sophisticated and powerful methods for analyzing such series is of importance when questions such as the testing of economic hypotheses are discussed. Many of the earlier methods have not proved satisfactory and it is thus clearly sensible to ask if methods used with success in other disciplines could not be used in economics. The most obvious of the new methods that needed to be considered was spectral analysis.

The main object of this volume is to report upon the methods developed by members of the Time Series Project at the Econometric Research Program of Princeton University. The Project was directed by Professor Oskar Morgenstern and was also particularly fortunate in being advised from its earliest days by Professor John Tukey who made available to us many of his unpublished methods of analysis. The other members of the Econometric Research Program particularly concerned with the Time Series Project were Michael Godfrey, Michio Hatanaka, Herman Karreman, Mitsuo Suzuki, Thomas Wonnacott, and the author.

Upon being initiated into the use of spectral methods by Professor Tukey, we were soon convinced of their potential importance, particularly the use of cross-spectral methods to discover and describe the possibly complex inter-relationships between economic variables. There were, however, two main obstacles to the direct use of these methods to economics. The first was that a re-orientation of many of our previous concepts of economic theory was required before the results of spectral analysis could be usefully interpreted. To non-mathematicians, the usefulness of presenting results in terms of frequencies is not immediately obvious but it is felt that once the great flexibility of this approach is appreciated it becomes important to recast many economic hypothesis in terms of frequencies instead of distributed lags or simple correlations.

Our second main obstacle was that, strictly, spectral methods may only be used on stationary data whereas it is obvious that few if any economic series are stationary. Much of the effort of the Project has been directed to the problems of either how to make economic data less non-stationary or to discovering whether or not spectral methods can extract useful information from series which are not completely stationary. The first of these problems chiefly concerns the development of efficient methods of removing trends in means. We are now confident, using the methods outlined in Chapter 8 and given sufficient data, that any undesirable effects due to such trends can be minimized. The effects of certain other forms of non-stationarity on spectral methods have been investigated both empirically and, in a non-rigorous manner, theoretically in Chapter 9. Although the study of non-stationary series is in its very early stages, we are at the moment confident that spectral methods can provide useful results when used with non-stationary series generated by processes which appear intuitively realistic for economics.

This book attempts both to promote the use of methods of analysis which are new to economics and to present and justify some entirely new methods in time series analysis. This has presented many problems of presentation as these two diverse objectives require two entirely different levels of mathematical sophistication. Thus an attempt has been made to follow each mathematically-orientated section or chapter by a non-mathematical discussion of the results. These non-mathematical sections often proceed in terms of analogies and intuitive reasoning. It should be remembered, however, that many of the basic concepts used in spectral methods are conceptually difficult, particularly the Cramér representation of a stationary series and the basic implications of the cross-spectrum. It is hoped that the non-mathematical sections will aid comprehension; but readers should be warned that if the analogies and the semi-intuitive reasoning are carried too far they are likely to give misleading results.

The presentation is chiefly aimed at graduate students taking advanced courses in econometrics, econometricians, and those statisticians who advise economists, although it is hoped that a much wider class of research workers will also find new concepts and techniques which will be useful to them.

It appears to be impossible to choose a perfect moment to record the methods of a quickly developing field. At all times, new and exciting possibilities are being considered, new results are appearing, and fresh experience is accumulated. Thus it is felt that any book on spectral methods appearing at the present time must be in many ways incomplete and should be considered as a progress report. Since the first draft was prepared, for example, a number of important and basic ideas in the field of non-stationary series have been proposed, new information is available concerning the problem of removing annual fluctuations from a series and a new method of constructing highly efficient filters has been discovered. If time were taken to insert these developments into the text, doubtless further results would by then become available, and so forth. Nevertheless these new results mainly represent further developments of a number of basic methods and as no full account of these methods is at present available it is hoped that their presentation here at this time is justified.

Although the whole Time Series Project has been a team effort, certain aspects of the work have been particularly connected with certain people and I feel that these should be acknowledged. The interpretation of cross-spectra and the demodulation technique were shown to us by John Tukey, the partial cross-spectral methods were developed by Thomas Wonnacott, and the considerable and important task of preparing the numerous computer programs for our various computers has been organized and, for the large majority, personally carried out by Herman Karreman. (A research memorandum, No. 59, giving the more important of these computer programs in Fortran language for use on an IBM 7090 computer is available from the Econometric Research Program, Princeton University, 92A Nassau Street, Princeton, N.J., U.S.A.)

I would like to thank Oskar Morgenstern for his continual encouragement and inspiration; Michio Hatanaka for his help at all stages in the preparation of this book and in particular for the two important studies using spectral methods which appear as chapters twelve and thirteen; John Tukey for showing us his extremely effective, if somewhat individualistic, methods of analyzing a time series; both Mitsuo Suzuki and Herman Karreman for advising and correcting the first draft of the manuscript; my wife Patricia for help with numerous details, and Mr. J. Wilson of Princeton University Press for preparing the book for publication. I would also like to thank numerous friends and acquaintances who by constant help and discussion have helped form the climate of opinion and experience within which this book was written. I would finally like to thank Professor Tew and Professor Pitt of the University of Nottingham, England, who have encouraged and enabled me to make the four trips to the United States which has made my part in this work possible.

I would like to emphasize that the views and opinions expressed in the book are mine alone and that any remaining errors are entirely my own responsibility.

The Time Series Project has been supported by a grant from the National Science Foundation and some individual members of the Project have been partially supported by grants from the office of Naval Research and the Rockefeller Foundation. My own first year in Princeton was as a Harkness Fellow of the Commonwealth Fund.

The manuscript was typed by Mrs. Lois Crooks, Mrs. Helen Peek, and Miss Helen Perna to whom I also wish to express my gratitude.

C. W. J. Granger,
Princeton, August, 1963.

CONTENTS

CONTENTS

Chapter 5. *Cross-spectral Analysis*

Chapter 6. *Cross-spectral Analysis*
of Economic Data

Chapter 7. *Processes Involving Feedback*

PART B.   NON-STATIONARY TIME SERIES
Chapter 8. *Series With Trending Means*

Chapter 9. *Series with Spectrum*
Changing with Time

⟨ xvi ⟩

CONTENTS

CONTENTS

SPECTRAL ANALYSIS
OF ECONOMIC TIME SERIES

CHAPTER 1

INTRODUCTION TO THE ANALYSIS OF TIME SERIES

1.1 Introduction

The world contains a very large number of phenomena which change with time, and any collection of data measuring some aspect of such phenomena and ordered with respect to increasing time may be thought of as comprising a time series. Simple examples would be hourly temperature readings, rainfall per month, daily stock prices, or weekly number of births, as these all determine a series of numbers with associated time parameter. The examples given are all discrete series, that is, readings which are taken at set times, usually equally spaced. If we consider a device which continually traces the local temperature on a roll of paper, we would now have a reading for every moment of time, an example of a continuous time series. Electrical engineers are almost solely concerned with such series, but economists, among others, are likely to meet only discrete series. It may be possible, for instance, to define theoretically the stock market price for Woolworth's for every instant of the day, but it would be less meaningfully defined when the stock market is closed. Alternatively, the daily opening price for the stock would comprise a more precisely defined series, and is much more likely to be used. Throughout this volume, we will be concerned only with discrete series.

Once data are available, there is immediately a desire to extract from them useful information and to put the data to use. The steps in the analysis of a single series might be considered as follows: (i) investigation, (ii) model fitting, and (iii) application.

The investigation stage will consist of forming useful summary statistics and making comments such as "the series is always positive," "feature X accounts for $\alpha\%$ of the total variance," or "the mean value of the series appears to be steadily increasing with time." Some of these results can be obtained by visual inspection, and the chart of the series, its components, and summary statistics calculated from it will play an important part in any analysis.

Concerning model building, Whittle [24][1] has written: "Suppose we are presented with a finite series of observations, and are asked to fit a model to it. We may regard the selection of the model as taking place in three stages:

[1] Numbers such as [24] refer to the list of references found at the end of each chapter.

(a) the limitation of the choice to a finite number of plausible model types,
(b) the selection of one of these types,
(c) the selection of a model from all the models possible within this type, i.e., the numerical selection of the parameters."

At one time the fitting of models to the available data was considered an essential part of the analysis but the more recent methods do not place any great emphasis on model-building. This is particularly true when relationships between series are considered, as the relationships are likely to be so complicated that only with great difficulty can they be fitted into an easily understood model.

Applications of the results derived from an analysis will be, for economics at least, either of a predictive nature or as "facts" to be compared to a particular economic theory. The interplay between experimental results and theories in physics has led to great advances in the subject, and it is hoped that the sequence of finding theories to fit the facts and finding new facts for theories to account for will also strengthen economics. As all of the data for the important dynamic aspects of an economy consist of time series, it is clear that powerful methods of analysis are required for dealing with such data.

Methods essentially pioneered by electrical engineers concerned with communication theory have been developed in the last decade or so, and it is the object of this volume to present these methods in a useful form and with particular reference to the difficulties associated with economic series.

1.2 Concise History of Time Series Analysis

The astronomers are usually given credit for being the first to analyze a time series, although certain meteorological and geophysical series had also been discussed by the middle of the nineteenth century. From the very beginning it had been obvious to statisticians and other research workers that most time series occurring in the actual world were not merely strings of independent data. The series were too "smooth" to be independent; that is, the fluctuations from one side of the mean to the other were not sufficiently violent. The most obvious feature of most of the series first considered was a constant fluctuation with set period, such as the eleven-year oscillation in sunspot data or the annual cycle in meteorological series, and this led to the idea that the smoothness of all series was due to the presence of an inherent periodic function. That is, it was felt that if one could determine the amplitude, period, and phase of a sine curve sufficiently accurately and subtract this from the data, then the remainder ought to be an independent, random series.

When, in fact, this was done and the remainder was still found to be somewhat too smooth, it was natural to re-use the current predominant idea of the cause of the smoothness and to look for yet further sine curves to fit to the data. Essentially, the model envisaged as fitting the data was

$$(1.2.1) \qquad x_t = \sum_{j=1}^{k} a_j \sin\left(\frac{2\pi t}{\theta_j} + b_j\right) + \varepsilon_t,$$

where ε_t is a series with the variable at time t uncorrelated with the variable at all other times, i.e., if $E[\varepsilon_t] = 0$, all the $E[\varepsilon_t \varepsilon_{t+s}] = 0$, all t, $s \neq 0$.[2] (Throughout the next two chapters, series such as ε_t will be called random series. In later chapters, however, such series will be called "white noise.") Equation (1.2.1) represents a model of how the given data have been generated and will be called the linear cyclic model. If $E[\varepsilon_t] = 0$, it should be noted that $E[x_t] = 0$, all t, and the variance is given by

$$(1.2.2) \qquad E[x_t^2] = \sigma_x^2 = \frac{1}{2} \sum_{j=1}^{k} a_j^2 + \sigma_\varepsilon^2.$$

Many methods of discovering the "hidden periodicities" θ_j were suggested by workers such as Lagrange [14] in 1772 and 1778, Buys-Ballot [4], and E. T. Whittaker [23], but the best known was the periodogram method made famous by Sir Arthur Schuster in 1898–1906 (e.g. [16], [17]), although Stokes [19] had suggested it earlier. In all these methods the random series ε_t in the model was assumed not to be important, that is, the term σ_ε^2 was assumed not to account for a major part of the variance of x_t. The Schuster periodogram consists of the function

$$(1.2.3) \qquad I_n(\omega) = \frac{1}{n}\left[\left(\sum_{j=1}^{n} x_j \cos\frac{2\pi j}{\omega}\right)^2 + \left(\sum_{j=1}^{n} x_j \sin\frac{2\pi j}{\omega}\right)^2\right]$$

with data x_t, $t = 1, \ldots, n$. It is easily shown that $I_n(\omega)$ will have a peak at $\omega = \omega_o$ if the data contains a periodic term of period ω_o and there will be subsidiary peaks at $\omega = \omega_o + \dfrac{2\omega_o}{n}$. Significance tests for the peaks so found have been proposed by several writers and a survey of these tests may be found in Jenkins and Priestley [10]. Such tests are very necessary, as the appearance of an estimated periodogram is invariably ragged, the fact that adjacent estimates are only slightly correlated causing many peaks to appear.

Examples of estimated periodograms for both random and economic series may be found in Davis [6], but the best known example is the

---

[2] Readers unfamiliar with the expectation notation should see the appendix at the end of Chapter 3.

diagram calculated by Sir William Beveridge [2], [3] (see also Kendall [11]) from a long series (trend-reduced) of European wheat prices. The data that Beveridge used will be described at the end of the next chapter. The periodogram of this data has so many peaks that at least twenty possible hidden periodicities may be picked out, though only five of these have any claim to corresponding to peaks of possible significance.

It was probably the excessive number of apparent "cycles" that the periodogram seemed to find, even in constructed series which contain no such cycles, that led research workers, and particularly G. U. Yule, to consider other possible models that could account for the kind of fluctuations observable in economic series. (It might, however, be noted that the periodogram approach proved useful in other fields. For instance, Whittaker and Robinson [23] show that the series recording the brightness or magnitude of a variable star at midnight on 600 successive days could be exactly fitted by the sum of two periodic terms with periods 24 and 29 days, i.e., $x_t = 17 + 10 \sin \dfrac{2\pi(t+3)}{29} + 7 \sin \dfrac{2\pi(t-1)}{24}$.)

Yule [20], [21], [22] noted that a time series generated in either of the following ways

$$(1.2.4) \qquad\qquad x_t = \sum_{j=0}^{k} b_j \varepsilon_{t-j}$$

or

$$(1.2.5) \qquad\qquad x_t + \sum_{j=1}^{k} a_j x_{t-j} = \varepsilon_t$$

had an appearance similar to many naturally occurring series. The first model, which is the weighted sum of a random series, is called a *moving-average process* and was studied in a particular form by Slutsky [18]. (The famous "Slutsky effect" is discussed in Chapter 3.) Equation (1.2.5) illustrates an *autoregressive process* in which the current value x_t is assumed to have been formed from a linear sum of past values of the series together with an independent term unconnected with the past. Series generated in either manner do not, of course, contain strictly periodic terms, although Kendall [12] showed empirically that the periodograms of such data still contained misleading peaks.

The reason why these models give smooth series can be quickly explained. Suppose that the data be plotted as in the diagram that follows and that it has mean zero:

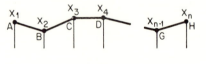

then obviously the length of the line ABCD$\cdots$GH will be a measure of the "smoothness" of the data. The square of this length is given by

$$k = \sum_{i=1}^{n-1} (x_i - x_{i-1})^2 + (n-1)H^2$$

where H is the distance between the readings. The expected (or mean) value of k is $2\sigma_x^2(1 - \rho) + (n-1)H^2$ where ρ is the correlation between x_{t-1} and x_t (assumed to be the same for all t), and so the nearer ρ is to 1, the smaller the mean of k. With the moving-average or autoregressive models, ρ can be made positive and large by suitable choice of the parameters a_j or b_j and so the smoothness of the series may be assured. We are here merely saying that if x_t is highly correlated to its immediate predecessor x_{t-1} then, on the average, $x_t - x_{t-1}$ will not be large.

For a comprehensive study of the use of the moving-average and autoregressive models see Wold [26], although more efficient methods of estimating the parameters involved in these and related models will be found in Durbin [7], [8]. It should be noted that the equation (1.2.5) can be "solved" in the form

$$(1.2.6) \qquad x_t = \sum_{j=0}^{k} c_j \theta_j^{t-T} + \sum_{j=0}^{\infty} b_j \varepsilon_{t-j},$$

i.e., as the sum of a function of time and an infinite moving average, it being assumed that the series started at time T. If all the roots (θ_j) of the equation $\theta^{k+1} + \sum_{j=1}^{k} a_j \theta^j = 0$ have modulus less than one and if the series is now assumed to have started in the very distant past, the terms involving θ_j^t can be ignored. If any of the roots have modulus greater than one the mean value of the series tends to infinity as t increases (as does the variance) and such a case is called an explosive autoregressive scheme. The problem of trends will frequently recur throughout the volume.

All the models so far considered have been particularly concerned with explaining series which have no apparent trends. Such series form a very important group and need to be correctly defined. A series has no trend in mean or variance if $E[x_t] = m$, $E[(x_t - m)^2] = \sigma_x^2$ for all t. A more particular class of series but also very important are those which have no trend in mean and variance and also for which $E[(x_t - m)(x_{t-k} - m)] = \mu_k$, all t, k. That is, the covariance between x_t and x_{t-k} depends only on k, the time-span between the terms, and not on the time t. Such series are called *stationary to the second order*, but, as the various classes of stationarity need not concern us in the book, all such series will henceforth be called merely *stationary*. μ_k is the kth autocovariance and $\rho_k = \frac{\mu_k}{\sigma_x^2}$ is called the kth autocorrelation coefficient and has the property that $-1 \leqq \rho_k \leqq 1$. It was shown above that ρ_1 was closely connected to a measure of the smoothness of a series, and more ambitious measures would involve several ρ_k. Estimates, respectively, of μ_k or ρ_k are formed by

$$C_k = \frac{1}{n-k} \left\{ \sum_{t=1}^{n-k} x_t x_{t+k} - \frac{1}{n-k} \sum_{t=1+k}^{n} x_t \sum_{t=1}^{n-k} x_t \right\}$$

$$r_k = \frac{C_k}{C_o},$$

and the plot of r_k against k is called the correlogram.

Bartlett [1] has studied the sampling properties of these estimates and found, for instance, that for a Gaussian process

$$E[C_k] = \rho_k \sigma^2, \qquad E[r_k] = \rho_k, \qquad \text{cov}\,(C_k, C_{k+s}) \sim \frac{1}{n-k} \sum_{v=-\infty}^{\infty} \varphi(v)$$

where

$$\varphi(v) = \sigma^4 (\rho_v \rho_{v+s} + \rho_{v+s+k} \rho_{v-s})$$

and, when $\rho_k \to 0$ as k increases,

$$\text{var}\,(r_k) \sim \frac{1}{n-k} \sum_{t=-\infty}^{\infty} \rho_v^2$$

$$\text{cov}\,(r_k, r_{k+s}) \sim \frac{1}{n-k} \sum_{j=-\infty}^{\infty} \rho_v \rho_{v+s}.$$

For many years the linear cyclic model, the moving average model and the autoregressive model were considered as the only possible alternatives, and so the problem of discriminating among them arose as to which was the best to fit. Theoretically, the correlogram would have discriminated as $\rho_k \to 0$ as k increases in different ways for a moving-average or autoregressive process, but $\rho_k \nrightarrow 0$ for a linear cyclic process. However, the large variance of the estimates of ρ_k invariably masks the relatively delicate theoretical behavior of the correlogram. Alternative methods of discrimination have been described by Rudra [15] and Granger [9], but neither is entirely satisfactory. In recent years the problem of discrimination has become considerably more difficult, as the above three models are no longer accepted as being the only possible alternatives. Mixtures of the models has become important, such as the linear regressive model

$$x_t + \sum_{j=1}^{k} a_j x_{t-j} = \sum_{j=0}^{m} b_j \varepsilon_{t-j},$$

but, using the spectral approach introduced in Chapter 3, series can be considered as having been generated by more complicated and unspecified mechanisms.

The methods described in this book have been developed from theoretical results by Kolmogoroff [13], Wiener [25], and Cramér [5], and are essentially generalizations of Fourier analysis. The transition from theoretical results to practical methods has been due to the efforts of many statisticians, but the leading group has been that of Tukey and his co-workers at the Bell Telephone Laboratories. These new methods are mathematically more subtle and statistically more powerful than earlier methods and require to a lesser extent the idea of a particular underlying model.

1.3 Plan of the Book

The purpose of this book has already been discussed in the preface and so need not be restated.

Chapter 2 briefly lists some of the more obvious characteristics of economic time series and various aspects of previous methods of analysis. Certain of the kinds of problems that may be tackled with spectral methods are also considered.

After Chapter 2, the book is divided into two main sections. As a rigorous statistical theory is available only for stationary (i.e., trend-free) series, Part A examines methods of analyzing such series.

Chapter 3 presents the ideas associated with and underlying the spectral theory for analyzing a single series and attempts to explain in simple terms some of the important, mathematically subtle concepts involved.

Chapter 4 gives an analogy that may help understand the idea of a spectrum and represents, in non-mathematical terms, the ideas of the previous chapter and the economic implications of these results. The practical aspects of estimating a spectrum and the interpretation of the estimate are discussed and several examples are presented.

Chapter 5 generalizes the results of Chapter 3 to deal with the problem of finding relationships between two (or more) stationary series.

In Chapter 6, the results of Chapter 5 are discussed further in non-mathematical terms, and the implications for economic theory are considered. Methods of estimating and interpreting cross-spectra are presented together with an example from economics.

Chapter 7 deals with the neglected but important problem of feedback between economic variables. Types of feedback are considered together with their effects on the cross-spectral methods discussed in the previous two chapters, and a test is presented for discovering whether feedback is present.

As the great majority of economic series are not stationary, Part B deals with methods of analyzing such series and considers the effect on the methods previously outlined of removing the assumption of stationarity.

Chapter 8 considers series which have merely a trend in mean and presents methods of isolating or removing this trend.

Chapter 9 deals with more realistic and complicated non-stationarity and shows by both a non-rigorous mathematical approach and by the evidence of experiments that the spectral and cross-spectral methods can still provide useful information providing the data are not too non-stationary.

Chapter 10 presents a method known as demodulation by which subtle types of non-stationarity might be detected and described. An example of its use is also given.

Chapter 11 considers briefly the many types of non-stationarity that appear to occur in economic series and also the effect on the statistical methods of many of the real phenomena of economic data such as missing data, changes in the definition, and the effect of the number of working days in a month not being a constant.

Chapters 12 and 13 contain applications of the new techniques to economic problems. The first of these two chapters discusses business cycle indicators and applies cross-spectral and demodulation techniques; the other applies partial cross-spectral methods to an investigation of the acceleration principle in inventory cycles.

REFERENCES

[1] Bartlett, M. S., *Stochastic Processes*, Cambridge, 1955.

[2] Beveridge, W. H., "Weather and harvest cycles," *Econ. J.*, 31 (1921), p. 429.

[3] Beveridge, W. H., "Wheat prices and rainfall in Western Europe," *J. Roy. Stat. Soc.*, vol. 85 (1922), p. 412.

[4] Buys-Ballot, C. D. H., "Les changements periodique de température," Utrecht, 1847.

[5] Cramér, H., "On the theory of stationary random processes," *Ann. of Math.*, vol. 41 (1940), pp. 215–230.

[6] Davis, H. T., *The Analysis of Economic Time Series*. Bloomington, Illinois: The Principia Press, 1941.

[7] Durbin, J., "Efficient estimation of parameters in moving average models," *Biometrika*, vol. 46 (1959), pp. 306–316.

[8] Durbin, J., "Estimation of parameters in time-series regression models," *J. Roy. Stat. Soc.* (B), vol. 22 (1960), 139–153.

[9] Granger, C. W. J., "Tests of discrimination and stationarity," Unpublished Ph.D. Thesis, Nottingham, 1959.

[10] Jenkins, G. M. and Priestley, M. B., "The spectral analysis of time series," *J. Roy. Stat. Soc.* (B), vol. 19 (1957), pp. 1–12.

[11] Kendall, M. G., *The Advanced Theory of Statistics*, vol. II, London, 1946.

[12] Kendall, M. G., *Studies in Oscillatory Time Series*, Cambridge, 1946.

REFERENCES

[13] Kolmogoroff, A., "Stationary sequences in Hilbert Space," *Bull. Math. Univ. Moscow*, vol. 2, No. 6 (1941) (Russian), 40 pp.

[14] Lagrange (1772, 1778). *Œuvres*, 6, p. 605; 7, p. 535.

[15] Rudra, "A method of discrimination in time series analysis," *Sankya*, vol. 15 (1955), pp. 9–34.

[16] Schuster, A., "On the investigation of hidden periodicities," *Terr. Mag.* (1898), 3:13.

[17] Schuster, A., "The periodogram of magnetic declination," *Trans. Cambridge Phil. Soc.*, 18 (1900), 107.

[18] Slutsky, E. (1927, 1937), "The summation of random causes as the source of cyclic processes," *Econometrica*, 5, 105 (reprint of paper earlier published in Russian).

[19] Stokes, G. C., "Note on searching for periodicities," *Proc. Roy. Soc.*, vol. 29 (1879), p. 122.

[20] Yule, G. U., "On the time correlation problem," *J. Roy. Stat. Soc.*, 84 (1921), 497.

[21] Yule, G. U., "Why do we sometimes get nonsense correlations," *J.R.S.S.*, 89 (1926), 1.

[22] Yule, G. U., "On a method of investigating periodicities in disturbed series," *Trans. Roy. Soc.* (A), 226, 267 (1927).

[23] Whittaker, E. T. and Robinson, G., *The Calculus of Observations*, London, 1924.

[24] Whittle, P., *Hypothesis Testing in Time Series Analysis*, Uppsala, 1951.

[25] Wiener, N., *The Extrapolation, Interpolation and Smoothing of Stationary Time Series*, New York, 1949.

[26] Wold, H., *Stationary Time Series*. Stockholm, 1938 (2nd Ed., 1958).

CHAPTER 2

NATURE OF ECONOMIC TIME SERIES

The main purposes of this chapter are to indicate some of the more obvious properties of economic series, thereby emphasizing some of the problems which need to be considered, and to point out a few of the advantages of the methods proposed in later chapters.

2.1   Classification of Economic Series from a Statistical Viewpoint

An important classification of economic time series is into (a) instantaneously recorded series, and (b) accumulated series. The former are discrete series that can be thought of as being the values of a continuous time series at certain moments of time. The temperature at noon at a particular location is a perfect example of such series. Economic series that may be considered to fall within this classification are price series, interest rate series, and series derived from concepts known to economists as stock concepts, such as amount of equipment, debt, financial assets, etc. In each case the variable can be thought of as existing at all moments of time and our series will be the values of the variable at the times chosen to record them.

The second class of series includes those which represent the sum or accumulation of a variable since the previous recording was taken. A good example of such series is rainfall measurements at a certain location. Examples from the field of economies are concerned with what economists call flow concepts, such as national income, production data, and volumes of transaction data.

Although the methods suggested for the analysis of series from either group will be essentially the same, occasionally problems arise in which the two types are affected differently. An example is the effect of the number of working days in a month not being a constant. The effect on instantaneously recorded series is slight, but accumulated series are changed in various ways. (This problem is discussed more fully in Chapter 11.)

A more subtle classification of economic series arises in connection with the problem of distinguishing causality and association between two series. The classification is: (a) series arising from micro-variables, and (b) series arising from macro-variables.

When we treat a firm in a competitive industry, the variables which it can control, such as the output of the firm, cannot significantly affect the important economy-wide variables such as aggregate output, overall price index, and national income. Variables unable to affect these primary economic quantities will be called micro-variables. Variables which are not micro will be called macro-variables.

If we are considering the problem of how to analyze a single series, this classification is not important, but when considering direction of causality the classification is of considerable importance since the problem for macro-variables is more difficult than for micro-variables. This is because for the latter we know a priori the mechanism of causality, which is usually very simple; for the former, feedback relationships (i.e., two-way causality) will usually occur.

The problems of how to test for the existence of feedback and how to disentangle the two-way causality are discussed in Chapter 7.

The statistically important classification of stationary or non-stationary as defined in the previous chapter is of less importance in economics as it is almost impossible to find a strictly stationary economic series.

Discussion of such topics as the quality of economic series and the effects of wars, crises, and strikes will be delayed until Chapter 11, by which time sharper tools for their dissection will be available.

2.2 Trends and Seasonal Variation

The problem of trends in economic series will continually recur throughout this work. Much of the theory upon which time series methods depend assumes that the series are trend-free. However, this is putting the problem into too simple a form, as we must distinguish between various types of trend.

The first and usually the most obvious visually is the trend in mean. A series might, loosely, be said to have an upward trend in mean if the series appears to be visually oscillating about a continually increasing value. One of the problems about such trends becomes obvious if the daily consumption of beer and ale in the United States is plotted throughout the months of April to July. Such a series has a visual "trend," whereas this "trend" is actually part of a cycle which is long compared to the time between adjacent terms in the series, in this case the seasonal variation. Thus, what we are forced to call a trend in mean is, at least partly, determined by the length of data available. Methods of defining and removing trends in mean are discussed in Chapter 8.

A second trend, also often visible in economic series, particularly in price and production data, is a trend in variance; that is, the extent of the oscillations about a (possibly trending) mean is changing with time. In practice, the change is usually an increase over time periods during which the economy is fairly stable. Frequently, a series with increasing mean will also have an increasing variance, although for many series the variance post-war is less than that for pre-war.

A third and more subtle type of trend is a change in the importance of one component (e.g., a decrease in the seasonal variation) or a change in the amount that the current value is correlated to the previous value in the series, say. This type of change in the series is rarely visible, yet is equally as important in analysis or in prediction of the series as the more obvious trends.

The importance of these second and third types of trend is discussed further in Chapter 9, and examples of many types of trends occurring in economic series are given in Chapter 11.

Whereas some series, such as population series, might appear to consist almost entirely of a trend in mean, other series equally appear to consist virtually of only a seasonal component; that is, they look like some shape of twelve months' duration simply repeated many times with only slight variations. Clearly these easily understood and appreciated seasonal variations (or the annual component, as it will often be referred to in later chapters) are due either to natural factors such as the weather or to social customs related entirely to the calendar year, such as Christmas. Examples of series containing important seasonal variations of various shapes and phases can easily be found in volumes such as the *Industrial Production Chart Book* produced by the U. S. Federal Reserve Bank, for instance: iron ore production (low in winter), natural gas production (high in winter), beer and ale production (very steady periodic movement accounting for almost the entire fluctuation of the series, high in July), confectionery production (high in September), dairy products production (low in November). Examples may also be found where the six-month cycle is the most important, and so there are two peaks and two troughs each year, such as women's outerwear (peaks in Spring and Fall) and newspaper production (lows every January and July).

Although the *period* of the seasonal variation is, of course, always known there is considerable variation of shape. Few if any of these shapes are reminiscent of a simple sine curve, but it is a well-known fact that any periodic function with period p may be approximated by a sum of sine curves with periods $p, p/2, p/3, \ldots$, i.e.,

$$f(t) = a_0 + \sum_{j=1}^{\infty} a_j \sin\left(\frac{2\pi jt}{p} + \theta_j\right).$$

Thus, if one attempted to describe the seasonal component of a series by an approach connected with Fourier representations such as periodogram analysis or spectral analysis, for many economic series not only will the term with twelve-month period be important but also the harmonics of this period will stand out. In many economic series it has been found that the harmonics with periods three and two-point-four months are of particular importance.

Many methods have been proposed for removing seasonal variation from a series but, unfortunately, most of these methods have undesirable side effects. When using the spectral approach the seasonal component need not be completely removed, but should usually be reduced, if of importance. The method recommended in the case of a seasonal component whose importance does not appear to be changing with time is merely to fit Fourier terms of period twelve months, and the harmonics of this period, and subtract from the series. When it is suspected that the component is changing with time the method called complex demodulation described in Chapter 10 should be used. A useful paper by Hannan [5] studies methods of estimating and removing seasonal variation in up-to-date terms although the demodulation technique is not mentioned. A computationally easy method is mentioned in Section 6 of Chapter 4.

Concerning the problem of whether to use raw data or data that have been seasonally adjusted by some government agency, no general rule can be suggested, but, as the method of adjustment used may have spoiled the data for spectral methods, it is frequently advisable to use the raw data and to "adjust" oneself. At least in this case the method used will be fully known and its effects can be estimated.

2.3 Business Cycles and Economic Fluctuations

The trend and annual components are frequently the most obvious features of an economic time series. However, if one examines a variable in which these components are not of great importance or if one can mentally filter out and disregard these components, the most obvious remaining feature of a sufficiently long time series is a series of long (two-year or more) irregular fluctuations.

By studying these fluctuations, some economists have suggested that they could have arisen as the sum of a number of more or less regular fluctuations. It is unfortunate that at an early stage of investigation the word "cycle" was applied to such fluctuations, as this term is apt to imply considerable regularity both in size and in period. Since many economists have discussed many cycles, the resulting concepts are likely to overlap, but any list of the more important of these suggested "cycles" must include the following:

(i) *Kondratieff Long Wave*

The Russian economist N. D. Kondratieff, in a study published in the 1920's, suggested a possible long wave of between 40 and 60 years' duration. The existence of these "Kondratieff" waves has been considerably questioned in recent years and there appears to be little conclusive evidence available to support Kondratieff's thesis.

(ii) *Kuznets Long Wave*

There has been an accumulation of evidence favoring the possibility of a cycle averaging some 20 years in duration from studies of Gross National Product, migration, and population variables. Studies in recent years indicate a close relationship between the Kuznets' wave and the building cycle, which was studied extensively in the 1920's and 1930's.

(iii) *Building Cycle*

There is some agreement that the building industries of various countries contain an important cycle of between 15 and 20 years' duration, and there is even some plausible theory available explaining this "building cycle."

(iv) *Major Cycle and Minor Cycle*

Hansen suggested a decomposition of economic cycles into major cycles, of duration six to eleven years, and minor cycles, of duration two to four years. Two of Schumpeter's three cycles also correspond to the major and minor cycles, although he used the terms Juglar and Kitchin, respectively. Hansen explains the minor cycle mostly in terms of the inventory cycle, whereas Schumpeter explains both the major and minor cycles as caused by a change in the rate at which new innovations generate changes in the economic system.

(v) *Business Cycles*

The National Bureau of Economic Research has defined business cycles as follows: "Business cycles are a type of fluctuation found in the aggregate economic activity of nations that organize their work mainly in business enterprises: a cycle consists of expansions occurring at about the same time in many economic activities, followed by similarly general recessions, contractions, and revivals which merge into the expansion phase of the next cycle; this sequence of changes is recurrent but not periodic; in duration business cycles vary from more than one year to ten or twelve years; they are not divisible into shorter cycles of similar character with amplitudes approximating their own." (Burns and Mitchell [1].)

In practice, the average duration of the National Bureau's business cycle is about four years and thus, as far as duration is concerned, there seems to be little difference between these cycles and the minor cycle.

(vi) *Mack's Sub-cycles*

Ruth Mack contends that she found cycles, which are shorter than the National Bureau business cycles, in many economic time series,

2.3 BUSINESS CYCLES AND ECONOMIC FLUCTUATIONS

especially in new orders, prices, inventories, etc. These are called sub-cycles, and their average duration is put at twenty-four months. One indication of these cycles is the pause observed in many economic series during the expansion period of the business cycle.

In all the above so-called cycles, in no sense is perfect regularity implied, the cycles being no more than fluctuations. This point is fully agreed upon by economists, but we quote from Gordon [3], p. 250: "Although business cycles represent *recurring* alternations of prosperity and depression, virtually all authorities agree that there is nothing *periodic* about these movements. There is no evidence that business cycles tend to recur over and over again in virtually the same form, with the same duration, and the same amplitude of movement. Some cycles are mild and others severe; some last two or three or four years, and others eight or ten years. In some the upswing is longer than the downswing; in others the reverse is the case." It is this very mixture of regularity and yet non-regularity that has provided the main difficulty in econometric model building and in statistically describing (and thus analyzing) economic series.

One of the advantages of using the spectral methods described in later chapters is that they provide a mathematically natural approach to this mixture of regularity and non-regularity. It might be noted that fluctuations similar to the business cycle could be described as the sum of a number of sine series with suitably chosen amplitudes and phases and all having *nearly* equal periods. The interactions between the terms would produce changes in both the duration and amplitude of the fluctuation, but nevertheless the average length of the fluctuation would remain constant. The spectral approach essentially describes fluctuations of the business cycle type by generalizing this idea, moving from a sum of sine terms to an integral of a sine function over a band of periods. This is one of the great advantages of spectral analysis over Fourier analysis (which was originally designed for strictly periodic functions of time). This and other advantages of using the spectral approach are discussed more fully in Chapter 4 after the idea of a spectrum has been introduced.

The spectral method also provides (theoretically) a robust way of determining the reality of the "cycles" described above by inquiring if the frequency bands to which they correspond provide an important part of the overall variance (see end of Section 4.2). However, the method requires data of at least seven times the length of the largest cycle one wishes to study for a proper determination to be made. Thus, to measure the reality of the Kuznets long wave, data of 140 years or so are required as a minimum. As reliable economic series are usually considerably shorter than this, it is seen that there is an insufficient amount of data available to make any test for such cycles. In the author's opinion no other method will find cycles correctly with data less than seven times the cycle length. (The figure seven was reached under the assumption that the series had no important trend in mean. As this is a very unreal assumption for economic series, even larger amounts of data are actually required to make a decision about the reality of a cycle.) In practice, few economic series are of sufficient length that a statistician may look for any business cycle other than the business cycles and Mack's sub-cycle. In fact, a minor cycle has been found in several series (such as pig-iron production and U.S. short-term interest rates), especially in the period prior to World War I. An example of a series containing a 40-month cycle is discussed in Chapter 4, Section 4.

One important point in the definition of the business cycle by the National Bureau of Economic Research is that business cycles are those fluctuations that are found in the aggregate economic activity. Burns [8], Mitchell [7], and Moore [9] made an extensive study to examine the extent to which economic time series move upward together during a certain length of period and then move downward together during the next period. The problem is not so much the regularity or irregularity of the cycle found in one economic time series as it is concerned with the "consensus" of the movements of different economic series. Some series are found to lead consistently some other series. Some series are found to lag consistently behind some others. With proper magnitudes of lead or lag, many important economic time series (with the exceptions of agriculture and finance) are found to move together. This is really the most important aspect of business cycles, and this aspect can be analyzed with the use of cross-spectral analysis, which will be explained in Chapters 5 and 6. The results of such an analysis will be found in Chapter 12.

2.4 Some Important Advantages in Using Spectral Methods of Analysis

The greatest contribution that the new statistical techniques are likely to make to the study of economics is the possibility of analyzing economic relationships in far more detail than the traditional econometric model-building methods have been capable. As is so often the case with innovations, some previous studies have come very close to the type of analysis which the new statistical techniques make available to us, and it is perhaps useful to illustrate the new ideas in the light of past studies.

Friedman [2] has presented an idea that both national income y and consumption c can be decomposed into two components, a permanent component (y_p, c_p) and a transitory component (y_t, c_t), so that $y = y_p + y_t$ and $c = c_p + c_t$. The decomposition is such that we should expect a certain relationship between y_p and c_p, but there is no reason to expect any meaningful relationship between y_t and c_p, between y_p and c_t, or between y_t and c_t.

According to Friedman, one way to define the permanent component of, say, national income, y, is,

$$y_p(T) = y_0 e^{\alpha T} + \beta \int_{-\infty}^{T} e^{\beta(t-T)}[y(t) - y_0 e^{\alpha t}]e^{\alpha(T-t)} \, dt$$

where $y_p(T)$ is the permanent component of y at time T, $y_0 e^{\alpha T}$ is the trend of y, $y(t) - y_0 e^{\alpha t}$ is the deviation of $y(t)$ from the trend in a time point t before T, $e^{\alpha(T-t)}$ is an adjustment factor to ensure a uniform variance of this deviation throughout the period under consideration (since the variance is less in the earlier period, it must be magnified), and $e^{\beta(t-T)}$ is the weight associated with the adjusted deviation at time point t in order to have the weighted average of $y(t)$ before T.

The point to be emphasized here is that, apart from the complications due to the trend in the mean and in the variance, the permanent component is essentially a weighted average of the past values. Actually, Friedman presents sophisticated economic reasons to support this idea, and it is grossly unfair to pick out this statistical technicality alone. However, from the standpoint of statistics, this is the essential point.

Now the question is, how are the permanent components of national income and consumption related to each other, i.e., how are the smoothed values of national income and consumption related to each other? This is one kind of problem which can be solved systematically by the new statistical technique of cross-spectral analysis.

In fact, cross-spectral analysis enables us to analyze the relationship between any meaningful components of a pair of time series. Thus, if there is any operational, meaningful definition of cyclical components, we can analyze the relationship between the cyclical components of two time series. If, apart from the traditional cyclical components, there is any meaning in the sub-cycles in which some economists are interested (see, for instance, Mack and Zarnowitz [6]), we might expect that the relationships between the traditional cyclical components of two series would be different from those between the sub-cycles of two series. In short, we can analyze the relationship between two series, *component by component*.

An interesting case is when a series x_t is closely related to a series y_t but not to the series z_t in regard to one component, but is closely related to z_t but not to y_t in regard to another component. An example would be that housing construction is very closely related to the situation in the mortgage market but not so closely to national income in regard to short-run fluctuations, whereas housing construction is closely related to national income in regard to the somewhat longer durations of fluctuations. (See Guttentag [4].)

Another important application is related to the long-run versus the short-run relationships. The necessity for distinguishing between the short-run relationship and the long-run relationship has been recognized in many fields of economics. For instance, the marginal propensity to consume in the short-run might be substantially less than that in the long-run. The reaction of supply to the change in price in the short-run would be significantly less than the corresponding reaction in the long-run. The acceleration principle explaining the movement of investment expenditures would be more successful in this explanation for the long-run than for the short-run. These problems can now be analyzed by the use of cross-spectral analysis, which will be explained in Chapters 5 and 6, provided that the long-run movement does not mean the trend component but rather oscillations that are somewhat longer than the short-run movements.

The parameters which the new statistical techniques estimate in regard to the relationship are the closeness of the relationship, the regression coefficient, and the lead or lag between each pair of components. One might say that the National Bureau method also estimates the lead or lag, but there is one important difference between the National Bureau method and the statistical techniques presented in the coming chapters. In the National Bureau method, the lead or lag is defined by the peaks and troughs only. Apart from the arbitrariness involved in the choice of peak and trough, this method does not consider the relationship during periods which are not turning points. (See Burns and Mitchell [1].) Unless we are particularly interested in the turning points only, this is a serious drawback. Unlike the National Bureau method, the methods presented later take into account all the time points for which the data are available in determining any lead or lag. Further, some of these methods can trace the changes over time in the extent of lead or lag, if such changes are significant.

Discussion of the use of spectral methods in determining relationships between economic variables is renewed in Chapter 6.

Apart from the advantages in determining relationships between pairs of variables and in accurately describing fluctuations of the business cycle type mentioned in the previous section, the other main advantages of spectral analysis seem to be increased mathematical rigour and generality, thus giving increased appreciation of the methods used, and a more flexible manner of considering the decomposition of a variable into components.

It might also be added that the increased generality of description will probably require economic theory to be phrased in new and more general forms, particularly when a model of some kind is involved.

2.5 Beveridge's Annual Wheat Price Series

The series analyzed in the examples throughout this book will be described along with the examples, but a series of historical importance which is mentioned on several occasions but is never analyzed in any detail is the Beveridge Wheat Price Series. This series consists of an attempt to construct an index for wheat prices in Western Europe for the period 1500–1869. It is thus a long and historically important series although, clearly, the index for the earlier years is of doubtful accuracy. The series and its periodogram are fully described in Beveridge (Chapter 1, references [2] and [3]), and the periodogram may also be found in Kendall (Chapter 1, reference [11]). The periodogram indicates a possibly significant peak corresponding to a cycle of 15 years. The original index was, naturally, not stationary, but the trends were removed by forming a series y_t from the original series x_t by

$$y_t = \frac{x_t}{\sum_{j=-15}^{15} x_{t+j}}.$$

This transformation proved extremely successful in removing the trends both in mean and variance.

REFERENCES

[1] Burns, A. F. and Mitchell, W. C., *Measuring Business Cycles*, New York, 1947.
[2] Friedman, M., *A Theory of the Consumption Function*, Princeton, 1957.
[3] Gordon, R. A., *Business Fluctuations* (2nd Ed.), New York, 1961.
[4] Guttentag, J. M., "The short cycle in residential construction, 1946–59," *American Economic Review*, vol. 51 (1961), pp. 275–298.
[5] Hannan, E. J., "The estimation of seasonal variation," *Aust. J. of Stats.*, vol. 2 (1960), pp. 1–15.
[6] Mack, R. and Zarnowitz, V., "Cause and consequence of change in retailers' buying," *American Economic Review*, vol. 8 (1958), pp. 18–49.
[7] Mitchell, W. C., *What Happens During Business Cycles*, New York, 1951.
[8] Burns, A. F., "New facts on business cycles," reprinted in Chapter 2 of *Business Cycle Indicators*, ed. by G. H. Moore, Princeton, 1961.
[9] Moore, G. H., "The diffusion of business cycles," reprinted in Chapter 8 of *Business Cycle Indicators*, Princeton, 1961.

PART A. STATIONARY TIME SERIES

CHAPTER 3

SPECTRAL THEORY

3.1 Definitions

A given time series $\{x_t, t = 1, 2, \ldots, n\}$ is here assumed to be a single sample from a particular generating process $\{X_t, t = -\infty, \ldots, -1, 0, 1, \ldots, \infty\}$. The generating process is merely supposed to indicate the *manner* in which the time series is formed for every moment of time but, due to its stochastic or probabilistic nature, it clearly cannot determine the *actual* value of the series at any moment of time. Simple examples of generating processes are

(3.1.1)

$$\text{(i)} \quad X_t = \varepsilon_t + b\varepsilon_{t-1}$$

$$\text{(ii)} \quad X_t = a \cos bt + \varepsilon_t$$

$$\text{(iii)} \quad X_t + aX_{t-1} = \varepsilon_t$$

$$\text{(iv)} \quad X_t = p(t) + q(t)\varepsilon_t$$

where ε_t is a random, independent series, $p(t)$ and $q(t)$ are polynomials in t. More complicated processes, for example, would be ones which took five terms from process (i) and followed them with four from process (iv) and then five more from (i), etc., or even consisted of terms taken randomly from process (ii) or (iii) in the ratio $p:1 - p$. Series derived from such complicated process will, however, usually prove too difficult to analyze.

By the "analysis" of a time series is meant the estimation and reconstruction of the properties of the underlying generating process from the given sample. The problem is analogous to drawing a random sample from a population and then attempting to estimate the properties of the population from the sample. It is clear in both cases that the simpler the properties one is attempting to discover and the more information available, i.e., the larger the sample, the more hope one has of correctly solving the problem. The use of such analysis, if correctly done, is to discover or indicate possible laws that the variable may obey and to allow prediction to occur. Once such an analysis has been performed it is the job of the economist to explain the laws and to use the predictions. The difference between the underlying generating process (denoted by capitals X_t, Y_t, etc.) and the available time series (denoted by x_t, y_t, etc.) considered as a sample from the generating process must be constantly borne in mind. Much of the theory will be considered in terms of the generating processes but the required estimates of parameters and suchlike will, of course, be derived from the actual (sample) series available.

It is usual to attempt to explain the properties of the generating process in terms of its first and second moments, i.e.,

(3.1.2)
$$m_t = E[X_t], \qquad \sigma_t^2 = E[(X_t - m_t)^2]$$
$$\mu(t, s) = E[(X_t - m_t)(X_s - m_s)]$$

$\mu(t, s)$ is termed the "autocovariance," between X_t and X_s (readers unfamiliar with the expectation notation $E[\;\;]$ should see the appendix to this chapter).

Suppose that we have available to us a number of independent samples from the same generating process, i.e., $\{x_t^{(k)}\}$, $k = 1, 2, \ldots, M$, then we can estimate m_t, for example, by

$$\bar{x}_t = \frac{1}{M} \sum_{k=1}^{M} x_t^{(k)}.$$

Such an average is called an "ensemble average" and has the property that

$$\lim_{M \to \infty} \bar{x}_t = m_t.$$

However, in economics we usually have only a single sample from the generating process and so $E[X_t]$ cannot be estimated by the use of ensemble averages.

In general, m_t, σ_t^2, and $\mu(t, s)$ will be functions of time but a very useful and important class of series are those generated by processes in which these first and second moments are not functions of time, i.e.,

(3.1.3)
$$E[X_t] = m, \qquad E[(X_t - m)^2] = \sigma^2$$
$$E[(X_t - m)(X_s - m)] = \mu(t - s) = \mu_\tau, \qquad \tau = t - s$$

for all t, s. Such series are called "stationary in the wide sense" or "stationary to the second order." (Henceforth such series will be termed "stationary" although the term is usually reserved for processes obeying stricter conditions than those imposed above.) Considerable interest has been shown in such series not only because they seem often to occur in practice but also because they allow powerful mathematical and statistical tools to be used in their analysis.

A particularly useful property of stationary series is that we can estimate the mean, etc., by averages over time instead of requiring ensemble averages, i.e.,

$$\bar{x} = \frac{1}{n} \sum_{t=1}^{n} x_t$$

$$s^2 = \frac{1}{n} \sum_{t=1}^{n} (x_t - \bar{x})^2$$

$$C_\tau = \frac{1}{n - \tau} \sum_{t=1}^{n-\tau} (x_t - \bar{x})(x_{t+\tau} - \bar{x})$$

provide efficient, unbiased estimates of m, σ^2, and μ_τ respectively.[1]

We may define a "stationary" process as a process generating stationary series. Simple examples of stationary processes are provided by example (i) and (ii) of (3.1.1) and example (iii) also, if $|a| < 1$. However, example (iv) is non-stationary as, if $E[\varepsilon_t] = 0$, $E[X_t] = p(t)$, i.e., the mean value is a function of time. If $p(t) \equiv 0$ then $E[X_t] = 0$, but $E[X_t^2] = q^2(t)\sigma_\varepsilon^2$ and so now the variance is a function of time.

In Part A of this book, stationary series only will be considered and methods of analysis for such series will be discussed. In Part B, the effect of removing the assumption of stationarity upon the method will be considered.

3.2 Power Spectra

To this point, the series considered have consisted of real numbers but it is mathematically more convenient to consider the series x_t as though it were a series of complex numbers. Although this step may appear to introduce an element of unreality into the argument, it clearly involves no loss in generality and is made well worth while by gains in ease and conciseness. Thus, $\{X_t\}$ will be thought of as a complex, stationary process with

$$(3.2.1) \qquad E[X_t] = 0, \qquad E[X_t\bar{X}_t] = \sigma^2, \qquad E[X_t\bar{X}_{t-\tau}] = \mu_\tau$$

where $\bar{X}$ is the conjugate of X.

Let us consider a *generating process* of the form

$$(3.2.2) \qquad\qquad X_t = \sum_{j=1}^{k} a_j e^{i\omega_j t}$$

where $(\omega_j, j = 1, \ldots, k)$ is a set of real numbers with $|\omega_j| \leq \pi$ and $(a_j, j = 1, \ldots, k)$ is a set of independent, complex random variables with $E[a_j] = 0$, all j, $E[a_j\bar{a}_j] = \sigma_j^2$, $E[a_j\bar{a}_k] = 0, j \neq k$.

Any term $a_j e^{i\omega_j t} = a_j (\cos \omega_j t + i \sin \omega_j t)$ of this generating process is a periodic function, with period $\dfrac{2\pi}{\omega_j}$. The frequency, measured in cycles per time unit, is given by the inverse $\dfrac{\omega_j}{2\pi}$. The angular frequency, measured in radians per time unit, is given by $2\pi \times$ frequency $= \omega_j$. Because of its convenience, the angular frequency ω_j will be used to describe the periodicity of the function, and its name will be shortened to frequency, when there is no danger of confusion.

Then, as the a_j's take different values so the different series that may be generated by (3.2.2) arise. For any *particular* series, the a_j's are

---

[1] For this to be true, we strictly require the series to possess also a property known as ergodic. The distinction has little practical importance.

constant throughout the time-span and the totality of all these series make up the process and the totality of the a_j's determine their distributions.

It is clear that $E[X_t] = 0$ and

$$\mu_\tau = E[X_t \bar{X}_{t-\tau}] = \sum_{j=1}^{k} \sigma_j^2 e^{i\omega_j \tau}$$

and so

$$\mu_\tau = \int_{-\pi}^{\pi} e^{i\omega\tau} \, dF(\omega)$$

where $F(\omega)$ is a step function with steps of size σ_j^2 at $\omega = \omega_j, j = 1, \ldots, k$, i.e., $F(\omega)$ will have the form shown in Fig. 3.1 and $F(-\pi) = 0$, $F(\pi) = \sum_{j=1}^{k} \sigma_j^2 = \text{variance } [X_t]$.

A process such as (3.2.2) is essentially a simple linear cyclic process with mean extracted as each sample is merely a sum of periodic functions.

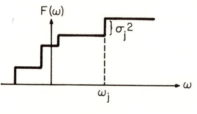

Figure 3.1

On considering such a process one may ask, why should k be a finite constant? The process

$$(3.2.3) \qquad X_t = \sum_{j=1}^{\infty} a_j e^{i\omega_j t}, \quad |\omega_j| \le \pi \text{ all } j$$

is more general and, if we suppose $\sum_{j=1}^{\infty} |a_j|^2 < \infty$, then the variance of X_t is finite. But again, why should only a discrete set of points of the line $(-\pi, \pi)$ be included. Cannot all the points on this line contribute something to the process. The answer is "yes" although considerable care has to be taken in correctly generalizing (3.2.3) to cover this situation. Not only is the answer yes, but it has been shown that the resulting generalization contains all possible stationary processes.

The work of Cramér, Kolmogoroff, Wiener, and others has given the following very important results:

(i) the sequence of autocovariances μ_τ for a stationary process can always be represented in the form

$$(3.2.4) \qquad \mu_\tau = \int_{-\pi}^{\pi} e^{i\tau\omega} \, dF(\omega)$$

⟨ 28 ⟩

where $\dfrac{F(\omega)}{\mu_0}$ is a distribution function, i.e., it is monotonically increasing (or, at least, non-decreasing) and bounded, $F(-\pi) = 0, F(\pi) = \mu_0 = \sigma^2$.

(ii) all stationary processes can be represented in the form

$$(3.2.5) \qquad X_t = \int_{-\pi}^{\pi} e^{it\omega}\, dz(\omega)$$

where $z(\omega)$ is a complex, random function called a process of non-correlated increments as it has the properties

$$E[(z(\omega_1) - z(\omega_2))(\overline{z(\omega_3) - z(\omega_4)})] = 0, \quad \omega_1 \geqq \omega_2 > \omega_3 \geqq \omega_4$$

$$E[|z(\omega_1) - z(\omega_2)|^2] = F(\omega_1) - F(\omega_2), \quad \omega_1 \geqq \omega_2$$

and so

$$E[dz(\omega_1)\,\overline{dz(\omega_2)}] = 0, \quad \omega_1 \neq \omega_2$$

$$= dF(\omega), \quad \omega_1 = \omega_2 = \omega.$$

Equation (3.2.4) is termed the spectral representation of the covariance function and $F(\omega)$ is the power spectral distribution function. Equation (3.2.5) will be called the Cramér representation of a stationary process and the equality must be understood to hold as a limit in mean square. (Methods of interpreting (3.2.4) and (3.2.5) are discussed at the end of this section.)

For real processes $\mu_t = \mu_{-t}$ and so $dF(\omega) = dF(-\omega)$ and also $dz(\omega) = \overline{dz(-\omega)}$. Putting $z(\omega) = \frac{1}{2}[u(\omega) - iv(\omega)]$ with real-valued $u(\omega)$, $v(\omega)$ one obtains $du(\omega) = du(-\omega)$, i.e., $du(\omega)$ is an even function, and $dv(\omega) = -dv(-\omega)$, i.e., $dv(\omega)$ is an odd function. Thus

$$E[du(\omega)^2] = E[dv(\omega)^2] = 2dF(\omega), \quad 0 < \omega < \pi$$

$$E[du(0)^2] = dF(0), \quad E[du(\pi)^2] = dF(\pi)$$

$$E[du(\omega_1)\, dv(\omega_2)] = 0, \quad 0 \leqq \omega_1, \quad \omega_2 \leqq \pi$$

and so, for real processes (3.2.4) and (3.2.5) become

$$(3.2.6) \qquad \mu_t = \int_0^{\pi} \cos \tau\omega\, dG(\omega)$$

where

$$dG(\omega) = 2dF(\omega), \quad 0 < \omega < \pi$$

$$dG(0) = dF(0), \quad dG(\pi) = dF(\pi)$$

and

$$(3.2.7) \qquad X_t = \int_0^{\pi} \cos t\omega\, du(\omega) + \int_0^{\pi} \sin t\omega\, dv(\omega)$$

An important implication of the spectral representation is seen by comparing the forms of the variances of the processes given by (3.2.3) and (3.2.5), i.e.,

$$\sigma_x^2 = \sum_{j=1}^{\infty} |a_j|^2$$

and

$$\mu_0 = \sigma_x^2 = \int_{-\pi}^{\pi} dF(\omega).$$

In the first case $|a_j|^2$ is the contribution to the overall variance of the component with frequency ω_j and, in the second case, when all the points on the line are included as for the Cramér representation, the contribution to the overall variance by the frequencies in the set $(\omega, \omega + d\omega)$ is $dF(\omega)$.

As $F(\omega)$ is monotonically increasing the classical decomposition holds, i.e.,

$$F(\omega) = F_1(\omega) + F_2(\omega) + F_3(\omega)$$

where $F_1(\omega), F_2(\omega), F_3(\omega)$ are non-decreasing, and are, respectively, an absolutely continuous function, a step function and a so-called singular function, continuous, but constant almost everywhere. The part corresponding to $F_3(\omega)$ does not appear to be meaningful observationally and we shall assume it to be zero in what follows.

Thus it can be shown that any stationary process can be decomposed into $X_t = X_1(t) + X_2(t)$ where $X_1(t)$ has an absolutely continuous power spectral distribution function and (3.2.4) becomes

$$(3.2.8) \qquad \mu_\tau' = E[X_1(t)\overline{X_1(t-\tau)}] = \int_{-\pi}^{\pi} e^{i\tau\omega} f(\omega)\, d\omega$$

and where $X_2(t)$ has form (3.2.3).

In this decomposition $X_1(t)$ and $X_2(t)$ are uncorrelated, $X_2(t)$ corresponding to a linear cyclic process such as (3.2.3) (called by Doob [13] a "deterministic component") and $X_1(t)$ is a member of a class of processes (called "non-deterministic") which contain the autoregressive, moving average and linear regressive processes. The terms deterministic and non-deterministic arise because if the process $\{X_t\}$ is deterministic, then, given X_t, $t = -\infty, \ldots, t_0$, i.e., an infinite number of past values, X_t, $t > t_0$, can be predicted exactly. However, if the process is non-deterministic and if P_t is the optimum least-squares, linear predictor of X_t using all past X_t, then the process defined by $\varepsilon_t = X_t - P_t$ will have non-zero variance, i.e., we are unable to predict X_t exactly.

The emphasis in the following work will be on non-deterministic processes, i.e., processes having power spectral density functions of the form $dF(\omega) = f(\omega)\, d\omega$ where $f(\omega)$ is absolutely continuous and is called the power spectrum of the process.

Thus, for processes with continuous spectrum, (3.2.4) and (3.2.6) become

$$(3.2.9) \qquad \mu_\tau = \int_{-\pi}^{\pi} e^{i\tau\omega} f(\omega) \, d\omega$$

$$(3.2.10) \qquad \mu_\tau = \int_{0}^{\pi} \cos \tau\omega \, g(\omega) \, d\omega$$

for a real process,

$$g(\omega) = 2f(\omega), \quad 0 < \omega < \pi$$

$$g(0) = f(0), \qquad g(\pi) = f(\pi).$$

As equations (3.2.4) and (3.2.5) represent the basic tools with which the majority of the results of this book will be fashioned and as they are by no means easy to understand, further discussion of them seems desirable.

Let us first concentrate on Cramér's representation in its form for real processes

$$(3.2.11) \qquad X_t = \int_{0}^{\pi} \cos t\omega \, du(\omega) + \int_{0}^{\pi} \sin t\omega \, dv(\omega).$$

We need to consider a generating process producing many *infinitely long*, discrete trend-free time series. If we look at a finite length of a particular sample series (i.e., particular series generated by the process) $(x_t, t = 1, \ldots, n)$ then this finite series can be exactly fitted by a finite Fourier series

$$x_t(n) = \sum_{j=0}^{n} a_j \cos \omega_j t + \sum_{j=1}^{n} b_j \sin \omega_j t$$

where $\omega_j = \dfrac{2\pi j}{n}$, and the a_j's, b_j's are chosen to make $x_t(n) = x_t$ at $t = 1, \ldots, n$. If we let $n \to \infty$, i.e., consider how a Fourier series can be made to fit an entire sample series, the first thing to be noticed is that $\omega_{j+1} - \omega_j \to 0$ and so the series becomes an integral and the representation needs to be of the form

$$(3.2.12) \qquad x_t = \int_{0}^{\pi} a(\omega) \cos \omega t \, d\omega + \int_{0}^{\pi} b(\omega) \sin \omega t \, d\omega.$$

This equation means that the infinite sequence $(x_t, t = 1, \ldots, \infty)$ can be exactly fitted by the mathematical function on the right hand side of (3.2.12) (except possibly at $t = 1$) if the functions $a(\omega)$, $b(\omega)$ are properly chosen. If $\{x_t\}$ contains a periodic element of period m (and, hence of frequency $\omega_1 = \dfrac{2\pi}{m}$) then $a(\omega)$, $b(\omega)$ will have sharp spikes at

$\omega = \omega_1$ but if $\{x_t\}$ contains no periodic elements, $a(\omega)$, $b(\omega)$ will be smooth.

If we now consider *all* the possible sample series generated by a particular process (in one sense, the totality of all such series defines the process) and then consider all the resulting $a(\omega)$'s, these functions make up an infinite population of functions. This population can be described as the population of the random function $\underline{a(\omega)}$ and similarly we can derive a random function $\underline{b(\omega)}$. Thus, as $\underline{a(\omega)}$, $\underline{b(\omega)}$ take on different values, we get different sample series from our generating process and it immediately follows that the *process* can be represented by

$$X_t = \int_0^\pi \underline{a(\omega)} \cos t\omega \, d\omega + \int_0^\pi \underline{b(\omega)} \sin t\omega \, d\omega$$

which is similar to Cramér's representation (3.2.7). (It must be firmly emphasized that the above heuristic description is very loose, non-rigorous, and may be sometimes even incorrect but it may help in understanding the concepts involved. The more subtle mathematical points have been ignored. Correct derivations and descriptions can be found in Hannan [10] and Grenander and Rosenblatt [11] but the mathematical equipment required to appreciate these accounts is considerable.)

We have said that, for a sample series, if we knew in advance the particular functions $a(\omega)$, $b(\omega)$ associated with this series, then all future values would be exactly known. However, we can never know these functions until the "complete," infinite series is known. As this is the case, it might fairly be asked, what can we estimate, knowing only a finite length of a sample series?

It is possible that an analogy might help at this stage. At any given time, the position of a man in relation to a particular point on the earth's surface can be represented by three variables; we might, for instance, use latitude, longitude, and height above sea-level. If we plot a man's position against time we would get a curve in four-dimensional space which will be called his "life-line." A completed life-line, from birth to death, could be simply represented by a set of three Fourier series of time. However, the terms of this "completed" Fourier series are never known (and cannot be known) at any stage of the man's life as, almost certainly, his future movements will be somewhat controlled by random events (or events which are so complex to explain that they appear to be random). Nevertheless, the life-line up to that point of his life will have put certain limitations on the eventual Fourier series representation.

Although the random effects are likely to affect the life-line, the main movements are likely to be due to laws or rules or circumstances which do not alter. He will rise, travel to work by a prescribed route at a prescribed time, eat lunch in a regular place, return home at a regular time; the weekends occur regularly and the annual vacations perhaps also. There will be in fact a large amount of regular, pseudo-periodic movement in the life-line of most persons. If we have a sample from the life-line, we can attempt to estimate these regularities and predict the person's position at some future time. The prediction will, of course, assume that the laws and circumstances that are operative in the sample will continue to operate in the future. If the man changes his home or his job or retires, then clearly this assumption will break down. This is essentially what we attempt to do with a time series. The assumption of stationarity we have required for a series to be analyzed is essentially an assumption that the same "rules" have been obeyed throughout the sample we have been given. From the sample we try to estimate those regularities or frequencies which appear to be most important and then we can use these estimates to predict the future values of the variable, assuming the same "rules" to continue to operate. The regularities of the person's life-line must not be confused with strictly period movements. A man's bed-time will rarely be exactly 10.30 P.M. each evening but will vary about such a time in a random way. Thus the length of the man's day will not be exactly 15 hours but will usually be somewhere between 13 and 19 hours, say. Many of the regularities will not be representable by a single periodic function but could usually be representable by a large weighted sum of such functions having nearly all the same period.

We have written above about finding which of the regularities are of most importance and to do this we obviously need a measure. It should be clear that the mean point of the man's life-line will be of little use to us (it will probably be somewhere between his home and his office or factory); it is the extent or importance of the fluctuations about the mean which we need to measure. To measure the importance of the regularities of a life-line we would probably need to take into account the length of journey involved, the cost, the time taken and the discomfort experienced but, fortunately, it is easier to introduce a measure of importance concerning the fluctuations of a time series.

The measure of importance we adopt is the amount contributed to the overall variance by the component we are considering. For a variable containing a periodic term, the importance of this term is the reduction in the variance when this term is removed. This, in fact, can be our definition of a variable containing a periodic term, i.e., there is a frequency which, if subtracted from the variable, will reduce the variance by a finite amount. If our model were $x_t = a \cos \omega_1 t + \varepsilon_t$ where ε_t is a random independent series, then $\sigma_x^2 = \frac{1}{2}a^2 + \sigma_\varepsilon^2$ and so removing the period term with frequency ω_1 will reduce σ_x^2 to σ_ε^2. However, for a series containing no such term we cannot reduce the variance in such a way. Thus, x_t is a random, independent series of infinite length and we cannot reduce σ_x^2 by a finite amount by subtracting from it terms of type $a \cos (\omega t + \theta)$.

Cramér's representation has told us that any stationary process can be considered as an integral over all the frequencies $(-\pi, \pi)$. If we define the function $F(\omega)$ by $F(\omega_2) - F(\omega_1)$

= amount of total variance attributable to the frequency band (ω_1, ω_2)

$$= \int_{\omega_1}^{\omega_2} [a^2(\omega) + b^2(\omega)] \, d\omega$$

then $F(\omega)$ is called the power spectral distribution function and is the function appearing in equation (3.2.5). If the process contains no periodic terms, then $a^2(\omega) + b^2(\omega)$ is absolutely continuous and the power spectral function can be defined as

$$f(\omega) = \frac{dF(\omega)}{d\omega}$$

and $f(\omega) \, d\omega$ is the contribution to the total variance by the frequency band $(\omega, \omega + d\omega)$. Thus, a peak in $f(\omega)$ indicates an important frequency band.

We can now discuss the important question of what we can attempt to estimate about the underlying process, given only one sample series of finite length. Let us first suppose that the process contains no periodic terms, i.e., has absolutely continuous power spectral distribution function. The process is well described if we know the power spectral function $f(\omega)$ (however, it should be noted that knowing $f(\omega)$ does not uniquely determine the process as many different processes can all have the same spectrum). If we had been given an infinite sample series, we might have attempted to find $a(\omega)$, $b(\omega)$ for all ω and then say that as $a(\omega)$ is a sample of one from the random variable $a(\omega)$ appearing in the (crude) Cramér representation of the *process*, and similarly, for $b(\omega)$, then $a^2(\omega) + b^2(\omega)$ is a crude estimate of $E[a^2(\omega) + b^2(\omega)]$. We have here assumed that $E[x_t] = 0$, all t, so that $E[a(\omega)] = 0$, $E[b(\omega)] = 0$. It might be thought, correctly, that using a sample of one to estimate the mean of its population is not a very good method, but $f(\omega)$ is absolutely continuous and thus smooth, so the average of $a^2(\omega) + b^2(\omega)$ over a small frequency band should give us an acceptable estimate of the average $f(\omega)$ in this band. In practice, we only have available a finite sample series and the length of the series together with the efficiency of our estimating techniques together determine over how many frequency bands we can attempt to estimate the average power spectrum and how good are our estimates.

If the generating process contains important periodic terms, we must also attempt to find at what frequencies these terms occur, and their amplitudes and phases. The Schuster periodogram attempted to do this and is a natural, but unsuccessful, method of estimating a spectrum. The important frequencies will correspond to high, sharp peaks in the estimated spectrum and the height of the peak will provide us with a rough estimate of the amplitude.

3.3 Black Boxes and Processes with Rational Spectral Functions

The term "black box" has been used for a considerable time by electrical engineers and workers in the field of communications theory in connection with continuous time series and it appears to be an appropriate term for use with a class of linear transformations applied to a series. A black box will be thought of as having an input $\{u_t, t = -\infty, \ldots, -1, 0, 1, \ldots, \infty\}$ and an output $\{v_t, t = -\infty, \ldots, -1, 0, 1, \ldots, \infty\}$, the two being connected by the conditions (which are not unrelated):

(3.3.1)

$$\text{(i)} \qquad v_t = \sum_{j=0}^{\infty} \alpha_j u_{t-j}$$

$$\text{(ii)} \quad \text{if} \quad u_t = ae^{i(t\theta + b)} \quad \text{then} \quad v_t = ce^{i(t\theta + d)},$$

i.e., the output is a linear function of past and present values of the input and if the input consists of a single frequency then the output consists only of the same frequency although the box may have altered the amplitude and phase. If $\sum_{j=0}^{\infty} |\alpha_j| < \infty$ and $\sum_{j=0}^{\infty} \alpha_j^2 < \infty$, and if u_t is a stationary process, then the output is a stationary process.

Simple examples of black boxes are

$$\text{(i)} \quad v_t = \alpha_0 u_t + \alpha_1 u_{t-1}$$

$$\text{(ii)} \quad v_t + \beta v_{t-1} = \alpha u_t$$

but the following are not black boxes:

$$\text{(iii)} \quad v_t = u_t + ae^{it\theta}$$

$$\text{(iv)} \quad v_t = u_t^2.$$

The concept of a black box will be found useful both later in this section and also in Part B of this volume.

The power spectrum of an independent random sequence is easily seen to be a constant over the range $(-\pi, \pi)$ as $\mu_\tau = 0$, $\tau \neq 0$, $\mu_0 = \sigma^2$ and such a sequence is given by

$$\mu_\tau = \frac{\sigma^2}{2\pi} \int_{-\pi}^{\pi} e^{i\tau\omega} \, d\omega$$

and so $f(\omega) = \dfrac{\sigma^2}{2\pi}, \; -\pi \leqq \omega \leqq \pi.$

It thus follows that, if ε_t is a random, independent series with $E[\varepsilon_t] = 0$ then Cramér's representation is given by

(3.3.2)
$$\varepsilon_t = \int_{-\pi}^{\pi} e^{it\omega} \, dz(\omega)$$

where

$$E[dz(\omega_1) \overline{dz(\omega_2)}] = 0, \quad \omega_1 \neq \omega_2$$

$$= \frac{1}{2\pi} \sigma_\varepsilon^2 \, d\omega, \quad \omega_1 = \omega_2$$

Such series are frequently called "white noise," an electrical engineering term.

Now consider the moving average process

(3.3.3)
$$X_t = \sum_{j=0}^{m} \alpha_j \varepsilon_{t-j}$$

then

$$X_t = \int_{-\pi}^{\pi} \sum_{j=0}^{m} \alpha_j e^{i(t-j)\omega} \, dz(\omega)$$

$$= \int_{-\pi}^{\pi} e^{it\omega} \left[\sum_{j=0}^{m} \alpha_j e^{-ij\omega} \right] dz(\omega)$$

and so

$$E[X_t X_{t-\tau}] = \frac{\sigma_\varepsilon^2}{2\pi} \int_{-\pi}^{\pi} e^{i\tau\omega} a(\omega)\overline{a(\omega)} \, d\omega,$$

and so the power spectrum of the process $\{X_t\}$ is given by

$$2\pi f(\omega) = \sigma_\varepsilon^2 a(\omega)\overline{a(\omega)} \quad \text{where}$$

(3.3.4)
$$a(\omega) = \sum_{j=0}^{m} \alpha_j e^{ij\omega}.$$

In a similar way, the power spectrum of an autoregressive process may be found. Suppose the process to be given by

(3.3.5)
$$X_t + \sum_{j=1}^{m} \beta_j X_{t-j} = \varepsilon_t.$$

Then if we suppose

$$X_t = \int_{-\pi}^{\pi} e^{it\omega} \, d\eta(\omega)$$

where

$$E[|d\eta(\omega)|^2] = f(\omega) \, d\omega,$$

$f(\omega)$ being the power spectrum of the process $\{X_t\}$, it follows that

$$\int_{-\pi}^{\pi} e^{it\omega}\left[1 + \sum_{j=1}^{m} \beta_j e^{-ij\omega}\right] d\eta(\omega) = \int_{-\pi}^{\pi} e^{it\omega}\, dz(\omega)$$

and so, considering $E[\varepsilon_t \bar{\varepsilon}_{t-\tau}]$, one gets

$$\int_{-\pi}^{\pi} e^{i\tau\omega} b(\omega)\overline{b(\omega)}\, f(\omega)\, d\omega = \frac{1}{2\pi}\sigma_\varepsilon^2 \int_{-\pi}^{\pi} e^{i\tau\omega}\, d\omega$$

and so

$$2\pi f(\omega) = \frac{\sigma_\varepsilon^2}{b(\omega)\overline{b(\omega)}} \quad \text{where}$$

(3.3.6)

$$b(\omega) = 1 + \sum_{j=1}^{m} \beta_j e^{-ij\omega}.$$

Combining the processes (3.3.3) and (3.3.5) into the more general linear regressive process

(3.3.7)
$$\sum_{j=0}^{b} \beta_j X_{t-j} = \sum_{j=0}^{a} \alpha_j \varepsilon_{t-j}, \qquad \beta_0 = 1$$

one finds that the power spectrum of this process is given by

(3.3.8)
$$2\pi f(\omega) = \frac{a(\omega)\overline{a(\omega)}}{b(\omega)\overline{b(\omega)}} \sigma_\varepsilon^2$$

where $a(\omega)$, $b(\omega)$ were defined in (3.3.4) and (3.3.6).

A process having a power spectrum of form (3.3.8) is said to have a rational spectrum.

For a general, real stationary process with power spectrum $f(\omega)$, the spectrum is assumed to be periodic outside $(-\pi, \pi)$ and is symmetric, i.e., $f(\omega) = f(-\omega)$. Clearly, if $f(\omega)$ is continuous it can always be expanded in the form

$$f(\omega) = \sum_{j=0}^{\infty} \gamma_j \cos j\omega$$

and so can be represented by

$$f(\omega) = g(\omega)\overline{g(\omega)}$$

where

$$g(\omega) = \sum_{j=0}^{\infty} g_j e^{-ij\omega}.$$

It thus follows that any real, non-deterministic, stationary process having continuous spectrum can be represented by

(3.3.9)
$$X_t = \sum_{j=0}^{\infty} g_j \varepsilon_{t-j},$$

i.e., an infinite moving average. It also follows that we may always approximate such a process as closely as we wish by a process having a rational spectrum, the "approximation" here meaning that the two processes will have approximately the same spectrum.

If we now consider a black box having an input ε_t which is a stationary, random, independent series, then from (3.3.1) the output may be represented by

$$v_t = \int_{-\pi}^{\pi} e^{it\omega} a(\omega)\, dz(\omega)$$

if

$$\varepsilon_t = \int_{-\pi}^{\pi} e^{it\omega}\, dz(\omega)$$

where

$$a(\omega) = \sum_{j=0}^{\infty} a_j e^{-ij\omega}$$

Thus, the power spectrum of the output will be $f_v(\omega) = \dfrac{1}{2\pi}\,\sigma_\varepsilon^2 a(\omega)\overline{a(\omega)}$ and it follows that, given a suitable black box with an independent series as input a sample from any stationary process with a given spectrum can be generated.

The function $a(\omega)$ will be called the *spectral transfer function* of the black box and it follows also from the above that if the input of the box has power spectrum $f(\omega)$ then the output will have spectrum $a(\omega)\overline{a(\omega)}\,f(\omega)$. It should be noted that it is not necessarily possible for any black box to have an inverse, i.e.,

as the box A may entirely cut out certain frequencies and these cannot be reconstituted by box B. If, however, $a(\omega) \neq 0$ for any ω, then an inverse black box is possible, having spectral transfer function $[a(\omega)]^{-1}$.

A special type of stochastic process of frequent interest is the so-called *normal process*. The process $\{X_t\}$ is said to be a normal process if the distribution of any subset $X_{\lambda_1}, X_{\lambda_2}, X_{\lambda_3}, \ldots, X_{\lambda_k}$ is a multivariate normal distribution. If the independent series ε_t is a sequence of normal variates, then the linear regressive process defined by (3.3.7) will be a normal process. It might also be noted that if a normal process is transformed by a black box transformation the resulting process will also be a normal process.

The important problem of prediction has been well covered by other writers (e.g., Grenander and Rosenblatt [11], Hannan [10], Bartlett [12], and Wiener [16]), and so need only be briefly mentioned here.

Given data $x_1, x_2, \ldots, x_n$, a clearly sensible method of predicting a future value x_{n+k} is by use of a linear sum of the available data such as

$$P[x_{n+k}] = \sum_{j=0}^{m} \alpha_j x_{n-j}$$

where the α_j are chosen to minimize

$$\sigma^2{}_P(k) = E[|x_{n+k} - P[x_{n+k}]|^2]; \text{ assuming } E[x_t] = 0, \text{ all } t.$$

Wiener [16] has considered the problem of choosing the α_k's when the power spectrum $f_x(\omega)$ of the series x_t is known and when the series is of infinite length. In this case Kolmogoroff [17] has shown that

$$\sigma^2{}_P(1) = \exp\left\{\frac{1}{2\pi} \int_{-\pi}^{\pi} \log 2\pi f_x(\lambda)\, d\lambda\right\}.$$

A more usual way in practice is to estimate the α_j's by fitting an autoregressive model to the series and then predicting from this model. Clearly, the further ahead one predicts the worse the prediction, and if the series contains a trend in mean or a periodic term account has to be taken of these components.

3.4   Filters

The occasion often arises in the analysis of a time series when we wish to alter the shape of the power spectrum, possible cases being:

(i) We wish to study only the frequency band (ω_1, ω_2).

(ii) We wish to remove entirely a particular frequency (ω_0) that is contributing a considerable amount to the variance with a view to better studying other frequencies, e.g., the annual component in a meteorological series.

(iii) We wish to "smooth" the series so as to study better the long-term movements in the series, i.e., remove the effect of high frequencies.

Clearly, these requirements are met if we could multiply the power spectrum of the series by functions $g(\omega)$ as in Fig. 3.2.

It is rarely that we are able to exactly find a black box with transfer function exactly to our requirements, but good approximations can usually be achieved. A *filter* is defined as a linear transformation of the series $\{x_t\}$ of the form

(3.4.1)
$$y_t \equiv L(x_t) = \sum_{j=a}^{m} \alpha_j x_{t+j}.$$

For computational and mathematical convenience it is usual to take $a = -m.$[2] From (3.4.1) it is seen that a filter is similar to a black box and can, in fact, be thought of as a time-lagged black box.

[2] The case $a = 0$ is considered in Section 4.6.

The effect of applying the filter (3.4.1) to a process is to multiply the power spectrum by $g(\omega) = a(\omega)\overline{a(\omega)}$ where

$$a(\omega) = \sum_{j=-m}^{m} \alpha_j e^{ij\omega}.$$

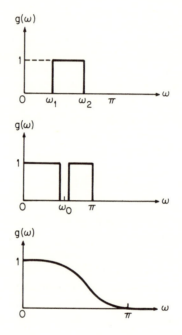

Figure 3.2

The problem of choosing the correct filter now becomes one of correctly choosing the coefficients α_j.

Consider the case where x_t is real and consists only of a single frequency, i.e.,

$$x_t = A \cos(\omega t + \theta),$$

then

$$y_t = A \sum_{j=-m}^{m} \alpha_j \cos(\omega(t+j) + \theta)$$

$$= A \cos(\omega t + \theta) \sum_{j=-m}^{m} \alpha_j \cos j\omega - A \sin(\omega t + \theta) \sum_{j=-m}^{m} \alpha_j \sin j\omega$$

and so the series $\{y_t\}$ still consists only of the single frequency ω but the amplitude has been multiplied by

$$S^2(\omega) = \left(\sum_{j=-m}^{m} \alpha_j \cos j\omega \right)^2 + \left(\sum_{j=-m}^{m} \alpha_j \sin j\omega \right)^2$$

and the phase has been changed by

$$\varphi(\omega) = -\tan^{-1} \frac{\sum \alpha_j \sin j\omega}{\sum \alpha_j \cos j\omega}$$

Although it depends to a large amount on what methods will consequently be used on the filtered data, it is usually very inconvenient to have the filter producing a phase-change and so we often require $\varphi(\omega) = 0$. This is easily achieved by taking $\alpha_j = \alpha_{-j}$ and such a filter will be called *symmetric* or *cosine* filter. Just occasionally, however, it is found useful to use an *asymmetric* or *sine filter*, i.e., a filter with $\alpha_j = -\alpha_{-j}$.

For a cosine filter, the phase is unaltered for every frequency and the power spectrum is multiplied by

$$S^2(\omega) = \left(\alpha_0 + 2 \sum_{j=1}^{m} \alpha_j \cos j\omega \right)^2,$$

$S^2(\omega)$ being called the *filter factor* and $S(\omega)$ the *transfer function*.

Discussion of how best to choose the coefficients α_j will be delayed until specific problems are considered, such as the removal of low frequencies (Chapter 8) and concentration on a particular frequency band (Chapter 10).

Many elementary textbooks of statistics warn of the use of filters or moving averages because "they might induce cycles into the data." Such warnings originate in a result by Slutsky [19], who found that if one forms a secondary, intercorrelated series from the primary, purely random series by m iterated summations of two consecutive terms, followed by n first differences, then, holding m/n constant, the resulting series tends to a sine curve as $n \to \infty$. This theorem can be proved easily using previous results. If the series $\{x_t\}$ has power spectrum $f(\omega)$ then the series $\{y_t\}$ formed by

$$y_t = x_t + x_{t+1}$$

has spectrum $A(\omega) f(\omega)$, where

$$A(\omega) = (1 + e^{-i\omega})(1 + e^{i\omega})$$
$$= 2(1 + \cos \omega)$$

and the series $\{z_t\}$ formed by

$$z_t = x_t - x_{t-1}$$

⟨ 41 ⟩

has spectrum $B(\omega)\,f(\omega)$ where

$$B(\omega) = (1 - e^{-i\omega})(1 - e^{i\omega})$$
$$= 2(1 - \cos \omega).$$

Thus, the effect of taking m sums of two followed by n first differences is to multiply the spectrum by $A^m(\omega)B^n(\omega)$. If we consider the special case of $m = n$, we multiply the spectrum by the function

$$2^n(1 - \cos \omega)^n 2^n(1 + \cos \omega)^n = 4^n(\sin \omega)^{2n}$$

which has the shape indicated in Fig. 3.3 and as n increases, the peak

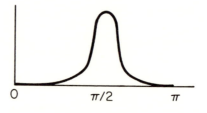

Figure 3.3

becomes higher and narrower. Thus a single frequency is very much emphasized by this process and a "cycle" results. If $m/n = \alpha \neq 1$, $n \to \infty$, then the result is similar but the frequency λ is emphasized where

$$\cos \lambda = \frac{1 - \alpha}{1 + \alpha}.$$

In a sense, the textbook warnings are correct, as the application of a moving average can emphasize a particular frequency band and persistent fluctuations will result, but as we are always able to determine the effect on the spectrum of any moving average, such occurrences need only occur when required. Thus, one effect of using the spectral approach is to give us greater understanding and control of filtering techniques.

3.5 Estimation of the Power Spectrum

From the relationship for real, stationary processes (3.2.10)

$$\mu_\tau = 2 \int_0^\pi \cos \tau \omega \, f(\omega) \, d\omega$$

the formal inversion gives

(3.5.1) $$f(\omega) = \frac{1}{2\pi}\left(\mu_0 + 2\sum_{j=1}^{\infty} \mu_j \cos j\omega\right)$$

⟨ 42 ⟩

and so, for a finite amount of data $\{x_t, t = 1, \ldots, n\}$ a sensible estimate would appear to be

$$(3.5.2) \qquad \hat{f}(\omega) = \frac{1}{2\pi}\left(C_0 + 2\sum_{j=1}^{n-1} C_j \cos j\omega\right)$$

where

$$(3.5.3) \qquad C_\tau = \frac{1}{n-\tau}\sum_{t=1}^{n-\tau}(x_t - \bar{x})(x_{t+\tau} - \bar{x}).$$

The estimate (3.5.2) is closely related to Schuster's periodogram

$$I_n(\omega) = \frac{1}{n}\left[(\sum x_t \sin \omega t)^2 + (\sum x_t \cos \omega t)^2\right].$$

Hannan [10], pages 52–53, shows that $E[I_n(\omega)] = 2\pi f(\omega)$, but

$$\text{var }[I_n(\omega)] \cong [2f(\omega)]^2 + 0(n^{-1})$$

and so $I_n(\omega)$ does not give a consistent estimate of $f(\omega)$, i.e.,

$$\text{var }[I_n(\omega)] \not\to 0 \text{ as } n \to \infty.$$

Also

$$\text{cov }\{I_n(\omega_1)I_n(\omega_2)\} = 0(n^{-1}),$$

at most, for $\omega_1 \neq \omega_2$ and so the periodogram does not provide a diagram that is at all smooth.

The failure of the periodogram as an estimate of the power spectrum has led to consideration of estimates of the form

$$\hat{f}(\omega) = \frac{1}{2\pi}\left\{C_0 \lambda_0(\omega) + 2\sum_{j=1}^{m-1} \lambda_j(\omega)C_j \cos j\omega\right\}$$

A considerable amount of discussion has occurred in deciding how to choose the weighting factors $\lambda_j(\omega)$. The arguments do not lie within the scope of this volume and have been carefully dealt with elsewhere, for instance in Chapter III of Hannan's book.

For a variety of reasons, the estimate used throughout the book is the Tukey-Hanning estimate, i.e.,

$$(3.5.4) \qquad \hat{f}(\omega) = \frac{1}{2\pi}\left[C_0 + \sum_{j=1}^{m} C_j\left[1 + \cos\frac{\pi j}{m}\right]\right]\cos j\omega$$

where m is an arbitrary integer to be chosen by the user, although it is suggested that $m < n/3$.

When, in statistics, a random sample of size n is drawn from a population, it is clearly impossible to estimate all parts of the population frequency function from the sample. Essentially, one is here saying that it is impossible to estimate an (uncountably) infinite number of points given only a finite amount of information. The usual procedure, then, is to approximate the frequency function by a histogram, as in Fig. 3.4,

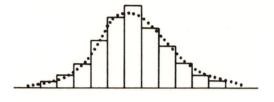

Figure 3.4

and, clearly, the larger the number of points one attempts to estimate, the larger the variance and so the worse the estimate for each point. The same problem and procedure holds in estimating the spectrum; we attempt to estimate the average value of the power spectrum over a finite set of frequency bands. It is not necessary but is usual to take the frequency bands to be of equal size. Thus, the estimate (3.5.4) is calculated at the points $\omega_k = \dfrac{\pi k}{m}$, $k = 0, 1, \ldots, m$.

One method of achieving such an estimate would be to apply a filter with filter factor

$$S(\omega) = 1 \qquad \omega_k - \frac{\pi}{2m} \leqq \omega < \omega_k + \frac{\pi}{2m}$$

$$= 0 \qquad \text{elsewhere}$$

and then to find the variance of the filtered data for $k = 0, 1, \ldots, m$. However, it is not possible to find a short filter having exactly such a sharp filter factor and one is forced to use a filter having transfer factor shaped like Fig. 3.5. (Such a filter is called a *"window"* since, by using it,

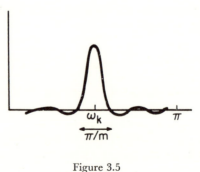

Figure 3.5

we look only at part of all that is to be seen.) If the spectrum has a large peak at some frequency other than ω_k, then it is possible that some of the power of this frequency will "leak" into the estimate of the spectrum at ω_k due to the presence of the side peaks in the filter factor.

It is very possible to have such important peaks in the spectrum of an economic series (due perhaps to trend or an important annual component), and so it is important to use a spectral estimate in which there is only a small amount of "leakage" between frequency bands. It is an important property of the Tukey estimate (3.5.4) that the side peaks of the window are never more than 2% of the main peak, and so the possibility of leakage spoiling the estimate at any frequency is small.

Further useful properties of the Tukey estimate are: (i) $\hat{f}(\omega_k)$ and $\hat{f}(\omega_{k+2})$ are effectively uncorrelated, (ii) approximate confidence bands are available, and (iii) it has been programmed for use on various digital computers. These properties will be further discussed in the next chapter.

Grenander and Rosenblatt [11] have shown that the variance of the Tukey estimate is approximately

$$\text{var}\,[\hat{f}(\omega)] \sim \frac{4m}{5n}\, f^2(\omega), \quad \omega \neq 0$$

$$\sim \frac{8m}{5n}\, f^2(0), \quad \omega = 0$$

and the estimate has bias approximately

$$0.46[\tfrac{1}{2}f(\omega + \pi/m) + \tfrac{1}{2}f(\omega - \pi/m) - f(\omega)].$$

The bias is clearly very small for sufficiently smooth spectral function, and although it is possible to find estimates having up to 15% less variance the above advantages seem to outweigh this possible gain.

Mention must here be made of a technique proposed by Tukey and Blackman to improve the estimate of a spectrum which is unlike the spectrum of white noise. The estimates proposed above assume the spectrum to be smooth, but if a certain frequency band is particularly important then leakage will occur. The Tukey-Blackman approach, known as "pre-whitening" is to estimate the spectrum and then, if any frequency band appears to be particularly important, to apply a filter to the series designed to de-emphasize (but not remove) this frequency band. Thus, new data is formed by application of the filter F with filter factor $S^2(\omega)$, $y_t = F(x_t)$ and the spectrum of y_t estimated. The "improved" estimate of the spectrum of the series x_t is now

$$\hat{f}_x(\omega) = \frac{\hat{f}_y(\omega)}{S^2(\omega)}.$$

There has been considerable disagreement in the literature about the usefulness of this technique, the majority consensus seeming to be against its use. (For the pros and cons of pre-whitening see, for instance, Blackman and Tukey [8], Tukey [4], Grenander and Rosenblatt [11], and Jenkins [7].)

Due to this controversy, and as some computer experiments investigating the importance of leakage (described in Chapter 8) indicated that leakage was not of too great importance except when tremendous peaks are present in the spectrum, the pre-whitening technique has not been used in the examples given in this book.

3.6 Nyquist Frequency, Aliasing

If we consider our sample series $\{x_t\}$ as being values taken from a continuous time series $x(t)$ at equally spaced intervals of time, certain important aspects of the interpretation of a spectrum need to be mentioned.

It should be clear that if $x(t)$ contains a frequency $\dfrac{2\pi}{k}$ where k is the length of time between recordings, then $\{x_t\}$ will contain no information about this frequency. As an example, if one recorded the temperature daily at noon one would have no information about the daily variation of temperature. However, if recordings were taken at noon and midnight, then the importance of the daily fluctuations could be estimated. In fact, the highest frequency about which we have direct information is $\dfrac{\pi}{k}$ and is known as the Nyquist frequency. The power of this frequency is recorded at $\omega = \pi$ in the power spectrum.

It must be remembered, however, that a fast cosine wave systematically sampled at regular intervals appears the same as a slow cosine wave. Figure 3.6 illustrates this in sketch form. Thus, after sampling,

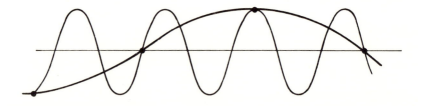

Figure 3.6

the apparent contribution of any frequency is the result of superimposing the contributions of many frequencies which now become aliases of one another. If ω_0 is the Nyquist frequency, then ω, $2\omega_0 - \omega$, $2\omega_0 + \omega$, $4\omega_0 - \omega$, $4\omega_0 + \omega, \ldots$, are confounded and are aliases of one another.

As an example, suppose we record temperature at 30 hour intervals. The daily, 24-hour variation in temperature corresponds to $\frac{30}{24} = 1.25$ oscillations per basic time unit and so will alias with the frequency of 0.25 oscillations per time unit. Thus, if the spectrum is estimated with m lags, the alias of the daily temperature variation in this case will affect the power of the kth spectral estimate, where k is the integer nearest $0.25 \cdot 2m = m/2$.

A second example, although more approximate, comes from the problem that there are not exactly four weeks in a real month. Taking into account leap years, the average number of days in a month is 30.437 and so there are 4.348 weeks in the average month. If an instantaneously recorded series, such as stock prices, measured every month, contained an important weekly cycle, it would thus correspond to the frequency 0.348. In the case when the spectrum is estimated with 60 lags, say, the weekly frequency will add power, due to aliasing, to the 42nd point, this being the integer nearest 41.76.

The effects of aliasing should be remembered when interpreting the peaks of a spectrum and when choosing sampling intervals.

3.7 Transformations of Stationary Processes

A transformation of a process $\{X_t\}$ into another process $\{Y_t\}$, of the form

$$Y_t = G(X_t)$$

where $G(x)$ is some function of x, may be called an instantaneous transformation or an amplitude distortion. Such transformations have been discussed by Grenander and Rosenblatt [11] and by Grenander [18], mostly under the assumption that $\{X_t\}$ is a normal process.

By far the most important transformation of this kind in economics is the logarithmic transformation

(3.7.1) $$Y_t = \log_e X_t$$

and it is important to determine the effect on the spectrum of this transformation.

It is clearly pointless to discuss the case where X_t is distributed normally as, regardless of the mean and variance of the process, Prob $(X < 0)$ will not be zero and so the process Y_t will not be real. Thus, we have to consider the case $X_t \geq 0$ and, if we assume X_t to be log normally distributed, the effect of the transformation is easily studied. Under this assumption, $\{Y_t\}$ will be a normal process. Let

$$E[X_t] = \alpha \qquad\qquad E[Y_t] = m$$
$$E[(X_t - \alpha)(X_{t-\tau} - \alpha)] = \beta R_x(\tau), \qquad E[Y_t Y_{t-\tau}] = \sigma^2 R_y(\tau) + m^2$$

where $|R_x(\tau)| \leq R_x(0) = 1$, $|R_y(\tau)| \leq R_y(0) = 1$. Using the fact that if x is distributed normally $N(m, \sigma)$ then $E[e^x] = \exp\left(\frac{1}{2}\sigma^2 + m\right)$, it is seen that

$$\alpha = E[X_t] = E[e^{Y_t}]$$

$$= \exp\left(\tfrac{1}{2}\sigma^2 + m\right)$$

and

$$E[X_t X_{t-\tau}] = E[\exp(Y_t + Y_{t-\tau})]$$

$$= \exp(\sigma^2 + 2m + \sigma^2 R_y(\tau)).$$

Thus

$$\beta R_x(\tau) = \exp(\sigma^2 + 2m)[\exp(\sigma^2 R_y(\tau)) - 1]$$

and so

$$(3.7.2) \qquad \sigma^2 R_y(\tau) = \log[1 + \mu^2 R_x(\tau)]$$

where $\mu^2 = \dfrac{\beta}{\alpha^2}$. ($\mu$ is called the coefficient of variation.) When $\mu^2 \leq 1$, the logarithm in (3.7.2) can be expanded as a power series, giving

$$\sigma^2 R_y(\tau) = \sum_{j=1}^{\infty} (-1)^{j+1} \frac{\mu^{2j}}{j}(R_x(\tau))^j$$

$$(3.7.3) \qquad\qquad = \sum_{j=1}^{\infty} (-1)^{j+1} \frac{(\beta R_x(\tau))^j}{j\alpha^{2j}}.$$

If $f_x(\omega)$ is the power spectrum of the process $\{X_t\}$, so that

$$\beta R_x(\tau) = \int_{-\pi}^{\pi} e^{i\tau\omega} f_x(\omega)\, d\omega$$

then

$$(3.7.4) \qquad [\beta R_x(\tau)]^n = \int_{-\pi}^{\pi} e^{i\tau\omega} f_x^{(n)}(\omega)\, d\omega$$

where the sequence of convolutions $f_x^{(j)}(\omega), j = 1, 2, \ldots$, are given by

$$(3.7.5) \quad f_x^{(1)}(\omega) = f_x(\omega), \qquad f_x^{(n)}(\omega) = \int_{-\pi}^{\pi} f_x^{(n-1)}(\lambda - \omega) f_x(\lambda)\, d\lambda$$

Thus, from equations (3.7.3), (3.7.4), and (3.7.5) the power spectrum of the process $\{Y_t\}$ is given by

$$(3.7.6) \qquad f_y(\omega) = \sum_{j=1}^{\infty} (-1)^{j+1} \frac{f_x^{(j)}(\omega)}{j\alpha^{2j}}$$

This equation is only true for processes $\{X_t\}$ containing no strictly periodic components and obeying the condition

$$(3.7.7) \qquad \frac{\sigma_x^2}{m_x^2} \leq 1.$$

That such a condition should arise is not surprising as the logarithm transformation is very sensitive to values near zero. When condition (3.7.7) is true, such values will be very rare. With this condition, the first one or two terms provide a reasonable approximation to the power spectrum of the formed series Y_t. In particular, if the mean is much larger than the standard deviation of the original series, the shape of the spectrum will be little changed by a logarithmic transformation.

Appendix

The Expectation Notation

If a random variable X has distribution function $F(x)$ then the expectation of the function $g(X)$ of X is defined as

$$E[g(X)] = \int_{-\infty}^{\infty} g(x)\, dF(x).$$

Thus, for a variable with discrete distribution function $p_j = \text{Prob}(X = X_j)$

$$E[g(X)] = \sum_{j=1}^{\infty} p_j\, g(X_j)$$

and for a variable with a differentiable distribution function such that $dF(x) = f(x)\, dx$,

$$E[g(X)] = \int_{-\infty}^{\infty} g(x) f(x)\, dx.$$

In particular, the mean and variance of such a variable are given by

$$m = E[X] = \int_{-\infty}^{\infty} x f(x)\, dx$$

and

$$\sigma^2 = E[(X - E[X])^2] = \int_{-\infty}^{\infty} (x - m)^2 f(x)\, dx.$$

For two random variables X, Y it may be noted that

$$E[aX + bY] = aE[X] + bE[Y]$$

and if the two variables are uncorrelated

$$E[XY] = E[X]E[Y].$$

These follow from the bivariate definition of expectation:

$$E[g(X, Y)] = \int_{-\infty}^{\infty} \int_{-\infty}^{\infty} g(x, y)\, dF(x, y)$$

where $F(x, y)$ is the bivariate distribution function for the variables X, Y.

For time series the expectation can only be used, correctly, in connection with the underlying generating process.

REFERENCES

NOTE. The following list of references includes the majority of the articles and books that attempt to present spectral analysis in a form useful to statisticians and economists. The list is, very roughly, in ascending order of mathematical sophistication. The books most recommended are Hannan [10] and Grenander and Rosenblatt [11].

[1] Hannan, E. J., "Some recent advances in statistics," *The Economic Record*, vol. 33 (1957), pp. 337–352.

[2] Granger, C. W. J., "First report of the Princeton economic time series project," *L'industria* (1961), pp. 194–206.

[3] Jenkins, G. M. and Priestley, M. B., "The spectral analysis of time series," *J. Roy. Stat. Soc. B.*, vol. 19 (1957), pp. 1–12.

[4] Tukey, J. W., "An introduction to the measurement of spectra," in *Probability and Statistics*, ed. by U. Grenander, Stockholm (1959), pp. 300–330.

[5] Tukey, J. W., "The estimation of (power) spectra and related quantities," in *On Numerical Approximation*, ed. by R. E. Langer, Madison, Wisconsin (1959), pp. 389–411.

[6] Tukey, J. W., "Discussion, emphasizing the connection between analysis of variance and spectrum analysis," *Technometrics*, vol. 3 (1961), pp. 191–219.

[7] Jenkins, G. M., "General considerations in the analysis of spectra," *Technometrics*, vol. 3 (1961), pp. 133–166.

[8] Blackman, R. B., and Tukey, J. W., *The Measurement of Power Spectra*, New York, 1958.

[9] Whittle, P., Appendix to second edition of *Stationary Time Series*, by H. Wold, Stockholm, 1954.

[10] Hannan, E. J., *Time Series Analysis*, London, 1960.

[11] Grenander, U. and Rosenblatt, M., *Statistical Analysis of Stationary Time Series*, New York, 1957.

[12] Bartlett, M. S., *Stochastic Processes*, Cambridge, 1955.

[13] Doob, J. L., *Stochastic Processes*, New York, 1952.

The problem of estimating the spectrum has been dealt with extensively in many of the above references, particularly by Hannan [10], Grenander and Rosenblatt [11], Jenkins [7] and Blackman and Tukey [8], but two other useful references are:

[14] Parzen, E., "Mathematical considerations in the estimation of spectra," *Technometrics*, vol. 3 (1961), pp. 167–190.

[15] Wonnacott, T. W., "Spectra analysis combining a Bartlett window with an associated inner window," *Technometrics*, vol. 3 (1961), pp. 235–244.

The two basic references concerning prediction of stationary time series are:

[16] Wiener, N., *The Extrapolation, Interpolation and Smoothing of Stationary Time Series*, New York, 1949.

[17] Kolmogoroff, A., "Sur l'interpolation et extrapolation des suites stationnaires," *C. R. Acad. Sci. Paris*, vol. 208 (1939), pp. 2043–2045.

REFERENCES

Two further references that occur in Chapter 3 are:

[18] Grenander, U., "Some nonlinear problems in probability theory," *Probability and Statistics* (the Harald Cramér volume) ed. by U. Grenander, Stockholm and New York, 1959.

[19] Slutzky, E., "The summation of random causes as the source of cyclic processes," *Econometrica*, vol. 5 (1937).

CHAPTER 4

SPECTRAL ANALYSIS OF ECONOMIC DATA

4.1 An Analogy

As the spectral concept is not a particularly easy one, this section is devoted to giving an analogy that has been found useful in the past. (Readers who feel that they already fully understand the concept should pass on to the next section.)

We consider the total amount of sound (or noise) coming over a very wide radio band. If we had a very crude instrument which transformed all the noise into sounds that the human ear can hear, the resulting cacophony would resemble the type of (stationary) time series that we are usually trying to analyze; that is, it is built up of many components, each of which we would like to know more about. Just as the ear can filter out sounds and concentrate on a particular one, so can a radio concentrate on a particular wave-band. It is certain that everyone has at some time swung the dial of a radio set across a wave-band, and the experience there gained can be used in an explanation of the spectrum. Suppose that we have a simple radio set that does not emit the actual words or sounds found at any frequency but only indicates the total power (or amount) of sound. By this we mean in effect that our simple radio set has the ability to look at one wave-length (frequency) at a time without being distracted by what is to be found at other frequencies. If we used our set in England at 3 A.M. (i.e., when no stations are broadcasting), the set would not register zero amount of sound at every point but rather a small, constant amount. This is due to all the "atmospherics" and internally produced noise of the set and thus corresponds to receiving a purely random signal. If, however, some stations are broadcasting at that time, theoretically each will be sending signals at one frequency only. The radio will now show the small, constant (background) noise at all frequencies except at a finite number (corresponding to the number of stations) where it will record the power put out by each station. The radio will thus find the position of the frequencies at which the stations are broadcasting together with the strength of signal being received at these frequencies.

In practice, as everyone knows, the sound from a particular station is not to be found only at a single point but rather is spread around the point, although with decreasing power. (Incidentally, if the sound were literally at only one point of the line it would be impossible to find with a perfect radio.) Diagrams i-iii illustrate the three types of signals discussed above.

We now define a *spectrum* as a diagram showing the size of the amplitude of each frequency to be found in a particular time series. It should not be surprising to learn that it may be proved that perfect knowledge of a spectrum will determine the *properties* of a time series, but not its

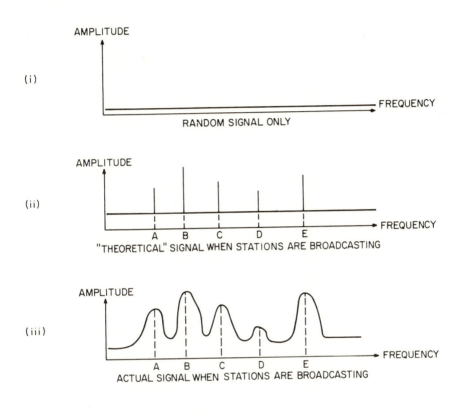

Diagrams i-iii

actual values, due to the probabilistic elements involved. In any case, the spectrum will certainly show which are the important components of the series.

Diagrams i–iii illustrate certain types of time series: (i) is, of course, the spectrum of a purely random, independent series (white noise), (ii) is the theoretical spectrum of the linear cyclic model, whereas (iii) represents the perfect estimate (should such a thing exist) of the spectrum of a time series of finite length generated by the linear cyclic model. (Diagram (iii) corresponds to the shape that Schuster was hoping his periodogram would take.)

It might be noted that even if the stations were broadcasting as in diagram (ii), a real radio is unable to concentrate on a single wave-length, but rather gives the output over a small wave-band, centered on this wave-length, possibly with weights decreasing from the center of the band outward. Thus, even if the stations were broadcasting as in (ii), the radio's output would resemble diagram (iii). This is the identical situation to that when we attempt to estimate the spectrum; having only a finite amount of data available, we are forced to estimate the spectrum over a finite number of frequency bands.

Suppose that our simplified radio was now attached to a radio tele-scope which is directed toward some point in the Milky Way. It is possible that the resulting plot of power against frequency looks like diagrams (i) or (iii), but it is also plausible to expect a more complicated diagram as in (iv) and (v). It is clear that such "spectra," as we may

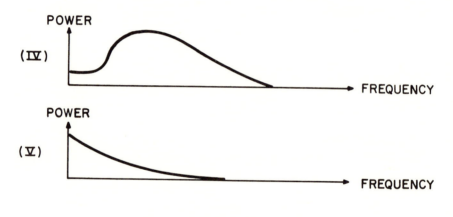

Diagrams iv-v

now think of them, cannot arise from series which are derived from a linear cyclic model. On the other hand, it is perfectly possible for a series from a linear regressive model to produce such a smooth spectrum, although a smooth spectrum does not necessarily indicate that a linear regressive model is the correct one. Many more complicated systems could also produce a similar shape.

By examining a spectrum the important *bands* of frequencies may be seen although little can be said about the underlying generating process (except, perhaps, that it is doubtful that it is linear cyclic).

It must be emphasized that the above analogy has been presented only to help understand the ideas involved in the concept of a spectrum and, like all analogies, it must not be taken too far or examined too deeply.

There are many problems concerned with estimating spectra (chiefly due to the rather obvious fact that one cannot satisfactorily estimate a continuous curve containing an infinite number of points when only given a finite amount of data), but there are now various satisfactory methods of estimation available, and these are discussed in Section 4.3.

The amount of information that an economist can gain from the estimation of a spectrum might at first sight seem insufficient to justify the amount of calculation involved. In a sense this is so, since information as to which frequency bands are most important cannot often be used unless evidence of peaks is found. However, the spectral idea proves to be a very useful tool in explaining what one is attempting to do in an analysis and for examining the effects of the various available methods (such as filtering) on the series. In the author's opinion, the spectral approach is mostly useful in easing comprehension when only a single series is involved, but the generalization of the approach to analyze two or more series together (dealt with in chapters 5 and 6) provides extremely useful and powerful methods; it is here that the approach takes on its true importance.

4.2 Economic Implications of Spectral Decomposition

Economists have long been aware that the variables with which they deal may be split into a set of components. Economic variables, for example, have often been represented by "trend," plus "cycles," plus a "random error term," or by the sum of "long-run" and "short-run" components. In both cases the terms used have been poorly defined, and quite correctly so, since it is only with the advent of the spectral approach that statistically acceptable definitions have been possible. It is perhaps worthwhile to discuss briefly the classical decompositions and some of their implications.

A casual glance at the plot of any data from a macroeconomic variable will almost certainly reveal that the data are apparently lying about an increasing curve of some nature, have some "long" swings away from the curve, occasionally of several years duration, and also contain a great many faster oscillations of lesser amplitude. Further, many economic series contain an important annual component. It is thus not at all unnatural to attempt to fit to the data a model consisting of the four components "trend," "cycles," "seasonal," and "error." The implications of such a model, however, have not always been fully realized. What is meant by "trend" in such a situation? If the data consist of n monthly readings of the variable, then they contain only a very slight amount of information concerning "cycles" of period considerably greater than n months. This is the same as saying that minute by minute temperature readings at a certain place for two thousand minutes will contain virtually no information about annual variations in temperature. The type of problem that one attempts to solve must be within the limitations of one's data. It would seem fair to include with the term "trend" all cycles with periods greater than $2n$ where n is the length of the series, as such cycles are indistinguishable from a polynomial trend over the time-span for which we have information. This definition will include polynomials (which have period infinity) and other non-periodic curves as merely part of the total, and once such a limitation in the definition of "trend" is realized, interpretation becomes easier. (The problems of trend in economic series are further discussed in Chapters 8 and 11.) It should be noted, however, that as we require half-a-dozen or so repetitions of a cycle before we are able to estimate its amplitude at all reasonably, the first frequency band in an estimated power spectrum will include such cycles together with the trend component just defined.

The "cycles" envisaged were usually of at least 20 months in length (except for the annual component), and it was not fully appreciated that to pick out such cycles by accurate statistical methods (as opposed to "eye") required a very large amount of data. A further difficulty of interpretation of the model was that each "cycle" was not thought of as having a constant, firmly fixed amplitude. If we slightly broaden the idea of a "cycle" to being a component corresponding to a narrow, important *band* of frequencies, the cycle will now have varying amplitude due to interference between the neighboring frequencies. This extension is essentially the same as moving from the theoretical to the actual broadcasting bands of the radio stations mentioned in the previous section, and the effect on the spectrum is the same.

The seasonal variation is far more regular than the "cycles" just discussed but its amplitude and phase do change over time and so even this component does not correspond to a set of frequency *points* (at twelve months, six months etc.) but rather to a set of narrow frequency *bands* centered on these points.

The vaguest of all the components is the "error," "random," or "irregular" component. It is envisaged as being an independent, random series whose power would almost be reduced to zero by the application of a moving average type of filter. It seems under the present interpretation that such a component consists of only high frequency terms, i.e., the spectrum of the component would be zero up to frequency $\frac{\pi}{4}$ (say) and is, perhaps, constant for higher frequencies.

The concepts of "long-run" and "short-run" and the more recently added "middle-run" can also be interpreted as an appreciation by students of economics that their variables consist of several components. The movements in the short-run, which are measured at an instant, could be thought of as being the responsibility of one component (high frequency), the length of the period being restricted so that the more ponderous components will have changed very little within it and thus can be neglected. The long-run movements which, strictly, should be measured as the change of the average value of the variable, will be mostly due to a component of low frequency, as the averaging will cut out the high frequency component. To give a highly naive model for such a variable, consider

$$x_t = \cos\left(\frac{\pi t}{5}\right) + 20 \cos\left(\frac{\pi t}{100}\right).$$

Between $t = 0$ and $t = 2$, the first component will have changed from 1 to 0.17 whereas the second component has changed from 20 to 19.96. Thus the high frequency component has accounted for 95% of the change over the period even though the low frequency component has a considerably larger amplitude. If, however, one considers the difference between the average value of x_t for $t = 1, 2, \ldots, 10$, and the value for $t = 91, 92, \ldots, 100$, then the entire (and very large) change is due to the second component.

The addition of the middle-run component appears to indicate that economists working in the field felt that the short and long-run components alone did not describe sufficiently well the fluctuations of economic variables.

One point that the author feels is interesting is that all early writers appear to be considering variables such that the power of low frequencies is considerably more than the power of higher frequencies. If such were not so, the long-run component would be hardly observable. The same applies to the "cycles" of macroeconomic theory; if they had not been "observed" the concepts would not have gained such importance in the theory. This suggests that casual observation of economic variables indicates that they have a spectrum that, in general, decreases as frequency increases. Such a spectrum can usually be very well represented by an autoregressive model employing few time-lags. We return to this point at the end of this section.

Using the frequency concept, the ideas of long-run, short-run, etc., may be defined specifically, e.g., long run $\equiv$ low frequencies (from 0 to $\frac{2\pi}{30}$, say, when using monthly data), short-run $\equiv$ high frequencies (from $\frac{\pi}{2}$ to π, say), and middle-run could correspond to the remaining frequencies. Such a decomposition is entirely arbitrary, there being no more reason for having three components than for having forty-three. To have only three components may appear to ease comprehension, but results in a considerable loss in generality of approach, particularly when "economic laws" are suggested or models of the economy are constructed. It is certainly possible, and indeed likely, that the variables ought to be split into more than three components, each of which will obey different laws. The reasonableness of this can be well shown when the relationships between two series are considered in Chapter 6. Unless there is some a priori reason for splitting into a set number of frequency components, the most general approach is to use either an obviously sufficiently large number (such as 40 or 60) or the largest number that the data allow. Thus, the Cramér representation, which essentially states that for a stationary (i.e., trend-free) series the whole continuum of frequencies from 0 to π is likely to be present to some extent in the generating process, should affect the manner in which models are constructed or economic laws (or relationships) are stated. It will usually be necessary to state the law which each of the components is supposed to obey, and this law will not always be the same for the various components.

The independence of the frequency components of a single variable, which is also part of the Cramér representation, has less economic significance. For a particular stationary series the only effect of this independence is that one would be very much surprised if the phases of all the frequencies obeyed some simple, linear function with frequency. Thus, the likelihood of all frequencies coming to a peak at the same time in a series of finite length is negligible. (This is similar to an argument from quantum physics. All the atoms at the base of the Washington Monument are moving in an independent random way, but if they all happened to be moving upward at the same instant the building would leap into the air. Fortunately, the probability of such an event occurring is so small that it may be considered to be zero.) This statistical independence is not the same as saying that frequencies not near one another have little effect on each other. This follows from the fact that the average value of the product of two sine curves with non-adjacent or equal periods is very small when taken over a sufficient length of time. Thus, any apparent fluctuation in the amplitude of any particular frequency will be entirely due to interference by a neighboring frequency.

Economists often doubt the independence of various components of the variables with which they deal, but when pressed for examples when independence is not a realistic assumption, almost invariably the example given is concerned with a non-stationary variable. Thus, for instance, an increase in short-run fluctuations in production may force a long-run decision to be made concerning expansion. However, for stationary variables, independence of components does seem to be more acceptable.

It was pointed out above that early investigations of economic data indicate that a typical power spectrum from an economic series decreases as frequency increases. In fact, experience shows that such spectra are very common among economic series. Thus, when the series contains no important seasonal component, a typical estimated power spectrum is similar to that found for Woolworth's stock prices (see Fig. 4.3), even when the series contains no trend in mean.

We may ask: does this experience contradict the "business-cycle" theories of economics? It is suggested that it does not. The brief account of business cycles given in Chapter 2 indicates that many cycles have been suggested, of many lengths. A typical sample from a process having a smooth spectrum, such as drawn in Fig. 4.3, will usually appear to have some of the low frequencies more important than other low frequencies but the spectral techniques need not find *peaks* corresponding to each of the suggested cycles. We would expect the frequency bands corresponding to the cycles to provide significant proportions of the over-all variance, which in fact we do find. The fact that the same important low frequencies have been visually observed in several series merely indicates that these series are closely associated at these frequencies.

It is thus suggested that the results from research into business cycles need not be interpreted as showing the underlying processes to have a series of peaks in the low frequencies, but can equally well be interpreted as having a shape such as found in Fig. 4.3.

The idea of a series being made up of a large number of frequency components has further, and perhaps more important, implications when the relationships between two series are considered. These implications are discussed in the next two chapters.

4.3 Spectral Estimation

All spectral estimates are of the form

$$(4.3.1) \qquad f(\omega_j) = \frac{1}{2\pi}\left\{\lambda_0 C_0 + 2\sum_{k=1}^{m}\lambda_k C_k \cos \omega_j k\right\}$$

$$\omega_j = \frac{\pi j}{m}, \qquad j = 0, \ldots, m$$

where the estimated covariances are given by a form similar to

$$(4.3.2) \qquad C_k = \frac{1}{n-k}\left\{\sum_{t=1}^{n-k} x_t x_{t+k} - \frac{1}{n-k}\sum_{t=1+k}^{n} x_t \sum_{t=1}^{n-k} x_t\right\}$$

with data $(x_t, t = 1, \ldots, n)$, and the weights, λ_k, are usually dependent upon m.

There is, at the moment, some controversy about whether C_k should be as in (4.3.2) or if the divisor $n - k$ ought to be replaced by n. The estimate of μ_k as given is unbiased, but the alternative estimate has lower variance and the resulting autocovariance matrix is necessarily positive definite. However, if $n \gg m$, the difference between the two estimates is negligible. (See Parzen [9] and Tukey [10].)

Various ways of choosing the weights λ_k have been suggested, but as this topic has been exhaustively discussed by other writers (e.g., Jenkins [5], Parzen [9], Hannan [4], and Grenander and Rosenblatt [3]), it need not concern us here. As mentioned in Chapter 3, the estimating procedure used throughout this volume is the Tukey-Hanning estimate. This has weights

$$\lambda_k = \frac{1}{2}\left[1 + \cos\frac{\pi k}{m}\right]$$

and the actual formulae used in estimating the spectrum are

$$C_k = \frac{1}{n-k}\left\{\sum_{t=1}^{n-k} x_t x_{t+k} - \frac{1}{n-k}\sum_{t=1+k}^{n} x_t \cdot \sum_{t=1}^{n-k} x_t\right\}$$

$$L_j = \frac{1}{2\pi}\left(C_0 + 2\sum_{k=1}^{m-1} C_k \cos\frac{\pi k j}{m} + C_m \cos \pi j\right)$$

$$U_j = 0.25L_{j-1} + 0.50L_j + 0.25L_{j+1}$$

where $L_{-1} = L_{+1}$, $L_{m+1} = L_{m-1}$.

The L_j are called the raw estimates and the U_j the smoothed estimates, so that in the original notation $U_j = f(\omega_j)$. [It should be noted that the Tukey estimate given is for the spectral mass in the interval $\left(\frac{\pi j}{m} \pm \frac{\pi}{2m}\right)$.]

Computer programs of this estimate have been prepared for the IBM 650 (known as Statisan II and III), the IBM 707, 709, 7090, the CDC 1604, and various other machines. The majority of these programs print out not only the U_j's but also the C_k's and the L_j's. It is doubtful if the latter will prove to be of use except in the hands of very experienced users.

The reasons for the Project using the Tukey-Hanning estimate were chiefly those of convenience (the computer programs being available) and due to the very small leakage from one frequency band to another that use of this estimate ensures, providing that the bands are not adjacent. It might be noted that, if the data is white noise, estimates for adjacent frequency bands will have correlation coefficients of (very approximately) 0.25. This correlation is due to the spectral window used and ensures that the spectrum is at least somewhat smooth. For non-adjacent bands the corresponding correlation coefficient will be 0.07 or less.

One trouble with this estimate is that it occasionally provides negative estimates of the spectrum (which is actually always positive). To be given a negative estimate of an object known to be positive can be annoying, and the usual remedy is to put the estimate at zero. Recently, however, Parzen [5] has introduced an estimate which allows even less leakage than the Tukey-Hanning estimate and which also has the useful property that it never gives negative estimates. The weights λ_k are

$$\lambda_k = 1 - \frac{6k^2}{m^2}\left(1 - \frac{k}{m}\right), \qquad 0 \leq k \leq m/2$$

$$= 2\left(1 - \frac{k}{m}\right)^3, \qquad m/2 \leq k \leq m$$

and so the estimating formula becomes

$$U_j^* = \frac{C_0}{2\pi} + \frac{1}{\pi}\sum_{k=1}^{m/2}\left[1 - \frac{6k^2}{m^2}\left(1 - \frac{k}{m}\right)\right]$$
$$C_k \cos\frac{\pi k}{m}\, j + \frac{2}{\pi}\sum_{k=(m/2)+1}^{m}\left(1 - \frac{k}{m}\right)^3 C_k \cos\frac{\pi k}{m}\, j.$$

Here the suggested estimate for the co-variance is

$$C_k = \frac{1}{n}\sum_{t=0}^{n-k}(x_t - \bar{x})(x_{t+k} - \bar{x})$$

where

$$\bar{x} = \frac{1}{n}\sum_{t=0}^{n}x_t$$

The Parzen estimate has a wider window (i.e., $f(\omega_j)$ and $f(\omega_{j+2})$ have higher correlation than for the Tukey estimate) but the leakage is less between estimates for non-neighboring frequency bands.

The integer m appearing in (4.3.1) and other formulae is called the cut-off point or "number of lags used." It essentially represents the number of frequency bands for which the spectrum is estimated. This number is entirely at the user's control apart from possible limitation due to the computer program (Statisan II for the IBM 650 limits m to less than or equal to sixty, for instance). The larger m the more points at which the spectrum is estimated, and consequently the larger the variance of the estimate at each point; the smaller m the better the estimate. No real agreement exists among statisticians as to suitable sizes for m but, with n pieces of data only rarely should m be as large as $n/3$; for n not large, m in the order of $n/5$ or $n/6$ would seem to be reasonable.

The amount of data required before it becomes sensible to attempt to estimate a spectrum would seem to be greater than about 100. $n = 200$ can be thought of as a desirable minimum, in general, although crude spectra have occasionally been estimated with n as low as 80.

It should be noted that we estimate the power spectrum at the $m + 1$ equi-distance points $\omega_j = \frac{j\pi}{m}, j = 0, \ldots, m$. There is, of course, no reason why other sets of points should not be chosen and the distances between the points need not be constant, but the estimation procedures suggested above assume the points ω_j to have been used and there is only rarely occasion to consider other points. If the data used is monthly data and one is interested in a particular frequency, say the annual $= \dfrac{2\pi}{12}$, then one looks at the point ω_j of the estimated spectrum nearest this number, e.g.,

$$\omega_j = \frac{j\pi}{m} \cong \frac{2\pi}{12}$$

$$j \cong \frac{m}{6}.$$

Thus, if we have used 60 lags, the annual component will lie at the 10th frequency point. Similarly, the "40-month cycle" component will lie at the third frequency point.

In the examples of estimated spectra discussed in the next section, it will be noted that $\log f(\omega_j)$ has always been plotted against j rather than $f(\omega_j)$ against j. The reasons for this are:

(i) it has been found for economic series that the low frequencies are generally considerably more important than the high frequencies and so plotting on a log scale allows all points to be shown conveniently,

(ii) confidence bands can be easily added to the estimated spectra when plotted on semi-log paper.

The latter is so because the approximate $(100 - \alpha)\%$ confidence band is given for all j by

$$(T_\alpha(m, n)\, f(\omega_j),\; T'_\alpha(m, n)\, f(\omega_j))$$

i.e., by

$$(\log f(\omega_j) + \log T_\alpha(m, n),\; \log f(\omega_j) + \log T'_\alpha(m, n)$$

on semi-log paper.

The factors $T_\alpha(m, n)$, $T'_\alpha(m, n)$ vary for the different estimation procedures used, but for the Tukey-Hanning estimates they may be found as follows:

$$T_\alpha(m, n) \text{ is } \frac{\chi^2_{100-\alpha}(k)}{k}$$

and

$$T'_\alpha(m, n) \text{ is } \frac{\chi^2_\alpha(k)}{k}$$

where $\chi^2_\beta(s)$ is the $\beta\%$ value of χ^2 with s degrees of freedom, and $k = \dfrac{2n}{m}$, n being the number of data used and m the number of lags used in the estimate. k is called the "equivalent degrees of freedom" and the value of k here given in terms of n and m is an approximation chosen to allow for the fact that the series under consideration is not necessarily exactly normally distributed. (For a fuller account of confidence bands and their underlying theory, see Jenkins [5].)

The table gives values of $T_\alpha(m, n)$, $T'_\alpha(m, n)$ for various values of $k (= 2n/m)$ and for $\alpha = 5\%$ and 10%.

$k = \dfrac{2n}{m}$	Exceeded by 95% of all values $[T_{5\%}]$	Exceeded by 90% of all values $[T_{10\%}]$	Exceeded by 10% of all values $[T'_{10\%}]$	Exceeded by 5% of all values $[T'_{5\%}]$
2	0.05	0.10	2.30	2.99
3	0.12	0.20	2.08	2.60
4	0.18	0.26	1.94	2.37
5	0.23	0.32	1.85	2.21
6	0.27	0.37	1.77	2.10
8	0.34	0.44	1.68	1.94
10	0.39	0.49	1.60	1.83
12	0.43	0.53	1.55	1.75
15	0.48	0.57	1.48	1.66
20	0.54	0.62	1.42	1.51
30	0.62	0.69	1.34	1.46
50	0.69	0.75	1.26	1.34
100	0.77	0.82	1.18	1.22

It should be noted that the variance of the spectral estimates is twice as large at $\omega = 0, \pi$ as it is at other frequencies. At these frequencies T and T' should be multiplied by 1.41. For ease of exposition, this change in the width of the confidence bands has not been shown in the diagrams in §4.4.

The theory underlying the confidence bands assumes the spectrum to be constant throughout the frequency band under consideration but, of course, the main use of the bands is to see if an apparent peak in the spectrum could really have arisen due to mere random fluctuation in the estimated spectrum.

A less sophisticated but often useful method of testing the reality of a peak is to look for its harmonics. As it is extremely unlikely that a true cycle will be shaped exactly like a sine curve at least the first harmonic and possibly others should also show up. For instance, the annual component of any series will almost certainly not be perfectly shaped and so six-month, four-month, three-month, etc., "cycles" should also be of importance if the twelve-month is important. In particular, it has been found in our calculations with economic variables, that quarterly and two–four month components are of importance. Thus, with $m = 60$, a peak at $j = 10$ due to the annual may not be of statistical significance, but the reality of this component will be made more likely if there are peaks also at $j = 20$, $j = 30$ (perhaps), and $j = 40$. There appears to be no statistical test available using this principal.

A final point concerning the plotting of the estimated spectrum should be made. Strictly, as the estimate at the "point" ω_j is the estimate average over a frequency band the plot ought to have the appearance of a histogram, with a horizontal line of length equal to the frequency band the appropriate height above the horizontal axis. However, as will be seen, the plotted estimated spectra given in this book will have the appearance of a frequency polygon, that is, single points centered at the mid-range of the frequency band and joined by straight lines. This method is used for convenience in plotting and because it is considered that the resulting diagram is easier to appreciate and contemplate.

4.4 Examples of Estimated Spectra

Example 1. Sunspot Numbers

This very long and old time series measures, very roughly, the number and size of the visible spots on the sun's disk. The annual series begins in 1750, but in the calculation the annual data for the years 1755 to 1952 were used. The series appears to be stationary.

A brief description of how the series is formed and the data used may be found in Granger [2], where a simple two-parameter model is fitted. The data has no apparent trend and an almost constant periodic fluctuation is observable with duration in the order of eleven years.

Schuster periodograms of the series are given in Davis [1], pages 317–319.

The series is really of only historical interest, being one of the first and most analyzed of any series, as better methods are now available for measuring the extent of disturbances on the sun's surface. Of course, these improved methods are represented by much shorter series.

The data used was for a period of 198 years and as the "cycle" of 11 years was of particular interest the spectrum was estimated with 44 lags, this being a multiple of 11. Refer to Fig. 4.1.

The effective degrees of freedom $k = \dfrac{2n}{m} = 9$ and the upper and lower 90% confidence limits are shown, the upper being found by multiplying the estimated spectrum by 1.63 and the lower by multiplying by 0.464.

Various features of the estimated spectrum may be noted:

(i) the sharp peak at $j = 8$ corresponding to a period of 11 years. One may have considerable confidence in the reality of this peak as it is clearly quite impossible to draw a smooth curve between the confidence limits which does not peak near $j = 8$.

(ii) the peak at $j = 15$ and 16, the center of which corresponds to a period of $5\frac{1}{2}$ years and is thus the first harmonic of the 11-year fluctuation.

(iii) the importance of the low frequencies, suggesting that the series contains real, long fluctuations although the length of data is insufficient to attempt to describe these fluctuations more accurately.

(iv) the general appearance of the spectrum, apart from the peaks, is of a gentle decrease as frequency increases.

(v) no explanation of the importance of the very high frequencies compared to the preceding frequencies can be suggested.

Example 2. New York Commercial Paper Rate, 1876–1914

The two most important short-term interest rates in the United States prior to World War I were the commercial paper rate and the New York call money rate. The first of these terms applies to "promissory notes on which merchants and manufacturers borrow money for use in the ordinary course of their businesses" and the second covers "loans to stock or bond brokers, or to investment bankers."

The two series and their properties are discussed in Macauley [7] (from which the above two quotations were extracted and wherein the data used may also be found) and in Morgenstern [8].

For this example and that of Chapter 6, monthly data were used for the period 1876–1914. Plots of the data over this period revealed no visible trends. The amount of data was $n = 462$ and the spectrum was estimated, using the Tukey estimate, with 120 lags ($m = 120$).

Figure 4.2 shows the estimate plotted on a semi-log scale with approximate 90% confidence limits indicated at zero frequency and in the neighborhood of the frequency corresponding to the annual component. The latter indicates that it would be impossible to insert a smooth curve between the upper and lower confidence limits without it having a peak corresponding to the annual component.

The peak around 40 months is of little significance by itself but peaks at 20 months and 10 months indicate the actual presence of a forty-month cycle. However, the width of the peak suggests that the "forty-month cycle" is really an important frequency *band* of, say, between 37 and 43 months.

The resulting spectrum is not a typical one for an economic series as the low frequencies are generally considerably more imposing and a peak has been found for a frequency other than that corresponding to the annual component.

Example 3. Woolworth's Stock Prices, 1946–1960

The monthly mid-range of Woolworth stock prices quoted on the New York Stock Exchange for the period January 1946 to December 1960

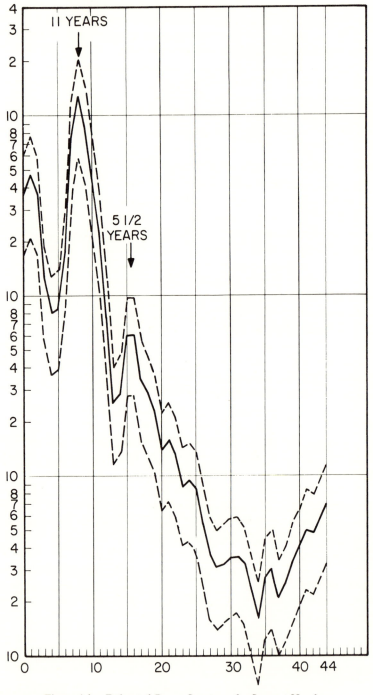

Figure 4.1.   Estimated Power Spectrum for Sunspot Numbers

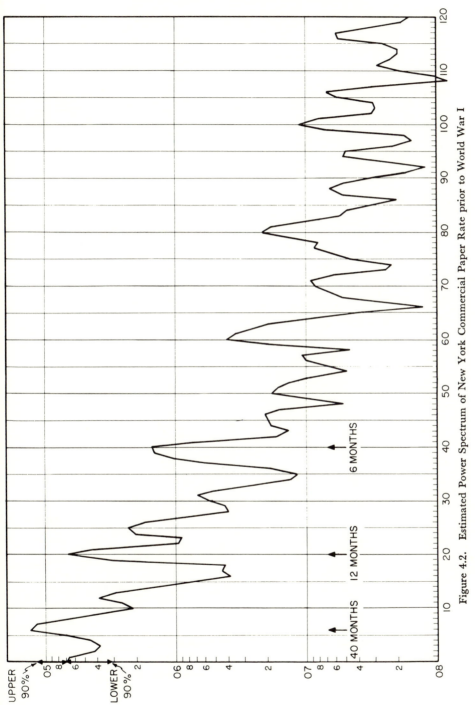

Figure 4.2. Estimated Power Spectrum of New York Commercial Paper Rate prior to World War I

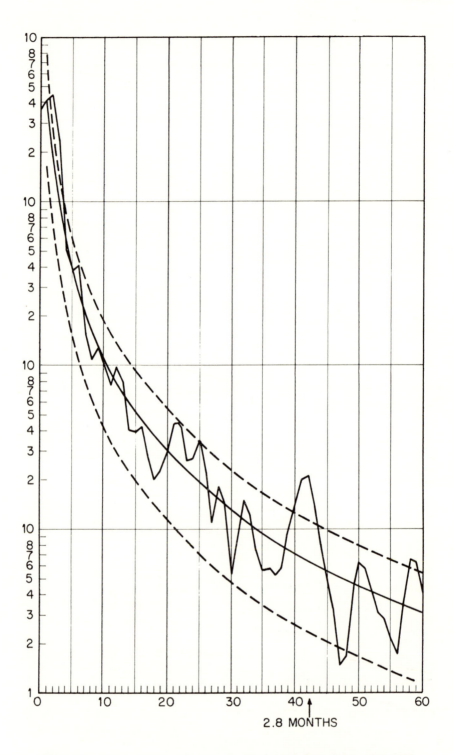

Figure 4.3.   Estimated Power Spectrum for Woolworth's Stock Prices, 1946–1950.

are used in this example. The spectrum was estimated with sixty lags, which is generally larger than would be recommended as the length of the series was $n = 180$, thus making the degrees of freedom $k = 2n/m = 6$. Refer to Fig. 4.3.

The spectrum is seen to be very smooth and with the low frequencies predominating, a shape frequently found for the spectrum of an economic series. There are no important peaks except that centered on $j = 42$. Thus no "forty-month cycle" or annual component is of importance in this series. (It might be added that extensive analysis of New York stock price series of various kinds and for all available periods of time has revealed no important annual component for any series.)

The diagram also illustrates an alternative method of using confidence bands. The central smooth line was fitted by freehand and the other two smooth curves indicate approximate 90% confidence limits.

As will be seen, only the peak around $j = 42$ lies outside these confidence limits. Such a peak would correspond to a "cycle" with period 2.8 months, but, as pointed out in Section 3.6, this point is also the alias of a weekly cycle. We might thus conclude that the data includes a weekly cycle, although it is surprising that this cycle is of sufficient importance to be noticeable since the data consisted of the average of the monthly high and the monthly low. Such a procedure does not remove a weekly cycle but is likely to reduce its importance considerably.

4.5 Normality of Economic Series

As spectral analysis deals exclusively with second moments, it is clearly best suited for use with normal or Gaussian processes (defined in Section 3.3) as all information about such processes is contained in their first and second moments. However, just as it is useful to discuss the correlation coefficient for non-normal statistical variables so is it useful to use spectral techniques on economic data although there is a certain amount of evidence that economic processes are not normal, having too much data in the tails. Such evidence has not taken non-stationarity into consideration nor the possibility of "contamination" (see Section 11.5). Thus the question of whether or not economic series are normal or can be made normal must be left open until more experience has been accumulated.

Few of the techniques presented in this volume require an assumption of normality, although some of the tests and confidence bands are based on such an assumption. As Lomnicki [6] has devised a test for normality of a stationary process, it may be worthwhile applying this test to any series being analyzed. Lomnicki's test is as follows:

Given data x_t, $t = 1, \ldots, n$ form

$$\bar{x} = \frac{1}{n} \sum_{t=1}^{n} x_t$$

$$M_j = \frac{1}{n} \sum_{t=1}^{n} (x_t - \bar{x})^j \qquad j = 2, 3, 4$$

$$G_1 = M_3 \cdot M_2^{-3/2}$$

and

$$G_2 = M_4 \cdot M_2^{-2} - 3.$$

Using the notation $A \sim N(\alpha, \beta)$ to mean the statistical variable A is asymptotically distributed normally with mean α and standard deviation β, Lomnicki proved that if the data is from a stationary, normal process, then

$$G_1 \sim N(0, R_1)$$
$$G_2 \sim N(0, R_2)$$

where

$$R_1^2 = 6 \sum_{q=-\infty}^{\infty} \rho_q^3$$

and

$$R_2^2 = 24 \sum_{q=-\infty}^{\infty} \rho_q^4.$$

Here ρ_q is the qth autocorrelation coefficient of the underlying process. As, in general, $\rho_q \to 0$ as $q \to \infty$, R_1 and R_2 can be estimated from the data by using truncated sums of the third and fourth powers of the estimated autocorrelation coefficients. The efficiency of the test with samples of sizes found in economics is not known and the test has not been applied to the series used in the examples in this volume.

4.6 Some Special Filters

The annual component of the series is frequently of considerable importance and in such cases it is usually advisable to reduce the importance of this component before further analyzing the series. In Chapter 10, a method known as demodulation is described which will efficiently achieve this reduction, even for non-stationary series, but as the computation involved is considerable, it is worth considering methods which are easier to use but less efficient. For this, a filter is required with transfer function that is fairly flat over the range $0 \leq \omega \leq \pi$ except for sharp dips at the 12-month component and its harmonics.

A simple set of filters having the property of reducing the annual component in monthly data while also removing or greatly reducing any trend in mean (a problem dealt with in detail in Chapter 8) is:

$$y_t = \sum_{j=-12}^{12} a_j x_{t-j}$$

where

$$a_0 = 6 + A$$

$$a_j = -\tfrac{1}{2}, \qquad j = 1, 2, \ldots, 6$$

$$= 0, \qquad j = 7, 8, \ldots, 11$$

$$= -A, \qquad j = 12$$

and

$$a_{-j} = a_j.$$

Thus, if there is little or no seasonal component, we take $A = 0$ and the trend only is removed; if the seasonal component is moderately important (say ten times the size of neighboring frequencies in the estimated spectrum) then we can take $A = 6$, and if the seasonal component is very large (as in the series of department store sales, for example) A may need to be as large as 20 or 30. (In Chapter 12, $A = 100$ is used at one point.) The filter function (i.e., the function which multiplies the spectrum of the unfiltered series) is

$$\left[A + 6 - \sum_{j=1}^{6} \cos j\omega - A \cos 12\omega \right]^2$$

and this function, with $A = 6$, is shown in Chapter 12.

The filter suggested has the advantage that only a fairly small amount of data is lost (twelve pieces at each end). If it is felt that too much of the frequency bands adjoining that of the annual component is being removed, filters having sharp dips can be constructed if a longer filter is used. In particular, the above filter could be used twice.

A second class of filters which are important in an entirely different situation are the "one-sided" filters, i.e.,

$$y_t = \sum_{j=0}^{m} a_j x_{t-j}.$$

When such a filter is used, the spectrum of x_t is multiplied by $|\sum_{j=0}^{m} a_j e^{-ij\omega}|^2$ but the series y_t has a phase-lag to x_t of amount

$$\Phi(\omega) = \tan^{-1} \left[\frac{\sum_{j=1}^{m} a_j \sin j\omega}{\sum_{j=0}^{m} a_j \cos j\omega} \right].$$

If one would like to smooth out high frequencies in a series right up to the present time, to determine if the business cycle has turned for instance, such a filter is appropriate. With this objective, the weights a_j would have to be chosen so that the transfer function is high at the low frequencies and low at the high frequencies and the phase-lag is small for the low frequencies. Experience indicates that these requirements oppose each other, thus one "buys" an efficient cut-off point in the filter function at the cost of a large phase-lag or one buys a small phase-lag with an inefficient filter function.

A particularly simple one-sided filter is that with exponentially decreasing weights. If we take

$$a_j = e^{-\alpha j}, \qquad \alpha > 0$$

then if $a = e^{-\alpha}$ is not near one and m is large, the filter function is approximately $(1 + a^2 - 2a \cos \omega)^{-1}$ and the phase-lag function is $\tan^{-1}\left[\dfrac{a \sin \omega}{1 - a \cos \omega}\right]$. Although by no means optimum, its properties are very satisfactory for a single-parameter filter except that the phase-change is tremendous near zero frequency. It is easily constructed by noting that

$$y_t = a y_{t-1} + x_t$$

and is being used successfully with various industrial problems.

NOTE.

The question of whether or not a given economic series contains "cycles" (i.e., strictly periodic components) other than the annual component is one that research workers considered prewar. Although, in the author's opinion, it is extremely unlikely that such cycles exist, it is worth noting that an effective but computationally laborious test is available to discover if a peak in the spectrum is due to the presence of such a cycle. The test is based on the periodogram and is given in "Testing for a jump in the spectral function," by E. J. Hannan, *J. Royal Statistical Society*, (B), vol. 23 (1961), pp. 396–404.

REFERENCES

[1] Davis, H. T., *The Analysis of Economic Time Series*, Bloomington, Indiana, 1941.
[2] Granger, C. W. J., "A statistical model for sunspot activity," *Astrophysical Journal*, vol 126 (1957), pp. 152–157.
[3] Grenander, U. and Rosenblatt, M., *Statistical Analysis of Stationary Time Series*, New York, 1957.
[4] Hannan, E. J., *Time Series Analysis*, London, 1960.
[5] Jenkins, G. M., "General considerations in the analysis of spectra," *Technometrics*, vol. 3 (1961), pp. 133–166.
[6] Lomnicki, A. A., "Tests for departure from normality in the case of linear stochastic processes," *Metrika* (1961), pp. 37–61.

REFERENCES

[7] Macauley, F. R., *Some Theoretical Problems Suggested by the Movements of Interest Rates, Bond Yields and Stock Prices in the United States Since 1856*, NBER, New York, 1938.

[8] Morgenstern, O., *International Financial Transactions and Business Cycles*, Princeton, 1959.

[9] Parzen, E., "Mathematical considerations in the estimation of spectra," *Technometrics*, vol. 3 (1961), pp. 167–190.

[10] Tukey, J. W., "Discussion, emphasizing the connection between analysis of variance and spectrum analysis," *Technometrics*, vol. 3 (1961), pp. 191–219.

CHAPTER 5

CROSS-SPECTRAL ANALYSIS

5.1 Cross-spectral Theory

In direct generalization to the univariate case, a real bivariate random generating process $\{X_t, Y_t\}$ is said to be stationary if the first and second moments of the bivariate process are all independent of time, i.e.,

$$E[X_t] = m_x, \; E[(X_t - m_x)^2] = \sigma_x^2$$

$$E[(X_t - m_x)(X_{t-\tau} - m_x)] = \mu_{xx}(\tau)$$

(5.1.1)
$$E[Y_t] = m_y, \; E[(Y_t - m_y)^2] = \sigma_y^2$$

$$E[(Y_t - m_y)(Y_{t-\tau} - m_y)] = \mu_{yy}(\tau)$$

$$E[(X_t - m_x)(Y_{t-\tau} - m_y)] = \mu_{xy}(\tau)$$

The spectral representation for bivariate processes becomes

$$\mu_{xx}(\tau) = 2 \int_0^\pi \cos \tau\omega \, dF_x(\omega)$$

(5.1.2)
$$\mu_{yy}(\tau) = 2 \int_0^\pi \cos \tau\omega \, dF_y(\omega)$$

$$\mu_{xy}(\tau) = 2 \int_0^\pi \cos \tau\omega \, dC_0(\omega) - 2 \int_0^\pi \sin \tau\omega \, dQ(\omega)$$

and for the case of processes with absolutely continuous spectral density functions, these become

$$\mu_{xx}(\tau) = 2 \int_0^\pi \cos \tau\omega \, f_x(\omega) \, d\omega$$

(5.1.3)
$$\mu_{yy}(\tau) = 2 \int_0^\pi \cos \tau\omega \, f_y(\omega) \, d\omega$$

$$\mu_{xy}(\tau) = 2 \int_0^\pi \cos \tau\omega \, c(\omega) \, d\omega - 2 \int_0^\pi \sin \tau\omega \, q(\omega) \, d\omega$$

$$= \int_{-\pi}^\pi e^{i\tau\omega} Cr(\omega) \, d\omega$$

Here $f_x(\omega)$ and $f_y(\omega)$ are the power spectra of the processes $\{X_t\}$, $\{Y_t\}$ respectively and

$$Cr(\omega) = c(\omega) + iq(\omega)$$

is known as the power cross-spectrum between $\{X_t\}$ and $\{Y_t\}$; $c(\omega)$ is known as the co-spectrum and $q(\omega)$ as the quadrature spectrum. These functions always obey the "coherence-inequality,"

$$(5.1.4) \qquad c^2(\omega) + q^2(\omega) \leq f_x(\omega) f_y(\omega)$$

If the equations of 5.1.3 are inverted they become

$$f_x(\omega) = \frac{1}{2\pi} \left(\mu_{xx}(0) + 2 \sum_{\tau=1}^{\infty} \mu_{xx}(\tau) \cos \tau\omega \right)$$

$$f_y(\omega) = \frac{1}{2\pi} \left(\mu_{yy}(0) + 2 \sum_{\tau=1}^{\infty} \mu_{yy}(\tau) \cos \tau\omega \right)$$

$$c(\omega) = \frac{1}{2\pi} \mu_{xy}(0) + \frac{1}{\pi} \sum_{\tau=1}^{\infty} (\mu_{xy}(\tau) + \mu_{yx}(\tau)) \cos \tau\omega$$

$$q(\omega) = \frac{1}{\pi} \sum_{\tau=1}^{\infty} (\mu_{xy}(\tau) - \mu_{yx}(\tau)) \sin \tau\omega$$

(except for a factor 2 at $\omega = 0$, π), and it should be noted that $q(0) = q(\pi) = 0$.

Expressing the series $\{X_t\}$ and $\{Y_t\}$ in terms of the complex form of the Cramér representation

$$X_t = \int_{-\pi}^{\pi} e^{it\omega} \, dz_x(\omega)$$

$$Y_t = \int_{-\pi}^{\pi} e^{it\omega} \, dz_y(\omega)$$

we have

$$E[dz_x(\omega_1) \, \overline{dz_y(\omega_2)}] = 0 \qquad \omega_1 \neq \omega_2$$
$$= Cr(\omega) d\omega \qquad \omega_1 = \omega_2 = \omega$$

When $\{X_t\}$ and $\{Y_t\}$ are each real stationary processes they may be written, using Cramér's representation,

$$X_t = \int_0^{\pi} \cos t\omega \, du_x(\omega) + \int_0^{\pi} \sin t\omega \, dv_x(\omega)$$

and

$$Y_t = \int_0^{\pi} \cos t\omega \, du_y(\omega) + \int_0^{\pi} \sin t\omega \, dv_y(\omega).$$

If $E[X_t] = E[Y_t] = 0$, the following relations hold[1]

---

[1] Strictly, the equations in (5.1.6) and (5.1.7) only hold for $0 < \omega < \pi$ and the factor 2 ought to be dropped for the equations to hold at $\omega = 0$ and π. As this is of little importance in practice it has been disregarded throughout the volume.

$$E[du_x(\omega)] = E[du_y(\omega)] = E[dv_x(\omega)] = E[dv_y(\omega)] = 0$$

$$E[du_x(\omega_1)\,du_x(\omega_2)] = E[dv_x(\omega_1)\,dv_x(\omega_2)]$$

$$= 0 \quad \text{if} \quad \omega_1 \neq \omega_2$$

$$= 2f_x(\omega)\,d\omega, \quad \text{if} \quad \omega_1 = \omega_2 = \omega$$

(5.1.6)
$$E[du_y(\omega_1)\,du_y(\omega_2)] = E[dv_y(\omega_1)\,dv_y(\omega_2)]$$

$$= 0 \quad \text{if} \quad \omega_1 \neq \omega_2$$

$$= 2f_y(\omega)\,d\omega \quad \text{if} \quad \omega_1 = \omega_2 = \omega$$

$$E[du_x(\omega_1)\,dv_x(\omega_2)] = E[du_y(\omega_1)\,dv_y(\omega_2)]$$

$$= 0, \quad 0 \leqq \omega_1,\ \omega_2 \leqq \pi$$

and also

$$E[du_x(\omega_1)\,du_y(\omega_2)] = E[dv_x(\omega_1)\,dv_y(\omega_2)]$$

$$= 0 \quad \text{if} \quad \omega_1 \neq \omega_2$$

$$= 2c(\omega)\,d\omega \quad \text{if} \quad \omega_1 = \omega_2 = \omega$$

(5.1.7)
$$E[du_x(\omega_1)\,dv_y(\omega_2)] = 0 \quad \text{if} \quad \omega_1 \neq \omega_2$$

$$= 2q(\omega)\,d\omega \quad \text{if} \quad \omega_1 = \omega_2 = \omega$$

$$E[dv_x(\omega_1)\,du_y(\omega_2)] = 0 \quad \text{if} \quad \omega_1 \neq \omega_2$$

$$= -2q(\omega)\,d\omega \quad \text{if} \quad \omega_1 = \omega_2 = \omega.$$

These equations suggest a method of interpreting the concepts of co-spectrum and quadrature spectrum (5.1.5). They can be roughly interpreted as stating that each of the processes can be represented by the integral over all frequencies in $0 \leqq \omega \leqq \pi$ and that each frequency can be decomposed into two components $\pi/2$ out of phase with each other. Each of the components has a random amplitude, i.e., $du_x(\omega)$, $dv_x(\omega)$ for the $\{X_t\}$ process and $du_y(\omega)$, $dv_y(\omega)$ for the $\{Y_t\}$ process, and for each process the amplitudes are uncorrelated not only between the components for any one frequency but also with the random amplitudes of the components for other frequencies. The random amplitudes for frequency ω_1 for one process are uncorrelated with the amplitudes of frequencies other than ω_1 in the other process. Thus we need only consider the relationships between a particular frequency in one process and the *same* frequency in the other process, i.e., between

$$\cos t\omega\,du_x(\omega) + \sin t\omega\,dv_x(\omega)$$

and

$$\cos t\omega\,du_y(\omega) + \sin t\omega\,dv_y(\omega).$$

Twice the co-spectral density, $2c(\omega)\,d\omega$, gives the covariance between the components that are "in phase," i.e., between $du_x(\omega)$ and $du_y(\omega)$ and also between $dv_x(\omega)$ and $dv_y(\omega)$, i.e.,

$$E[du_x(\omega)\, du_y(\omega)] = E[dv_x(\omega)\, dv_y(\omega)] = 2c(\omega)\, d\omega.$$

Twice the quadrature spectral density, $2q(\omega)\, d\omega$, gives (to within a factor ± 1) the covariance between the components that are in quadrature (i.e., $\pi/2$ out of phase), that is between $du_x(\omega)$ and $dv_y(\omega)$ and between $du_y(\omega)$ and $dv_x(\omega)$, i.e.,

$$E[du_x(\omega)\, dv_y(\omega)] = 2q(\omega)\, d\omega$$

$$E[du_y(\omega)\, dv_x(\omega)] = -2q(\omega)\, d\omega.$$

Thus, if $q(\omega) = 0$, $c(\omega) \neq 0$ this shows that the components of the two processes with frequency ω are somewhat connected and are exactly in phase with each other. If $q(\omega) \neq 0$, $c(\omega) \neq 0$, then the two components will be both somewhat connected and somewhat out of phase.

It also follows from the above approach that to know fully the relationship between two stationary processes one needs to know the extent to which the frequency ω component of $\{X_t\}$ is correlated to the frequency ω component of $\{Y_t\}$ and also how much the two components are out of phase. It is by the use of cross-spectra that we are able to measure such relationships.

5.2 Coherence, Phase, Gain, and Argand Diagrams

A measure of the correlation between the frequency components of the two processes is given by

(5.2.1) $$C(\omega) = \frac{c^2(\omega) + q^2(\omega)}{f_x(\omega)\, f_y(\omega)}$$

$C(\omega)$ is called the *coherence at* ω and, from (5.1.4), it is seen that

(5.2.2) $$0 \leq C(\omega) \leq 1.$$

$C(\omega)$ is analogous to the square of the correlation coefficient between two samples and is interpreted in a similar way, i.e., the larger $C(\omega)$ the more closely related are the two components. This is further seen by the use of information theory. If we draw a bivariate sample $(x_i, y_i; i = 1, \ldots, n)$ from a bivariate normal distribution with correlation coefficient ρ, then, for n large, the amount of information about the x's contained in the y's is $i(x, y) = -\frac{1}{2} \log (1 - \hat{\rho}^2)$ where $\hat{\rho}$ is an estimate of ρ. It has been shown by Gel'fand and Yaglom [2] that the *average* amount of information per unit of time concerning one series derivable from the other is

(5.2.3) $$i(x, y) = -\frac{1}{2\pi} \int_{-\pi}^{\pi} \log (1 - C(\omega))\, d\omega.$$

The plot of $C(\omega)$ against ω over $0 \leq \omega \leq \pi$ will be called the *coherence diagram*.

A measure of the phase difference between the frequency components of the two processes is $\psi(\omega) = \tan^{-1}\left(\dfrac{q(\omega)}{c(\omega)}\right)$ and the plot of $\psi(\omega)$ against ω $(0 < \omega < \pi)$ will be called the *phase diagram*.

A further diagram that has proved useful in analysis is the *Argand diagram* (or frequency-response diagram) in which the points

$$\left(\frac{c(\omega)}{f_x(\omega)}, \frac{q(\omega)}{f_x(\omega)}\right)$$

are plotted for various values of ω.

A final diagram frequently used in discussing the relationship between two series is the *gain diagram*. The *gain* $R_{xy}(\omega)$ is defined by $f_y(\omega)R_{xy}^2(\omega) = f_x(\omega)C(\omega)$; the gain diagram is $R_{xy}(\omega)$ plotted against ω. $R_{xy}(\omega)$ is essentially the regression coefficient of the process $\{X_t\}$ on the process $\{Y_t\}$ at frequency ω.[2]

The estimation problem for the cross-spectrum is essentially the same as for the spectrum. Estimation can only occur at a set number of points (in fact, over a set number of frequency bands) and the method used throughout this volume is a direct generalization of the Tukey estimate for the power spectrum. The estimates are of the form

(5.2.4) $$\hat{c}(\omega_j) = \frac{1}{\pi}\left\{\frac{a_0\lambda_0(\omega_j)}{2} + \sum_{k=1}^{m-1}\lambda_k(\omega_j)a_j\cos k\omega_j\right\}$$

$$\hat{q}(\omega_j) = \frac{1}{\pi}\sum_{k=1}^{m-1}\lambda_k(\omega_j)b_k\sin k\omega_j$$

$$\omega_j = \frac{\pi j}{m}, \qquad j = 0, 1, \ldots, m$$

where

(5.2.5) $$a_k = \frac{1}{n-k}\sum_{j=1}^{n-k}(x_jy_{j-k} + y_jx_{j-k})$$

(5.2.6) $$b_k = \frac{1}{n-k}\sum_{j=1}^{n-k}(x_jy_{j-k} - y_jx_{j-k}), \qquad k = 0, 1, \ldots, m$$

it being assumed that $\bar{x} = \bar{y} = 0$. The actual formula used will be found in the next chapter.

Goodman [3] has studied the distribution of these estimates under the assumptions that the process $\{X_t, Y_t\}$ is distributed in a bivariate normal distribution, that $(f_x(\omega), f_y(\omega), \hat{c}(\omega), \hat{q}(\omega))$ is distributed in a complex Wishart distribution and that the estimation procedure used

---

[2] It will be remembered that the regression coefficient β of the equation $x = \beta y + u$ is estimated by $\dfrac{\Sigma_t x_t y_t}{\Sigma y_t^2}$. The analogy is obvious.

has perfect (no leakage) windows. In particular, this study allows one to consider the distribution of the sample coherence $\hat{C}(\omega_j)$ given by

$$\hat{C}(\omega) = \frac{\hat{c}^2(\omega) + \hat{q}^2(\omega)}{\hat{f}_x(\omega)\,\hat{f}_y(\omega)}$$

$$\omega = \omega_j, \qquad j = 0, 1, \ldots, m.$$

If the sample size is n and we estimate the cross-spectrum over m frequency bands, then the distribution of $\sqrt{\hat{C}}(\omega_j)$ for any j when the true coherence is zero at this frequency (i.e., $C(\omega_j) = 0$) is

(5.2.7) $$F(u) = 1 - (1 - u^2)^{n/m-1}, \ldots.$$

The following table shows certain relevant values for $\sqrt{\hat{C}}(\omega)$ when $C(\omega_j) = 0$:

n/m	4	6	8	10	12	16	20
median	0.454	0.361	0.307	0.272	0.247	0.212	0.190
90 percent	0.732	0.607	0.529	0.475	0.435	0.377	0.338
95 percent	0.795	0.672	0.590	0.532	0.488	0.425	0.382

The last two rows list the values of u such that $F(u) = 0.90$ and $F(u) = 0.95$.

Thus, if $n = 300$, $m = 50$ then $n/m = 6$ and 95% of the sample coherences would lie, on the average, below $\sqrt{0.672}$.

Goodman's work also provides a frequency function for the estimated phase angle $\hat{\Phi}(\omega)$ given by

$$\hat{\Phi}(\omega) = \tan^{-1}\left\{\frac{\hat{q}(\omega)}{\hat{c}(\omega)}\right\}.$$

if Γ^2 is the true coherence, $\delta = 1 - \Gamma^2$, then the frequency function is given by

(5.2.8) $$p(\Phi) = \frac{\delta^k}{2\pi} - \frac{K\delta^k S}{2\pi(1 - S^2)^{k+\frac{1}{2}}}\left[\frac{\Gamma(\frac{1}{2})\Gamma(k+\frac{1}{2})}{\Gamma(k+1)} \pm B_s 2(\frac{1}{2}, k+\frac{1}{2})\right]$$

where $k = \dfrac{n}{m}$, $S = -\Gamma\cos(\Phi - \Phi_0)$, $E[\hat{\Phi}(\omega)] = \Phi_0$ and $B_x(p, q)$ represents the incomplete Beta function. The plus sign applies if $|\Phi - \Phi_0| \leq \frac{1}{2}\pi$, and the minus sign applies if $\frac{1}{2}\pi \leq |\Phi - \Phi_0| \leq \pi$. We note that

(i) if $\Gamma^2 = 0$, $p(\Phi) = \dfrac{1}{2\pi}$, i.e., when the coherence is zero, $\hat{\Phi}$ is rectangularly distributed over the entire admissible range of values.

(ii) if $\Gamma^2 = 1$, $p(\Phi) = 0$, i.e., when the true coherence is one, the variance of $\hat{\Phi}$ is zero.

Equation (5.2.8) can be used to find confidence bands for Φ but two assumptions have to be made: (i), $\hat{C}(\omega_j) = \Gamma$, i.e., the estimated coherence will have to be used as though it were the true coherence and (ii), leakage is not important. This assumption weakens these results considerably.

An alternative form of approximation for the distribution of the estimated phase has been given by Jenkins "Cross-spectral analysis and the estimation of linear open loop transfer functions," in *Symposium on Time Series Analysis*, edited by M. Rosenblatt, John Wiley & Sons, 1963. Both methods of approximation are considered by the author to be extremely crude; and the confidence bands derived from them should be used with considerable caution until experience of their properties has been accumulated. However, as the availability of confidence bands, even very approximate ones, is desirable, Table 5.1, derived from Jenkins' results, is presented.

TABLE 5.1. CONFIDENCE BANDS FOR PHASE ANGLE, IN DEGREES

Coherence n/m	0.1	0.2	0.3	0.4	0.5	0.6	0.7	0.8	0.9	1.0
4	56	45	37	31	27	22	18	14	4	0
6	50	39	31	26	22	18	15	11	3	0
8	46	35	27	23	19	16	12	10	3	0
10	43	32	26	21	17	14	11	9	2	0
12	41	30	23	19	16	13	10	8	2	0
16	36	26	20	17	14	11	9	7	2	0
20	33	23	18	15	12	10	8	6	2	0

The table is used as follows: if sample size is n and the cross-spectrum, estimated at m frequency bands, gives an estimated coherence $\hat{C}(\omega)$, then the appropriate figure in the table, on being added to and subtracted from the estimated phase in degrees, will indicate the upper and lower 95% confidence bands. Thus, for example, with $n = 300$, $m = 50$, $\hat{C}(\omega) = 0.7$, if $\hat{\Phi}(\omega)$ is the estimated phase at ω, the 95% confidence bands will be $(\hat{\Phi}(\omega) \pm 15°)$.

The use of the estimated coherence diagram in considering the relationships between two series should now be clear, but certain practical aspects will be further discussed in the next chapter. To consider the importance of the other two diagrams and the place of phase-relationships we need to consider series that differ from each other only in phase. This forms the subject of the next section.

5.3 Processes Differing Only in Phase

It was stated in Chapter 3 that any real stationary process could be represented by

$$(5.3.1) \qquad X_t = \int_0^\pi \cos t\omega \, du(\omega) + \int_0^\pi \sin t\omega \, dv(\omega)$$

where, if $E[X_t] = 0$, $E[du(\omega)] = E[dv(\omega)] = 0$ and

$$E[du(\omega_1)\, du(\omega_2)] = E[dv(\omega_1)\, dv(\omega_2)] = 0, \quad \omega_1 \neq \omega_2$$
$$= 2f(\omega)\, d\omega, \quad \omega_1 = \omega_2 = \omega$$

and

$$E[du(\omega_1)\, dv(\omega_2)] = 0, \quad 0 \leq \omega_1, \; \omega_2 \leq \pi.$$

Consider a second process denoted by X_t^φ and defined by

$$(5.3.2) \quad X_t^\varphi = \int_0^\pi \cos\,[t\omega - \varphi(\omega)]\, du(\omega) + \int_0^\pi \sin\,[t\omega - \varphi(\omega)]\, dv(\omega)$$

where $\varphi(\omega)$ is a real, always finite function for $|\omega| < \infty$.

It is seen that $E[X_t^\varphi] = 0$ and

$$E[X_t^\varphi X_{t-\tau}^\varphi] = E[X_t X_{t-\tau}] = 2\int_0^\pi \cos \tau\omega\, f(\omega)\, d\omega.$$

Thus the processes $\{X_t\}$ and $\{X_t^\varphi\}$ have the same power spectrum $f(\omega)$ and so can differ only in phase. By its construction X_t^φ has a phase-lag of $\varphi(\omega)$ to X_t at frequency ω.

If, for a moment, we consider the more compact form of Cramér's representation,

$$(5.3.3) \qquad\qquad X_t = \int_{-\pi}^\pi e^{it\omega}\, dz(\omega)$$

then as X_t is a real process $dz(\omega) = \overline{dz(-\omega)}$. The corresponding representation for X_t^φ is

$$(5.3.4) \qquad\qquad X_t^\varphi = \int_{-\pi}^\pi e^{it\omega} e^{-i\Phi(\omega)}\, dz(\omega)$$

where

$$\Phi(\omega) = \varphi(\omega), \qquad \omega > 0$$
$$= 0, \qquad \omega = 0$$
$$= -\varphi(-\omega), \qquad \omega < 0.$$

If we defined a process by (5.3.4) but did not impose the condition that $\Phi(\omega)$ be an odd function [i.e., $\Phi(\omega) \neq -\Phi(-\omega)$] then the X_t^φ process need not be a real process.

Let us now consider the cross-spectrum between $\{X_t\}$ and $\{X_t^\varphi\}$. From (5.3.1) and (5.3.2)

$$E[X_t X_{t-\tau}^\varphi] = 2\int_0^\pi \cos\,[\tau\omega + \varphi(\omega)]\, f(\omega)\, d\omega$$

$$= 2\int_0^\pi \cos \tau\omega \cdot \cos \varphi(\omega)\, f(\omega)\, d\omega$$

$$-2\int_0^\pi \sin \tau\omega \cdot \sin \varphi(\omega)\, f(\omega)\, d\omega.$$

Thus

(5.3.5)
$$c(\omega) = \cos \varphi(\omega) \, f(\omega)$$
$$q(\omega) = \sin \varphi(\omega) \, f(\omega)$$

$$0 \le \omega \le \pi$$

and

$$C(\omega) = \frac{f^2(\omega)}{f^2(\omega)} \left[\cos^2 \varphi(\omega) + \sin^2 \varphi(\omega) \right] = 1$$

for all ω, $0 \le \omega \le \pi$ as would be expected from the definition of X_t^φ. The coherency diagram will thus be a constant for all ω.

The phase-diagram, however, will vary as

$$\psi(\omega) = \tan^{-1} \left(\frac{q(\omega)}{c(\omega)} \right)$$

$$= \varphi(\omega), \quad 0 < \omega < \pi,$$

i.e., the phase-diagram will directly give $\varphi(\omega)$.

The Argand diagram will consist of points lying on a circle, although the angle (or "speed" of circulation) will vary with $\varphi(\omega)$.

5.4 Special Cases

In this section we consider the special case of $\varphi(\omega)$ being a linear function in ω, i.e., $\varphi(\omega) = a + b\omega$ and some other simple models. Before dealing with the general linear case, however, we consider the particular cases when $a = 0$ or $b = 0$.

(i) $\varphi(\omega) = b\omega$, $\omega \ge 0$. Substituting into (5.3.2),

(5.4.1) $$X_t^{b\omega} = \int_0^\pi \cos (t - b)\omega \cdot du(\omega) + \int_0^\pi \sin (t - b)\omega \cdot dv(\omega)$$

i.e., $X_t^{b\omega} = X_{t-b}$ if b is an integer.

For this case the phase diagram will be linearly increasing (if $b > 0$) with ω and so a simple time-lag relationship between two series will be detectable from the phase-diagram. The length of the time-lag will be measurable from the angle at which the phase-diagram is increasing (or decreasing).

(ii) $\varphi(\omega) = k$, k a constant. Substituting into (5.3.2) gives

(5.4.2) $$X_t^k = \int_0^\pi \cos (t\omega - k) \, du(\omega) + \int_0^\pi \sin (t\omega - k) \, dv(\omega)$$

and such a process is said to have a *fixed angle lag* to the process.

When $k = \pi/2$ (5.4.2) becomes

(5.4.3) $$X_t^{\pi/2} = \int_0^\pi \sin t\omega \, du(\omega) - \int_0^\pi \cos t\omega \, dv(\omega)$$

and $X_t^{\pi/2}$ may be called the *Hilbert transform* of X_t and will be denoted by X_t^H. Thus, every frequency of X_t is exactly out of step (i.e., $\pi/2$ out of phase) with the corresponding frequency of X_t^H.

Expanding $\cos(t\omega - k)$ and $\sin(t\omega - k)$ in (5.4.2) it is seen that

$$X_t^k = \cos k \cdot X_t + \sin k \cdot X_t^H$$

and so, if one wished to construct X_t^k it would be a simple matter once X_t^H were constructed. (This question is dealt with further in Section (5.5).)

Considering the cross-spectrum between the processes $\{X_t\}$ and $\{X_t^k\}$ shows that the phase-diagram will be a constant (k) and the Argand diagram will consist of the single point $(\cos k, \sin k)$. Thus, if the estimated phase diagram from samples from two processes appears to be randomly oscillating about a non-zero constant and, if the points of the Argand diagram appear to be lying about a point in the plane other than the origin these would be indications that one process had merely a fixed angle lag to the other.

(iii) $\varphi(\omega) = k + b\omega$, k, b *constants.* Using the above results it is seen that

$$X_t^{k+b\omega} = X_{t-b}^k$$

i.e., if $\varphi(\omega)$ is a linear function then the new process has both a fixed time lag *and* a fixed angle lag to the original process.

From the cross-spectrum of the processes $\{X_t\}$ and $\{X_t^{k+b\omega}\}$ the phase diagram will be linearly increasing with ω (if $b > 0$) and b may be estimated from the slope of the line and k from the line's intersection with the vertical axis at $\omega = 0$. The more practical problems of estimation will be further discussed in the next chapter.

Certain simple relationships hold when $\varphi(\omega)$ is a linear function, for example if two processes are related by

$$X_t^{a+b\omega} = Y_t^{c+d\omega}$$

then

$$X_t = Y_t^{(a-c)+(d-b)\omega}$$

$$= Y_{t+b-d}^{a-c}$$

(iv) *Sum of processes with linear $\varphi(\omega)$.* If two processes $\{X_t\}$, $\{Y_t\}$ are related by an equation such as

(5.4.5) $$Y_t = \alpha X_t^{a+b\omega} + \beta X_t^{c+d\omega} \quad (\alpha \geq 0, \beta \geq 0)$$

$$= \alpha X_{t-b}^a + \beta X_{t-d}^c$$

then

$$E[Y_t Y_{t-\tau}] = 2(\alpha^2 + \beta^2) \int_0^\pi \cos \tau\omega\, f(\omega)\, d\omega$$

$$+ 2\alpha\beta \int_0^\pi \{\cos [(\tau + d - b)\omega + c - a]$$

$$+ \cos [(\tau + b - d)\omega + a - c]\}\, f(\omega)\, d\omega$$

$$= 2 \int_0^\pi \{\alpha^2 + 2\alpha\beta \cos [(d - b)\omega + c - a] + \beta^2\}$$

$$\cos \tau\omega\, f(\omega)\, d\omega$$

and

$$E[X_t Y_{t-\tau}] = 2 \int_0^\pi \cos \tau\omega\, [\alpha \cos (b\omega - a) + \beta \cos (d\omega - c)]\, f(\omega)\, d\omega$$

$$- 2 \int_0^\pi \sin \tau\omega\, [\alpha \sin (b\omega - a) + \beta \sin (d\omega - c)]\, f(\omega)\, d\omega$$

thus

$$\frac{c(\omega)}{f_x(\omega)} = \alpha \cos (b\omega - a) + \beta \cos (d\omega - c)$$

and

$$\frac{q(\omega)}{f_x(\omega)} = [\alpha \sin (b\omega - a) + \beta \sin (d\omega - c)].$$

Clearly, the three cross-spectral diagrams will be complicated (and, in particular, the coherence diagram will vary with ω) but certain special cases can sometimes be distinguished:

(a) If $\alpha > \beta$ then the Argand diagram will be an epi-cycloid (i.e., the curve generated by a fixed point on a circle which rolls externally upon a fixed circle) with the central circle having radius α and the outer circle radius β.

(b) If $\alpha \gg \beta$, then

$$\psi(\omega) = \tan^{-1} \left(\frac{q(\omega)}{c(\omega)}\right) \cong (b\omega - a)$$

and so a and b could be roughly estimated from the estimated phase diagram.

(c) If $\alpha = \beta$

$$\psi(\omega) = -\tfrac{1}{2}(b + d)\omega + \tfrac{1}{2}(a + c)$$

and so $(b + d)$, $(a + c)$ can be estimated from the estimated phase diagram.

(d) If $|\alpha - \beta|$ is very small compared to α then the results of (c) will be approximately true.

(e) If $a = 0$, $d = 0$ (case where Y_t is the sum of a fixed angle lag series and fixed time lag series), the Argand diagram will be a circle of radius α about the point $(\beta \cos c, \beta \sin c)$.

(f) If b (say) is known or estimated (as in the case (b) above) and if it is an integer, then

$$Y_{t+b} = \alpha X_t^a + \beta X_{t+b-d}^c$$

and the Argand diagram derived from considering the processes $\{X_t\}$, $\{Y_{t+b}\}$ would consist of a circle of radius β with centre at the point $(\alpha \cos a, \alpha \sin a)$. Thus a, α, β could perhaps be immediately estimated and possibly $d - b$ could be estimated from the "speed" at which the points go around the circle on the estimated Argand diagram. Probably $\hat{\alpha}$ and $\hat{\beta}$ would be better derived by least squares after a, c and d had been estimated.

It should be clear from this last section that analysis of linear models more complicated than (5.4.5) is quite unfeasible with the tools so far presented.

However, one further model can be mentioned:

$$Y_t = \alpha(X_{t+k}^a - X_{t-k}^{-a}) + \beta X_t$$

then

$$\frac{c(\omega)}{f_x(\omega)} = \beta, \qquad \frac{q(\omega)}{f_x(\omega)} = 2\alpha \cos a \cdot \sin k\omega.$$

Thus, for this highly contrived model, the points of the Argand diagram lie on a straight line perpendicular to the real axis. It may be noted that α and a cannot be separately estimated by use of cross-spectral methods.

5.5 Estimation of $\{X_t^\varphi\}$

The problem considered in this section is as follows: Given a particular realization (i.e., sample) from the $\{X_t\}$ process how to best estimate the corresponding sample from the process $\{X_t^\varphi\}$?

It was shown in Chapter 3 (Section 3.4) that if a filter was applied to the data, i.e.,

$$(5.5.1) \qquad L(x) = \sum_{k=-m}^{m} a_k x_{t+k}$$

the effect on a particular frequency ω would be to multiply its amplitude by $M^2(\omega) + N^2(\omega)$ and change its phase by adding

$$\tan^{-1}\left[\frac{N(\omega)}{M(\omega)}\right]$$

where

$$M(\omega) = \sum_{k=-m}^{m} a_k \cos k\omega$$

and

$$N(\omega) = \sum_{k=-m}^{m} a_k \sin k\omega.$$

Thus, the sample from $\{X_t^{\varphi}\}$ would be formed if

$$M^2(\omega) + N^2(\omega) \cong 1$$

and

$$\tan^{-1} \frac{N(\omega)}{M(\omega)} \cong \Phi(\omega)$$

where

$$\begin{aligned} \Phi(\omega) &= \varphi(\omega), & \omega &> 0 \\ &= 0, & \omega &= 0 \\ &= -\varphi(-\omega), & \omega &< 0. \end{aligned}$$

Hence, it appears sensible to choose the a_k's such that

$$G = \int_{-\pi}^{\pi} |M(\omega) + iN(\omega) - 1e^{-i\Phi(\omega)}|^2 \, d\omega$$

is minimized.

$$G = \int_{-\pi}^{\pi} \{[M(\omega) - \cos \Phi(\omega)]^2 + [N(\omega) + \sin \Phi(\omega)]^2\} \, d\omega$$

and so

$$\frac{\partial G}{\partial a_k} = 2 \int_{-\pi}^{\pi} \{\cos k\omega[M(\omega) - \cos \Phi(\omega)]$$

$$+ \sin k\omega[N(\omega) + \sin \Phi(\omega)]\} \, d\omega$$

and, to minimize G we put $\dfrac{\partial G}{\partial a_k} = 0, k = -m, \ldots, m.$

i.e.,

$$2\pi a_k - \int_{-\pi}^{\pi} \cos k\omega \cdot \cos \Phi(\omega) \, d\omega$$

$$+ \int_{-\pi}^{\pi} \sin k\omega \cdot \sin \Phi(\omega) \, d\omega = 0,$$

(5.5.2)
$$a_k = \frac{1}{2\pi} \int_{-\pi}^{\pi} \cos [k\omega + \Phi(\omega)] \, d\omega.$$

Thus, applying the filter (5.5.1) with the coefficients a_k given by (5.5.2) to the available data $\{x_t, t = 1, \ldots, n\}$ will give an estimate of $\{x_t^\varphi, t = 1, \ldots, n\}$ which is, in a certain sense, the best available.

If $\varphi(\omega) = b\omega$, with b an integer, than (5.5.2) gives

$$a_k = 0, \quad k \neq -b$$

$$a_k = 1, \quad k = -b$$

and so $L(x) = x_{t-b}$ as required.

If $\varphi(\omega) = \pi/2$, then (5.5.2) gives

$$a_{2k+1} = \frac{2}{(2k+1)\pi}, \quad k = 0, 1, \ldots, [m/2]$$

$$a_{2k} = 0, \quad k = 0, 1, \ldots, [m/2]$$

$$a_{-k} = -a_k$$

where $[p]$ means the largest integer smaller than p.

This happens to be the filter of length $2m$ that has transfer function that best approximates (in a least squares sense) the function

$$p(\omega) = 1 \qquad 0 < \omega < \pi$$

$$= 0 \qquad \omega = 0, -\pi, \pi$$

$$= -1 \qquad -\pi < \omega < 0$$

i.e.,

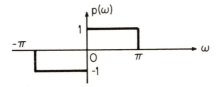

As noted before, estimation of x^k for any constant k can be easily accomplished once $x^H = x^{\pi/2}$ has been estimated by using the formula

$$x_t^k = \cos k \cdot x_t + \sin k \cdot x_t^H.$$

A further point that should be noticed here is that the filter function of the filter with coefficients given by (5.5.3) vanishes at frequency zero and thus the process $\{X_t^H\}$ has no zero frequency even should the process $\{X_t\}$ have a value there.

5.6 Case when Coherence is not a Constant

To emphasize the method of interpreting phase-diagrams and for ease of exposition, Sections 5.3 and 5.4 dealt with the case where the two series differed only in phase. When two series also have different power spectra, the interpretations still hold true.

Suppose that the series $\{X_t\}$ has power spectrum $f_x(\omega)$ and Cramér representation

$$(5.6.1) \qquad X_t = \int_{-\pi}^{\pi} e^{it\omega} \, dz(\omega)$$

and that a second series has Cramér representation

$$(5.6.2) \qquad Y_t = \int_{-\pi}^{\pi} e^{it\omega} \cdot a(\omega) e^{-i\Phi(\omega)} \, dz(\omega)$$

where

$$\Phi(\omega) = \varphi(\omega), \qquad \omega > 0$$
$$= 0, \qquad \omega = 0$$
$$= -\varphi(-\omega), \qquad \omega < 0$$

and $a(\omega)$ is a real, non-negative and even function of ω.

The power-spectrum of the series $\{Y_t\}$ is given by $f_y(\omega) = a^2(\omega) f_x(\omega)$ and we shall denote a series Y_t related to a second series X_t in the manner of equation (5.6.2) by

$$(5.6.3) \qquad Y_t = X_t\{a(\omega), \varphi(\omega)\}$$

It should be noted that the coherence between X_t and $X_t\{a(\omega), \varphi(\omega)\}$ is unity for all ω but there will be a phase-lag of $\varphi(\omega)$ between the two series.

Some properties of this notation are

    (i) $X_t^{\varphi(\omega)} \equiv X_t\{1, \varphi(\omega)\}$

    (ii) if $Y_t = X_t\{a(\omega), \varphi(\omega)\}$

    and

$$(5.6.4) \qquad Z_t = Y_t\{b(\omega), \theta(\omega)\}$$

    then

$$Z_t = X_t\{a(\omega)b(\omega), \varphi(\omega) + \theta(\omega)\}$$

    (iii) $\sum_{j=1}^{m} X_t\{a_j(\omega), \varphi_j(\omega)\} = X_t\{a(\omega), \varphi(\omega)\}$

$(5.6.5)$

    where $a(\omega), \varphi(\omega)$ are given by

$$\sum_{j=1}^{m} a_j(\omega) \exp\{i\varphi_j(\omega)\} \equiv a(\omega) \exp\{i\varphi(\omega)\}$$

and where m need not be a finite integer providing certain obvious convergence properties are obeyed.

The case when the coherence is not a constant is that for which all the fluctuations of frequency ω for the series Y_t cannot be attributed entirely to the fluctuations of frequency ω of the X_t series.

Thus, essentially, we have the model

(5.6.6) $$Y_t = X_t\{a(\omega), \varphi(\omega)\} + U_t$$

where the coherence between the series $\{X_t\}$ and $\{U_t\}$ is zero for all ω, $\{U_t\}$ being some stationary series.

As $f_y(\omega) = a^2(\omega) f_x(\omega) + f_u(\omega)$,

$$C(\omega) = \frac{a^2(\omega) f_x^2(\omega)}{f_y(\omega) f_x(\omega)} = \frac{a^2(\omega) f_x(\omega)}{f_y(\omega)}$$

we see that $a^2(\omega)$ and $f_u(\omega)$ can be estimated from the estimated power spectra of the X_t and Y_t series and from the coherence-diagram. $\varphi(\omega)$ is estimated directly, as usual, from the phase-diagram.

As, frequently, it will be the phase-diagram which will prove of most interest, we need to consider the effect of fluctuations in the coherence diagram upon it. It should be first noted that if the coherence is small at frequency ω, then both $c(\omega)$ and $q(\omega)$ will be small and so the estimate of $\dfrac{q(\omega)}{c(\omega)}$ is likely to have very large variance. It is clear, then, that the points in the phase-diagram corresponding to frequencies with low coherence will generally contain less useful information than points corresponding to frequencies with high coherence. Thus, if one is searching for a trend, say, in the phase-diagram, one should pay more attention to the points with high coherence than to those with low. If a visual judgment is to be made, this might be achieved by marking the more important points more heavily.

Fluctuations in the coherence do not affect the theory behind the suggested interpretation of the phase-diagram but merely alters the variance of the estimate of the phase. If one wished to fit a polynomial trend to the phase-diagram it would clearly be advisable to take this effect into account. If the cross-spectrum is estimated at the m frequency points $\omega_j, j = 0, \ldots, m$, with estimated coherence $\hat{C}(\omega_j)$ and estimated phase $\hat{\psi}(\omega_j)$ and we wished to fit a polynomial $p(x)$ to the (estimated) phase-diagram the optimum method would be to minimize

(5.6.7) $$G = \sum_{j=0}^{m} F(\hat{C}(\omega_j))[\hat{\psi}(\omega_j) - p(\omega_j)]^2$$

where $F(\hat{C}(\omega))$ is some function of $\hat{C}(\omega)$ chosen so that

$$E\{F(\hat{C}(\omega_j))[\hat{\psi}(\omega_j) - E\{\hat{\psi}(\omega_j)\}]^2\}$$

is a constant for all j. However, it is not at all clear how to choose the function F as $\hat{C}(\omega_j)$ and $\hat{\psi}(\omega_j)$ are not independent and the work of Goodman [3] does not appear to be able to help us. It is thus suggested that the function

$$(5.6.8) \qquad G' = \sum_{j=0}^{m} \hat{C}(\omega_j)[\hat{\psi}(\omega_j) - p(\omega_j)]^2$$

be minimized. Although this is doubtlessly not the optimum method, it is likely to be considerably better than the use of an unweighted sum of least squares.

5.7 Sums and Products of Related Series

In this section we consider the power spectra of the sum and the product of two related series.

Let the series be $\{X_t\}$, $\{Y_t\}$ with zero means, power spectra $f_x(\omega)$, $f_y(\omega)$ and power cross-spectrum $f_{xy}(\omega) = c_0(\omega) + iq(\omega)$.

For the sum, the autocovariance between the new variable at times t and s is

$$\gamma(s - t) = E[(X_t + Y_t)(X_s + Y_s)]$$
$$= E[X_t X_s] + E[Y_t Y_s] + E[X_t Y_s + Y_t X_s]$$

and as the power spectrum is the Fourier transform of the autocovariance sequence it follows immediately that the power spectrum of $Z_t = X_t + Y_t$ is $f_z(\omega) = f_x(\omega) + f_y(\omega) + 2c_0(\omega)$.

If X_t, Y_t are Gaussian processes, then a formula by Isserlis [4] states that

$$\mathrm{cov}\,(X_t Y_t, X_s Y_s) = E[X_t X_s]E[Y_t Y_s] + E[X_t Y_s]E[Y_t X_s]$$

and again it follows immediately using Fourier transforms and the convolution theorem that the power spectrum of $Z_t = X_t Y_t$ is[3]

$$f_z(\omega) = \int_{-\pi}^{\pi} f_x(\omega - \lambda) f_y(\lambda)\, d\lambda + \int_{-\pi}^{\pi} c_0(\omega - \lambda)c_0(\lambda)\, d\lambda$$
$$+ \int_{-\pi}^{\pi} q(\omega - \lambda)q(\lambda)\, d\lambda.$$

Thus, in particular, the spectrum of the square of the stationary series X_t, i.e., of $Z_t = X_t^2$ is

$$f_z(\omega) = 2 \int_{-\pi}^{\pi} f_x(\omega - \lambda) f_x(\lambda)\, d\lambda.$$

[3] I am grateful to Professors E. J. Hannan and E. Parzen for pointing this result out to me.

5.8 The Partial Cross-spectrum and other Generalizations

When attempting to find relationships between two variables each of which is associated with other variables, a generalization of the above approach will usually be required. The method involves partial cross-spectra and interpretation is parallel to the idea of partial correlation coefficients used in multivariate statistical analysis.

We may regard spectral analysis as a form of analysis of variance, the components of variance being associated with various frequencies instead of the conventional rows and columns. (See Tukey [5].) Extending this idea to multiple time series $(X_1, X_{2t}, \ldots, X_{mt})$, we can regard the matrix of (auto) spectra and cross-spectra

(5.8.1) $$\Sigma = (S_{ij}(\omega))$$

as estimating the *covariance matrix of the time series around frequency ω*. The term "around" being deliberately chosen as a reminder that spectral estimates are estimates of an average over a frequency band. In equation (5.8.1), $S_{ii}(\omega)$ denotes the estimated power spectrum of X_{it} and $S_{ij}(\omega)$ denotes the estimated power cross-spectrum for the series X_{it}, X_{jt} and so $S_{ij}(\omega)$ will be a complex quantity with $S_{ij}(\omega) = \overline{S_{ji}(\omega)}$. Fixing frequency temporarily (at ω), we may proceed to compute from (1) such (complex-valued) quantities as correlations between frequency ω components, coefficients of determination (the squared absolute value of correlation, usually denoted in this complex time series case as the coherency), and partial correlations.

A summary account of partial correlation is given in Anderson [1], from which the relevant formulae are quoted below; with a careful regard to the fact that in this time series case, the complex covariance matrix is Hermitian instead of merely symmetric; and with a slight change of notation to conform with the actual computation method employed.

Denote the component of the ith time series around frequency ω, by $X_i(\omega)$. Without loss of generality (for the time series can be ordered arbitrarily), we consider the computation of $p_{12}(\omega)$ the partial correlation estimates of the ordered pair $(X_1(\omega), X_2(\omega))$. We first partition Σ into submatrices as follows

$$\Sigma = \left[\begin{array}{c|c} \Sigma_{11} & \Sigma_{12} \\ \hline \Sigma_{21} & \Sigma_{22} \end{array}\right]$$

The partitioning lines are between the second and third rows, and second and third columns. Next form the matrix

$$\Sigma_{12 \cdot k} = \Sigma_{11} - \Sigma_{12}\, \Sigma_{22}^{-1}\, \Sigma_{21},$$

⟨ 91 ⟩

then

$$\Sigma_{12 \cdot k}(\omega) = \begin{bmatrix} S_{11 \cdot k}(\omega) & S_{12 \cdot k}(\omega) \\ S_{21 \cdot k}(\omega) & S_{22 \cdot k}(\omega) \end{bmatrix}$$

is the partial auto and cross-spectral matrix for the series X_{1t} and X_{2t} with k denoting the set 3, 4, ..., m.

The partial coherence is given by

$$C_{12 \cdot k}(\omega) = \frac{|S_{12 \cdot k}(\omega)|^2}{S_{11 \cdot k}(\omega) S_{22 \cdot k}(\omega)}$$

and the partial angle by

$$\varphi_{12 \cdot k}(\omega) = \text{amp.}\ S_{12 \cdot k}(\omega)$$

$$= \tan^{-1} \frac{\text{Imag. part of } S_{12 \cdot k}(\omega)}{\text{Real part of } S_{12 \cdot k}(\omega)}$$

Suppose that an optimum linear combination of the series X_{3t}, X_{4t}, ..., X_{mt} has been subtracted from X_{1t} leaving residual $\tilde{X}_{1t}$, and similarly for X_{2t}, leaving $\tilde{X}_{2t}$, then the above functions can now be used and interpreted as being the spectra, coherence and angle for the two series $\tilde{X}_{1t}$, $\tilde{X}_{2t}$.

Thus $S_{11 \cdot k}(\omega)$ is the spectrum of $\tilde{X}_{1t}$, $C_{11 \cdot k}(\omega)$ measures the amount that the frequency ω component of $\tilde{X}_{1t}$ is related to the frequency ω component of $\tilde{X}_{2t}$ and so forth. The uses of the partial coherence and partial angle diagrams are thus similar to those of the ordinary coherence and angle diagram as described previously in this chapter.

Formally, if the information (or predictive ability)[4] of the processes $X_{jt}, j \in k$, is removed from both X_{1t} and X_{2t}, giving residual processes

$$\tilde{X}_{1t} = X_{1t} - E[X_{1t} | X_{jt}, j \in k]$$

$$\tilde{X}_{2t} = X_{2t} - E[X_{2t} | X_{jt}, j \in k]$$

then $S_{ij \cdot k}(\omega)$ is the Fourier transform of the covariance sequence

$$\mu_{ij \cdot k}(\tau) = E[\tilde{X}_{it}, \tilde{X}_{j,t-\tau}]$$

assuming all means to be zero.

As a simple example, consider a three variable set of series X_{1t}, X_{2t} and X_{3t}. If X_{1t} and X_{3t} are related for all frequencies and X_{2t} and X_{3t} are also related, there is no reason why X_{1t} and X_{2t} should be. If, for example, X_{1t} were sale of ice cream, X_{2t} sale of air conditioners, and X_{3t} was a temperature series, then the coherence between X_{1t} and X_{3t} and between X_{2t} and X_{3t} would probably be large for many frequencies. The coherence between X_{1t} and X_{2t} might also be large but this would be a spurious relationship, as X_{1t}, X_{2t} are connected only via X_{3t}. In such

[4] Both of these concepts are considered fully in Chapter 7.

a case the *partial* coherence between X_{1t}, X_{2t} ought to be zero (in theory) or small (in practice) for all frequencies.

The effectiveness of techniques using partial spectra has to be investigated and little experience has been accumulated at present.

The quantity

$$R_{12 \cdot k}(\omega) = \frac{S_{12 \cdot k}(\omega)}{S_{22 \cdot k}(\omega)}$$

is also of importance and may be called the complex partial regression coefficient at frequency ω. Thus, if a model for frequency ω,

$$X_{1t}(\omega) = a_2(\omega) X_{2t}(\omega) + \sum_{j=3}^{m} a_j(\omega) X_{jt}(\omega) + \varepsilon_t(\omega)$$

is proposed, where ε_t is a process independent of all X_{jt}, $R_{12 \cdot k}(\omega)$ will be, in practice, an estimate of the regression coefficient $a_2(\omega)$.

When there are only two processes (X_{1t}, X_{2t}) in the set being considered, the regression coefficient becomes

$$R_{12}(\omega) = \frac{c_0(\omega) + iq(\omega)}{f_2(\omega)}$$

If $R_{12}(\omega) = A(\omega)e^{i\varphi(\omega)}$, then the real function $A(\omega)$ is the *gain* or amplitude gain of X_{1t} over X_{2t} and $\varphi(\omega)$ may be called the phase gain. These terms arise from the model at each frequency ω,

$$X_{1t}(\omega) = R_{12}(\omega) X_{2t}(\omega) + \varepsilon_t(\omega)$$

which can be considered as a noisy black box with X_{2t} as input and X_{1t} as output. In this case, the transfer function of the black box is $A(\omega)e^{i\varphi(\omega)}$.

Just as the partial cross-spectrum generalizes the concept of the partial correlation coefficient so we can also generalize the idea of a multiple correlation coefficient.

If the matrix of (auto) spectra and cross-spectra $\Sigma(\omega)$ introduced above is portioned into submatrices

$$\Sigma(\omega) = \left| \begin{array}{c|c} S_{11}(\omega) & \Gamma_{12}(\omega) \\ \hline \Gamma_{21}(\omega) & \Gamma_{22}(\omega) \end{array} \right|$$

the portioning lines being between the first and second rows and the first and second columns, the function

$$\Sigma_{1,p}(\omega) = S_{11}(\omega) - \Gamma_{12}(\omega) \Gamma_{22}^{-1}(\omega) \Gamma_{21}(\omega)$$

is the partial (auto) spectrum of the series X_{1t} defined as

$$\bar{X}_{1t} = X_{1t} - E[X_{1t}|X_{jt}, j \in p]$$

where p is the set $(2, 3, \ldots, m)$. Thus $\bar{X}_{1t}$ is the residual process when all the information about X_{1t} contained in the processes $X_{2t}, X_{3t}, \ldots, X_{mt}$ has been removed. The function

$$M_{1,\,p}(\omega) = 1 - \frac{\Sigma_{1,\,p}(\omega)}{S_{11}(\omega)}$$

is a direct generalization of the multiple correlation coefficient squared. We note that when $m = 2$, i.e., only two processes are involved,

$$M_{1,2}(\omega) = \frac{|S_{12}(\omega)|^2}{S_{11}(\omega)S_{22}(\omega)}$$

$$= C(\omega),$$

$C(\omega)$ being the coherence, which agrees with the interpretation of coherence introduced earlier.

REFERENCES

[1] Anderson, T. W., *Introduction to Multivariate Statistical Analysis*, New York, 1958.

[2] Gel'fand, I. M. and Yaglom, A. M., *American Math. Soc. Translations*, Ser. 2, vol. 12 (1959), p. 99.

[3] Goodman, N. R., Scientific Paper No. 10, Engineering Statistics Laboratory, New York University, 1957 (also Ph.D. Thesis, Princeton University).

[4] Isserlis, L., *Biometrika*, vol. 12 (1918), pp. 134–139.

[5] Tukey, J. W., *Technometrics*, vol. 3 (1961), pp. 191–220.

CHAPTER 6

CROSS-SPECTRAL ANALYSIS OF ECONOMIC DATA

6.1 Introduction

In Chapter 4 it was pointed out that any stationary series could be considered as a sum of components or frequency bands, each component being statistically independent of the others. In this chapter we consider the effect of such a decomposition when investigating the relationships between two stationary series.

Although, theoretically, we can divide any variable into an infinite number of components in practice, due to limitations on the amount of data available and to ease interpretation, we can suppose there to be only m components. If we divide the line $(0, \pi)$ into m sections of equal length then each one of our m components can be taken as those frequencies lying in a particular section. Suppose the jth section to have centre ω_j, then we can talk of the component having frequency band centred on ω_j, where j can take the values $1, 2, \ldots, m$.

One of the important things that the theory of stationary processes tells us is that not only is the component with centre ω_j independent of all the other components of the variable but it is independent of all components of another variable except the component centred on ω_j. If, as in Diagram a, we split our two variables X_t, Y_t into m components

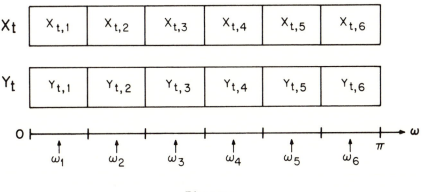

Diagram a

(with $m = 6$), then each of the $X_{t,i}$, $Y_{t,i}$ are statistical variables and, for instance, $X_{t,3}$ is independent of $X_{t,1}$, $X_{t,2}$, $X_{t,4}$, $X_{t,5}$, and $X_{t,6}$ and is also independent of $Y_{t,1}$, $Y_{t,2}$, $Y_{t,4}$, $Y_{t,5}$ and $Y_{t,6}$. It may or may not be independent of $Y_{t,3}$ depending on whether or not the variables X_t and Y_t are related in any way.

Suppose that X_t, Y_t are not independent and so at least one of the pairs $X_{t,i}$, $Y_{t,i}$ are correlated. There is, however, no reason to suppose that the correlation between $X_{t,1}$ and $Y_{t,1}$ is the same as the correlation between $X_{t,3}$ and $Y_{t,3}$ or, stating the same again but in a more general form, the correlation between corresponding frequency components need not be constant for all frequencies. We could consider drawing a diagram showing the amount of correlation for any particular pair of components which, for the case $m = 6$, considered above, might look like Diagram b. However, for the case when $m \to \infty$, i.e., when there are

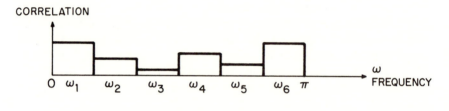

Diagram b

a very large number of components, the diagram would be smooth, as in Diagram c. $C(\omega)$ is called the coherence between the variables $\{X_t\}$

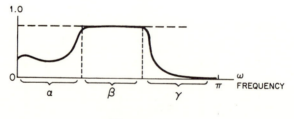

Diagram c

and $\{Y_t\}$ at frequency ω and is a direct measure of the square of the correlation of the amplitudes of frequency ω. Thus, in the diagram shown, the frequency bands in X_t and Y_t in α are partly dependent, those in β are entirely dependent, while those in γ are almost independent.

Even if the amplitudes are fully correlated, it is possible that the corresponding frequency components will have different phases. Thus, for instance, the annual cycle in milk production may exactly account for the annual cycle in the production of canned milk but the two cycles may not have peaks at the same moment of time. In fact, one would expect the peak in milk production to slightly precede the peak in canned milk production. In this example the two annual components might be represented by:

Milk $\qquad\qquad a_t \cos (\omega t + \theta)$

Canned Milk $\quad a_t \cos (\omega t + \varphi)$

and $\theta > \varphi$, $\theta - \varphi$ being the phase-lag at frequency $\omega = \dfrac{2\pi}{12}$ if the basic time unit is a month. This indicates that, when considering the relationship between two stationary series, we need not only the coherency-diagram but also the phase-diagram in which the phase-lag for each frequency is plotted against the frequency. As here presented, the phase-diagram may appear to be more difficult to interpret than the coherency diagram but, in fact, this need not be so and the phase-diagram often proves the more useful of the two. This can best be shown by considering the form of the phase-diagram when one of the variables has a fixed time-lag to the other, i.e., $Y_t = X_{t-k}$. If we consider the ω-frequency of X_t, it can be represented by

$$a_t \cos (t\omega + \theta)$$

and the corresponding component of Y_t by

$$a_{t-k} \cos [(t - k)\omega + \theta] = a_{t-k} \cos [t\omega + (\theta - k\omega)].$$

As the amplitudes a_t, a_{t-k} come from the same sequence of stochastic variables, the coherence will be one and the phase-lag at frequency ω is $k\omega$. Thus, the phase-diagram is, as shown in Diagram d, a straight

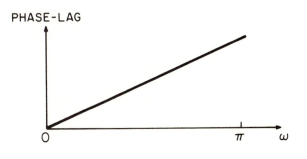

Diagram d

line through the origin with slope depending on the length of the fixed time-lag k.

There is, of course, no reason why the relationship between two variables should always be one of a simple time-lag; or, to put it another way, it is possible for some pairs of components to be time-lagged by different amounts than other pairs. Thus, one could interpret a phase-diagram of the form shown in Diagram e, such that the components of

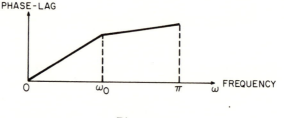

Diagram e

each variable consisting of the frequencies between 0 and ω_0 have one time-lag between them and the components consisting of the other frequencies have a different time-lag. In economic terms this could be thought of as the case of two variables with the short-run fluctuations time-lagged by a certain amount and the long-run fluctuations by a different amount.

A case of particular interest, due to its simplicity, is when the phase-diagram has the form shown in Diagram f, i.e., the phase-lag is the same

Diagram f

constant for all frequencies. If we consider the components of the variables X_t, Y_t with frequency ω, in this case they would be of the form

$$X_t; \quad a_t \cos (t\omega + \theta)$$
$$Y_t; \quad a_t \cos (t\omega + \theta - c).$$

Rewriting the latter as

$$a_t \cos \left(\omega \left(t - \frac{c}{\omega} \right) + \theta \right)$$

we see that it can be interpreted as a time-lag of $\frac{c}{\omega}$ at frequency ω, i.e., the smaller the frequency the larger the time-lag between the corresponding components. Such a relationship is called a "fixed angle lag" and is discussed further in the next section.

If $X_t(\omega)$, $Y_t(\omega)$ are the components of X_t, Y_t at frequency ω, we may be interested in models of the form

$$X_t(\omega) = R_{xy}(\omega) \cdot Y_t(\omega) + \varepsilon_t(\omega)$$

i.e., the linear regression of $X_t(\omega)$ on $Y_t(\omega)$. $R_{xy}(\omega)$ is called the gain at frequency ω and the plot of $R_{xy}(\omega)$ against ω is the *gain-diagram*.

We may sum up, and slightly generalize the above, in the following way: consider two stationary variables X_t and Y_t each of which can be thought of as the sum of (a very large number of) frequency components. Each variable will have a spectrum which will indicate to us the distribution of the total "power" or "energy" (i.e., variance). If the two variables are in some way related then some of the power of the component of frequency ω of Y_t may be induced by the component of frequency ω of X_t (and/or vice-versa), for example the production of canned milk may have an annual variation (or component of frequency $2\pi/12$) which is caused or induced by the annual variation of the production of milk series. [On the other hand, it is easy to think of two series each having an important annual component but with these components being entirely unrelated, e.g., sale of New Year cards, sale of ice cream.] We also have a theorem which states that the component of Y_t of frequency ω can only possibly be affected by the component of X_t of frequency ω and not by other components of X_t. The diagram which plots the amount of correlation per pair of frequency components against frequency is called the coherence-diagram. There may also be phase differences (which can be interpreted as time-lag differences) between the related components, and the diagram plotting the phase-differences against frequency is called the phase-diagram.

It must be emphasized that the account given in this section is not rigorous and has ignored many of the subtle difficulties involved in interpretation of the mathematical results of Chapter 5. In practice, of course, we would expect any stochastic process to have all frequencies present and if the phase at frequency ω is $\Phi(\omega)$, this will be a *continuous random curve*. Intuitively, a random curve is such a difficult concept that a simple explanation becomes extremely difficult and perhaps impossible. This is particularly so when we move from the theoretical underlying processes to the actual available series, being samples from these processes.

In the next section some of the economic consequences of the frequency approach to the problem of relationships between series are discussed, and in the final section to this chapter some actual coherence and phase-diagrams are presented.

6.2 Relationships between Economic Series

Let us consider pairs of economic series denoted by X_t, Y_t such that one is intrinsically lagged to the other; a simple example might be the labor input in man-hours and the production of some firm or industry. In such cases we might reasonably expect the relationship to be a single-direction one, that is, there is little or no feedback present. (Feedback problems will be considered in the next chapter.) It has been usual, in such cases, for a simple time lag to be envisaged such as $X_t = Y_{t-1}$ or $X_t = aY_{t-1} + \varepsilon_t$. Although superficially such a model appears reasonable, when it is remembered that each variable may be split into a sum of independent components it becomes much less realistic. Is it really sensible to expect the long-run components to be lagged by exactly the same amount as the short-run, the minor cycles to be lagged the same as the month-to-month fluctuations? Almost certainly, for intrinsically lagged variables, the lag will vary with frequency. It is for this reason that we need to carefully consider the phase-diagram, which estimates the relevant lag for each pair of frequency components. In many cases it would probably be reasonable to expect the lag to be greater for the low frequencies (i.e., longer periods) than for the high frequencies. In fact, if a very simple type of lag relationship needs to be considered, a better assumption than a fixed time-lag is that of a fixed angle-lag, in which the lag is proportional to the inverse of the frequency (i.e., lag $\sim$ period of component). An example of such a lag arising in practice is given in the last section of this chapter.

A second consideration arising from the frequency components concept is that the amount to which components are related may not be a constant. Thus, for instance, it would not be difficult to construct examples of series for which the long and middle-run components were closely related but the short-run entirely unrelated. It is suggested that knowledge of the relevant correlations and time-lags between components of economic laws might be suggested, and such information ought to be incorporated in economic models. The phase and coherence diagrams provide powerful methods of investigating such relationships between series in which there is no feedback and which are stationary. It will be shown in Chapter 9 that the stationarity assumption need not be an important stumbling block in finding the time-lags between components of non-stationary series.

6.3 Estimating Cross-spectra

If we define, for data $\{x_t, y_t; t = 1, \ldots, n\}$

$$C_{xy}(-k) = C_{yx}(k) = \frac{1}{n-k} \left\{ \sum_{t=1}^{n-k} x_t y_{t+k} - \frac{1}{n-k} \sum_{t=k+1}^{n} y_t \sum_{t=1}^{n-k} x_t \right\}$$

$$C_{yx}(-k) = C_{xy}(k) = \frac{1}{n-k} \left\{ \sum_{t=1}^{n-k} y_t x_{t+k} - \frac{1}{n-k} \sum_{t=k+1}^{n} x_t \sum_{t=1}^{n-k} y_t \right\}$$

$$\text{for } k = 0, 1, \ldots, m,$$

then estimates of the power co-spectrum and quadrature spectrum are of the form

$$\hat{c}(\omega_j) = \frac{\lambda_0}{4\pi} (C_{xy}(0) + C_{yx}(0)) + \frac{1}{2\pi} \sum_{k=1}^{m} \lambda_k (C_{xy}(k) + C_{yx}(k)) \cos \omega_j k$$

$$\hat{q}(\omega_j) = \frac{1}{2\pi} \sum_{k=1}^{m} \lambda_k (C_{xy}(k) - C_{yx}(k)) \sin \omega_j k$$

$$\omega_j = \frac{\pi j}{m}, \quad j = 0, \ldots, m.$$

The weights λ_k are the same as used in estimating the power spectrum and so there are various estimates to choose from. Throughout this volume, the examples have been estimated using the Tukey-Hanning weights

$$\lambda_k = \frac{1}{2} \left[1 + \cos \frac{\pi k}{m} \right]$$

but the weights recently suggested by Parzen, i.e.,

$$\lambda_k = 1 - \frac{6k^2}{m^2} \left(1 - \frac{k}{m} \right), \quad 0 \leq k \leq \frac{m}{2}$$

$$= 2 \left(1 - \frac{k}{m} \right)^3, \quad \frac{m}{2} \leq k \leq m$$

have certain advantages if used with the following estimates of the cross-covariances;

$$C_{yx}(k) = \frac{1}{n} \sum_{t=1}^{n-k} (x_t - \bar{x})(y_{t+k} - \bar{y})$$

$$C_{xy}(k) = \frac{1}{n} \sum_{t=1}^{n-k} (y_t - \bar{y})(x_{t+k} - \bar{x})$$

where

$$\bar{x} = \frac{1}{n} \sum_{t=1}^{n} x_t$$

and

$$\bar{y} = \frac{1}{n} \sum_{t=1}^{n} y_t$$

Using the Tukey-Hanning weights, the usual steps are to form first the raw estimates

$$(L_c)_j = \frac{1}{2\pi}\left(C_{xy}(0) + \sum_{k=1}^{m-1}(C_{xy}(k) + C_{yx}(k))\cos\frac{\pi jk}{m}\right.$$
$$\left. + \tfrac{1}{2}(C_{xy}(m) + C_{yx}(m))\cos\pi j\right)$$

$$(L_q)_j = \frac{1}{2\pi}\left(\sum_{k=1}^{m-1}(C_{xy}(k) - C_{yx}(k))\sin\frac{\pi jk}{m} + \tfrac{1}{2}(C_{xy}(m) - C_{yx}(m))\sin\pi j\right)$$

and from these, the smooth estimates,

$$\hat{c}(\omega_j) = 0.25(L_c)_{j-1} + 0.50(L_c)_j + 0.25(L_c)_{j+1}$$
$$\hat{q}(\omega_j) = 0.25(L_q)_{j-1} + 0.50(L_q)_j + 0.25(L_q)_{j+1}$$

with

$$(L_c)_{-1} = (L_c)_{+1}, \qquad (L_c)_{m+1} = (L_c)_{m-1}$$
$$(L_q)_{-1} = -(L_q)_{+1}, \qquad (L_q)_{m+1} = -(L_q)_{m-1}.$$

There is, however, little point in printing out the raw estimates produced by the computer. We have little use for $\hat{c}(\omega_j)$, $\hat{q}(\omega_j)$ as they stand, and so the more useful coherence, angle and gain, must be estimated, using

$$\hat{C}(\omega_j) = \frac{\hat{c}(\omega_j)^2 + \hat{q}(\omega_j)^2}{\hat{f}_x(\omega_j)\cdot\hat{f}_y(\omega_j)}$$

$$\hat{\phi}(\omega_j) = \tan^{-1}\left[\frac{\hat{q}(\omega_j)}{\hat{c}(\omega_j)}\right]$$

and

$$\hat{f}_y(\omega_j)\,\hat{R}^2_{xy}(\omega_j) = \hat{f}_x(\omega_j)\hat{C}(\omega_j).$$

where $\hat{f}_x(\omega_j)$, $\hat{f}_y(\omega_j)$ are the estimated power spectra of the series $\{x_t\}\{y_t\}$ respectively.

It has been found better, in general, to record the estimated angle in degrees rather than in radians.

As the Tukey-Hanning estimate does occasionally give a negative estimate of the power spectrum and as all estimates do allow some leakage, it is possible for the estimated coherence to be either negative or greater than one, although we know that the true coherence (from the underlying generating process) must lie between zero and one. If the Parzen estimate is used, no negative coherences or values greater than one will be found.

When $\hat{C}(\omega_j)$ lies outside $0 - 1$, interpretation becomes extraordinarily difficult and it has been the practice of the program at Princeton not to plot such frequencies. Nevertheless, some rough rules can be given to help interpret these cases:

(i) If $\hat{C}(\omega_j)$ is negative, set it equal to zero. The suggested logic behind this is that a negative number will be due to one or the other of the series having very little power in the frequency band being considered and so nothing of interest can occur in this band.

(ii) If $\hat{C}(\omega_j) > 1$ and if either of the estimated power spectra is very small for this frequency band, put $\hat{C}(\omega_j) = 0$ for the same reason as above. However, if neither of the power spectra is particularly small for this band, treat the estimated coherence as if $\hat{C}(\omega_j) = 1$.

It should be noted that it is possible to get a value of $\hat{C}(\omega_j)$ between zero and one but with both power spectra negative for this band. Such occurrences will be very rare and $\hat{C}(\omega_j)$ should be treated as zero.

Confidence bands for the coherence-diagram and phase-diagram are discussed in Section 5.2.

It should be noticed that as $\hat{\phi}(0) = \hat{\phi}(\pi) = 0$, these points need not be marked on the estimated phase-diagram as they contribute nothing to the investigation.

One piece of advice is perhaps permissible at this point. It should always be remembered that as $\hat{\phi}(\omega)$ is an angle derived from arctan it can be altered by the addition or subtraction of a multiple of 2π. In practice, to aid the interpretation of the phase-diagram, some such alterations are often required. Great care, however, must be taken, and only intelligent use of the alteration should be made. This can be emphasized by pointing out that the points $\hat{\phi}(\omega_j) - 2k_j\pi, j = 0, \ldots, m$, can doubtlessly be made to lie on virtually any curve one cares to consider by suitably choosing the integers k_j.

It is just because the above alteration is always allowable that it is doubtful if the interpretation of phase-diagrams could be made entirely mechanical.

Although most of the decisions concerning the shape of the phase-diagram must be made entirely on visual evidence (and experience) it is possible to provide quick and fairly powerful tests of significance for the two problems:

(i) Time-lag? Question: Is there a trend in the phase diagram?

(ii) Angle-lag? Question: Is the phase-diagram oscillating about a constant other than zero?

In the two tests proposed, the fact that some points of the phase-diagram are more significant than others due to non-constant coherence, has not been taken into account. It is very possible that better tests can be invented but the gains in making correct decisions are unlikely to be great. Both the tests use the result that, although adjacent estimates of the phase are correlated, non-adjacent estimates are only slightly correlated when either the Tukey or the Parzen estimating procedure is used. Thus, for each test, the data used is the estimate of the phase at the first, third, fifth, etc., frequency points, i.e., $\hat{\varphi}(\omega_1)$, $\hat{\varphi}(\omega_3)$, ..., $\hat{\varphi}(\omega_{k-1})$ if an even number of lags (k) were used in estimating the spectrum. However, for ease of presentation the data used in the tests will be denoted $x_1, x_2, \ldots, x_m$.

Test 1 (Records Test)

Null hypothesis (H_0): there is no trend in the data.
Alternative hypothesis (H_A): there is a trend present.
We take x_j as an upper record if $x_j > x_k$, all $k < j$, and, similarly, as a lower record if $x_j < x_k$, all $k < j$. Starting at x_1 and proceeding to x_m, count the number of upper records and lower records occurring. Let d equal the number of upper records minus the number of lower records. The process is now repeated, starting at x_m and proceeding to x_1 counting upper and lower records, giving a second statistic d', defined as for d. Denoting $D = d - d'$, Foster and Stuart[1] proved the following: when H_0 is true, $E[d] = E[D] = 0$, and d and D are asymptotically distributed normally with the variance of d given by (approximately) $2 \log_e m - 0.845$. The variance of D is more complicated but can be approximately interpolated from the following table which lists the standard deviation of D for certain values of m:

m	10	25	50	75	100	125
$\sigma(D)$	3.26	3.80	4.05	4.30	4.41	4.45
$\sigma(d)$	1.94	2.44	2.64	2.79	2.89	2.97

The corresponding values for the standard deviation of d are also given. There is no simple relationship between $\sigma(D)$ and $\sigma(d)$ as d and d' are correlated.

The test consists merely of finding d or D and then using the usual standard errors technique, e.g., if $d_{\text{obs.}} > 2\sigma(d)$ then H_0 can be rejected at the 95% confidence level, etc. The test using d, known as the simple records test against trend, is quicker but less powerful than the test using the statistic D, known as the round-trip records test.

Foster and Stuart investigated the power of these tests using a Monte Carlo method. They were found to be more powerful than other "quick and easy" tests. A sample of the powers found with H_A consisting of

[1] Foster, F. G. and Stuart, A., "Distribution-free tests in time series based on the breaking of records," *J. Roy. Stat. Soc.* (B), vol. 16 (1954), p. 1.

data $x_t + \Delta t$, x_t being a random, independent series normally distributed $N(0, 1)$ are:

Using d	m	Δ	0.02	0.04	0.07
	25		0.09	0.15	0.34
	50		0.18	0.38	0.69

Using D	m	Δ	0.02	0.04	0.07
	25		0.11	0.20	0.49
	50		0.25	0.55	0.87

Test 2 (Sign test)

   H_0: $E[x_j] = 0$

   H_A: $E[x_j] \neq 0$

Find the number of the x_j $(j = 1, \ldots, m)$ which are positive, and test this number k against H_0 by using the binomial theorem, i.e., probability of getting k or more positive with H_0 true is

$$\left(\frac{1}{2}\right)^m \sum_{j=k}^{m} {}_mC_j.$$

For m not small (> 10, say) a reasonable approximation is that, with H_0 true, $k \sim N\left(\frac{m}{2}, \frac{1}{2}\sqrt{m}\right)$, and so, again, the standard error technique may be used.

The power efficiency of the sign test is about 90% for $m = 10$ and decreases as m increases to an asymptotic efficiency of 63%.

6.4   An Example of Estimated Cross-spectra

New York Call Money Rate, Commercial Paper Rate, 1876–1914

The data used in this example has been described in Chapter 4 and the estimated power spectrum for the commercial paper rate was also discussed in Chapter 4. The estimated spectrum of the call money rate was similar in general appearance to that of the commercial paper rate but with less prominent peaks corresponding to the annual and 40-month components and their harmonics.

In Fig. 6.1 the coherence will be seen to be of varying size for different frequency bands indicating that the two series have some components closely related and other components almost unrelated.

The angle diagram is seen to oscillate about a horizontal line around 340° and thus indicates a fixed angle lag relationship between the two

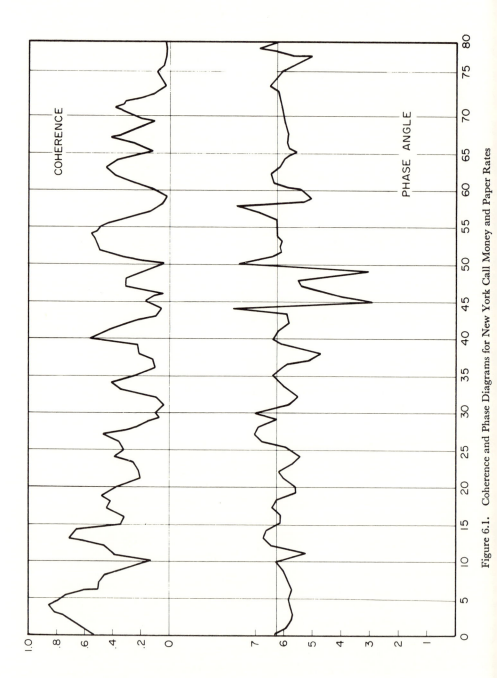

Figure 6.1.   Coherence and Phase Diagrams for New York Call Money and Paper Rates

series, with the call money rate leading. This relationship is even more obvious when it is noted that the biggest deviations from the line 340° or so occur when the coherence is low. It is of interest to note that earlier studies had suggested that the New York commercial paper rate was lagged to the call money rate prior to World War I although the lag had, of course, been assumed to be a simple time-lag.

If one uses a simple average the angle diagram seems to fluctuate about 336.35° and if the coherence-weighted least squares method is used, as suggested in Section 5.6, the average angle becomes 336.36°.

The binomial test of the hypothesis (H_0) that the angles are oscillating around 360° rejects this hypothesis with high confidence as thirty-one are below 360° and only nine above of the sequence $\hat{\phi}_1, \hat{\phi}_3, \hat{\phi}_5, \ldots, \hat{\phi}_{79}$. Thus $k = 9$, and if H_0 were true $k \sim N(20, 2.24)$ and the probability of getting a k as low as 9 from a normal distribution with mean 20 and standard deviation 2.24 is approximately 0.0000005. H_0 is clearly rejected.

Further examples of estimated cross-spectra will be found in Chapters 12 and 13.

6.5 A Note on the Interpretation of Coherence

If a high coherence throughout the frequency band $(0, \pi)$ is found between two aggregate series, the following should be remembered when interpreting this result:

If $X_t = A_{1t} + B_{1t}$, $Y_t = A_{2t} + B_{2t}$, where A_{1t} and A_{2t} have high coherence for most frequencies as do B_{1t} and B_{2t}, but where the coherence is low between any A series and any B series, then the coherence between the two series X_t, Y_t will, in general, be moderate to high for most frequencies.

As a simple example of this, consider the model where $A_{1t} = \lambda_1 A_{2t}$, $B_{1t} = \lambda_2 B_{2t}$, i.e., A_{1t}, A_{2t} are unlagged and have coherence one and similarly for the B's and let A_{it}, B_{jt} be independent, $i = 1, 2; j = 1, 2$. If we let $\lambda_1/\lambda_2 = \alpha$ and suppose that $f_{B_1}(\omega) = \beta f_{A_1}(\omega)$, i.e., all four series have power spectra of the same shape, then the coherence between $X_t = A_{1t} + B_{1t}$ and $Y_{1t} = A_{2t} + B_{2t}$ is given by

$$C_{xy}(\alpha, \beta) = \frac{(\alpha + \beta)^2}{(1 + \beta)(\alpha^2 + \beta)}.$$

As $\alpha \geqq 0$, $\beta \geqq 0$, $C_{xy}(\alpha, \beta)$ will generally be near one for any α, β and has a minimum value of $\frac{1}{2}$, when $\alpha = 0$, $\beta = 1$.

Situations similar to this simple model occur when stock exchange price series are used. It has been found, for example, that if X_t is the Securities and Exchange Commission stock price index for manufacturers of durable goods and Y_t is the SEC's stock price index for manufacturers of non-durable goods, then the coherence between X_t and Y_t is high for almost all frequencies. On the other hand, if A_t is the SEC index for TV and radio manufacturers and B_t is the SEC index for the stock prices of motor manufacturers, then A_t and B_t are important components of X_t, yet the coherence between A_t and B_t is, generally, small. It may, incidentally, be noted that the estimated power spectra for the weekly indices over the period 1939–1960 for these four series, and for all the other major SEC indices, are all of remarkably similar shape. No "cycles" are observed, even an annual component is missing, but the frequency corresponding to a monthly period is slightly, but consistently, larger than its neighbors.[2]

---

[2] Further application of spectral methods to stock market data will be found in "Spectral Analysis of New York Stock Market Prices" by C. W. J. Granger and O. Morgenstern, *Kyklos* No. 16 (1963), pp. 1–27.

CHAPTER 7

PROCESSES INVOLVING FEEDBACK

7.1 Feedback and Cross-spectral Analysis

In the previous two chapters we have been considering the case in which one process $\{X_t\}$ is "causing" or is intrinsically leading another process $\{Y_t\}$. Such relationships can be expressed as

$$(7.1.1) \qquad Y_t = X_t\{a(\omega), \varphi(\omega)\} + U_t$$

using the notation introduced in Section 5.6, U_t being a stationary process independent of X_t. Such models may be reasonable in the field of micro-economics, but in macro-economics there is often also a feedback equation, perhaps of the form

$$(7.1.2) \qquad X_t = Y_t\{b(\omega), \theta(\omega)\} + V_t.$$

It should be fairly clear that when feedback is present in a system the methods described in Chapter 5 will be less appropriate. This may be shown more exactly by considering further the pair of equations (7.1.1) and (7.1.2). Assuming $E[U_t] = E[V_t] = E[U_t V_{t-\tau}] = 0$, all t, τ, they may be rewritten

$$(7.1.3) \quad \begin{aligned} X_t &= X_t\{a(\omega)b(\omega), \varphi(\omega) + \theta(\omega)\} + U_t\{b(\omega), \theta(\omega)\} + V_t \\ Y_t &= Y_t\{a(\omega)b(\omega), \varphi(\omega) + \theta(\omega)\} + V_t\{a(\omega), \varphi(\omega)\} + U_t \end{aligned}$$

and if

$$P_t = \int_{-\pi}^{\pi} e^{it\omega} \, dz_p(\omega)$$

$$E[dz_p(\omega) \, \overline{dz_p(\lambda)}] = 0, \quad \omega \neq \lambda$$

$$= f_p(\omega)d\omega, \quad \omega = \lambda$$

for $P = X, Y, U, V$, then

$$dz_x(\omega) = [b(\omega)e^{-i\theta(\omega)} \, dz_u(\omega) + dz_v(\omega)]/A(\omega), \quad \omega > 0$$

$$dz_y(\omega) = [a(\omega)e^{-i\varphi(\omega)} \, dz_v(\omega) + dz_u(\omega)]/A(\omega), \quad \omega > 0$$

where

$$A(\omega) = 1 - a(\omega) \, b(\omega) \exp\{-i(\theta(\omega) + \varphi(\omega))\}$$

$$dz_x(-\omega) = \overline{dz_x(\omega)}, \qquad dz_y(-\omega) = \overline{dz_y(\omega)},$$

and if $C_r(\omega) = c_0(\omega) + iq(\omega)$ is the power cross-spectrum between $\{X_t\}$ and $\{Y_t\}$, then

$$B(\omega) f_x(\omega) = b^2(\omega) f_u(\omega) + f_v(\omega)$$

$$B(\omega) f_y(\omega) = a^2(\omega) f_v(\omega) + f_u(\omega)$$

$$B(\omega) c_0(\omega) = a(\omega) f_v(\omega) \cos \varphi(\omega) + b(\omega) f_u(\omega) \cos \theta(\omega)$$

$$B(\omega) q(\omega) = a(\omega) f_v(\omega) \sin \varphi(\omega) - b(\omega) f_u(\omega) \sin \theta(\omega),$$

where

$$B(\omega) = 1 + a^2(\omega) b^2(\omega) - 2a(\omega) b(\omega) \cos [\varphi(\omega) + \theta(\omega)].$$

Thus, the coherence is

$$C(\omega) =$$

$$\frac{a^2(\omega) f_v^2(\omega) + b^2(\omega) f_u^2(\omega) + 2a(\omega) b(\omega) f_u(\omega) f_v(\omega) \cos [\varphi(\omega) + \theta(\omega)]}{[b^2(\omega) f_u(\omega) + f_v(\omega)][a^2(\omega) f_v(\omega) + f_u(\omega)]}$$

$$= 1 - \frac{f_u(\omega) f_v(\omega)}{B(\omega) f_x(\omega) f_y(\omega)}.$$

and the phase-diagram varies as

$$\psi(\omega) = - \tan^{-1} \left\{ \frac{b(\omega) f_u(\omega) \sin \theta(\omega) - a(\omega) f_v(\omega) \sin \varphi(\omega)}{b(\omega) f_u(\omega) \cos \theta(\omega) + a(\omega) f_v(\omega) \cos \varphi(\omega)} \right\}.$$

The coherence, of course, still measures the degree of dependence between the processes at each frequency, but, as now no one process is continually lagged to the other, the phase diagram is unlikely to provide useful information unless the feedback is weak ($b(\omega)$ small for all ω, $a(\omega)$ not small, say).

It should further be noted that as there are six unknown functions ($a(\omega)$, $b(\omega)$, $\varphi(\omega)$, $\theta(\omega)$, $f_u(\omega)$, $f_v(\omega)$)) and only four estimated functions ($f_x(\omega)$, $f_y(\omega)$, $c_0(\omega)$, $q(\omega)$)) it is not possible to estimate the unknown functions. Even if the processes $\{U_t\}$ and $\{V_t\}$ are assumed to be white noise, the estimation problem cannot be solved using spectral methods.

Thus, consideration of feedback suggests a variety of problems which will be considered in this chapter:

(i) How to define feedback and test it if it is occurring in a system.

(ii) How to measure the feedback-lag (length of time taken for feedback to occur) and the strength of any feedback.

(iii) How to consider whether feedback is varying in importance and direction with frequency.

7.2 Some Preliminary Results

If the $q \times 1$ vector $\mathbf{X}_t$ with[1]

$$\mathbf{X}'_t = \{X_{1t}, X_{2t}, \ldots, X_{qt}\},$$

$$E[X_{jt}] = 0, j = 1, \ldots, q,$$

is a multivariate, stationary, non-deterministic[2] process, Zashuin [7] has shown that it may be represented by

(7.2.1)
$$\mathbf{X}_t = \mathbf{B}(U)\boldsymbol{\varepsilon}_t$$

where $\mathbf{B}(U)$ is the matrix

$$\mathbf{B}(U) = [B_{jk}(U)]$$

$$B_{jk}(U) = \sum_{m=0}^{\infty} b_{jkm} U^m,$$

U being the shift operator defined by

$$UX_t = X_{t-1},$$

and $\boldsymbol{\varepsilon}_t$ is a $q \times 1$ multivariate white noise vector with mean zero, i.e.,

$$\boldsymbol{\varepsilon}'_t = \{\varepsilon_{1t}, \varepsilon_{2t}, \ldots, \varepsilon_{qt}\}, \quad E[\varepsilon_{jt}] = 0, \quad j = 1, \ldots, q;$$

$$E[\boldsymbol{\varepsilon}_t \boldsymbol{\varepsilon}'_t] = \mathbf{I}_q; \qquad E[\boldsymbol{\varepsilon}_t \boldsymbol{\varepsilon}'_{t+s}] = \mathbf{0}_q, \quad s \neq 0.$$

Here, $\mathbf{I}_q$ is the unit matrix and $\mathbf{0}_q$ the zero matrix, both of the qth order. (7.2.1) may be called the "moving average" representation of the process.

Defining the theoretical autocovariances and power spectral functions by[3]

$$\Gamma_{jk}(s) = E[X_{j, t+s} X_{kt}]$$

$$F_{jk}(\omega) = \sum_{s=-\infty}^{\infty} \Gamma_{jk}(s) e^{i\omega s}$$

$$\mathbf{F}(\omega) = [F_{jk}(\omega)], j, k = 1, \ldots, q,$$

it is easy to show that

$$\mathbf{F}(\omega) = \mathbf{B}(e^{i\omega})\mathbf{B}'(e^{-i\omega}).$$

If the equation in z, $|\mathbf{B}(z)| = 0$, has no roots on or within $|z| = 1$, we may invert (7.2.1) to get the "autoregressive" representation

(7.2.2)
$$\mathbf{A}(U)\mathbf{X}_t = \boldsymbol{\varepsilon}_t$$

---

[1] Matrix $\mathbf{A}'$ is the transpose of matrix $\mathbf{A}$.

[2] Defined in Chapter 3.

[3] For ease of exposition, the definition of spectra differs by a factor 2π from the earlier definition. The difference can be easily seen by considering the spectrum of white noise.

where

$$\mathbf{A}(U) = \mathbf{B}^{-1}(U) = \sum_{j=0}^{\infty} \mathbf{A}_j U^j.$$

If we write (7.2.2) as

(7.2.3) $\mathbf{A}_o\mathbf{X}_t + (\text{past values of } \mathbf{X}_t) = \boldsymbol{\varepsilon}_t$

we have

$$\mathbf{X}_t = \mathbf{A}_o^{-1}\boldsymbol{\varepsilon}_t + (\text{past } \mathbf{X}_t)$$

(7.2.4) $= \mathbf{B}_o\boldsymbol{\varepsilon}_t + (\text{past } \mathbf{X}_t).$

Equation (7.2.3) will be called the *basic representation* of the vector process $\{\mathbf{X}_t\}$ and equation (7.2.4) the *reduced-form representation*.

It is important to note that (7.2.3) is not a unique representation. If $\boldsymbol{\Lambda}$ is an orthogonal matrix, i.e., a square matrix having the property $\boldsymbol{\Lambda}\boldsymbol{\Lambda}' = \mathbf{I}_q$, then, if $\boldsymbol{\varepsilon}_t$ is a white noise vector, so is the vector $\boldsymbol{\eta}_t$ defined by $\boldsymbol{\eta}_t = \boldsymbol{\Lambda}\boldsymbol{\varepsilon}_t$, as

$$E[\boldsymbol{\eta}_t\boldsymbol{\eta}'_{t+s}] = \boldsymbol{\Lambda}E[\boldsymbol{\varepsilon}_t\boldsymbol{\varepsilon}'_{t+s}]\boldsymbol{\Lambda}' = \boldsymbol{\Lambda}\mathbf{I}_q\boldsymbol{\Lambda}' = \mathbf{I}_q, \quad \text{if } s = 0$$

$$= \boldsymbol{\Lambda}\mathbf{0}_q\boldsymbol{\Lambda}' = \mathbf{0}_q, \quad \text{if } s \neq 0.$$

Thus an alternative representation to (7.2.3) having exactly the same form is achieved by pre-multiplying (or post-multiplying) throughout by any orthogonal matrix, getting

$$\boldsymbol{\Lambda}\mathbf{A}_o\mathbf{X}_t + (\text{past } \mathbf{X}_t) = \boldsymbol{\eta}_t.$$

It follows that, as any matrix can be written as the product of an orthogonal matrix and a triangular matrix, we lose no generality by assuming $\mathbf{A}_o$ to be a triangular matrix in any basic representation. On the other hand, we are unable, in general, to assume $\mathbf{A}_o = \mathbf{I}_q$ and still retain a basic representation having white noise as the residual term.

Viewing the reduced-form representation (7.2.4) with regard to prediction possibilities, we see that if given all past values of $\mathbf{X}_t$ we can predict all of the present $\mathbf{X}_t$ apart from the terms $\mathbf{B}_o\boldsymbol{\varepsilon}_t$. The determinant of the covariance matrix of these terms,

(7.2.5)
$$V = |E[(\mathbf{B}_o\boldsymbol{\varepsilon}_t)(\mathbf{B}_o\boldsymbol{\varepsilon}_t)']|$$
$$= |\mathbf{B}_o\mathbf{B}'_o| = |\mathbf{B}_o|^2$$

is called the *total predictive variance* of the process $\{\mathbf{X}_t\}$. We note that pre-multiplying the basic form by any orthogonal matrix $\boldsymbol{\Lambda}$ has no effect on V as $|\boldsymbol{\Lambda}| = 1$.

Let us denote the set of q stochastic processes $\{X_{it}\}$, $i = 1, \ldots, q$, by Q and let $Q(j)$ be the set of processes $\{X_{it}\}$, $i = 1, \ldots, j - 1, j + 1, \ldots,$

q, i.e., the set Q excluding $\{X_{jt}\}$, let $Q(j, k)$ be the set of processes Q excluding $\{X_{jt}\}$ and $\{X_{kt}\}$, and so forth.

For any one of the processes in the set Q, say $\{X_{it}\}$, we can form an optimum linear predictor using only those processes belonging to some subset J of Q by defining

$$(7.2.6) \qquad P_{it}[J] = \sum_{j} \sum_{k=1}^{\infty} a_{jk} X_{j,t-k}, \quad j \in J,$$

and choosing the coefficients a_{jk} so that the prediction error variance

$$(7.2.7) \qquad V_i[J] = E[(X_{it} - P_{it}[J])^2]$$

is a minimum. Thus, $P_{it}[J]$ is the best (in a least-squares sense) predictor of X_{it} available to us if we restrict ourselves to using only the past values of the set of processes $\{X_{jt}\}$, $j \in J$. Clearly, the better the prediction, the lower will be the value of $V_i[J]$, and thus

$$0 < V_i[J] \leq \sigma_i^2$$

where $\sigma_i^2 = E[X_{it}]^2$. If and only if the process X_{it} is deterministic, $V_i[J] = 0$.

7.3 Definitions of Causality and Feedback

We shall initially restrict ourselves to vector stochastic processes having basic representation

$$\mathbf{A}_o \mathbf{X}_t = (\text{past } \mathbf{X}_t) + \boldsymbol{\varepsilon}_t,$$

where $\boldsymbol{\varepsilon}_t$ is white noise and $\mathbf{A}_o$ is a *diagonal* matrix. As explained above, this is a restrictive assumption, but the class of such processes is important because each process $\{X_{it}\}$, $i = 1, \ldots, q$, is now "caused" only by *past* values of $\mathbf{X}_t$. The removal of this assumption is discussed below. We note that for such processes (7.3.1) can be written

$$\mathbf{X}_t = (\text{past } \mathbf{X}_t) + \mathbf{B}_o \boldsymbol{\varepsilon}_t,$$

where

$$\mathbf{B}_o \mathbf{B}_o' = \mathbf{V} = [V_i \delta_{ij}]$$

with

$$\delta_{ij} = 0, \quad i \neq j$$
$$= 1, \quad i = j.$$

Thus, V_i will be the prediction error variance of the process $\{X_{it}\}$ if all processes in the set Q are used, i.e.,

$$V_i = E[(X_{it} - P_{it}[Q])^2],$$

and the total prediction variance is given by

$$V = \prod_{i=1}^{q} V_i.$$

Using the notation of the previous section, we shall define causality of the process $\{X_{jt}\}$ by the process $\{X_{kt}\}$ within the set Q if

$$V_j[Q(k)] - V_j[Q] > 0.$$

Such a causality will be denoted by

$$\{X_{kt}\} \Rightarrow \{X_{jt}\}.$$

If

$$V_j[Q(k)] - V_j[Q] = 0,$$

there is no causality, denoted by $\{X_{kt}\} \not\Rightarrow \{X_{jt}\}$. Thus, we say that the process $\{X_{kt}\}$ is causing the process $\{X_{jt}\}$ if we are better able to predict X_{jt} using past values of X_{kt} than if we do not use these values.[4]

If we find $\{X_{kt}\} \Rightarrow \{X_{jt}\}$ and $\{X_{jt}\} \Rightarrow \{X_{kt}\}$, i.e., we have both $V_j[Q(k)] - V_j[Q] > 0$ and $V_k[Q(j)] - V_k[Q] > 0$, we say that direct feedback is present and denote this by

$$\{X_{jt}\} \Leftrightarrow \{X_{kt}\}.$$

Two other types of feedback will also be distinguished:

(i) If $V_j[Q(j)] - V_j[Q] > 0$, we say that there is "internal feedback."
(ii) If causality chains are found of the type $\{X_{kt}\} \Rightarrow \{X_{it}\} \Rightarrow \{X_{jt}\} \Rightarrow \{X_{kt}\}$ we may talk of "indirect feedback."

Strictly speaking, we should always indicate the basic set Q of processes within which we are working whenever the causality or feedback notation is used. A possible notation is:

$$\{X_{jt}\} \Rightarrow \{X_{kt}\}|Q.$$

The reason why we must be careful on this point is because it is possible, for instance, that there exists a stochastic process $\{Y_t\}$ outside of Q such that

$$\{X_{kt}\} \Rightarrow \{Y_t\}|R$$
$$\{Y_t\} \Rightarrow \{X_{jt}\}|R$$

and

$$\{X_{kt}\} \not\Rightarrow \{X_{jt}\}|R$$

but

$$\{X_{kt}\} \Rightarrow \{X_{jt}\}|Q,$$

where R is the set Q plus the process $\{Y_t\}$. In such a case we are finding

---

[4] This definition of causality agrees with that proposed by Wiener [6].

causality within Q due to the indirect causality via $\{Y_t\}$ in the larger set R. Putting this another way, causality is found in Q between X_{kt} and X_{jt} because X_{kt} contains information about the missing process Y_t which itself contains information about X_{jt}. However, whenever the basic set of processes Q within which we are working is clearly evident the generalized notation will not be used.

7.4 Time-Lags Connected with Causality and Feedback

Suppose that we have a set Q of stochastic processes and that a causality has been found between two of them $\{X_{kt}\} \Rightarrow \{X_{jt}\}$, so that we have optimum linear predictors $P_{jt}[Q]$, $P_{jt}[Q(k)]$ and prediction error variances $V_j[Q]$, $V_j[Q(k)]$ associated with them and having the property $V_j[Q(k)] > V_j[Q]$.

Define the k-truncated optimum linear predictor of X_{jt} as

$$P_{jt}[Q; k, \tau] = \sum_{p \in Q(k)} \sum_{i=1}^{\infty} a_{pi} X_{p, t-i} + \sum_{i=\tau}^{\infty} a_{ki} X_{k, t-i}$$

where the coefficients a_{ji} are chosen to minimize

$$V_j[Q; k, \tau] = E[(X_{jt} - P_{jt}[Q; k, \tau])^2],$$

$V_j[Q; k, \tau]$ being the minimum thus achieved.

If now, we find that

$$V_j[Q(k)] > V_j[Q; k, \tau] = V_j[Q],$$

then there is a *causality lag* of at least τ time units. $V_j[Q; k, \tau]$ will be a non-decreasing sequence as τ increases, and the least value of $\tau(\tau_0)$ such that

$$V_j[Q; k, \tau_0 - 1] = V_j[Q; k, \tau_0] < V_j[Q; k, \tau_0 + 1]$$

will be called the *integer causality lag* of the causality $\{X_{kt}\} \Rightarrow \{X_{jt}\}$.

We are saying here that if the causality $\{X_{kt}\} \Rightarrow \{X_{jt}\}$ occurs, but that we do not worsen our prediction of X_{jt} by not using any of the terms $X_{kt}, X_{k, t-1}, \ldots, X_{k, t-\tau+1}$, then the causality lag must be at least τ units.

The true causality lag may be $\tau_0 + a$ time units, where $0 \leq a < 1$, as the discrete processes being considered may be samples from continuous stochastic processes and the causality need not occur exactly at one of the sampling points. To introduce such sophistication would not appear to be worth while in practice, but this point will be discussed again later when there is a possibility of a causality lag of less than one time unit occurring (see Section 7.7).

If the integer causality lags of $\{X_{kt}\} \Rightarrow \{X_{jt}\}$ and $\{X_{jt}\} \Rightarrow \{X_{kt}\}$ are τ_0 and τ_1 respectively, we shall call $\tau_0 + \tau_1$ the *integer feedback lag*.

7.5 Strength of Causality and Feedback

Using the notation of the previous two sections, we define the *strength* of the causality $\{X_{kt}\} \Rightarrow \{X_{jt}\}$ as

$$(7.5.1) \qquad C(k, j) = 1 - \frac{V_j[Q]}{V_j[Q(k)]}$$

and the strength of the feedback $\{X_{kt}\} \Leftrightarrow \{X_{jt}\}$ is defined as

$$(7.5.2) \quad S(k, j) = C(k, j)\, C(j, k) = \left(1 - \frac{V_j[Q]}{V_j[Q(k)]}\right)\left(1 - \frac{V_k[Q]}{V_k[Q(j)]}\right).$$

These quantities have the properties

$$0 \leq C(k, j) \leq 1, \qquad 0 \leq S(k, j) \leq 1, \qquad S(k, j) = S(j, k).$$

The quantities measuring strength are chosen so that $C(k, j) = 0$ when $\{X_{kt}\} \not\Rightarrow \{X_{jt}\}$ and $S\{k, j\} = 0$ when there is no feedback between the two processes. Although these measures have useful properties, it must be emphasized that they are arbitrarily-chosen measures and that various alternative measures could be proposed.

To indicate how these measures of strength or importance are related to alternative measures such as coherence and information, we consider the case when $q = 2$, i.e., the set Q contains only the two processes $\{X_{1t}\}$ and $\{X_{2t}\}$. Suppose that $f_1(\omega), f_2(\omega)$ are the power spectra of these processes and $C(\omega)$ is the coherence between them.

For the case $q = 2$, $V_1[Q(2)]$ will be the minimum prediction error variance of X_{1t} when only past values of X_{1t} are used, and $V_1[Q]$ will be the minimum prediction error variance of X_{1t} when past values of both X_{1t} and X_{2t} are used. $V_2[Q(1)]$ and $V_2[Q]$ are similarly defined, and $V = V_1[Q]V_2[Q]$ is the minimum total prediction variance. Kolmogoroff [4] has shown that

$$\log V_1[Q(2)] = \frac{1}{2\pi} \int_{-\pi}^{\pi} \log f_1(\omega)\, d\omega$$

and

$$\log V_2[Q(1)] = \frac{1}{2\pi} \int_{-\pi}^{\pi} \log f_2(\omega)\, d\omega,$$

and Whittle [5] has shown that

$$\log V = \log V_1[Q] + \log V_2[Q]$$

$$= \frac{1}{2\pi} \int_{-\pi}^{\pi} \log\left[f_1(\omega)\, f_2(\omega)(1 - C(\omega))\right] d\omega.$$

Thus,

$$\log V_1[Q] + \log V_2[Q] = \log V_1[Q(2)] + \log V_2[Q(1)] - I$$

where

$$(7.5.3) \qquad I = -\frac{1}{2\pi} \int_{-\pi}^{\pi} \log\,(1 - C(\omega))\,d\omega,$$

has been defined by Gel'fand and Yaglom [2] as the average amount of information per unit of time contained in $\{X_{1t}\}$ about $\{X_{2t}\}$ and vice-versa. Substituting from (7.5.1) into this equation, we have

$$\log\,(1 - C(1, 2)) + \log\,(1 - C(2, 1)) = -I$$

or

$$(7.5.4) \qquad 1 + S(1, 2) - C(1, 2) - C(2, 1) = e^{-I}.$$

Thus, in the case of two variables, the important quantities of strength of feedback, information, and coherence are connected by equations (7.5.3) and (7.5.4). In the case of q variables, similar equations exist if coherence is replaced by partial coherence (defined in Section 5.9), and a new concept of "partial information" is introduced.

7.6 Tests for Causality and Feedback

The previous sections of this chapter have been chiefly concerned with the theoretical aspects of causality and feedback, and we have been able to assume that we have available knowledge of all past values of the processes belonging to the set Q. In practice, of course, we will have only the past values of $\{\mathbf{X}_t\}$ over a finite time interval of N units, i.e., $\mathbf{x}_1, \mathbf{x}_2, \ldots, \mathbf{x}_N$. Thus we are forced to use *approximate* linear predictors of the type

$$(7.6.1) \qquad \tilde{P}_{jt}[J] = \sum_{p} \sum_{k=1}^{m_j} a_{pk} x_{p,\,t-k}, \quad p \in J$$

which, for sufficiently large m_j, $j \in J$, will be an approximation to $P_{jt}[J]$ defined in equation (7.2.6). Although it is more general to put no limit on the truncation values m_j, we shall henceforth take all the m_j's to be equal, i.e., $m_j = m$, $j \in J$, and denote the resulting approximate linear predictor $\tilde{P}_{jt}[J, m]$. This will be an optimum predictor if the coefficients a_{jk} are chosen so that

$$\hat{V}_j[J, m] = \frac{1}{N - m} \sum_{t=m+1}^{N} (x_{jt} - \tilde{P}_{jt}[J, m])^2$$

is minimized, $\hat{V}_j[J, m]$ being the resulting minimum value. In general, $E[\hat{V}_j[J, m]] > V_j[J]$, but

$$\lim_{m \to \infty} E[\hat{V}_j[J, m]] = V_j[J],$$

and so if we choose m sufficiently large the approximate linear optimum predictor will be a good approximation of the true optimum predictor.

If it is assumed that all the processes $\{X_{jt}\}, j \in Q$, are Gaussian, some results due to Whittle [5] provide a test for causality. He proves that under the null hypothesis of no causality $\{X_{kt}\} \Rightarrow \{X_{jt}\}$, the statistic

$$\psi^2 = (N - q - m) \log_e \left[\frac{\hat{V}_j[Q(k), m]]}{\hat{V}_j[Q, m]} \right]$$

is distributed as chi-squared with m degrees of freedom.[5] Thus, if $\hat{V}_j[Q(k), m]/\hat{V}_j[Q, m]$ becomes too large, the null hypothesis of no causality will be rejected. If, and only if, both causalities $\{X_{kt}\} \Rightarrow \{X_{jt}\}$, $\{X_{jt}\} \Rightarrow \{X_{kt}\}$ are found, it can be said that feedback exists between the two processes.

The same test may be used to find the causality lag. Suppose that the null hypothesis $\{X_{kt}\} \not\Rightarrow \{X_{jt}\}$ has been rejected and that a pre-truncated approximate linear optimum predictor of X_{jt} is found,

$$\tilde{P}_{jt}[Q, m; k, \tau] = \sum_{p \in Q(k)} \sum_{i=1}^{m} a_{pi} x_{p, t-i} + \sum_{i=\tau}^{m} a_{ki} x_{k, t-i}$$

being an approximation to the predictor introduced in Section 7.4, with the coefficients minimizing

$$\hat{V}_j[Q, m; k, \tau] = \frac{1}{N - m} \sum_{t=m+1}^{N} [x_{jt} - \tilde{P}_{jt}]^2,$$

$\hat{V}_j[\ \ ]$ being the minimum.

The null hypothesis that the integer causality lag is at least $\tau + 1$ units is tested by forming the statistic

$$\psi_\tau^2 = (N - q - m) \log_e \left[\frac{\hat{V}_j[Q, m; k, \tau]}{\hat{V}_j[Q, m]} \right]$$

which, if the null hypothesis is true, will be distributed as chi-squared with $\tau - 1$ degrees of freedom. If the null hypothesis is rejected, the integer causality lag will be τ units or less.

How important is the assumption that $\{\mathbf{X}_t\}$ is a Gaussian vector process is uncertain. No equivalent test for non-normal data exists at present, but the test given is likely to be appropriate asymptotically as $N \to \infty$. The question of whether economic series may be considered to be

---

[5] If the simplifying assumption $m_j = m$, all j, had not been made, the test statistic should be

$$\psi^2 = (N - q - M/q) \log_e [\hat{V}[Q(k), m]/\hat{V}[Q, m]]$$

where $M = \sum_{j=1}^{q} m_j$, and ψ^2 is distributed as chi-squared with m_k degrees of freedom under the null hypothesis.

Gaussian, possibly after "decontamination," has been briefly mentioned in Chapter 4, but considerably more research is required before a more definite answer can be given.

7.7 Removing the Basic Assumption of Section 7.3

The previous four sections have all been based on the assumption that the vector process $\{\mathbf{X}_t\}$ can be represented by

$$(7.7.1) \qquad \mathbf{A}_o\mathbf{X}_t = (\text{past } \mathbf{X}_t) + \boldsymbol{\varepsilon}_t,$$

where $\boldsymbol{\varepsilon}_t$ is white noise and $\mathbf{A}_o$ is a diagonal matrix. Using the terms since introduced, the assumption can be restated as assuming all causality lags occurring in the system to be of at least one time unit. For certain economic series such as monthly production data, such an assumption may be a realistic one, but it is certainly not so for all economic series. It will be the object of this section to study the effect of removing this assumption.

First, however, a test of whether or not the assumption holds for a given set of processes will be considered. Suppose that, using the notation of the previous section, an approximate optimum linear predictor of x_{jt} is found for all $j = 1, \ldots, q$, involving all the processes in the set Q, i.e.,

$$\tilde{P}_{jt}[Q, m] = \sum_{p=1}^{q} \sum_{k=1}^{m} a_{pk} x_{p, t-k}, \quad \text{for each } j = 1, \ldots, q.$$

Now, forming the estimated prediction error series

$$(7.7.2) \qquad \hat{\varepsilon}_{jt} = x_{jt} - \tilde{P}_{jt}[Q, m]$$

for $j = 1, \ldots, q$ and $t = m + 1, \ldots, N$, we need to consider two possible sources of error in our approach:

(i) m has not been chosen sufficiently large, so that one or more of the approximate predictors $\tilde{P}_{jt}[Q, m]$, $j = 1, \ldots, q$, are not good approximations of the true optimum predictors $P_{jt}[Q], j = 1, \ldots, q;$

(ii) the assumption that $\mathbf{A}_o$ is a diagonal matrix in representations such as $(7.7.1)$ is untrue.

The possibility of complication (i) occurring can be investigated by testing for serial correlation in any of the series $\{\hat{\varepsilon}_{jt}\}$. Various tests for serial correlation are available, the best known being that by Durbin and Watson [1].

If these tests indicate that the m chosen is sufficiently large (or if new predictors and error series with m larger have been constructed) the basic assumption of (ii) can be investigated by testing for correlation between any two error series $\{\hat{\varepsilon}_{jt}\}$, $\{\hat{\varepsilon}_{kt}\}$ considered as independent samples. Any of the usual tests for correlation will suffice, but generally, since $N - m$ will be large, one of the quick and easy tests will be appropriate. If any correlation coefficient is found that is significantly non-zero, the assumption that $\mathbf{A}_o$ is diagonal will have to be rejected.

Once the assumption that $\mathbf{A}_o$ is diagonal is rejected, the problems of defining and testing for causality and feedback become not merely more difficult but perhaps impossible. This is shown by considering a simple example. Suppose that the set Q consists of the two processes $\{X_t\}$, $\{Y_t\}$ only, and that there is a causality $\{X_t\} \Rightarrow \{Y_t\}$ but no feeedback, and let the causality lag be exactly one time unit. Suppose now that instead of sampling the processes at times $t = 1, 2, \ldots$, the sampling had taken place at times $t = 1, 3, 5, \ldots$. In this case, the time lag is now twice the causality lag. Let the processes sampled at twice the original time unit be denoted by $\{X_T\}$, $\{Y_T\}$, and suppose further that the original representation of the process $\{X_t\}$, $\{Y_t\}$ was

(7.7.3)
$$X_t = \sum_{j=1}^{\infty} a_j X_{t-j} + \varepsilon_t$$

$$Y_t = \beta X_{t-1} + \sum_{j=1}^{\infty} b_j Y_{t-j} + \eta_t$$

which, incidentally, has a causality lag of exactly one time unit. The representation for the new processes would be

(7.7.4)
$$X_T = a_o X_{T-\frac{1}{2}} + \sum_{j=1}^{\infty} a'_j X_{T-j} + \varepsilon_T$$

$$Y_T = \beta X_{T-\frac{1}{2}} + b_o Y_{T-\frac{1}{2}} + \sum_{j=1}^{\infty} b'_j Y_{T-j} + \eta_T$$

if one could define $X_{T-\frac{1}{2}}$, $Y_{T-\frac{1}{2}}$, but

$$X_{T-\frac{1}{2}} = \int_{-\pi}^{\pi} e^{iT\omega} e^{-i\omega/2} \, dz(\omega)$$

and

$$e^{-i\omega/2} = \sum_{j=0}^{\infty} d_j e^{-ij\omega}$$

and so

$$X_{T-\frac{1}{2}} = \sum_{j=0}^{\infty} d_j X_{T-j},$$

and the representation becomes

(7.7.5)
$$X_T = \sum_{j=1}^{\infty} a''_j X_{T-j} + \varepsilon'_T$$

$$Y_T = \beta' X_T + \sum_{j=1}^{\infty} b''_j Y_{T-j} + \eta'_T,$$

i.e., $\mathbf{A}_o$ is no longer diagonal.

These steps have several important implications concerning the problems of defining and testing for causality. For the original processes represented by (7.7.3), we cannot "predict" X_t any better by knowing Y_t, but this is not true for the new processes, as Y_T contains information about $X_{T-\frac{1}{2}}$ which can be used to better "predict" X_T. Similarly, if we know all past X_T and Y_T, we could better "predict" Y_T if we also knew X_T than if we did not, as X_T contains information about $X_{T-\frac{1}{2}}$. Hence, the definitions of causality and feedback using the idea of linear predictors are no longer appropriate. Due to the lack of uniqueness of the general representation (7.7.1) when $\mathbf{A}_o$ is not diagonal, it seems unlikely that causality can be defined or tested for when the causality lag is less than the time-lag. In brief, the data are unsuitable for the problem being considered when $\mathbf{A}_o$ is not a diagonal matrix.

In such a case, the only appropriate method of analysis would seem to be that of classical model-building, and we are brought face-to-face with the usual problems of identification, simultaneous equation estimation, and interpretation. However, it must be emphasized that the preceding techniques have little in common with model-building methods, being based on a different philosophy. The techniques, given certain assumptions, are entirely general, whereas model-building attempts to use all the a priori knowledge and economic theory that is available.

In Section 7.9 below, the possibility of causality strength and causality lag varying with frequency is considered. It is plausible that causality lag decreases with increasing frequency, and that by suitably filtering out high frequencies the resulting data will have a causality lag longer than the time unit. Clearly, no general rules can be laid down about such a method of making data suitable for causality testing, and each particular set of data will have to be dealt with in the light of available a priori knowledge or theory.

A further question that can be mentioned is whether or not instantaneous causality or feedback occurs in economic systems. It is the author's personal belief that instantaneous feedback does not occur, and so one can always, by sampling the processes sufficiently often, make all causality lags not less than the time unit. If this view is true, an implication is that the majority of the work on feedback and feedback control which is available in the field of electrical engineering cannot be applied to economics.

7.8 Calculations Involved in Testing for Feedback

The main calculations involved in testing for a causality $\{X_{kt}\} \Rightarrow \{X_{jt}\}$ are the formation of the approximate linear predictors of the type

$$\tilde{P}_{jt}[Q, m] = \sum_{p=1}^{q} \sum_{r=1}^{m} a_{pr} x_{p, t-r}$$

and of the resulting prediction error variance,

$$\hat{V}_j[Q, m] = \min \frac{1}{N - m} \sum_{t=m+1}^{N} (x_{jt} - \tilde{P}_{jt}[Q, m])^2$$

together with the corresponding quantities when Q is replaced by $Q(k)$.

The equations for a_{pk} when the prediction error variance is minimized are asymptotically the same as

(7.8.1)
$$\mu_j = \mathbf{Ma},$$

where $\mathbf{a}$ is the $qm \times 1$ vector of the unknown coefficients, i.e.,

(7.8.2) $\mathbf{a}' = [\mathbf{a}_1', \mathbf{a}_2', \ldots, \mathbf{a}_q']$ with $\mathbf{a}_i' = [a_{i1}, a_{i2}, \ldots, a_{im}]$

and μ_j, $\mathbf{M}$ are $qm \times 1$ and $qm \times qm$ matrices of the estimated cross- and autocovariances, i.e.,

(7.8.3) $\mu_j' = [\mu_{j1}', \mu_{j2}', \ldots, \mu_{jq}']$

with $\mu_{jp}' = [\hat{\mu}_{jp}(1), \hat{\mu}_{jp}(2), \ldots, \hat{\mu}_{jp}(m)];$

(7.8.4)
$$\mathbf{M} = \begin{bmatrix} \mathbf{M}_{11} & \mathbf{M}_{12} & \mathbf{M}_{13}\cdots\mathbf{M}_{1q} \\ \mathbf{M}_{21} & \mathbf{M}_{22} & \mathbf{M}_{23}\cdots\mathbf{M}_{2q} \\ \cdot & \cdot & \cdot \\ \cdot & & \cdot & \cdot \\ \cdot & & & \cdot & \cdot \\ \cdot & & & \cdot \\ \mathbf{M}_{q1} & \mathbf{M}_{q2} & \mathbf{M}_{q3}\cdots\mathbf{M}_{qq} \end{bmatrix}$$

where $\mathbf{M}_{rs} = [\hat{\mu}_{rs}(k - i)]$, i.e., the matrix with $\hat{\mu}_{rs}(k - i)$ in the ith row and k^{th} column. Here $\hat{\mu}_{rs}(k - i)$ is the estimate of the cross-covariance as introduced in Chapter 6,

$$\hat{\mu}_{rs}(\tau) = \frac{1}{N - \tau} \left[\sum_{i=\tau+1}^{N} x_{ri}x_{s, i-\tau} - \frac{1}{N - \tau} \sum_{i=\tau+1}^{N} x_{ri} \sum_{i=1}^{N-\tau} x_{si} \right]$$

where

$$E[\hat{\mu}_{rs}(\tau)] = \mu_{rs}(\tau) = E[X_{rt}X_{s, t-\tau}]$$

assuming $E[X_{rt}] = 0$, all r, t.

(These quantities already appear in the cross-spectral computer programs and so need not be re-programmed.)

Thus, the coefficients in $\mathbf{a}$ are found by forming

(7.8.5)
$$\mathbf{a} = \mathbf{M}^{-1}\mu_j$$

and, once these are known, $\hat{V}[Q, m]$ is formed by

(7.8.6)
$$\hat{V}[Q, m] = \frac{1}{N - m} \sum_{t=m+1}^{N} (x_{jt} - \tilde{P}_{jt}[Q, m])^2.$$

To find $\hat{V}[Q(k), m]$, the same matrices are involved except that all components involving the parameter k are removed, e.g.,

$$\mathbf{a}' = [\mathbf{a}'_1, \mathbf{a}'_2, \ldots, \mathbf{a}'_{k-1}, \mathbf{a}'_{k+1}, \ldots, \mathbf{a}'_q], \text{ etc.}$$

Clearly, the calculations will invariably be sufficiently complicated that a high-speed electronic computer will need to be used.

The only decisions that must be made before computation starts are the size of q and m. The size of q will almost certainly be determined by the economic system being considered, and the size of k will almost certainly be limited by the ability of the computer being used to invert large matrices. A value for m of at least 10 or 12 is recommended, although experience may indicate that a larger value is required or that a smaller value is sufficient.

7.9 Causality and Feedback Varying with Frequency

One of the important features of spectral and cross-spectral analysis is that it provides ways of observing how certain quantities vary with frequency. Just as it is possible for the strength of the relationship between two series (coherence) and the phase-lag to vary with frequency, so also is it possible that the strength of causality (and thus of feedback) and the causality lag to change with frequency. A simple (and highly unreal) example will perhaps help to show this. Consider two stock exchanges in some country, one of major importance (A) and the other of lesser importance (B). Clearly, B will be likely to follow all the fluctuations, both long-run and short-run, of A, and so we have $A \Rightarrow B$. However, A will be unlikely to be affected by the short-run fluctuations of B, but may be concerned by the long-run fluctuations. Thus, if a subscript L denotes the low-frequency component and a subscript H the high-frequency component, we may have

$$B_L \Rightarrow A_L$$
$$B_H \nRightarrow A_H.$$

Thus, in this example, feedback will only occur in the low frequency range.

A conceptually simple way of considering the possibility of causality and feedback changing with frequency is as follows:

Let $F_j[\ ], j = 1, \ldots, m$, be a set of mutually exclusive filters such that if $\{X_t\}$ is a stationary process with Cramér representation,

$$X_t = \int_{-\pi}^{\pi} e^{it\omega} \, dz(\omega),$$

then

$$F_j[X_t] = \int_{-\pi}^{\pi} g_j(\omega) e^{it\omega} \, dz(\omega)$$

where $g_j(\omega)$ is the real function

$$g_j(\omega) = \frac{1}{m}, \quad \frac{(j-1)\pi}{m} \leqq \omega < \frac{j\pi}{m},$$

$$= 0 \quad \text{elsewhere.}$$

Thus, applying the filter $F[\ \ ]$ cuts out all frequencies except in the band

$$\delta_j = \left(\frac{(j-1)\pi}{m}, \frac{j\pi}{m}\right)$$

and leaves the phase angle unaltered.

Let $F_j'[\ \ ]$ be a set of symmetric, moving-average filters approximating the set $F_j[\ \ ]$. If the new time series vector $\{\mathbf{y}_t(j)\}$ is formed from the original vector $\{\mathbf{x}_t\}$ by

$$F_j'[\mathbf{x}_t] = \mathbf{y}_t(j),$$

we can study the causality strengths and lags for the frequency band by carrying out the techniques introduced in the previous sections on the data $\mathbf{y}_t(j)$. Similarly, other frequency bands can be studied by using $\mathbf{y}_t(j)$ for the other j's.

Such a procedure will not be studied in any further detail here as the amount of computation required would be considerable in practice, and would be superimposed on what is already likely to be a very large amount of computation. However, if an intensive study of feedback within a certain group of economic series is required, the suggested technique should provide useful and interesting information, always remembering that all results will depend to a certain amount on the particular filters $F_j'[\ \ ]$ that are chosen.

Although the procedure outlined above is intrinsically reasonable, it has connected with it certain formidable theoretical problems. It is not possible to justify the technique theoretically by considering the perfect case when information of all the past and the actual filters $F_j[\ \ ]$ are available. This is because the resulting process $Y_t(j) = F_j[X_t]$ will have a frequency set of finite measure for which its spectrum is zero. Wherever this occurs, the process is deterministic, i.e., prediction can be made perfectly and so the definition of causality via prediction becomes of no use. In practice such problems have little consequence since no finite moving average filter $F_j'[\ \ ]$ can produce a process Y_t having zero spectrum over a set with finite measure unless the input process X_t in the definition of Y_t, i.e., $Y_t = F_j'[X_t]$, is already deterministic.

7.10 Summary and Conclusions

The main results of this chapter can be summarized as follows:

(i) If feedback is present in a system of processes the coherence diagram will still provide useful information but the phase-diagram is unlikely to do so. (Section 7.1.)

(ii) We say that, given a set of processes $\{X_{jt}\}, j = 1, \ldots, q$, there is causality of $\{X_{jt}\}$ by $\{X_{kt}\}$ if we can better predict X_{jt} using past values of X_{kt} than if we do not use these values. (Section 7.3.)

(iii) If $\{X_{jt}\}$ causes $\{X_{kt}\}$ and also $\{X_{kt}\}$ causes $\{X_{jt}\}$, we say that feedback is present. (Section 7.3.)

(iv) If causality $\{X_{kt}\} \Rightarrow \{X_{jt}\}$ is found, but we cannot better predict X_{jt} using the values $X_{k,t-1}, X_{k,t-2}, \ldots, X_{k,t-\tau}$ than if we did not use these values, we say that there is a causality lag of at least τ units. A measure of causality strength can be defined. (Sections 7.4 and 7.5.)

(v) If we assume all processes to be Gaussian, a test for causality is available. The test is likely to be appropriate asymptotically for non-Gaussian processes. (Section 7.6.)

(vi) When any causality lag is less than the time unit involved in the processes, no appropriate way of defining or testing for causality is suggested. (Section 7.7.)

(vii) It is possible that causality and feedback vary with frequency. (Section 7.7.)

If the tests for causality are found to be efficient in practice, the theory proposed in this chapter should prove useful in testing many currently important economic hypotheses and theories, in model building, and in suggesting control methods for the economy.

One essential assumption involved in the techniques here proposed is that of stationarity. Methods of removing trends in mean are discussed in the next chapter, but the effects of more complicated non-stationarities are not known at present. The definitions of causality, feedback, lags, etc., are easily generalized to the non-stationary case by the use of non-stationary predictors, but the effect on the tests involved is likely to prove more difficult to determine.

Clearly, the basic assumption of this chapter is that the future is caused by the past. It is possible to propose that the future is also caused by the expected future, but as the expectation must be based on past and present knowledge, the basic assumption still holds true.

More research is required into the field of feedback problems, particularly with respect to how feedback varies with frequency. Economic theory occasionally suggests that the direction of causality between two series will be different for the long-run and the short-run. In such a case, the overall method will indicate a (spurious?) feedback. The method suggested in this chapter for investigating the variation with frequency is clumsy, and it is to be hoped that a better and more direct method can be evolved, possibly as a generalization of the spectral method.

Finally, it should be emphasized that the "causality" defined in this chapter is strictly only a second-moment causality. For non-normal processes the true causality may be more complicated. However, just as "second-moment" prediction is a useful method, so is "second-moment" causality and feedback.

REFERENCES

[1] Durbin, J. and Watson, G. S., "Testing for serial correlation in least squares regression," *Biometrika*, 37 (1950), 159–177.

[2] Gel'fand, I. M. and Yaglom, A. M., *American Math. Soc. Translations*, Series 2, vol. 12 (1959), p. 99.

[3] Klein, L. R., *Textbook of Econometrics*. Evanston: 1953.

[4] Kolmogoroff, "Sur l'interpretation et extrapolation des suites stationnaires," *Comptes Rendus Acad. Sci. Paris*, 208 (1939), pp. 2043–2045.

[5] Whittle, P., "The analysis of multiple stationary time series," *Journal Royal Stat. Soc.* (B), 15 (1953), pp. 125–139.

[6] Wiener, N., "The theory of prediction," Chapter 8 of *Modern Mathematics for Engineers* (Series 1), edited by E. F. Beckenback, 1956.

[7] Zashuin, *Comptes Rendus (Doklady) de l'Acad. Sc. de L'URSS*, 23 (1941), pp. 435–437.

PART B. NON-STATIONARY TIME SERIES

CHAPTER 8

SERIES WITH TRENDING MEANS

8.1 Introduction

In this chapter we consider the class of non-stationary series having trend only in their means, i.e., generated by

$$(8.1.1) \qquad Y_t = m(t) + X_t$$

where X_t is a stationary series. This class is probably the simplest class of non-stationary processes and has been the most studied. The term $m(t)$ will be assumed to be either smoothly changing with time or to have only a small number of widely separated discontinuities, and throughout this chapter it will be called the *trend*.

Several problems will need to be considered and in particular the following will be dealt with in detail:

(a) effect of presence of trend on spectral and cross-spectral analysis,
(b) estimation of $m(t)$,
(c) removal of $m(t)$, and
(d) definition of "trend" in a sample.

It is clear that these problems are interrelated, but before considering them some generalities are required.

If, in equation (8.1.1), we assume $E[X_t] = 0$ then $E[Y_t] = m(t)$. Given a sample $\{y_t, t = 1, \ldots, n\}$ from Y_t the sample mean will be

$$\bar{y} = \frac{1}{n} \sum_{t=1}^{n} y_t$$

i.e.,

$$(8.1.2) \qquad \bar{y} = \frac{1}{n} \sum_{t=1}^{n} m(t) + \bar{x}$$

and the sample variance is

$$s_y^2 = \frac{1}{n} \sum y_t^2 - (\bar{y})^2 = \frac{1}{n} \sum_{t=1}^{n} (m(t) + x_t)^2 - (\bar{y})^2$$

$$= \frac{1}{n} \sum m^2(t) + \frac{2}{n} \sum m(t)x_t + \frac{1}{n} \sum x_t^2 - (\bar{y})^2$$

$$= \frac{1}{n} \sum m^2(t) + \frac{2}{n} \sum m(t)x_t$$

$$\qquad\qquad - \frac{1}{n^2} \left[\sum m(t)\right]^2 - \frac{2}{n} \bar{x} \sum_{t=1}^{n} m(t) + s_x^2$$

$$(8.1.3) \qquad = \frac{1}{n} \sum m^2(t) - \frac{1}{n^2} \left[\sum m(t)\right]^2 + \frac{2}{n} \sum m(t)[x_t - \bar{x}] + s_x^2$$

and so

(8.1.4) $$\sigma_y^2 = E[s_y^2] = \frac{1}{n} \sum m^2(t) - \frac{1}{n^2} [\sum m(t)]^2 + \sigma_x^2.$$

Thus, the variance of the $\{Y_t\}$ process can be split up into a component due to the trend and a component due to the stationary process $\{X_t\}$.

The term

(8.1.5) $$V(m) = \frac{1}{n} \sum m^2(t) - \left[\frac{1}{n} \sum m(t)\right]^2$$

will be called the *variance of the trend* although strictly it only relates to a particular sample.

Let us consider the Fourier transform of the function $m(t)$ and suppose that

(8.1.6) $$m(t) = \int_{-\pi}^{\pi} e^{it\omega} \, d\mu(\omega)$$

or, as $m(t)$ is real,

$$m(t) = \int_{0}^{\pi} \cos t\omega \, d\mu_1(\omega) + \int_{0}^{\pi} \sin t\omega \, d\mu_2(\omega).$$

If

$$m(t) = A \cos t\omega_0 + B \sin t\omega_0,$$

then

$$d\mu_i(\omega) = 0, \qquad \omega \neq \omega_0, \qquad i = 1, 2$$

that is, if $m(t)$ consists only of the single frequency ω_0 then $d\mu(\omega)$ vanishes everywhere except at that frequency. It is usual to suppose a trend $m(t)$ that is monotonically increasing or, at least, to be non-periodic. For instance, if $m(t)$ was a polynomial in t, e.g.,

$$m(t) = \sum_{j=1}^{p} a_j t^j$$

then it would be non-periodic or, putting it another way, the "period" of $m(t)$ is infinity. This is so because the "period" of a periodic function is the time taken before the function begins repeating itself and this, for a polynomial, is infinity. Thus a non-periodic $m(t)$ has period infinity which, of course, corresponds to zero frequency, and so, for such a trend, the $d\mu(\omega)$ of (8.1.6) vanishes for all $\omega \neq 0$. It is for this reason that we say that the power spectrum of a non-random, non-periodic function is zero everywhere except for a jump at the origin, the size of the jump being proportional to the variance of the function.

It now follows from (8.1.1) that the power spectrum of the process $\{Y_t\}$ is identical to that of the process $\{X_t\}$ except for a jump at the origin.

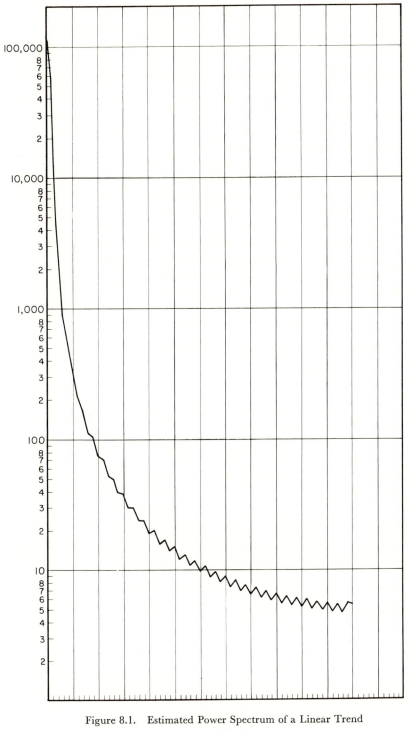

Figure 8.1.   Estimated Power Spectrum of a Linear Trend

〈 131 〉

Although this statement is true for the process $\{Y_t\}$ the situation when dealing with a sample $\{y_t, \; t = 1, \ldots, n\}$ is more complicated. This is so because, for instance, the straight line $a + bt, \; t = 1, \ldots, n$ is virtually unrecognizable from the function $a \cos \dfrac{t}{N} + bM \sin \dfrac{t}{M}$ where $N \gg n$, $M \gg n$. Thus we are unable to differentiate between a true trend and a very low frequency. However, as far as a spectral estimate is concerned, this fact is of no consequence as we estimate over frequency bands and the first band will include both zero frequency and also very low frequencies. It has been found useful by the author to consider as "trend" in a sample of size n all frequencies less than $\tfrac{1}{2}n$ as these will all be monotonic increasing if the phase is zero, but it must be emphasized that this is an arbitrary rule. It may also be noted that it is impossible to test whether a series is stationary or not, given only a finite sample as any apparent trend in mean *could* arise from an extremely low frequency. (The problem of testing for stationarity has been discussed by Granger [2], [3].)

It is of interest to record the spectrum of a linear function of time taken over a finite time period. The diagram Fig. 8.1 shows the "spectrum" of $3.039t$ with $t = 1, \ldots, 400$ and with a maximum lag of 60 used in the spectral estimate. The spectrum decreases with frequency ω in proportion to $\dfrac{1}{\omega^2}$ as the coefficients in the Fourier expansion of a linear trend decrease $\sim \dfrac{1}{\omega}$, i.e.,

$$at = \frac{4a}{\pi} \sum_{j=1}^{n} (-1)^{j+1} \frac{\sin \pi jt}{j}, \qquad t = -n, \ldots, n.$$

8.2 Leakage Problems

We see from the previous section that, theoretically, the addition of a trending mean to a stationary series will affect only the spectral estimate at the first frequency band and so we could continue with a spectral or cross-spectral analysis simply by ignoring the first frequency band.

However, as explained in Chapter 3, all estimates allow leakage between frequency bands, i.e., the estimate of the spectrum for a particular frequency band will, in fact, include part of the overall variance really due to other bands. This can be illustrated as follows (refer to Diagrams 1 and 2): if we multiply a spectrum such as is shown in Diagram 1 by a

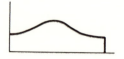

Diagram 1

function $g(\omega)$ shown in Diagram 2 (as, for instance, when we apply a filter having $g(\omega)$ as filter function to a series) then the resulting function can be thought of as an estimate of the spectrum over the frequency band

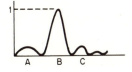

Diagram 2

B. However, due to the side-peaks of $g(\omega)$, this estimate will, in fact, include parts of the spectrum due to frequency bands A and C. The Tukey estimate has been chosen to keep this leakage small and for a power spectrum that is a constant over the whole range $(0, \pi)$ the leakage between estimates is less than 2%. However, if the spectrum had a very large peak at a certain frequency band, up to 1% of this may leak into other estimates and this could provide an important bias in the estimate.

To investigate the importance of leakage, particularly from the zero frequency, a series of experiments were carried out at Princeton, using an IBM 650 computer. Series of the form $y_t = x_t + m(t)$ were generated and in every case the data used for the stationary series x_t were Kendall's series 5a (i.e., generated by $x_{t+2} - 1.1x_{t+1} + 0.5x_t = \varepsilon_t$). The trending means $m(t)$ used and the "visual" results were as follows:

$m(t)$	variance ratio	frequencies affected
0.430t	1:1	0–3
0.744t	1:3	0–4
1.360t	1:10	0–5
3.039t	1:50	all
0.00328t²	1:10	0–5
0.01036t²	1:100	all

The term "variance ratio" in the table means the ratio var x_t:var $m(t)$; thus, for instance, in the last case the variance due to the trending mean is a hundred times the variance of the stationary series part of y_t. Linear and quadratic trends did not appear to affect the estimated spectrum differently and the tentative conclusion from the experiments was that the leakage effect for moderate trends was not important. In all the above experiments, the Tukey estimate of the spectrum was used with 400 pieces of data and 60 lags. If a Parzen estimate had been used, the leakage would have been slightly less.

In the illustration, Fig. 8.2, the estimated spectra of x_t, $x_t + 1.360t$ and $x_t + 3.039t$ are shown.

8.3 Regression Analysis

Although leakage effects will usually be small it is invariably advisable to remove at least the majority of the trend in the mean. In Section 8.4 methods of estimating the trend factor (and so allowing one to remove it by subtracting the estimated trend) by the use of filters are considered and in this section regression methods are investigated. The essential difference between the two sections is that filtering is a black-box transformation of the series whereas regression analysis involves non-black box transformations. By this we mean that if the basic series is $y_t = x_t + m(t)$ where x_t is a stationary series, then removing $m(t)$ by filtering merely multiplies the spectrum of x_t by a known function, whereas removing $m(t)$ by regression methods will have a more complex effect on the spectrum of x_t.

Two regression methods will be considered:

(i) polynomial regression, i.e., $m(t)$ is approximated by the polynomial $p(t) = \sum_{j=0}^{k} \alpha_j t^j$, and

(ii) harmonic regression, i.e., $m(t)$ is approximated by the trigonometric polynomial

$$T(t) = \sum_{j=0}^{k} \left(a_j \cos \left(\frac{\pi j t}{n} \right) + b_j \sin \left(\frac{\pi j t}{n} \right) \right).$$

In each case we shall suppose $t = 1, \ldots, n$. The coefficients α_j are chosen so that

$$I = \sum_{t=1}^{n} [m(t) - p(t)]^2$$

is minimized, and the coefficients a_j, b_j are chosen so that

$$I' = \sum_{t=1}^{n} [m(t) - T(t)]^2$$

is minimized.

The full theory for such estimates need not concern us here (it is dealt with by Hannan [5, Chapter 5] and Grenander and Rosenblatt [4, Chapter 7]) but the relevant facts are:

(i) the least-squares estimates of the coefficients α_j, a_j and b_j are all efficient;

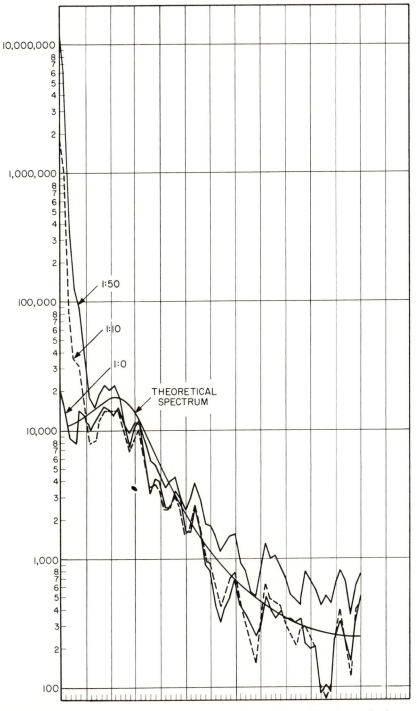

Figure 8.2. Effect on Estimated Spectrum of Adding a Linear Trend to a Stationary Series

(ii) the spectrum of the residuals is biased but only by a function that is $O(n^{-1})$ at most;

(iii) the variance of the residuals is not a constant over time, i.e., if $\bar{m}(t)$ represents the least squares approximation to $m(t)$, then var $[y_t - \bar{m}(t)]$ is a function of time of form

$$c + O\left[\left(\frac{2t - n}{n}\right)^2\right].$$

The latter two effects are not usually very important and a big advantage of regression techniques is that one loses little or none of the data, whereas if a filter of length $2m + 1$ is used, m pieces of data at each end are lost. Thus, regression techniques are particularly useful for data of moderate length ($150 \leq n \leq 500$, say) although they require a large amount of computation with large amounts of data.

It is known both from theory (cf. Blackman and Tukey [1, pp. 139–146]) and experience that polynomial regression and subtraction does not affect to any worthwhile extent the spectral estimates of frequency bands other than the band centred on zero frequency, which it effectively removes.

The theory for harmonic regression has been little explored but experiments carried out at Princeton indicate that its use efficiently removes a very narrow frequency band near zero frequency and appears to have no unfortunate effects on other frequencies.

8.4 Filters for Determining Trend

It was shown in Chapter 3 that if the filter $F[\ \ ]$ was applied to the stationary process $\{X_t\}$, i.e.,

(8.4.1)
$$F[X] = \sum_{j=-m}^{m} a_j X_{t-j}$$

then the power spectrum $f_x(\omega)$ of the process $\{X_t\}$ is multiplied by the filter function $s(\omega)\,\overline{s(\omega)}$ where the transfer function $s(\omega)$ is given by

(8.4.2)
$$s(\omega) = \sum_{j=-m}^{m} a_j e^{-ij\omega}.$$

In this section we shall consider only cosine filters, i.e., $a_j = a_{-j}$, and so the transfer function becomes

(8.4.3)
$$s(\omega) = a_0 + 2 \sum_{j=1}^{m} a_j \cos j\omega.$$

If we wish to estimate the trend component of a series by means of filters we would want to cut out (or, at least, considerably diminish) all frequencies except those near zero, i.e., the perfect transfer function would be that shown in Diagram 3. ω_0 would have to be chosen to correspond to the definition of "trend" that one adopts.

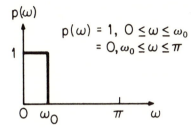

Diagram 3

It is clear that, for finite m, the coefficients a_j of (8.4.3) cannot be chosen so that $s(\omega)$ has exactly the perfect shape and so some kind of approximation has to be used. An apparently sensible approach would be to choose the a_j's so that $s(\omega)$ is the truncated Fourier series of the function $p(\omega)$, i.e.,

(8.4.4)
$$a_j = \frac{2 \sin j\omega_0}{j\pi} \qquad j = 1, \ldots, m$$

$$a_0 = \frac{\omega_0}{\pi}.$$

This filter will give a reasonably good approximation to $s(\omega)$ if m is large and ω_0 not too small; however, it will be usual to expect ω_0 to be small and m cannot be too large as the application of a filter of length $2m + 1$ loses $2m$ pieces of data and for a sample that is not large this can determine an important upper limit to the length of filter that one is able to apply.

For small ω_0 and m not large the resulting transfer function may be shaped as in Diagram 4; there will be large side peaks and these can be extremely important.

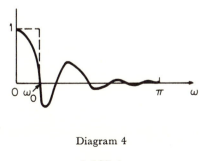

Diagram 4

As $\cos j\omega$ is flat near $\omega = 0$ the usual shape of $s(\omega)$ defined by (8.4.3) will be of a major, first peak followed by a series of smaller side peaks and so the problem of investigating good approximations to $p(\omega)$ really boils down to the problem of controlling the size of the side peaks.

One possible approach would be to make $s(\omega)$ obey a set of equations of the type

(8.4.5)

$$s(\omega_i) = 0, \qquad i = 1, \ldots, q$$

$$\frac{ds(\omega_j)}{d\omega} = 0, \qquad j = 1, \ldots, r$$

$$s(\omega_j) = m_j, \qquad j = 1, \ldots, r .$$

$$q + 2r = m,$$

i.e., to fix a set of zeros for $s(\omega)$ and attempt to fix the size and position of some of the side peaks. (This method has, for instance, been advocated and applied by J. M. Craddock (*J. Royal Stat. Soc.* (A), 1957, p. 387.) The equation (8.4.5) together with $s(0) = 1$ provide $m + 1$ linear equations in the $m + 1$ unknowns $a_j, j = 0, \ldots, m$ and so can, in general, be be solved. This method will provide useful filters unless ω_0 is made very small and m not sufficiently large, in which case large side peaks may occur. The reason for this is easy to see as one row of the matrix to be inverted for the solution of the a_j's is $(\frac{1}{2}, 1, 1, \ldots, 1)$ while another row is

$$(\tfrac{1}{2}, \cos \omega_0, \cos 2\omega_0, \ldots, \cos m\omega_0)$$

and, for m not sufficiently large and ω_0 small these two rows will be nearly identical. Thus, the inverse matrix will have a determinant that is very large and so some of the elements of the inverse matrix will be very large. This means that some of the a_j's are very large and the side peaks become large compared to $s(0)$. As an example, if $\omega_0 = \dfrac{2\pi}{40}$, $m = 7$, with $s(0) = 1$ the first side peak can be of magnitude 10,000 or more.

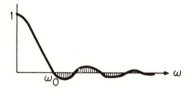

Diagram 5

Another approach, which is a combination of the previous two, is to assume that $s(\omega)$ has a shape of the form shown in Diagram 5, and to choose the coefficients a_j so that

$$s(0) = 1$$

$$s(\omega_0) = 0 \quad \text{and} \quad I = \int_{\omega_0}^{\pi} s^2(\omega)\, d\omega \text{ is minimized,}$$

i.e., the absolute value of the area between $s(\omega)$ and the line $s(\omega) = 0$ is minimized. These give the equations

$$a_0 + 2a_1 + \cdots + 2a_m = 1$$

$$a_0 + 2a_1 \cos \omega_0 + \cdots + 2a_m \cos m\omega_0 = 0$$

(8.4.6)

$$2 \sum_{j=1}^{m} a_j K(j) - a_0 K(0) + \lambda + \mu = 0$$

$$a_0 K(k) + \sum_{j=1}^{m} a_j [K(j+k) + K(j-k)] + \lambda + \mu \cos k\omega_0 = 0$$

$$k = 1, \ldots, m$$

where

$$K(x) = \frac{\sin x\omega_0}{x}, \quad x \neq 0$$

$$K(0) = \pi - \omega_0.$$

Thus there are $m + 3$ equations for the $m + 3$ unknowns μ, λ, and $a_j, j = 0, \ldots, m$; μ and λ being Lagrange multipliers. Again, these equations may be solved but the result is, once more, satisfactory only if ω_0 is not small when m is not large.

It is clear, from the above, that we can choose suitable filters with ease once we have more knowledge of the kind of ratio between ω_0 and m that provides small side peaks, i.e., we need to know how to choose ω_0 and m so that we do not attempt to construct a filter having impossible properties. In particular we require to know the relationships between ω_0, m, and the maximum size of the largest side peak.

The problem may be stated in the following form: find coefficients a_j so that $s(\omega)$ is bounded by the function

$$m(\omega) = 1, \quad 0 \leq \omega \leq \omega_0$$

$$|m(\omega)| \leq a, \quad \omega_0 < \omega \leq \pi$$

with $a \leq 1$ having a certain, given size with given ω_0, m. This is illustrated in Diagram 6. It will be seen later that certain combinations of ω_0, m, and a are impossible.

As

$$s(\omega) = a_0 + 2 \sum_{1}^{m} a_j \cos j\omega$$

and

$$\cos n\omega = \sum_{j=0}^{n} c_j \cos^j \omega$$

it follows that

$$(8.4.7) \qquad s(\omega) = \sum_{j=0}^{m} b_j \cos^j \omega$$

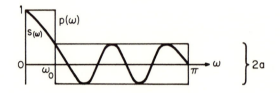

Diagram 6

and so the problem of finding the "optimum" filter with $|s(\omega)| \leq |m(\omega)|$ can be stated in the form: Find the polynomial of order m,

$$P_m(x) = \sum_{j=1}^{m} b_j x^j, \qquad -1 \leq x \leq 1$$

with the properties

$$(8.4.8) \qquad \begin{aligned} |P_m(x)| &\leq 1, \qquad x_0 \geq x \geq -1 \\ P(1) &\quad \text{a maximum} \end{aligned}$$

where

$$x_0 = \cos \omega_0.$$

It is a property of the Tchebycheff polynomials $T_n(x)$ given by

$$(8.4.9) \qquad T_n(x) = \cos(n \cos^{-1} x)$$

that in the range $-1 \leq x \leq 1$, $|T_n(x)| \leq 1$ and just outside this range it rises faster than any other polynomial of the same order that obeys this condition.

Thus the required polynomial obeying conditions (8.4.8) is $P_m(x) = T_m(\xi)$ where

$$(8.4.10) \qquad \xi = \frac{2x - (x_0 - 1)}{1 + x_0}.$$

(ξ is chosen so that $\xi = 1$ at $x = x_0$, $\xi = -1$ at $x = -1$, as then the following statements hold for both odd and even m.)

The parametric equations of the Tchebycheff polynomials are:

$$T_n(x) = \cos n\theta, \qquad |x| \leq 1$$
$$x = \cos \theta$$
$$T_n(x) = \cosh n\theta, \qquad |x| \geq 1$$
$$x = \cosh \theta.$$

It thus follows that

$$P_m(1) = T_m(\xi_1)$$

where

$$\xi_1 = \frac{2 - (x_0 - 1)}{1 + x_0}$$

or

$$\xi_1 = \frac{3 - \cos \omega_0}{1 + \cos \omega_0}$$

but, as ω_0 is assumed small, we may replace $\cos \omega_0$ by $1 - \frac{1}{2}\omega_0^2$, so

$$\xi_1 \cong \frac{2 + \frac{1}{2}\omega_0^2}{2 - \frac{1}{2}\omega_0^2}$$

$$\approx 1 + \frac{1}{2}\omega_0^2 + 0(\omega_0^4).$$

$T_m(\xi_1)$ is given by the parametric equation

$$T_m(\xi_1) = \cosh m\varphi$$

$$\xi_1 = \cosh \varphi$$

and so

$$\cosh \varphi \approx 1 + \frac{1}{2}\omega_0^2 + 0(\omega_0^4)$$

or

$$\varphi \approx \omega_0.$$

Hence, to a good degree of approximation for small ω_0

(8.4.11) $$P_m(1) \approx \cosh m\omega_0$$

and this represents the ratio of the height of the main peak to the maximum possible height of the subsidiary peaks (which are all of the same height).

The zeros of the system may be found from the zeros of $T_m(x)$ and then using (8.4.10), i.e.,

$$\cos (m \cos^{-1} x) = 0$$

or

$$m \cos^{-1} (x)^k = \frac{(2k - 1)}{2} \pi$$

and so

$$(x)^k = \cos \left[\frac{(2k - 1)}{2m} \pi \right]$$

where $(x)^k$ is the kth zero.

Thus, the first zero, ω_1 in terms of ω_0 is

$$\cos \omega_1 = \frac{1}{2}(\cos \omega_0 - 1) + \frac{1}{2}(\cos \omega_0 + 1)(x)^1$$

$$= \frac{1}{2}(\cos \omega_0 - 1) + \frac{1}{2}(\cos \omega_0 + 1) \frac{\cos \pi}{2m}.$$

This gives an exact equation for ω_1 but a good approximation is

$$(8.4.12) \qquad \omega_1^2 \approx \omega_0^2 + \left(\frac{\pi}{2m}\right)^2$$

provided m is sufficiently large that we may write

$$\cos \frac{\pi}{2m} \approx 1 - \frac{1}{2}\left(\frac{\pi}{2m}\right)^2.$$

From (8.4.11) and (8.4.12) we can derive the following table show-ing the relationship between the ratio between the height of the main peak and largest side peak and the smallest zero for given m.

Ratio main peak to side peak	Smallest zero	m when smallest zero $\cong \pi/20$
1	$\pi/2m$	10
2	$\pi/1.54m$	13
5	$\pi/1.13m$	18
10	$\pi/0.93m$	21
20	$\pi/0.78m$	26
50	$\pi/0.65m$	31
100	$\pi/0.57m$	35

Although the table has been drawn up using Tchebycheff polynomials and assumes ω_0 small, m sufficiently large for certain approximations to be true, it nevertheless does give an indication of the kind of limitation on the length of filter that one needs for it to obey required conditions regardless of the type of approximation used.

Thus, for example, if one requires all side peaks to be at most one-fifth of the height of the main peak and if the filter length to be used is 13 so that $m = 6$ (as $2m + 1 = 13$) then the smallest possible zero one can hope for is

$$\frac{\pi}{1.13 \times 6} = \frac{\pi}{6.78}.$$

As another example consider the requirement that the ratio between main and side peak height is 10 and the first zero is to be at $\frac{\pi}{20}$, then the smallest possible filter length that can obey these conditions will be somewhere near $2.21 + 1 = 43$.

If such limitations are borne in mind any of the previously mentioned methods of finding "optimum" filters should prove satisfactory.

Two particular further filters will be considered as they do have certain advantages over those filters mentioned previously.

The moving average of length $2m + 1$ having all $a_j = \dfrac{1}{2m + 1}$ will have transfer function given by

$$(2m + 1)s(\omega) = 1 + 2 \sum_{k=1}^{m} \cos k\omega$$

$$= \frac{\sin (m + \frac{1}{2})\omega}{\sin \omega/2}.$$

The first zero is at $\omega = \dfrac{2\pi}{2m + 1}$ and the side peaks are decreasing in magnitude (as $(\sin \omega/2)^{-1}$ decreases with ω) and the ratio of the main peak to the first side peak is, in absolute terms

$$(2m + 1) \sin \left[\frac{3\pi}{2(2m + 1)}\right] : 1.$$

This ratio decreases with increasing m and a few values of m show that it quickly approaches its limit:

$$
\begin{aligned}
\text{for} \quad m = 1 \quad &\text{ratio is} \quad \approx 3:1 \\
m = 2 \quad &\text{,, \quad ,,} \quad \approx 4:1 \\
m = 3 \quad &\text{,, \quad ,,} \quad \approx 4.4:1 \\
m = 4 \quad &\text{,, \quad ,,} \quad \approx 4.5:1 \\
m \to \infty \quad &\text{,, \quad ,,} \quad \approx 4.7:1
\end{aligned}
$$

Hence, increasing the length of the moving average does little to improve the relationship between the height of the main peak to the side peak but the position of the first zero is continually improved. A moving average having equal weights will henceforth be called a *simple moving average*.

The filter with $a_j = \dfrac{1}{2m}$, $j = 0, \ldots, m - 1$, $a_m = a_{-m} = \dfrac{1}{4m}$ has transfer function $2ms(\omega) = \dfrac{\cos \frac{1}{2}\omega \sin m\omega}{\sin \frac{1}{2}\omega}$ and so has zeros at $\dfrac{k\pi}{m}$, $k = 1$, $\ldots$, m. (Such a filter might be thought of as a simple moving average of length $2m$.)

The ratio of the heights of the main peak to the first side peak is

$$(2m + 1) \tan \left(\frac{3\pi}{4m}\right) : 1$$

and this tends to the same limit as the previous case as $m \to \infty$.

The two big advantages of using such simple moving averages is that one can pick the length so that a zero appears in a particular place and the calculations involved are easy. Thus, if one wanted an estimate of the trend in a series in which it is suspected that the annual component is of importance then if one chooses the filter so that the transfer function vanishes at the frequency corresponding to the annual component the estimate will not be biased due to leakage.

Although by no means an optimum filter, a very conveniently understood and easily computed filter is to apply two or more simple moving averages of different lengths in sequence. Thus, for instance, if the simple moving average of length 12 is used after a simple moving average of length 5, we know that the transfer function has zeros as $\frac{\pi}{12}, \frac{\pi}{6}, \frac{\pi}{5}, \frac{\pi}{4}, \frac{\pi}{3},$ etc.

As an illustration of the kind of transfer function resulting from a combination of moving averages, Fig. 8.3 shows the transfer function of the combination of two simple moving averages of length 20 and 12. The square of the transfer function, this being the function that multiplies the spectrum when such a pair of moving averages is applied, is also shown.

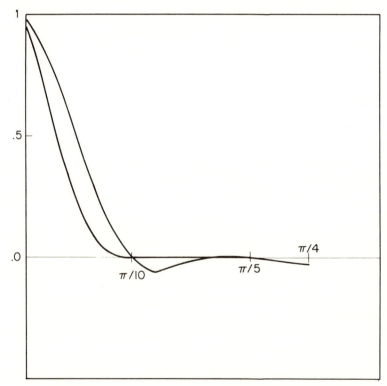

Figure 8.3. Transfer Function $S(\omega)$ and $S^2(\omega)$ for the Pair of Moving Averages with Lengths 20 and 12

The filters considered so far in this section belong to the class with transfer functions having zeros in the range $-\pi \leqq \omega \leqq \pi$. It should be noted that a transfer function need not have such zeros. An example of such a filter is one with weights $a_j = a^j, 0 \leqq a < 1, a_{-j} = a_j, j = 0, \ldots,$ m. For m large, a not near 1, the transfer function will be approximately

$$\frac{1 - a^2}{1 + a^2 - 2a \cos \omega}$$

which has no zeros. Although this class of filter can be useful in certain circumstances, as it does not appear to have any worthwhile advantages over the class of filters previously considered, when trends are being estimated or removed, it will not be considered further.

8.5 Conclusion

Three techniques for dealing with trending means have been discussed in the two previous sections, i.e., polynomial regression, harmonic regression, and filtering. The leakage experiments (and connected theoretical work) seem to indicate that as long as *most* of the trend in mean is removed then the spectral and cross-spectral methods may be used with confidence. As any of the three methods considered effectively remove a very large part of the trend it would seem that in most cases it is of little consequence which method one uses.

The method to be used for removing trend, then, really depends on what subsequent analysis one intends to perform. If, for instance, one wishes to consider the possibility of the data containing long cycles then the filtering methods appear to be inappropriate as the frequencies one wishes to look at would almost certainly be removed by a cosine filter unless a filter of extreme length and with very carefully chosen properties were used. It is thus impossible to lay down any general rules for trend removal or estimation, and readers may use their own preferences, always bearing in mind the reservations about each type that is mentioned in the previous two sections. However, the author feels that he ought to place on record his (present and purely personal) recommendations:

(i) to *estimate* the trend term, use a combination of two or more simple moving averages. If n pieces of data are available then the largest moving average should be of length between 40 and $\frac{n}{10}$. If the annual component is likely to be large in monthly data, a second simple moving average of length 12 should be used. (Any other *very* important component should similarly be removed.) A final smoothing average of length 3 or 5 may also be appropriate.

(ii) to *remove* trend, when one is not particularly interested in the very low frequency bands and for data of moderate length ($n \leqq 400$, say), a polynomial regression and subtraction will usually be sufficiently effective. Rarely will one need to fit a polynomial of order greater than two and a linear regression will very often be sufficient. For very large amounts of data ($n \geq 1000$, say) a quicker and usually better method will be to estimate the trend by filtering, as above, and then subtract. However, if the ratio between variance due to trend and variance of residual appears to be particularly large (i.e., greater than 15:1, say), then filtering should not be used.

(iii) to *remove* trend, when one is also very interested in the possibility of long cycles being present, the harmonic regression and subtraction is the most appropriate. For very large amounts of data, a computationally easier method is to use a sine filter, i.e., form the Hilbert transform of the series by the method suggested in Chapter 5. This latter method should be used when the subsequent analysis of the data *only* involves spectral and cross-spectral techniques.

REFERENCES

[1] Blackman, R. B. and Tukey, J. W., *The Measurement of Power Spectra*, New York, 1958.

[2] Granger, C. W. J., "Tests of discrimination and stationarity for time series," unpublished Ph.D. Thesis, Nottingham, 1959.

[3] Granger, C. W. J., "First report of the Princeton economic time series project," *L'industria* (1961), pp. 194–206.

[4] Grenander, U. and Rosenblatt, M., *Statistical Analysis of Stationary Time Series*, New York, 1957.

[5] Hannan, E. J., *Time Series Analysis*, London, 1960.

CHAPTER 9

SERIES WITH SPECTRUM CHANGING
WITH TIME

9.1 Definitions

In economics, and probably in various other subjects that are potential users of time series analysis, it is highly unreal to suppose all series to be stationary. In fact, most economic series are highly non-stationary with not only the mean but also the variance and autocovariances changing with time. As the frequency approach has been so useful in stationary series, it is sensible to ask if the approach could not be generalized in some way to cover, at the very least, an important class of non-stationary series. A series can be envisaged, for instance, that is made up of the sum of frequency bands but for which the amplitudes of the bands are changing with time. This suggests the idea of a power spectrum that changes with time. However, the phrase "time-changing spectrum" is an oxymoron, as the essential condition on a series that it should have a spectrum is that it be stationary. In the following, a class of non-stationary series is proposed with which one can associate the idea of a spectrum that changes with time and which may be useful when building econometric models.

In Chapter 3 the concept of a black box was introduced having spectral transfer function $a(\omega)$, i.e., if the power spectrum of the input $\{u_t\}$ is $f_u(\omega)$ then the power spectrum of the output $\{v_t\}$ is

$$f_v(\omega) = a(\omega) \, \overline{a(\omega)} \, f_u(\omega).$$

Let us consider a set of black boxes with associated parameter k, $k = -\infty, \ldots, -1, 0, 1, \ldots, \infty$ and such that the kth box has spectral transfer function $a(k, \omega)$. If the *same* independent, random sequence $\{\varepsilon_t\}$ is used as input for all the boxes a set of stationary time series $\{X_t(k)\}$ will be generated, with

$$X_t(k) = \int_{-\pi}^{\pi} e^{it\omega} \, a(k, \omega) \, dz(\omega)$$

where

$$\varepsilon_t = \int_{-\pi}^{\pi} e^{it\omega} \, dz(\omega)$$

(9.1.1)
$$E[dz(\omega_1) \, \overline{dz(\omega_2)}] = 0, \qquad \omega_1 \neq \omega_2$$
$$= Cdw, \quad \omega_1 = \omega_2$$
$$-\pi \leqq \omega_1, \quad \omega_2 \leqq \pi.$$

Clearly, the power spectrum of $\{X_t(k)\}$ will be $C\, a(k,\omega)\, \overline{a(k,\omega)}$ and if $E[e_t] = 0$, all t, then $E[X_t(k)] = 0$, all t, k.

We now define the series

(9.1.2) $$Y_t = X_t(t).$$

$\{Y_t\}$ will be a non-stationary series as

(9.1.3) $$E[Y_t Y_{t-\tau}] = C \int_{-\pi}^{\pi} e^{i\tau\omega}\, a(t,\omega)\, \overline{a(t-\tau,\omega)}\, d\omega$$

and, in general, this is a function of time.

However, it can be claimed that the "spectrum" of Y_t is the same as $X_t(t)$, and so we are able to associate with the series $\{Y_t\}$ a power spectrum that changes with time, i.e.,

$$f_y(t,\omega) = C\, a(t,\omega)\, \overline{a(t,\omega)}.$$

In what sense is $f_y(t,\omega)$ a spectrum? If we apply a filter F to all the series $\{X_t(k)\}$ with transfer function

$$b(\omega) = 0, \qquad \omega \neq \omega_1, \quad -\pi \leqq \omega \leqq \pi$$
$$= 1, \qquad \omega = \omega_1$$

then the resulting series (corresponding to that of (9.1.2)),

$$Y(F,t) = \{FX_t(t)\}$$

will consist only of the single frequency ω_1 and the curve $f_y(t,\omega_1)$ plotted against t will represent how the amplitude of the frequency ω_1 is changing with time.

From (9.1.1) and (9.1.2)

(9.1.4) $$Y_t = \int_{-\pi}^{\pi} e^{it\omega}\, a(t,\omega)\, dz(\omega)$$

and if $a(t,\omega)$ changes slowly with time it is clear that one can, approximately, speak of the series $\{Y_t\}$ consisting of a sum of frequency bands with random amplitudes and phases but with the means of these amplitudes and phases changing (slowly) with time.

It should be noted that a series representable in the form (9.1.4) is a special case of a class of series considered by Karhunen [2] and by Cramér [1].

From the same set of black boxes various other non-stationary time series can be defined. If

(9.1.5) $$Z_t = X_t(t - b)$$

then $\{Z_t\}$ represents a series that has power spectrum $f_z(t,\omega)$ which is lagged to the spectrum of the series $\{Y_t\}$, i.e.,

$$f_z(t + b, \omega) = f_y(t,\omega).$$

Thus, $\{Y_t\}$, $\{Z_{t+b}\}$ are each samples from the same non-stationary process but are clearly not independent samples. The type of relationship between the two samples can be seen diagrammatically as follows:

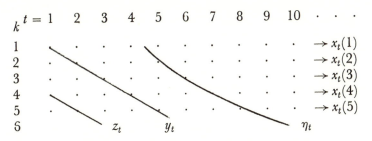

where the dots represent terms in the various time series.

A more general class of non-stationary series can be derived from the same set of black boxes by

$$(9.1.6) \qquad \eta_t = X_t([g(t)])$$

where $[p] \equiv$ smallest integer larger than p. If $g(t) = t - b$ then we have the series Z_t defined in (9.1.5). Such series will be called "diagonal" series. If $g(t) = $ constant, then we have a stationary series. An example of η_t is shown on the above diagram. If the set of black boxes is such that k can take on all values in $(-\infty, \infty)$ then a suitable transformation of the k scale will ensure that η_t given by (9.1.6) is a diagonal series provided that $g(t)$ is monotonically increasing.

However, $g(t)$ need not be monotonically increasing. Important cases when it is not necessarily monotonic are

$$(i) \quad u.b.|g(t) - c| \downarrow 0 \quad \text{as} \quad t \to \infty$$

for some constant c. In this case the series

$$\eta_t = X_t(c) \quad \text{for} \quad t \geq t_0$$

and so such a series may be termed *asymptotically stationary*.

$$(ii) \quad g(t + K) = g(t) \quad \text{for all} \quad t,$$

i.e., $g(t)$ is periodic with period K (assumed an integer). Clearly, only the series $X_t(k)$, $k = 1, \ldots, K$ will be involved in the non-stationary series η_t, and if η_t were sampled at wider intervals, i.e., at $t_0 + jK$, $j = 1, 2, \ldots$, then the resulting series would be stationary for any value of t_0. This property leads the author to suggest the title *almost-stationary* for such series.

Many other "types" of non-stationary series can perhaps be distinguished by imposing conditions on $g(t)$ but this is likely to be an unworthwhile exercise until more experience of non-stationarity is acquired.

The class of non-stationary series given by (9.1.4), could equally as well have been achieved by passing a stationary random series through a time-varying black box, but such an approach makes a proper definition of the time-changing spectrum more difficult and also the concept of an ensemble of samples could less easily be used if required.

An even more general class of non-stationary series can be envisaged with the use of the same set of black boxes as before, but all having different inputs, i.e., the box with spectral transfer function $a(k, \omega)$ will have as input a random, independent series

$$\varepsilon_t(k) = \int_{-\pi}^{\pi} e^{it\omega} \, dz(k, \omega)$$

and so the output will be

$$X_t(k) = \int_{-\pi}^{\pi} e^{it\omega} \, a(k, \omega) \, dz(k, \omega)$$

However, even if $E[dz(k, \omega)] = 0$, all k, ω, it need not follow that $E[dz(k_1, \omega_1 \overline{dz(k_2, \omega_2)})]$ will vanish for $\omega_1 \neq \omega_2$ and so equation (9.1.3) will become considerably more complicated.

If $\varepsilon_t(k) = c(k) \cdot \varepsilon_t$ then no new type of series is involved, as such a case is the same as before except that the kth black box will have transfer function $c(k) \, a(k, \omega)$.

The class of non-stationary series that can be represented in the form (9.1.4) will be the most general dealt with in detail in this volume.

9.2 Particular Cases

In this section various models of non-stationary time series that may be represented in the form

$$(9.2.1) \qquad Y_t = \int_{-\pi}^{\pi} e^{it\omega} \, a(t, \omega) \, dz(\omega)$$

will be considered.

(i) *Exploding autoregressive scheme*

It has been shown by various authors that a necessary condition that the autoregressive scheme

$$(9.2.2) \qquad x_t + \sum_{j=1}^{m} a_j x_{t-j} = \varepsilon_t$$

be stationary is that the roots of the equation

$$1 + \sum_{j=1}^{m} a_j z^j = 0$$

should all have moduli greater than unity.

For instance, if with $\{\varepsilon_t\}$ white noise

$$x_t = \rho x_{t-1} + \varepsilon_t, \qquad x_o = 0, \qquad E(\varepsilon_t) = 0$$

and $\rho > 1$ then

(9.2.3) $$x_t = \varepsilon_t + \rho \varepsilon_{t-1} + \rho^2 \varepsilon_{t-2} + \cdots + \rho^{t-1} \varepsilon_1$$

and

$$E(x_t) = 0$$

$$E(x_t^2) = \frac{\rho^{2t} - 1}{\rho^2 - 1} \cdot \text{var } \varepsilon$$

Thus, the variance is exponentially increasing and, as $E(x_t|x_{t-1}) = \rho x_{t-1}$, the series will tend to diverge from the mean value and to fall into an exponential trend. It should be noted that the series is assumed to have started at $t = 1$. If $\rho < 1$ it is usual for (9.2.3) to be extended to include ε_{-m}, $m \to \infty$, i.e., to consider the series starting at $t = -\infty$.

If

$$\varepsilon_t = \int_{-\pi}^{\pi} e^{it\omega} \, dz(\omega)$$

from (9.2.3) it is seen that

$$x_t = \int_{-\pi}^{\pi} e^{it\omega} \sum_{j=0}^{t-1} \rho^j e^{-ij\omega} \, dz(\omega),$$

i.e.,

(9.2.4) $$x_t = \int_{-\pi}^{\pi} e^{it\omega} a(t, \omega) \, dz(\omega)$$

where

$$a(t, \omega) = \frac{(\rho e^{-i\omega})^t - 1}{\rho e^{-i\omega} - 1}$$

and so is of the form (9.2.1). The "spectrum" at time t of the series is

$$\frac{\rho^{2t} - 2\rho^t \cos t\omega + 1}{\rho^2 - 2\rho \cos \omega + 1}.$$

The theory for the more general autoregressive scheme (9.2.2) is similar and so all explosive autoregressive schemes fall into the class of non-stationary processes defined in Section 9.1.

(ii) *Autoregressive scheme with time-trending coefficients*

The scheme

(9.2.5) $$\sum_{j=0}^{m} a_j(t) z_{t-j} = b(t) \varepsilon_t$$

⟨ 151 ⟩

is an autoregressive scheme with time-trending coefficients and has been considered by various writers as a plausible non-stationary model for certain economic series (see, e.g., Kendall [3]).

If

$$\varepsilon_t = \int_{-\pi}^{\pi} e^{it\omega} \, dz(\omega)$$

is the input series of a set of black boxes generating series $x_t(k)$ given by

(9.2.6)
$$\sum_{j=0}^{m} a_j(k) x_{t-j}(k) = b(k) \varepsilon_t$$

then

$$x_t(k) = \int_{-\pi}^{\pi} e^{it\omega} \, a(k, \omega) \, dz(\omega)$$

where

$$a(k, \omega) = \frac{b(k)\sigma_\varepsilon^2}{\sum_{j=0}^{m} a_j(k) e^{-ij\omega}}.$$

If we now consider the non-stationary series given by $y_t = x_t(t)$ and if $a_j(t)$, $b(t)$ are changing sufficiently slowly with time, then $y_t \simeq z_t$ where z_t is generated by (9.2.5).

Thus z_t can be (approximately) represented by

(9.2.7)
$$z_t \simeq \int_{-\pi}^{\pi} e^{it\omega} \, a(t, \omega) \, dz(\omega)$$

where

$$a(t, \omega) = \frac{b(t)\sigma_\varepsilon^2}{\sum a_j(t) e^{-ij\omega}}$$

and the spectrum of z_t will be approximately $a(t, \omega) \, \overline{a(t, \omega)}$ at time t.

As all the $x_t(k)$ are stationary series we have, in fact, only considered the scheme (9.2.5) in the case when the roots of

$$\sum_{j=0}^{m} a_j(t) z^j = 0$$

are all of modulus greater than unity for any integer t.

Let us assume that z_t given by (9.2.5) can be exactly represented by

(9.2.8)
$$z_t = \int_{-\pi}^{\pi} e^{it\omega} \, a(t, \omega) \, dz(\omega)$$

then substituting into (9.2.5) we get the equation

(9.2.9)
$$\sum_{j=0}^{m} a_j(t) \, a(t-j, \omega) e^{-ij\omega} = b(t)\sigma_\varepsilon^2.$$

This is a very complicated difference equation for the function $a(t, \omega)$ and cannot, in general, be solved. However, as indicated above, if $a_j(t)$, $b(t)$ are changing sufficiently slowly with t, i.e., if m is not too large and $a(t - j, \omega) \cong a(t, \omega)$ then we get the approximate solution (9.2.7).

Although no solution to (9.2.8) can usually be written down, theoretically a solution always exists providing $a_j(t)$, $b(t)$ obey certain smoothness conditions. In particular, if $a_j(t)$, $b(t)$ are polynomials in t a solution will exist. Thus, in these cases, representation (9.2.8) is correct.

For $m = 1$ and 2, solutions to (9.2.8) are known for particular cases. For example:

(α) The solution of the equation

$$\varphi(x) f(x + k) - \chi(x) f(x) = \psi(x)$$

is

$$f(x) = f_2(x)/f_1(x)$$

where

$$\frac{f_1(x + k)}{f_1(x)} = \frac{\varphi(x)}{\chi(x)}$$

and

$$f_2(x + k) - f_2(x) = \frac{\psi(x)}{\chi(x)} - f_1(x).[1]$$

(β) Concerning the equation

$$(*) \qquad f(x + 2) + p(x) f(x + 1) + q(x) f(x) = r(x),$$

if a solution $Y(x)$ is known to the equation

$$f(x + 2) + p(x) f(x + 1) + q(x) f(x) = 0$$

then

$$Y(x + 2)v(x + 1) - q(x) Y(x)v(x) = r(x)$$

where

$$v(x) = u(x + 1) - u(x), \qquad u(x) = f(x)/Y(x)$$

and so a solution to (*) is possible once $Y(x)$ is known.

(γ) Consider the equation

$$A(x) f(x + 1) - B(x) f(x) + C(x) f(x - 1) = 0$$

with $A(x)$, $B(x)$ never zero, x a positive integer, then if we put

$$f(n + 1) = \frac{B(0)B(1) \cdots B(n)}{A(0)A(1) \cdots A(n)} \cdot v_{n+1},$$

$$f(0) = v_0,$$

[1] From E. W. Barnes, "The linear difference equation of the first order," *Proc. Lond. Math. Soc.* (II) 2 (1904), pp. 438–469.

the equation becomes

(**)
$$v_{n+1} = v_n + \alpha_n v_{n-1},$$

where

$$\alpha_n = -\frac{C(n) \cdot A(n-1)}{B(n) \cdot B(n-1)}.$$

Watson has considered the solution of equation (**), the majority of the solutions proving to be continued fractions.[2]

(δ) Webb has considered the equation

$$(a_n x + b_n) f(x+n) + (a_{n-1} x + b_{n-1}) f(x+n-1) + \cdots$$
$$+ (a_0 x + b_0) f(x) = 0$$

and proves that if the roots of the equation

$$a_n t^n + a_{n-1} t^{n-1} + \cdots + a_0 = 0$$

are all different then the solution is a hypergeometric function of the nth order. The case when the roots are not all the same is also considered.[3]

Although occasionally useful, these and similar available results usually prove to be too complicated for use and it will invariably be assumed that the approximation (9.2.7) is sufficiently good for the model under consideration.

Two particular cases can be noted:

(a) If

$$b(t) = b_0 t^p + b_1 t^{p-1} + \cdots + b_p$$

$$a_j(t) = \alpha_0(j) t^p + \alpha_1(j) t^{p-1} + \cdots + \alpha_p(j)$$

then

$$a(t, \omega) \to \frac{b_0 \sigma_\varepsilon^2}{\sum \alpha_0(j) e^{-ij\omega}} \quad \text{as} \quad t \to \infty,$$

i.e., the series is asymptotically stationary.

(b) If $b(t)$, $a_j(t)$ are all periodic functions with common period K (an integer), then the series will be almost-stationary.

The model (9.2.5) can be generalized to

(9.2.10)
$$\sum_{j=1}^{A} a_j(t) z_{t-j} = \sum_{j=1}^{B} b_j(t) \varepsilon_{t-j},$$

---

[2] G. N. Watson, "The solution of the homogeneous linear difference equations of the second order," *Proc. Lond. Math. Soc.* (II), 8 (1910), pp. 125–161, and 10 (1912), pp. 211–248.

[3] H. A. Webb, "On the solution of linear difference equations by definite integrals," *Messenger of Mathematics*, vol. 34 (1905), pp. 40–45.

i.e., the linear regressive model with time-trending coefficients, the theory being essentially similar to that already discussed in this section.

(iii) *Multiplicative trend*

It is suggested in Chapter 11 that the model

(9.2.11) $$Y_t = g(t)[X_t + a(t)]$$

where X_t is a stationary series with mean zero sometimes appears to be appropriate to certain economic series.

If, in Section 9.1 of this chapter we suppose $x_t(k)$ to have mean $a(k)$ then, clearly, a model such as (9.2.11) can arise from the set of black boxes.

The power spectrum of $\{Y_t\}$ is $g^2(t) f_x(\omega)$ at time t.

(iv) *Trend in annual component*

In a dynamic economy in which the agricultural sector is becoming less important, it is clearly conceivable to get series in which the amplitude of the frequency band centered on the annual component is either decreasing or is changing at a different rate to the amplitudes of other frequency bands. Obviously, such a situation can easily be represented in a form such as (9.2.1).

9.3 Effect of Non-stationarity on Estimated Spectrum and Cross-spectrum

Consider a non-stationary series $\{Y_t\}$ representable by

(9.3.1) $$Y_t = \int_{-\pi}^{\pi} e^{it\omega} a(t, \omega) \, dz(\omega).$$

with

$$E[dz(\omega) \, dz(\lambda)] = 0, \quad \omega \neq \lambda$$
$$= 1, \quad \omega = \lambda.$$

In this section we consider the effect of carrying out spectral and cross-spectral estimations on samples from such series, using the samples as though they were from stationary processes.

If $E[Y_t] = m(t)$ then, by filtering, $m(t)$ can be (almost) entirely removed provided that it is sufficiently smooth. (This problem is considered further in Section 9.5 of this chapter.) Without loss of generality, then, it will be assumed that $E[Y_t] = 0$.

Given a sample $\{y_t, t = 1, \ldots, n\}$ from the process $\{Y_t\}$ we form the statistics

(9.3.2) $$C_\tau = \frac{1}{n - \tau} \sum_{t=1}^{n-\tau} y_t y_{t+\tau}.$$

From (9.3.1)

$$E[C_\tau] = \frac{1}{n-\tau} \int_{-\pi}^{\pi} e^{i\tau\omega} \left[\sum_{t=1}^{n-\tau} a(t,\omega)\,\overline{a(t-\tau,\omega)} \right] d\omega.$$

If $n \gg \tau$, τ not large, and if $a(t,\omega)$ changes very slowly with t, we have

$$(9.3.3) \qquad E[C_\tau] \cong \int_{-\pi}^{\pi} e^{i\tau\omega} \left[\frac{1}{n} \sum_{t=1}^{n} a(t,\omega)\,\overline{a(t,\omega)} \right] d\omega$$

Thus, if an estimate of the power spectrum is formed using C_τ as though the $\{Y_t\}$ were stationary, the function we should actually be estimating would be approximately

$$(9.3.4) \qquad \tilde{f}(n,\omega) \cong \frac{1}{n} \sum_{t=1}^{n} f(t,\omega),$$

i.e., the average spectrum of the series $x_t(k)$ generated by our set of black boxes.

The approximation is only likely to be satisfactory for series having very slowly changing spectra. In Section 9.4 of this chapter, various sampling experiments are described which investigate further how good equation (9.3.4) is as an approximation.

Suppose that we now have two sets of black boxes, all having common input ε_t and generating the stationary series $\{X_t(k)\}$, $\{X'_t(k)\}$ where

$$(9.3.5) \qquad \begin{aligned} X_t(k) &= \int_{-\pi}^{\pi} e^{it\omega} a(k,\omega)\,dz(\omega) \\ X'_t(k) &= \int_{-\pi}^{\pi} e^{it\omega} a'(k,\omega)\,dz(\omega). \end{aligned}$$

Let the coherence and phase relationships between $\{X_t(k)\}$ and $\{X'_t(k)\}$ be $C(k,\omega)$ and $\varphi(k,\omega)$ respectively, i.e.,

$$(9.3.6) \qquad a(k,\omega)\,\overline{a'(k,\omega)} = r(k,\omega)e^{i\varphi(k,\omega)}, \qquad \omega > 0$$

where

$$(9.3.7) \qquad r^2(k,\omega) = C(k,\omega)\,f_x(k,\omega)\,f_{x'}(t,\omega).$$

We now consider the cross-spectral relationships between the two series $\{Y_t\}$, $\{Y'_t\}$ where $Y_t = X_t(t)$, $Y'_t = X'_t(t)$. It should be noted that not only are $\{Y_t\}$, $\{Y'_t\}$ non-stationary but the relationships between them are also changing with time.

$$E[Y_t Y'_{t-\tau}] = \int_{-\pi}^{\pi} e^{i\tau\omega} a(t,\omega)\,\overline{a'(t-\tau,\omega)}\,d\omega,$$

and if $a'(t, \omega)$ changes slowly with time,

$$E[Y_t Y'_{t-\tau}] \cong \int_{-\pi}^{\pi} e^{i\tau\omega} \, a(t, \omega) \, \overline{a'(t, \omega)} \, d\omega$$

$$= 2 \int_{0}^{\pi} \cos \tau\omega \, r(t, \omega) \cos \varphi(t, \omega) \, d\omega$$

$$- 2 \int_{0}^{\pi} \sin \tau\omega \, r(t, \omega) \sin \varphi(t, \omega) \, d\omega$$

and so

(9.3.8)
$$c(t, \omega) \cong r(t, \omega) \cos \varphi(t, \omega)$$
$$q(t, \omega) \cong r(t, \omega) \sin \varphi(t, \omega)$$

where $c(t, \omega)$, $q(t, \omega)$ are, respectively, the co-spectrum and the quadrature spectrum between $\{Y_t\}$ and $\{Y'_t\}$.

If we are given samples $\{y_t, \ t = 1, \ldots, n\}$, $\{y'_t, \ t = 1, \ldots, n\}$ from $\{Y_t\}$, $\{Y'_t\}$, respectively, and if we form estimates of the co-spectrum and the quadrature spectrum as though the samples were from stationary processes (as in Chapter 5), then the functions we actually estimate are approximately given by

(9.3.9) $\quad \overline{c(\omega, n)} \cong \dfrac{1}{n} \sum_{t=1}^{n} c(\omega, t) \quad$ and $\quad \overline{q(\omega, n)} \cong \dfrac{1}{n} \sum_{t=1}^{n} q(\omega, t)$

the proof being identical to that deriving equation (9.3.4).

Thus, if we form "estimates" of the coherence and phase we shall actually be estimating

(9.3.10)
$$\overline{C(\omega, n)} \cong \frac{[\sum c(\omega, t)]^2 + [\sum q(\omega, t)]^2}{[\sum f_x(\omega, t)][\sum f_{x'}(\omega, t)]}$$
$$= \frac{[\sum r(t, \omega) \cos \varphi(t, \omega)]^2 + [\sum r(t, \omega) \sin \varphi(t, \omega)]^2}{[\sum f_x(\omega, t)][\sum f_{x'}(\omega, t)]}$$

and

(9.3.11) $\qquad \overline{\psi(\omega, n)} \cong \tan^{-1} \left\{ \dfrac{\sum r(t, \omega) \sin \varphi(t, \omega)}{\sum r(t, \omega) \cos \varphi(t, \omega)} \right\}.$

These equations are extremely complicated, but if we suppose that the phase-relationship is *not* changing with time, e.g., the two series are non-stationary but one has a fixed time lag or angle lag to the other, then $\varphi(t, \omega) = \varphi(\omega)$ and (9.3.10) and (9.3.11) become:

(9.3.12) $\qquad \overline{C(\omega, n)} \cong \dfrac{[\sum r(\omega, t)]^2}{[\sum f_x(\omega, t)][\sum f_{x'}(\omega, t)]}$

and

$$\overline{\psi(\omega, n)} \cong \tan^{-1} \left\{ \frac{\sin \varphi(\omega)}{\cos \varphi(\omega)} \right\}$$

(9.3.13)

$$= \varphi(\omega).$$

These equations show that when the phase relationship between two series is unchanging with time, the cross-spectral approach investigated in Chapters 5 and 6 is still likely to be successful in discovering this relationship, always providing that the power spectrum of each series is not altering too quickly with time.

As

$$r^2(\omega, t) = C(\omega, t) f_x(\omega, t) f_{x'}(\omega, t),$$

(9.3.12) shows that we shall be able to estimate approximately a kind of "average" coherence for any frequency band between the two series.

Equation (9.3.13) probably represents the most important result in this chapter as it does indicate that non-stationarity need not be of any great worry to us if we are searching for permanent or long-standing relationships between economic variables.

9.4 Some Experiments Designed to Check the Results of the Previous Section

As the important results of the previous section (i.e., equations (9.3.4) and (9.3.13)) required various approximations in their proofs, several sampling experiments were carried out to check the accuracy of the results.

Data having spectra changing with time in three different ways were used to test (9.3.4):

(i) A stationary series with mean zero and multiplied by a linearly increasing factor, representing a series with variance monotonically increasing with time.

(ii) A stationary series multiplied by a decreasing factor added to an independent stationary series multiplied by an increasing factor. The multiplying factors were chosen to keep the total variance constant throughout time. Thus the series to the eye appears to be stationary in mean and variance, while it undergoes changes in predominant frequencies.

(iii) A series generated by an autoregressive scheme having time-varying parameters.

Each of the experiments and their results will be described separately. All computations were done on an IBM 650 electronic computer and the spectral estimation program used was "Statisan II," which uses the Tukey estimate.

(i) *Increasing variance*

The data may be represented by

$$Y_t = g(t)X_t$$

where X_t is a stationary series with mean zero for all t.

X_t was generated by the second order autoregressive scheme

$$X_{t+2} - 1.1X_{t+1} + 0.5X_t = \varepsilon_t$$

where $\{\varepsilon_t\}$ is a series of independent terms taken from the RAND table of normal deviates [4] (as were the "error" terms in the other experiments).

As pointed out in 9.2 (iii), the "spectrum" of Y_t at time t is $g^2(t)f_x(\omega)$, i.e., we would expect the *shape* of the spectrum to remain the same, but the *level* or total power of the spectrum constantly increases.

Thus, from equation (9.3.4), the expected estimated "average spectrum" of $\{Y_t\}$ should be

$$\hat{f}(\omega, n) \cong f_x(\omega) \frac{1}{n} \sum_{t=1}^{n} g^2(t).$$

In the example illustrated in Fig. 9.1, the length of data used was 397, the spectrum was estimated with 60 lags, and $g(t) = kt$ with $k = 0.005$. Thus $\hat{f}(\omega, n) \cong f_x(\omega)\ 1.32.$

(ii) *Changing spectrum, constant variance*

The data can be represented by

$$Y_t = tX_t^{(1)} + (n - t)X_t^{(2)}$$

for Y_t, $t = 1, \ldots, n$, where $X_t^{(1)}$, $X_t^{(2)}$ are stationary series with zero means, generated by

$$X_{t+2}^{(1)} - 1.1X_{t+1}^{(1)} + 0.5X_t^{(1)} = \varepsilon_t^{(1)}$$

$$X_{t+2}^{(2)} + 1.1X_{t+1}^{(2)} + 0.5X_t^{(2)} = \varepsilon_t^{(2)}$$

and where $\varepsilon_t^{(1)}$ is independent of $\varepsilon_t^{(2)}$.

The theoretical spectra $f^{(1)}(\omega)$, $f^{(2)}(\omega)$ of the series $\{X_t^{(1)}\}$, $\{X_t^{(2)}\}$ are shown in Fig. 9.2 and thus the spectrum of Y_t is shown to change considerably with time (from $f^{(2)}(\omega)$ at $t = 0$ to $f^{(1)}(\omega)$ at $t = n$). As the series $tX_t^{(1)}$ and $(n - t)X_t^{(2)}$ are independent, the "spectrum" of their sum, Y_t, is the sum of their spectra, i.e.,

$$\hat{f}(\omega, n) \cong f^{(1)}(\omega) \frac{1}{n} \sum_{t=1}^{n} t^2 + f^{(2)}(\omega) \frac{1}{n} \sum_{t=1}^{n} (n - t)^2.$$

(Due to the independence of $X_t^{(1)}$ and $X_t^{(2)}$ the results of this experiment

---

[4] The RAND Corporation, *A Million Random Digits with 100,000 Normal Deviates*. Glencoe, Ill.: The Free Press, 1955.

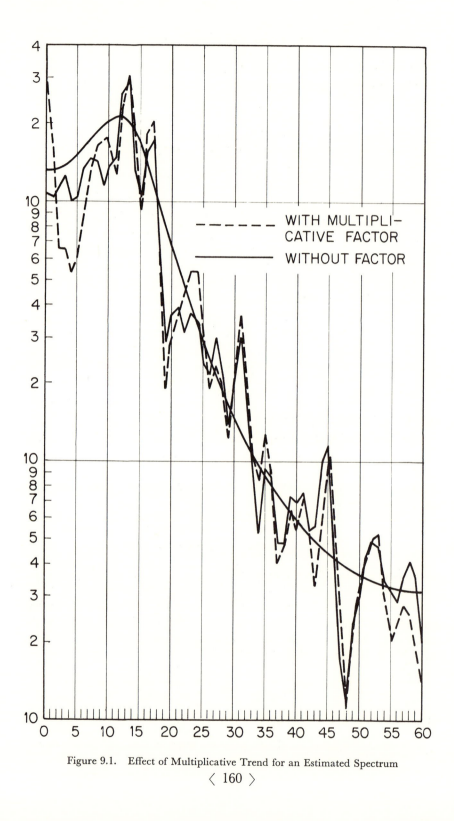

Figure 9.1.   Effect of Multiplicative Trend for an Estimated Spectrum

could have been derived, in an approximate sense, from those of the previous experiment.)

Figure 9.3 shows the expected spectrum $\hat{f}(\omega, n)$ and the estimated spectrum with $n = 397$, and with 60 lags used in the estimation.

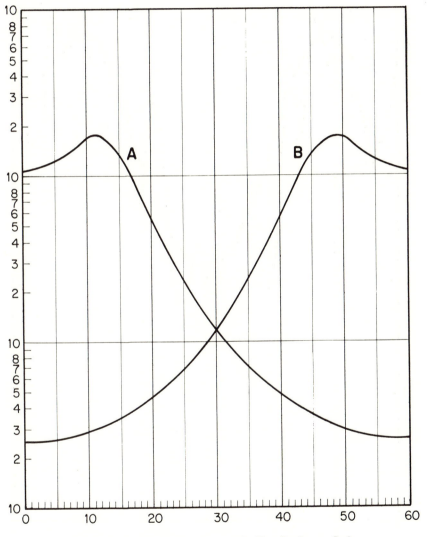

Figure 9.2.   Theoretical Spectra of the Two Stationary Series

(iii) *Autoregressive with changing parameter*

Six sets of data from a first-order autoregressive scheme with time-trending coefficient were generated.

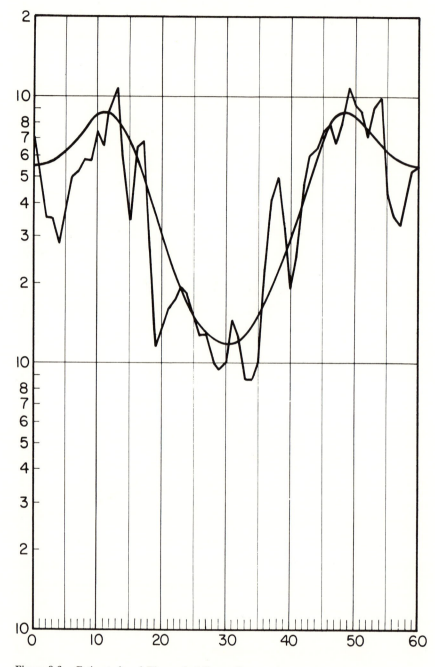

Figure 9.3.   Estimated and Theoretical Power Spectra for a Series with Time-Changing
Spectra

The first set, of length 397, was generated by

$$y_{t+1} + 0.9 \left(\frac{t}{200} - 1 \right) y_t = \varepsilon_t,$$

and five sets of length 290 were generated by

$$y_{t+1} + (0.006t - 0.9)y_t = \varepsilon_t$$

where the ε_t in each case were taken from the Rand tables of normal deviates.

Thus, for instance, the coefficient of y_t in the latter case varies from -0.9 at $t = 0$ to 0.84 at $t = 290$, which is a faster change than might be expected in practice.

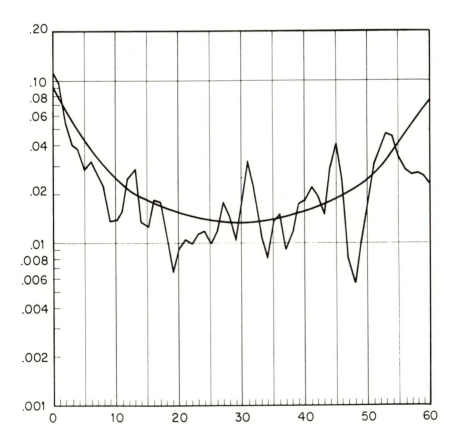

Figure 9.4. Estimated and Theoretical Power Spectra for a First-Order Autoregressive Series with Time-Changing Parameter

For such schemes, using (9.3.4), the expected or "average spectrum" for y_t is given by

$$f(\omega, 397) \simeq \frac{1}{397} \sum_{t=0}^{396} \frac{1}{1 + 0.81 \left(\dfrac{t}{200} - 1\right)^2 + 2 \cos \omega \, 0.9 \left(\dfrac{t}{200} - 1\right)}$$

for the first set, and

$$f(\omega, 290) \simeq \frac{1}{290} \sum_{t=0}^{289} \frac{1}{1 + (0.006t - 0.9)^2 + 2 \cos \omega (0.006t - 0.9)}$$

for the second set of data.

In Fig. 9.4 the expected and estimated spectra (using lag 60) are shown for the longer set of data and as an illustration of the amount of variation found in the experiments, the estimated spectra for all five sets of data of length 290 are superimposed, using lag 20 in estimating the spectra, in Fig. 9.5.

(iv) *Cross-spectral experiments*

To check the result (9.3.13), concerning the phase and coherence diagrams of pairs of non-stationary series, a number of experiments were conducted on such data. In most cases the pairs of series were formed in the following way: If $\{y_t\}$ is a non-stationary series, a second series $\{z_t\}$ is formed by using

$$z_t = \frac{1}{12} [y_t + 2y_{t+1} + 3y_{t+2} + 3y_{t+3} + 2y_{t+4} + y_{t+5}],$$

i.e., a simple moving average of length 4 was applied to the y_t series, and then a further simple moving average of length 3 was applied to get z_t. This z_t is a black box transform of y_t and has an intrinsic and constant time lag to y_t of $2\frac{1}{2}$ time units. If the data were stationary, we would expect the phase diagram to show a downward trend.

Figure 9.6 shows the results of one of these experiments where y_t is generated by

$$y_{t+1} + 0.9 \left(\frac{t}{200} - 1\right) y_t = \varepsilon_t, \qquad t = 1, \ldots, 400.$$

Figure 9.7 illustrates a slightly different experiment. Data of length 400 was first generated by

$$u_{t+2} - 1.1u_{t+1} + 0.5u_t = \varepsilon_t,$$

i.e., u_t is a stationary series, and a second stationary series (v_t) was then formed by taking moving averages of u_t of length 4 and 3, in the same way as z_t was formed from y_t above. Figure 9.7 shows the phase and coherency diagrams for this pair of stationary series. Non-stationary series

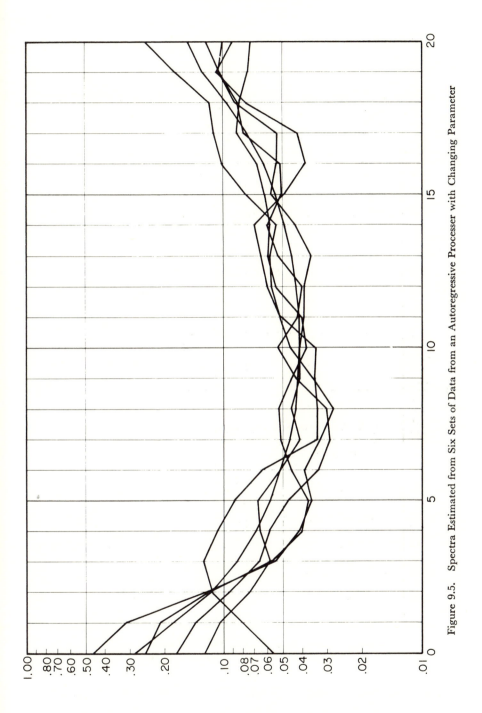

Figure 9.5.   Spectra Estimated from Six Sets of Data from an Autoregressive Processer with Changing Parameter

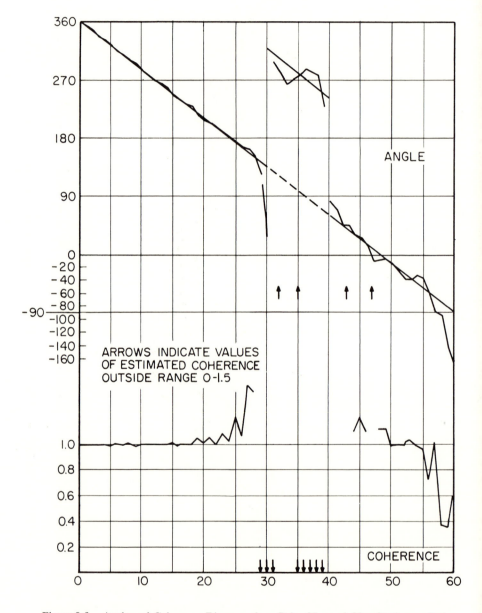

Figure 9.6. Angle and Coherence Diagrams for a Pair of Lagged, Non-Stationary Series

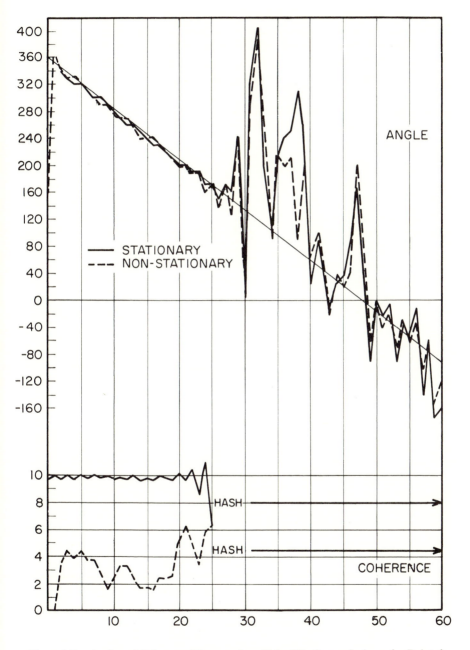

Figure 9.7.   Angle and Coherence Diagrams for a Pair of Stationary Series and a Related
Pair of Non-Stationary Series

were then formed by $y_t = 0.005\ tu_t$ and $z_t = (2.000 - 0.005t)v_t$, and the phase and coherence diagrams for the non-stationary series are shown by a broken line.

It will be noticed that in all cases, stationary and non-stationary, the phase-diagram has picked out the time-lag very accurately, except around the frequency band $(\frac{1}{4}, \frac{1}{3})$ where the spectrum of the series v_t and z_t almost vanishes. As has been pointed out earlier, where the power is low, the variance of the phase and coherence will be very large, as one is trying to measure effectively the relationship of a series with another series that is so small that it hardly exists.

Conclusions

The conclusions from both the experiments here illustrated and also from other experiments carried out at Princeton are that the results (9.3.4) and (9.3.13) appear to hold satisfactorily. That is, for non-stationary series with time-changing spectra, we are able to estimate the average spectrum and also find relationships between pairs of such series perfectly satisfactorily, using the methods devised for stationary series, always providing that the spectrum does not change *too* fast with time.

As would be expected, the variance of the estimates is increased due to the non-stationarity, and in the estimate of the average spectrum the variance is particularly high for the very high and very low frequency bands.

9.5   The Use of Filters with Non-Stationary Series

If the filter

$$(9.5.1) \qquad F(x) = \sum_{j=-m}^{m} a_j x_{t+j}$$

is applied to all the stationary series $\{X_t(k)\}$ generated by the set of black boxes considered in Section 9.1, and if then the non-stationary series

$$(9.5.2) \qquad Z_t = F(X_t(t))$$

is defined, it should be clear that

$$(9.5.3) \qquad Z_t \neq F(Y_t)$$

where

$$Y_t = X_t(t).$$

This is so because $F(X_t(t))$ will involve terms such as $X_{t+1}(t)$ which do not appear in $F(Y_t)$. Using the Cramér representation

$$X_t(k) = \int_{-\pi}^{\pi} e^{it\omega} a(k, \omega)\, d\omega$$

then

$$F(X_t(k)) = \int_{-\pi}^{\pi} e^{it\omega} \left(\sum_{j=-m}^{m} a_j e^{ij\omega} \right) a(k, \omega)\, d\omega$$

and so

$$Z_t = \int_{-\pi}^{\pi} e^{it\omega}\, b(t, \omega)\, d\omega$$

where

(9.5.4)
$$b(t, \omega) = a(t, \omega) \left[\sum_{j=-m}^{m} a_j e^{ij\omega} \right];$$

whereas

$$F[Y_t] = \int_{-\pi}^{\pi} e^{it\omega}\, b'(t, \omega)\, d\omega$$

where

(9.5.5)
$$b'(t, \omega) = \sum_{j=-m}^{m} a_j e^{ij\omega}\, a(t + j, \omega).$$

Thus $b'(t, \omega) \neq b(t, \omega)$, and so the effect of applying a filter with known filter factor will not be merely to multiply the power spectrum of the non-stationary series by this factor. However, if m is not large and $a(t, \omega)$ is changing only slowly with time, then $b'(t, \omega) \cong b(t, \omega)$ and so if the filter factor is $s(\omega)$ the approximate effect of applying the filter to the non-stationary series will be to alter its power spectrum to $s(\omega) f(t, \omega)$.

This result is extremely useful as it means that if the non-stationary series has a trending mean then this mean can be filtered out in a manner exactly as in Chapter 8.

If, however, the spectrum is trending quickly or if for some reason a long filter is used, then the approximation may not be satisfactory. In such cases it may be better to use a time-trending filter, e.g.,

(9.5.6)
$$F(x, t) = \sum_{j=-m}^{m} a_j(t) x_{t+j},$$

but the selection of the coefficients $a_j(t)$ becomes very complicated, especially as the form of $a(t, \omega)$ is usually not known.

REFERENCES

[1] Cramér, H., "A contribution to the theory of stochastic processes," *Proc. Second Berkeley Symposium in Math. Stat. and Probability*, Berkeley, 1951, pp. 329–339.

[2] Karhunen, K., Über die Struktur stationärer zufälliger Funktionen,"*Ark. Mat.*, 1 (1949), pp. 141–160.

[3] Kendall, M. G., "The analysis of economic time series; Part 1: Prices," *J. Royal Stat. Soc.* (A), 96 (1953), pp. 11–25.

CHAPTER 10

DEMODULATION

10.1 Introduction

If we have a non-stationary process $\{Y_t\}$ representable by

$$(10.1.1) \qquad Y_t = \int_{-\pi}^{\pi} e^{it\omega} a(t, \omega) \, dz(\omega)$$

where $a(t, \omega)$ is changing slowly with t, then it would be clearly of interest to know *how* $a(t, \omega)$ is changing with time for all ω. Given a finite sample $\{y_t, \ t = 1, \ldots, n\}$ from the process $\{Y_t\}$, it is not possible to estimate $a(t, \omega)$ for all t, ω, but it will be shown later that it is possible to estimate

$$(10.1.2) \qquad A(t, \omega_j) = \int_{\omega_j - \delta}^{\omega_j + \delta} a(t, \omega) \, d\omega$$

or, at least, something approximating to $A(t, \omega_j)$, for most values of t and

$$\omega_j = \frac{\pi j}{m}, \quad j = 0, 1, \ldots, m; \qquad \delta = \frac{\pi}{2m},$$

i.e., the average of $a(t, \omega)$ over a small frequency band.

It should be remembered that $a(t, \omega)$ (and hence $A(t, \omega)$) is a complex function and, as it is the changes in the amplitude and phase of any particular frequency band that are of most interest to us, we shall need to estimate $|A(t, \omega)|$ and $\varphi_A(t, \omega)$ where

$$A(t, \omega) = |A(t, \omega)| \exp \{i\varphi_A(t, \omega)\}.$$

If we divide $[0, \pi]$ into $m + 1$ parts

$$L_j(m) = \left[\frac{\pi}{2m} (2j - 1), \ \frac{\pi}{2m} (2j + 1) \right], \quad j = 1, \ldots, m - 1$$

$$(10.1.3) \quad L_0(m) = \left[0, \frac{\pi}{2m} \right]$$

$$L_m(m) = \left[\frac{\pi}{2m} (2m - 1), \ \pi \right]$$

and if the filter $F_j[\ \ ]$ is symmetric and has transfer function

$$S(\omega) = 1, \qquad \omega \in L_j(m)$$

$$= 0, \qquad \text{elsewhere } 0 \leqq \omega \leqq \pi,$$

then, using the results of the last section of Chapter 9,

$$(10.1.4) \qquad F_j[Y_t] \cong \int_{L_j(m)} e^{it\omega} \, a(t, \omega) \, dz(\omega),$$

and so the group of filters $F_j[\ \ ]$, $j = 0, \ldots, m$ decompose the series $\{Y_t\}$ into $m + 1$ (almost) uncorrelated non-stationary series

$$(10.1.5) \qquad Z_{t,j} = F_j[Y_t] \quad \text{with} \quad \sum_{j=0}^{m} Z_{t,j} \cong Y_t$$

Thus estimating the amplitude and phase of $Z_{t,j}$ at time t will give us the required knowledge of $A(t, \omega)$. It would be an extremely tedious task to form the filters $F_j(m)$ for various values of m and various filter-lengths but, fortunately, this is not required. In the next section, methods of "moving" the frequency one is interested in to the place originally occupied by the zero frequency are discussed, as once such a shift is made any of the narrowband filters mentioned in Chapter 8, which cut out all but very low frequencies, may be used.

10.2 Demodulation

If the real, stationary series $\{X_t\}$ is multiplied by the complex, non-random function $A(t)$ where

$$(10.2.1) \qquad X_t = \int_{-\pi}^{\pi} e^{it\omega} \, dz(\omega)$$

$$A(t) = \int_{-\pi}^{\pi} e^{it\omega} \, d\alpha(\omega)$$

and a filter (F) is applied to the new series which cuts out all but zero frequency, i.e., has transfer function

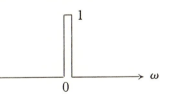

the result is

$$Z_t = F[X_t A(t)] = \int_{-\pi}^{\pi} \int_{\substack{-\pi \\ \omega + \lambda = 0}}^{\pi} dz(\omega) \, d\alpha(\lambda)$$

$$(10.2.2)$$

$$= \int_{-2\pi}^{2\pi} dz(\omega) \, d\alpha(-\omega)$$

and Z_t will be complex.

We now consider two important particular cases:

(i) If

$$d\alpha(\omega) = 0 \qquad \omega \neq \omega_0$$
$$= 1 \qquad \omega = \omega_0$$

i.e.,

corresponding to

$$A(t) = e^{it\omega_0},$$

then

$$Z_t = dz(\omega_0),$$

and so the modulus and angle of $E[Z_t]$ will give us the amplitude and phase of the frequency ω_0 at time t.

For a strictly stationary series, the amplitude and phase of any frequency do not vary with time, but it should be clear that, for a non-stationary series that can be represented by

$$Y_t = \int_{-\pi}^{\pi} e^{it\omega} a(t, \omega) \, dz(\omega),$$

the same procedure will produce

$$Z_t \cong a(t, \omega_0) \, dz(\omega_0).$$

(ii)

$$d\alpha(\omega) = \frac{1}{2\delta} \qquad c - \delta \leq \omega \leq c + \delta$$
$$= 0 \qquad \text{elsewhere,}$$

then

$$Z_t = \frac{1}{2\delta} \int_{c-\delta}^{c+\delta} dz(\omega),$$

and so the modulus and angle of $E[Z_t]$ will give us the average amplitude and phase of the frequency band $(c - \delta, c + \delta)$.

In this case $A(t) = \dfrac{\sin \delta t}{\delta t} [\cos ct + i \sin ct]$ and as $\delta \to 0$, $A(t) \to e^{ict}$ as in the first case.

This theory suggests a method of looking at the amplitude and phase of a particular frequency or a particular frequency band at a given time t. If we multiply the sample $\{x_t, t = 1, \ldots, n\}$ by $\sin \omega_0 t$, $\cos \omega_0 t$, giving $x'_t = x_t \sin \omega_0 t$, $x''_t = x_t \cos \omega_0 t$ and then apply a low pass filter F (i.e., a filter which passes only the low frequencies), we have

$$z'_t = F(x_t \sin \omega_0 t)$$

$$z''_t = F(x_t \cos \omega_0 t)$$

and so $2[(z'_t)^2 + (z''_t)^2]^{\frac{1}{2}}$ will be an estimate of the amplitude of the frequency ω_0 at time t and $\tan^{-1} \dfrac{z'_t}{z''_t}$ will be an estimate of the phase at time t.

$R^2_t = 2[(z'_t)^2 + (z''_t)^2]$ may be called the "instantaneous spectrum" and it should be noted that

$$R^2 = \frac{2}{n - 2m} \sum_{t=m}^{n-m} R^2_t$$

is an estimate of the spectrum at frequency ω_0 based on all the data, assuming a filter of length $2m + 1$ to have been used.

The method of multiplying a series by a function and then applying a low pass filter is called *demodulation*.

As a simple example of this procedure consider the series x_t generated by

$$x_t = a \sin (\omega_0 t + \theta).$$

If now we demodulate at frequency ω_0, we form

$$x_t \sin \omega_0 t = \tfrac{1}{2} a \cos \theta - \tfrac{1}{2} a \cos (2\omega_0 t + \theta)$$

and

$$x_t \cos \omega_0 t = \tfrac{1}{2} a \sin \theta + \tfrac{1}{2} a \sin (2\omega_0 t + \theta)$$

and, applying a filter F which leaves in only the zero frequency, we have

$$z'_t = F[x_t \sin \omega_0 t] = \tfrac{1}{2} a \cos \theta$$

$$z''_t = F[x_t \cos \omega_0 t] = \tfrac{1}{2} a \sin \theta.$$

Thus,

$$2[(z'_t)^2 + (z''_t)^2]^{\frac{1}{2}} = a$$

and

$$\tan^{-1} \left(\frac{z'_t}{z''_t}\right) = \theta$$

as required.

If we wish to study the average amplitude and phase of the frequency band $(c - \delta, c + \delta)$ we have (theoretically) two alternative methods.

We may use either of the following two combinations of multiplying factor and filter:

Multiplying factor with Fourier transform:

Filter with filter function:

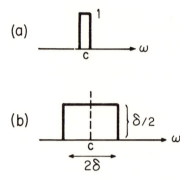

(a)

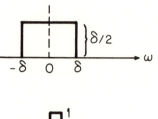

(b)

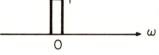

(a) gives

$$Z_t = \frac{1}{2\delta} \int_{c-\delta}^{c+\delta} dz(\omega)$$

and (b) gives

$$Z_t = \frac{e^{-ict}}{2\delta} \int_{c-\delta}^{c+\delta} e^{i\omega t} \, dz(\omega)$$

but for δ small the difference is unimportant.

In practice it is easier to get a filter approximating that used in (a) than that in (b) (as discussed in Chapter 8), and so method (a) has been used in the various calculations presented in the next section, i.e., x_t is multiplied by $\cos \omega_0 t$, $\sin \omega_0 t$ and an approximation to a square filter is applied to each of the new series. The estimates of amplitude and phase now follow as for the single-frequency case.

If the series is non-stationary and representable by (10.1.1), the method here described will provide estimates of amplitude and phase for a particular frequency or frequency band if $a(t, \omega)$ changes sufficiently slowly with time. The phrase "sufficiently slowly" here means that $a(t, \omega)$ has not appreciably altered in the time period over which the filter is operating.

If we wish to see visually how the annual (or twelve-month) component of a given monthly series is altering in reality rather than looking at the amplitude and phase separately, we *remodulate* the data. That is, we first form z_t', z_t'' as above and then calculate

(10.2.3) $$\eta_t = 2z_t' \sin t\omega_0 + 2z_t'' \cos t\omega_0$$

⟨ 174 ⟩

η_t is the same as if we applied a filter to the original data x_t that cuts out all but the frequencies near ω_0. The use of the demodulation, re-modulation technique, however, means that we need not construct a special filter for every frequency ω_0, and also provides extra information concerning the average amplitude and phase of the frequency band.

The demodulation-remodulation technique can be used when the series contains an important annual component whose amplitude is changing with time. If the series is remodulated at twelve months, six months, and perhaps also at three months, and these then subtracted from the original series, the annual component will have been largely removed. The sum of the parts removed provide an estimate of the actual shape of the annual component for any year.

When a time series contains an extremely important component corresponding to a very high but narrow peak in the spectrum, this peak, due to leakage, may disrupt many of the methods proposed in earlier chapters. This is particularly true of the cross-spectral methods. If, for instance, two economic variables are related by a simple time lag of four months except for their respective annual fluctuations which we suppose are lagged by eight months, then if the annual component contributes the majority of the total variance of the series, the phase-diagram method is likely to show only the 8-month lag, because of the not inconsiderable leakage. In such cases it is necessary to remove the majority of the overpowering component. It may be asked why all of the component is not removed. It is not usually desirable to create gaps in the spectrum, as these can prove almost as disrupting to the phase-diagram as was the original component but, in any case, just as it was impossible, with a series of finite length, to remove entirely the frequency band adjoining the zero frequency, it is equally impossible to remove any other frequency band entirely.

The demodulation-remodulation method suggested above will usually prove to be sufficiently efficient in reducing the importance of the component. However, when the amplitude and phase of the component are actually changing slowly and smoothly with time an alternative, and frequently more efficient, method is available. The series is de-modulated at the relevant frequency, as before, and the resulting esti-mates of amplitude and phase plotted against time. Simple trends are then fitted to these graphs, either by "eye" or by least squares, and the series corresponding to these trends is formed by remodulation. The resulting series should then be subtracted from the original series. Experience seems to indicate that a greater percentage of the effect of the large component is removed by this method, possibly due to the invariably poor point estimate of the phase at time t, which thus spoils the originally proposed method of simple demodulation-remodulation and subtraction.

Just as we obtained the "instantaneous spectrum" above, so we can obtain an "instantaneous cross-spectrum." If we have samples $\{y_t, t = 1, \ldots, n\}$, $\{y'_t, t = 1, \ldots, n\}$ from two non-stationary processes (of the type discussed in Chapter 9) and if $F[\ \ ]$ is a filter passing only frequencies near zero, then, as above,

$$R_t^2 = F[y_t \sin \omega_0 t]^2 + F[y_t \cos \omega_0 t]^2 = |F[y_t e^{i\omega_0 t}]|^2$$

is the estimate of the amplitude of frequency ω_0 at time t and

$$\varphi_t = \tan^{-1}\left(\frac{F[y_t \sin \omega_0 t]}{F[y_t \cos \omega_0 t]}\right)$$

is an estimate of the phase of frequency ω_0 at time t, i.e.,

$$F[y_t e^{i\omega_0 t}] = R_t e^{i\varphi_t},$$

and likewise,

$$F[y'_t e^{i\omega_0 t}] = R'_t e^{i\varphi'_t}.$$

The "instantaneous cross-spectrum" is then

$$V_t = F[y_t e^{i\omega_0 t}]\, F[y'_t e^{-i\omega_0 t}]$$
$$= R_t R'_t e^{i[\varphi_t - \varphi'_t]},$$

thus the instantaneous coherence is

$$\frac{|V_t|^2}{R_t^2 R_t'^2} \equiv 1$$

and the instantaneous phase-difference is $\varphi_t - \varphi'_t$.

We are thus unable to estimate changes in coherence with time by this direct method, and changes in phase-difference are found merely by estimating the instantaneous phase for each series separately by demodulation and then taking the difference. This agrees with the intuitive notion of the cross-spectrum outlined in Chapter 5.

By using the assumption of smoothly-changing non-stationarity, the instantaneous coherence can be crudely estimated. If we are interested in the coherence at time t, we form averages of the functions entering into the coherence, i.e.,

$$\bar{V}_t = \frac{1}{2m+1} \sum_{j=-m}^{m} F[y_{t-j} e^{i\omega_0(t-j)}]\, F[y'_{t-j} e^{-i\omega_0(t-j)}]$$

$$\bar{R}_t^2 = \left|\frac{1}{2m+1} \sum_{j=-m}^{m} F[y_{t-j} e^{i\omega_0(t-j)}]\right|^2,$$

and similarly $\bar{R}_t'^2$. A crude estimate of the instantaneous coherence will be

$$\bar{C}(t, \omega) = \frac{|\bar{V}_t|^2}{\bar{R}_t^2 \bar{R}_t'^2},$$

and an alternative estimate of the phase-difference between the series at frequency ω and at time t is the angle of $\bar{V}_t$, i.e., the arctan of the imaginary part of $\bar{V}_t$ divided by the real part.

Using these methods there is a possibility of detecting how the relationship between two series changes with time. It might be noted that, theoretically at least, the relationship can be estimated almost up to the last piece of data. This is achieved by using a one-sided filter (discussed in Section 4.6) for $F[\ \ ]$ instead of a symmetric filter. A one-sided filter will change the phase of each series equally and so the phase-difference is not affected.

10.3 Practical Aspects of Demodulation

In Chapter 3 it was pointed out that it was not sensible, given a finite amount of data, to attempt to estimate the spectrum for any given *point*. One must always estimate the average spectrum over a given frequency band, although the band may be very narrow (e.g., $\frac{2\pi}{60}$ is used in many of the examples in this book). For exactly the same reasons, it is not sensible to try and demodulate at a single frequency, but one should rather consider a frequency band. It is likely, for most series, that the spectrum changes little over a narrow band. However, it might be argued that at least one frequency component is both very important and is concentrated at a single frequency point, that is, the twelve-month component in monthly series. Although it is doubtful if the annual component is really concentrated at a single frequency point, if one demodulated a narrow band centered on frequency $\frac{2\pi}{12}$ the twelve-month component would be likely to be so much more important than any other of the frequency components in the band (even the third harmonic of the "forty-month cycle" often found in economic series) that all one would be *effectively* looking at would be the annual component.

The stages in demodulation of the frequency band $(\omega_0 - \delta, \omega_0 + \delta)$ are, as proved in the previous section, given data $(x_t, t = 1, \ldots, n)$:

(i) form $x_t \cos \omega_0 t$, $x_t \sin \omega_0 t$,

(ii) with filter $F[\ \ ]$, form

$$z_t'' = F[x_t \cos \omega_0 t], \qquad z_t' = F[x_t \sin \omega_0 t]$$

(iii) form and plot $R_t^2 = 2[(z_t')^2 + (z_t'')^2]$ and $\theta_t = \tan^{-1}\frac{z_t'}{z_t''}$.

Then, if the filter $F[\ \ ]$ has been correctly chosen, R_t^2, θ_t represent, respectively, estimates of the "average" amplitude and "average" phase of the frequency band $(\omega_0 \pm \delta)$ at time t.

Thus, the only step requiring further discussion is how to choose the filter F. The "perfect" F would have transfer function:

but, as pointed out in Chapter 8, although it is not possible to find a perfect filter of finite length, there are many ways of choosing filters which approximately have the correct properties.

Users of the demodulation method are at liberty to choose the filter best satisfying their own needs but a recommended method is to use combinations of simple moving averages as discussed in Chapter 8. The simple moving average of length $2m + 1$ is given by

$$y_t = \frac{1}{2m + 1} \sum_{j=-m}^{+m} x_{t+j}$$

and the simple moving average of length $2m$ is given by

$$y_t = \frac{1}{2m} \sum_{j=-m+1}^{+m} x_{t+j}.$$

Strictly, however, this last formula centers y_t not at time t but at time $t + \frac{1}{2}$ and so an alternative formula having similar properties to a simple moving average of length $2m$ is

$$y_t = \frac{1}{2m} \left[\sum_{j=-m+1}^{m-1} x_{t+j} + \tfrac{1}{2}x_{t-m} + \tfrac{1}{2}x_{t+m} \right],$$

i.e., the two end terms are given half weights. As its properties are so similar this latter filter will not be differentiated in name from a simple moving average of length $2m$.

The simple moving average of length k has transfer function with first zero at $\frac{2\pi}{k}$ and the ratio (in absolute values) of the first side peak to the main peak is $1:4.7(\approx 21\%)$.

If one uses first a simple moving average of length k and then one of length p with $p \leq k$, the first zero will be unaltered (i.e., the window-width is the same) and the ratio of side peak to main peak is reduced. The reduction is considerable if p is nearly as large as k and if a moving average of length k is used twice, the ratio becomes $1:22.1$ (4.5%).

Thus, if we wish to demodulate the frequency band $(\omega_0 \pm \delta)$, the length (k) of the longest moving average used should be such that $\left(\frac{2\pi}{k} - \delta\right)$ is small. It is advisable, to reduce leakage, to also use a second moving average of length p with $p \leqq k$, always assuming that sufficient data is available, i.e., $n \gg k + p$. Additional simple moving averages might also be used if it is felt there is sufficient need, but all must be of length less than k.

A good rule for choosing the length of the second moving average, p, is to rid oneself of the possibility of leakage from some component of the series that is known to be important. We know, for instance, that if we move the frequency ω_0, by demodulation to the zero frequency point, then what was the zero frequency will now be at ω_0. As the zero frequency often contains a very large amount of power, it would be good strategy to choose p so that $\omega_0 - \dfrac{2\pi}{p}$ is as small as possible. If one of the other zeros of the filter factor of the moving average of length k lies near ω_0, this latter precaution may be unnecessary. Similarly, if the annual component of the series is large then it will shift to frequency $\left|\dfrac{2\pi}{12} - \omega_0\right|$ after demodulation and it may be worth while ensuring that one of the zeros of one of the moving averages lies near this frequency point.

The cutting down of leakage is very important in the phase part of the demodulated series, as any considerable leakage will immediately induce a trend in the phase. (This is discussed further in the next section.) Although more sophisticated filters than a mere combination of simple moving averages may provide better protection, the main advantages of the suggested filters are their flexibility and their ease of comprehension and calculation. Leakage can be reduced in the case where the annual component is particularly important by applying a filter to reduce this component, as introduced in Section 4.6, before demodulating.

Perhaps the most important advice about the use of demodulation is, "do not ask the technique to do too much," i.e., do not attempt to look at too narrow a frequency band. The logic of this is as follows: if one uses too narrow a window the correlation between adjacent R_t^2 (and θ_t) become very high and also var (R_t^2) (and var (θ_t)) become large. Thus, for a series of moderate length (n up to 400 even) there is a good chance that one will get a "visible trend" in the amplitude R_t^2 or in the angle θ_t. This effect is well illustrated by one of the experiments carried out at Princeton. A purely random, independent series (i.e., white noise) of length 294 was used, which was demodulated at frequency $\dfrac{2\pi}{12}$ by using various filters. The first filter (A) was a combination of moving averages of length 20 and 12, the second (B) consisted of moving averages of length 50 and 20, and the third (C) included moving averages of length 100, 50, and 20. Thus, the window-width was made progressively smaller. The experiment was repeated five times and one of the series gave the results illustrated in Fig. 10.1.

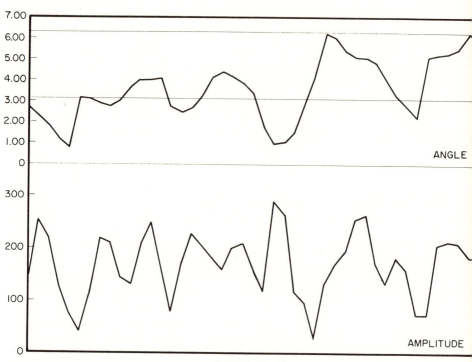

FILTER 20, 12

Figure 10.1 (i). Demodulation of White Noise at Frequency 1/12 with Filter 20, 12

As one of the important uses of the demodulation technique was to enquire whether the amplitude of a particular frequency band is trending with time, visual judgments about the "existence" of trend in the $\frac{2\pi}{12}$ frequency of the white noise were made, with the following results:

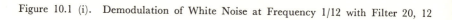

		Filter A (20, 12)	Filter B (50, 20)	Filter C (100, 50, 20)
	"Trend"	0	0	1
Amplitude	"Perhaps"	0	1	2
	"No trend"	5	4	2
	"Trend"	0	2	2
Angle	"Perhaps"	1	1	3
	"No trend"	4	2	0

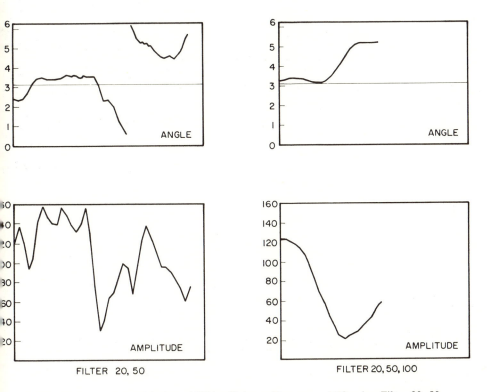

Figure 10.1 (ii). Demodulation of White Noise at Frequency 1/12 using Filter 20, 50 and 20, 50, 100

Clearly, no trend should have been found at any point and although the fairly narrow filter A gave satisfactory results the very narrow filter C gave very misleading results.

When data of length 700 was used, however, trends were "seen" hardly at all, even with filter C.

Although such experiments *prove* nothing, they can help in giving one experience as to what to expect in practice. The above (and other) experiments performed at Princeton emphasize the danger in trying to look at too narrow a frequency band and suggest that it is easier to detect real trends or changes in the amplitude than in the phase.

It will be remembered that, for a stationary series, the amplitude of each frequency is constant throughout time. However, if we demodulate a narrow frequency band there will be apparent fluctuations in the resulting estimated amplitude. These fluctuations must not be thought of as evidence of changes in the amplitudes but are due to "interference" by nearby frequencies.

10.4 Uses and Examples of Demodulation

The main use of demodulation in connection with economic time series is to try to provide answers to questions such as:

(i) Are the low frequencies trending in amplitude faster than the high frequencies?

(ii) Is the amplitude of the annual component increasing as fast as the amplitudes of other frequencies?

(iii) Is the "forty-month cycle" as important now as it was pre-war?

(iv) Has the phase of the annual component changed at all over the years, e.g., does the peak in ice cream sales occur later now than in 1930?

(v) Has the intrinsic time-lag between series A and series B decreased in the last few years?

Answers to the questions involving specific frequencies are provided by merely demodulating a band centred on the frequency, but for more complex questions (such as (i) and (v)) we will need to demodulate several bands. Thus, for instance, one might split the frequency range $(0, \pi)$ into ten bands of equal size and demodulate each. Question (i) would be answered by comparing the trends (if any) in the amplitudes of the high and low frequency bands. Taking such a sequence of "cross-sections" ought to provide useful and important information about the way in which a time-tending spectrum is changing with time (always assuming the change to be slow and smooth).

If we take cross-sections for two series and subtract the phases in pairs, we can attempt to answer question (v). If there is a constant time-lag between the two series, all the plots against time ought to be oscillating about constants, but the sequence of constants should be increasing or decreasing with increasing frequency (c.f., Chapter 5). If, however, the phase-difference diagrams appear to lie about trending lines, then the relationship between the series would appear to be changing with time.

A further use of the demodulation technique is to find the exact location of a fixed, important cycle. Suppose that such a cycle exists in our series, at frequency ω_1, and we demodulate near it, at ω_0. If the window used was not sufficiently narrow or if a large amount of leakage occurred, then the resulting phase of the demodulated series will contain a linear trend. This is seen by considering the simple case of a (complex) series $x_t = ae^{i\omega_1 t}$, containing only the frequency ω_1. If we demodulate at ω_0, the series becomes $z_t = be^{i(\omega_1 - \omega_0)t}$ and so (if $b \neq 0$) the phase is $(\omega_1 - \omega_0)t$, i.e., a linear trend. $\omega_1 - \omega_0$ can be determined (or estimated) from the trend line and so the true position of ω_1 may be estimated. Great care, however, should be used in this method. If we have two important cycles near one another (ω_0 and ω_1) and if we demodulate near one (say, ω_0) the phase is still likely to trend some what due to ω_1.

However, the trend will be a complicated mixture of the influences of the two cycles and no useful information is likely to be gained in such a case.

Using the trending phase idea it is just possible that we would be able, given sufficient data, to answer a question of the sort: "It is suspected that the short business cycle used to be of 40 months but in later years has become 38 months. Can we check this?" If the surmise were true, demodulating at the frequency $\frac{1}{40}$ (assuming monthly data) would give a trending phase only over the last part of the time-span being considered.

As an example of demodulation, the monthly data for pig iron production in the United States for the years 1877–1936 were used. If this data is plotted there is visual evidence of both a trend in mean and in variance. To show how the *shape* of the power spectrum appears to have changed with time, Fig. 11.1, found in the next chapter, has the spectra for the years 1877–1906, 1907–1936, and 1937–1956 superimposed.

Monthly figures for the production of pig iron in the United States for the period 1877–1956 were made available to us by the National Bureau for Economic Research, New York. This series, of extraordinary length for an economic series, was important in early work on business cycles, being the only long production series available and being regarded as an adequate measure of industrial production as a whole or often as an indicator of investment activity.

The post-1946 character of the series has undoubtedly been affected by the industry-crippling strikes of 1949, 1952, and 1956. The data are adjusted for the different number of working days in different months by taking the average per working day within the month.

The series for the years 1877–1936 were demodulated at frequencies $\frac{1}{40}, \frac{2}{40}, \frac{3}{40}, \frac{4}{40}, \frac{5}{40}, \frac{6}{40}, \frac{7}{40}, \frac{8}{40}, \frac{9}{40}$ and $\frac{10}{40}$ and the amplitudes are shown in Fig. 10.2. Similarly, the amplitudes of the annual and half-annual components (frequencies $\frac{1}{12}, \frac{1}{6}$) are shown in Fig. 10.2 (vi). In every case the length of data is 720 and the filter used is a combination of two simple moving averages of lengths 48 and 30.

The main implications of the diagrams are:

(i) The major trend or increase in size of amplitude occurred during the World War I, for all frequencies.

(ii) There is some evidence that the amplitudes of the low frequencies (up to $\frac{1}{10}$) have continued to increase after World War I but the amplitudes of the higher frequencies did not increase.

(iii) There appears to be a *considerable* increase in the importance of the annual component after 1920.

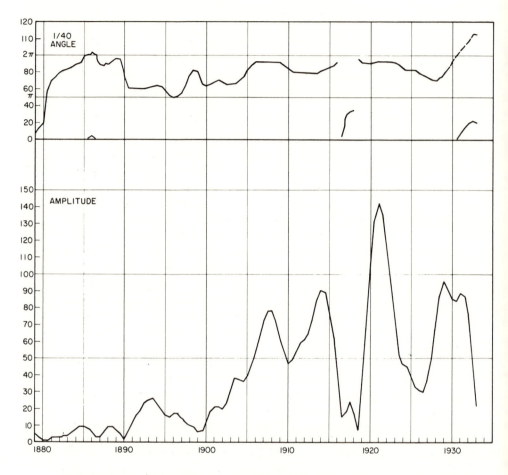

Figure 10.2 (i). Demodulation of Pig Iron Production at Frequency 1/40, Angle and Amplitude

The demodulations were not continued after 1936 as the frequent and considerably effective strikes after this date have an important but unpredictable effect on the data, making interpretation very difficult.

The phases of the frequencies demodulated are not shown in all cases as they contain little useful information. However, the phases for frequencies $\frac{1}{40}$, $\frac{2}{40}$ and $\frac{3}{40}$ are shown in Fig. 10.2 (i), (ii), and (iii). The phase of frequency $\frac{1}{40}$ appears to be constant throughout the time-span, whereas the phase of frequency $\frac{2}{40}$ is typical of the uninformative

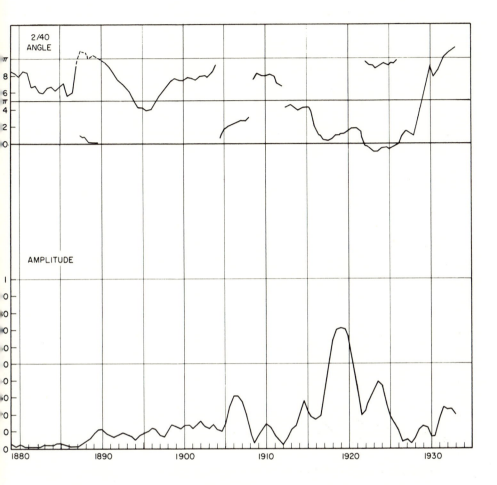

Figure 10.2 (ii).   Demodulation of Pig Iron Production at Frequency 2/40, Angle and Amplitude

diagrams one is inclined to get. The phase-diagram for frequency $\frac{3}{40}$ illustrates the slope effect described earlier when there is a nearby important frequency, in this case the frequency $\frac{1}{12}$ corresponding to the annual component of the series.

One of the more obvious observable phenomena in Fig. 10.2 is that the larger the amplitude R_t^2, the larger the variance of R_t^2. To show theoretically that this is so, we need a theorem originally proved by Rice [1] and generalized in Chapter 5, Section 7.

⟨ 185 ⟩

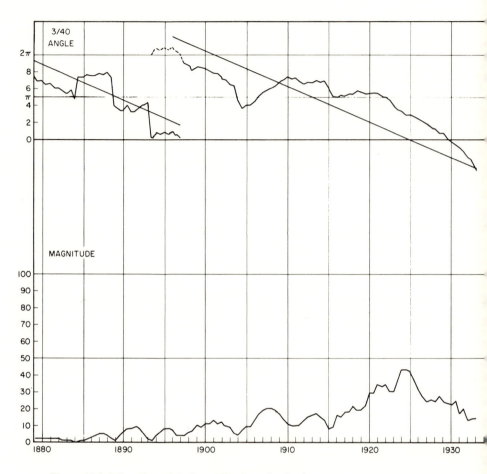

Figure 10.2 (iii).   Demodulation of Pig Iron Production at Frequency 3/40, Angle and
Amplitude

THEOREM.   *If the power spectrum of a complex, stationary, Gaussian process $\{X_t\}$ is $f(\omega)$, the power spectrum of the process $\{X_t \bar{X}_t\}$ is given by*

$$2 \int_{-\pi}^{\pi} f(\lambda) f(\omega - \lambda) \, d\lambda.$$

It will be recalled that demodulation is essentially the application of a filter $F[\ ]$ with transfer function

$$F_0(\omega) = \frac{1}{2\delta}, \qquad \omega_0 - \delta \leqq \omega \leqq \omega_0 + \delta$$

$$= 0 \qquad \text{elsewhere,}$$

⟨ 186 ⟩

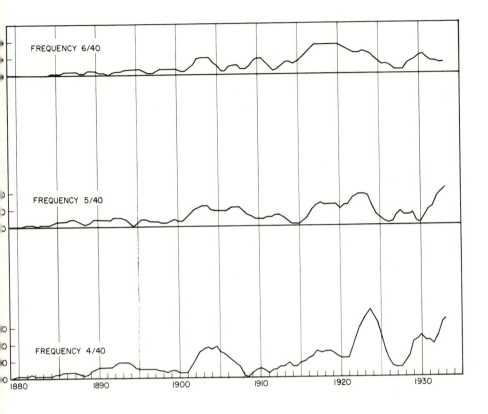

Figure 10.2 (iv). Demodulation of Pig Iron Production at Frequencies 4/40, 5/40, and 6/40, Amplitudes Only

and so, if the original process has spectrum $f(\omega)$ and can be represented by

$$X_t = \int_{-\pi}^{\pi} e^{it\omega} \, dz(\omega),$$

the demodulated process can be represented by

$$Y_t = \int_{-\pi}^{\pi} e^{it\omega} F_0(\omega) \, dz(\omega)$$

with spectrum $F_0^2(\omega) f(\omega) = \frac{1}{2\delta} F_0(\omega) f(\omega)$.

Thus, using the above theorem, the spectrum of $R_t^2 = Y_t \overline{Y}_t$ is proportional to

$$2 \int_{-\pi}^{\pi} F_0(\lambda) F_0(\omega - \lambda) f(\lambda) f(\omega - \lambda) \, d\lambda,$$

⟨ 187 ⟩

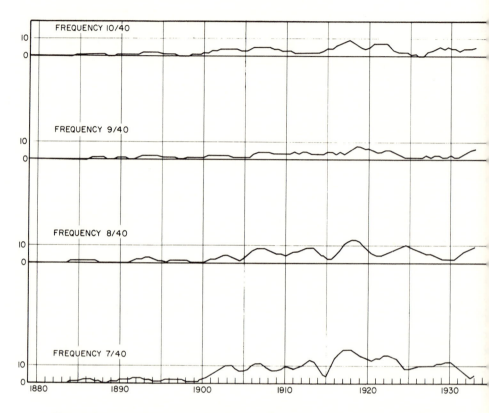

Figure 10.2 (v). Demodulation of Pig Iron Production at Frequencies 7/40, 8/40, 9/40, and 10/40, Amplitudes Only

and so the variance of R^2 is proportional to

$$I_0 = \int_{-\pi}^{\pi} \int_{-\pi}^{\pi} F_0(\lambda)\, F_0(\omega - \lambda)\, f(\lambda)\, f(\omega - \lambda)\, d\lambda\, d\omega.$$

The term $F_0(\lambda)\, F_0(\omega - \lambda)$ vanishes everywhere except in the rectangle $\omega_0 - \delta \leqq \lambda \leqq \omega_0 + \delta$, $2(\omega_0 - \delta) \leqq \omega \leqq 2(\omega_0 + \delta)$, and if we assume $f(\omega)$ to be almost constant throughout the range $2(\omega_0 \pm \delta)$, we have

$$I_0 \approx 2f^2(\omega_0)$$

and so, approximately, the standard deviation of R_t^2 is proportional to the "power" of the frequency at which we demodulate (or at the central frequency of the band we demodulate). Thus, the greater the power the greater are the deviations, as is the case in the example illustrated.

One implication of this result is that if one wishes to fit a trend to R_t^2 (by regression methods, say) then it will usually be better to fit a polynomial to $\log R_t^2$.

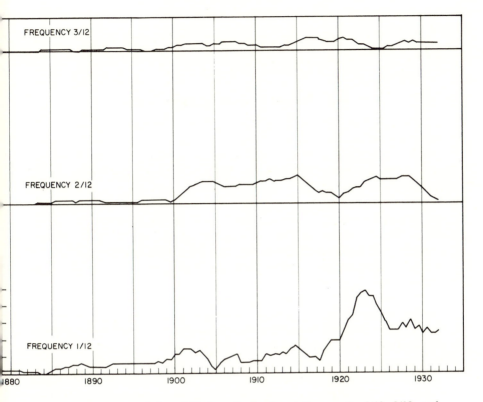
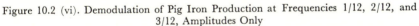

Figure 10.2 (vi). Demodulation of Pig Iron Production at Frequencies 1/12, 2/12, and 3/12, Amplitudes Only

REFERENCES

[1] Rice, S. O., "Mathematical analysis of random noise," *Bell System Technical Journal*, 23 (July 1944), pp. 282–332; 24 (January 1956), pp. 46–156. (This article also appears in *Selected Papers on Noise amd Stochastic Processes*, edited by N. Wax, Dover Publ., New York, 1954, pp. 133–294.)

CHAPTER 11

NON-STATIONARITY AND ECONOMIC SERIES

11.1 Visual Trends in Time Series

Virtually the most obvious feature of any economic time series is its non-stationarity; that is, it is likely to contain an "obvious" or visual trend in its mean and also possibly in variance. Although such trends are extremely important, they are very difficult to analyze properly, for the reason that what appears to be a trend in a small amount of data may become a part of a long cycle in a larger amount of data. Thus, for instance, the minute by minute temperature readings for a typical summer day in Princeton from 6 A.M. to 1 P.M. would probably visually indicate a steady increasing trend. However, the same figures viewed as part of a week's temperature readings become merely the upswing of a daily oscillation.

It is always the case in statistics that one must make the best decision possible using the data available, and so if all the information one has indicates an upward trend then one's decision must be that the trend is a real one. The great danger of such analysis is, of course, to rely too much on an extrapolation of the trend when making further decisions.

It is not without interest to mention examples of different visual trends that appear to be present in United States economic series. (Many of the following examples are taken from "Historical Supplement to the Federal Reserve Chart Book on Financial and Business Statistics," Federal Reserve, September 1960.)

(i) *No trends visible:*
Freight car loadings index, 1918–1960.
Common stock yields (earnings/price ratio and dividend/prices ratio), 1910–60.

(ii) *No trends but a large jump in over-all level after war years:*
Gross debt of U.S. Government, 1928–60.
Index of Employment of Production Workers in Manufacturing, 1919–60.
(Such series appear to be almost stationary before and after the war, but the postwar level is considerably higher than the prewar level.)

(iii) *Very fast, smooth, upward trend:*
Population of United States, 1900–60.
Private debt, 1915–60.

Total assets, life insurance companies, 1921–60.

Bankers' earnings and expenses, 1918–60.

(The last three of these series appear to be exponentially trending from about 1935 onward.)

(iv) *Fast expanding, with constant variation about trending mean:*

Personal income, 1928–60.

Corporate profits after taxes by major industry, 1928–60.

Gross National Product, 1928–60.

Stock Market price index, 1870–1960.

(The last series appears to have no trend in the periods 1870–1900 and 1917–1942.)

(v) *Increasing trend in mean and variance:*

Balance of payments, 1918–60.

Merchandise Exports and Imports, 1913–60.

Pig iron production, 1877–1960.

Beveridge's European wheat-price index, 1545–1844.

(vi) *Decreasing trend in mean only:*

High-grade preferred stock dividend/price ratio, 1910–60.

Average hours worked by production workers in manufacturing, 1900–60.

(vii) *Constant mean, decreasing variance:*

Exchange rate in pounds per 100 dollars, 1878–1912.

(viii) *Other "trends":*

Number of commercial banks, 1915–60. (This very smooth series increases until 1921, decreases faster and faster until 1933, rises sharply in 1934, and decreases slowly 1935–60.)

Rates charged by banks on short-term loans to business, 1919–60. (The "trend" in mean appears to be U-shaped, decreasing 1919 to 1940 and increasing since 1940.)

This highly incomplete list of examples should at least illustrate forcefully the large variety of trends that can occur in economic series. The only "general" law that one can formulate is that each series must be treated on its own merits.

11.2 Trends in Mean

It is clear that we are living in a growing international economy. The pure growth of population is undoubtedly sufficient to ensure a growing economy, and the aims of increasing our standard of living and scientific knowledge are sufficiently important to us for large gains to be made, further forcing growth. Economic series which are obviously closely connected with these factors, such as housing construction, production data, amount of money in circulation, and G.N.P. will clearly contain important trends in mean.

If one of the objects of an analysis is to attempt to predict some distance into the future, we shall need to efficiently extract the "trend" factor from the rest of the data. As has been emphasized before, such a procedure is fraught with difficulties. One needs to use all the data that are available, but even then one can only extrapolate under the assumption that the laws or generating processes that have existed in the past will hold true for the future. Although such an assumption is usually reasonable in the physical sciences, it is less likely to be so in economics and elsewhere in the social sciences.

Methods for determining the trend in mean have been suggested in Chapter 8. The leakage experiments also discussed in Chapter 8 indicated that if we wished to study that part of the series that is not trend then spectral analysis can be used provided that the trend in mean was not too large. However, it will usually be very poor practice not to remove a "visible" trend in mean. The important point about the leakage experiments is that one need not worry about a slight trend existing in the data that one has missed (or that an important trend has not been entirely removed).

There appear to be no published tests of whether or not data contain a trend in mean that are suitable for all types of data. (There are many tests which deal with the simpler problem of whether random data contain a trend, e.g., Foster and Stuart [1].) The problem of testing for trends in means (and for complete stationarity) has been discussed by Granger [2], and a short account of a proposed test is given in Granger [3]. Since, however, such tests are likely to be of little use in analyzing economic series, they will not be discussed further here.

There does not appear to have been a complete study in recent years of trends in economic series, but a series of studies carried out some twenty years ago are worth mentioning, chiefly as a further example of the difficulties of working with trends.

Around 1938, one of the statements that could be made about the visual appearance of many series was that the mean was trending upwards at a decreasing rate, and so an apparently sensible curve to fit to the mean was the logistic curve

$$y = \frac{k}{1 + be^{-at}}.$$

The important properties of this curve are that y increases with t but y tends to k as $t \to \infty$, the constant k being called the maturity (or saturation) level. It was found that many biological populations grow along such a curve and that various charts of production data appeared to lie about such curves, e.g., production of passenger automobiles,

1913–1939, industrial production, 1884–1937. Various ways of fitting the logistic curve were invented, and examples of the saturation levels found were, for instance, a U.S. population of 190 million to be reached by 2040 (current estimation is about twice this number) and a U.S. automobile production of 300,000 per month (production in 1960 was in excess of 550,000 per month). The present (and longer) series show no indication that the logistic curve is a reasonable one to fit. This example is not a slight on the analysts of 1940, who were merely doing their best with the available data, but it does illustrate the dangers of fitting an apparently sensible trend line and then extrapolating from it.

11.3 Trends in Variance

It is easy to suggest reasons for the variance of a series about a trend in mean to be also trending, If, for instance, 10% of a population of 100 million put off buying a car in a slight depression and, many years later, a similar proportion postponed purchase when there is a population of 150 million and a depression occurs, the *number* of cars affected is very different. However, it is not only in production series that the phenomenon of increasing variance occurs with increasing mean, as many price series, for instance, also display this characteristic. It would be possible to promote models such as $y_t = a(t)[x_t + m]$ where x_t is a stationary series, to account for the dual increase in the mean and the variance of the residual. One can easily test whether such a model is correct for production data (which is always positive) by forming the logarithm of the series. If $\log y_t$ has trend only in mean then the model would appear to be a reasonable one, but if there is still a trend in variance then the model is clearly incorrect. Analysis shows, for instance, that pig iron production in the U.S. (1887–1956) does not obey the model, whereas the famous Beveridge European wheat price series does so very well. In general one would expect the variance to be changing with time in a complicated way, and so we have to consider how the various components of the variance are changing with time, which leads us to the notion of a time-changing spectrum.

11.4 Spectrum Changing with Time

Not only do we live in an expanding economy, but the basis and structure are also continually altering. The relative importance of agriculture and the manufacturing industries, the proportion of office workers to manufacturing workers, the proportion of those who work for the government, the decline in some industries and the rise of others, the difference in rate of growth of some countries and states—all these and many other phenomena introduce more subtle non-stationarities in the series than mere growth and its consequences. We might think of each series as coming from a generating process which is itself altering with time. In a sense this makes the problem of analysis almost impossible, but fortunately, except in times of war or economic crisis, the economic structure changes slowly and smoothly. We are thus led to consider the possibility of the series having a "spectrum that changes with time" as defined in Chapter 9. We showed there that the methods earlier introduced to determine which were the important frequencies and how pairs of series were related would still work sufficiently well with this non-stationary data, always provided that the underlying structure was not changing too quickly with time.

As an example of how the *shape* of a spectrum can change with time, the "average" spectrum for monthly pig-iron production was calculated for each of the periods 1877–1906, 1907–1936, and 1937–1956. For each of the first two periods, 60 lags were used, and for the last period, 40 lags were used, so making the degrees of freedom the same for all the estimated points. In Fig. 11.1 the three spectra are superimposed and have been scaled as if there were equal power in each period. In actual fact, of course, the power (i.e., variance) becomes considerably larger with later years. The large trend in mean was not removed from the data before the spectra were estimated.

There appears to be little difference between the spectra for the first two periods, although the frequency bands corresponding to components with periods between 40 months and 12 months are relatively more important in the second period. The fact that all middle and high frequencies are more prominent for the period 1937–1956 is possibly due to the important strikes that occurred in this period. (See the next section.)

The idea of a spectrum changing with time as considered in Chapter 9 was essentially developed to deal with variables in which the importance of one or more of the components altered with time. The annual component provides good examples of such changes, as the following quotation from R. A. Gordon's *Business Fluctuations* (1961, 2nd Edition, page 222) shows:

> Gradual changes in seasonal patterns are fairly common. The development of an elastic credit supply and centralized banking reserves under the Federal Reserve System steadily reduced the amplitude of the seasonal swings in short-term interest rates until they virtually disappeared in the 1930's. The spread of air conditioning has significantly increased the residual use of electricity in the summer months. Increasing emphasis on style and fashion has altered seasonal patterns in numerous industries. Changing consumers' tastes, aided by advertising, have significantly reduced the contrast between the winter low and the summer high point in the production of ice cream.

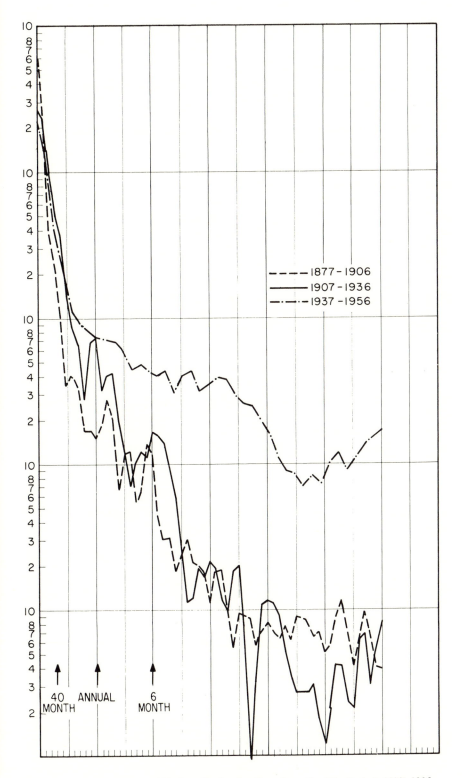

Figure 11.1. Power Spectra of Pig Iron Production Data for each of the Periods 1877–1906, 1907–1936, and 1937–1958

Other components also are doubtlessly changing in importance. Almost certainly, for example, the long fluctuations known as business cycles have now relatively smaller amplitudes due to the methods of control developed from Keynesian theory.

11.5 Contamination: Gaps, Strikes, Crises, and Wars

In this section the effects on the spectrum of some important phenomena that occur in economic series are considered in an approximate fashion.

(i) *Gaps in data.* It occasionally occurs in economic data that certain terms are missing, particularly during periods of war. The series may, however, be of great importance and interest, and so it is relevant to ask what form of analysis can be used with such data. The soundest method would be to analyze each of the two segments separately, assuming there to be only one gap, but frequently either one or both of the segments are of insufficient length to be properly analyzed.

If we suppose for a moment that the series has no trend in mean and that it has a single gap, and is denoted by $x_1, x_2, \ldots, x_{p-1}, x_{p+s}, \ldots, x_n$ with

$$\sum_{j=1}^{p-1} x_j + \sum_{j=p+s}^{n} x_j = 0,$$

then an apparently reasonable method is to proceed as if all the missing values were zero. However, some alterations are needed in the program for estimating the spectrum. Suppose, when all the data is known, that the kth autocovariance μ_k is estimated by

$$R_k = \frac{1}{n-k} \sum_{j=1}^{n-k} x_j x_{j+k},$$

then R_k provides an unbiased estimate. If we call the missing data zero, we shall be estimating the autocovariance by

$$R'_k = R_k - \frac{1}{n-k} \sum_D x_j x_{j+k}$$

where D denotes the set $j = p, p+1, \ldots, p+s-1$ and $j+k = p$, $p+1, \ldots, p+s-1$. Then

$$E[R'_k] = \mu_k - \frac{q(k, s)}{n-k} \mu_k$$

$$= \left[\frac{n-k-q(k,s)}{n-k} \right] \mu_k$$

where

$$q(k, s) = s + k, \quad k \leq s$$

$$= 2s, \quad k \geq s.$$

Thus,

$$\frac{1}{n - k - q(k, s)} \sum_{k=1}^{n} x_j x_{j+k}$$

provides an unbiased estimate of μ_k, with the gap of length s filled by zeros. This correction factor can be simply fitted into the computer program for estimating the spectrum and should provide an acceptable estimate if the gap is less than about 10% of the total length of the series.

The gap will lessen the degrees of freedom for the estimate and so the confidence limits need to be calculated as though the series were of length $n - s$.

If the series contains a trend in mean, merely putting zeros throughout the gap will not be sufficient. A modified polynomial regression will probably be better, with the missing values interpolated from the polynomial. A filtering method of removing trend would not appear to be appropriate.

(ii) *Strikes.* Many economic series, particularly production series, have large dips with associated side humps due to strikes. It can be argued that a strike has a multiplicative effect on a production series, but as it is usually preferable to deal with the logarithm of such series (to reduce trends in mean and variance) we can consider the effect as being the addition to the log series of a function $G(t)$ of the shape of Diagram 1. Clearly, the strike expectation and post-strike extra production humps are being ignored and it is assumed that the (single) strike is of short duration. Consideration of a strike in such a form will give *some indication* of the effect of real strikes on the spectrum.

The Fourier series of such a function is proportional to

$$\sum_{j=0}^{\infty} \left(\frac{\cos\left(p + \frac{q}{2}\right)\omega_j \cdot \sin\frac{q}{2}\omega_j}{\omega_j} \cos \omega_j t \right.$$

$$\left. + \sum_{j=1}^{\infty} \frac{\sin\left(p + \frac{q}{2}\right)\omega_j \cdot \sin\frac{q}{2}\omega_j}{\omega_j} \sin \omega_j t \right)$$

where $\omega_j = \dfrac{2\pi j}{n}$.

Thus, if the spectrum of the total series is estimated at m frequency bands, the strike will add a term

$$\left[\frac{\sin\dfrac{qm\lambda_j}{2n}}{\dfrac{m}{n}\lambda_j} \right]^2$$

at frequency $\lambda_j = \dfrac{2\pi j}{m}$, which if $\dfrac{qm}{2n} \leq \dfrac{1}{2}$ will be a fairly flat curve. As it is usual for the low frequencies to be considerably more important than the high frequencies in economic series, the only important *visual* effect of a strike is to raise the spectrum for high frequencies.

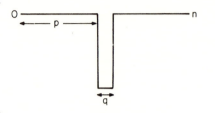

Diagram 1

If several strikes occur, at random intervals, the same holds true, but if the interval between the strikes appears to be almost constant, then the frequency having this interval as a period will be emphasized in the spectrum.

It has been proposed that the logarithm of a non-stationary production series will usually be easier to analyze, but if a strike is sufficiently general for no production to occur, the logarithmic transformation will no longer be appropriate as the log of zero is infinity. It is suggested that in such a case a short, simple moving average be first applied (of longer length than the longest strike) before forming logarithms, but as such a moving average will decrease the high frequencies, allowance for this should be made when interpreting the spectrum. As is often the case, no general rules can be laid down as what is most appropriate varies from series to series and varies also with the intended subsequent methods of analysis.

(iii) *Major Crises.* If one looks upon a major crisis such as occurred around 1930 as a special, non-recurrent event, the approximate effect on the spectrum can be estimated by considering the crisis as the addition

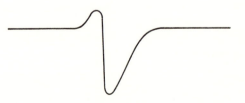

Diagram 2

to the series of a function such as that in Diagram 2. The spectrum of such a function will be of the form shown in Diagram 3. The rate of decrease of $f(\omega)$ and the ratio of $f(0)$ to $f(\pi)$ depend on the size of the crisis and the length of the effects of the crisis as compared to the length of the series.

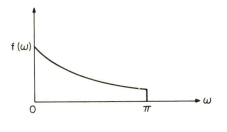

Diagram 3

As all frequencies are affected, there seems to be little point in attempting to flatten out the crisis by using moving averages.

(iv) *Wars.* Certain series, particularly price series, may appear to be reasonably stationary both before and after a major war but seem to have a considerably larger mean value postwar. Lead (St. Louis) and Zinc (East St. Louis) prices, for example, received large boosts during the last war. Such increases may be thought of roughly as the addition to the series of a function such as is shown in Diagram 4.

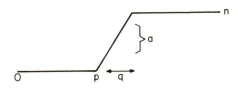

Diagram 4

Providing that both p and q are not very small, the coefficients in the Fourier series of such a function are $0(\omega_j^{-1})$ for frequency $\omega_j = \dfrac{2\pi j}{n}$ and so the spectrum of the function will be of the same form (roughly) as that for a linear trend, which is illustrated in Chapter 8. Thus, the low frequencies only will be affected to any great degree, and so a filter removing such frequencies will largely remove the war-component of the series.

For most series, however, the effect of wars will be considerably more complicated, but possibly some rough idea of how the spectrum of the series is altered may be derived using methods similar to that used above.

(v) *Contamination.* Just as most statistical data is liable to be contaminated by misreadings, misprints or highly exceptional events, so may economic series be contaminated by wars, strikes, major crises and the like. Doubtless some kind of economic law still operates during these periods, but it is unlikely to be the same law that operates during normal times, and it is these "normal laws" which spectral analysis attempts to discover. Thus, any economic series may be thought of as $X_t = Y_t + Z_t$ where Y_t is the "usual series" and Z_t is the "contaminating series" with $Z_t = 0$ except at the time points $t = t_j$ when $Z_t = \gamma_j$. The stochastic processes γ_j and $T_j = t_{j+1} - t_j$ (intervals between occurrences) may be white noise but are not necessarily so. For the contamination to be important $\sigma_\gamma^2 \gg \sigma_y^2$ and $E[T_j] \leq n$, where n is the sample size or length of the series being considered. It is possible that $\sigma_\gamma^2 = \infty$, but in any case the effect of the contamination on the underlying theory is important, even if the previous sections of 11.5 indicate that the effects need not be overpoweringly important in practice.

It is clear that if $E[T_j] \ll n$, it would be best to decontaminate the data by methods analogous to that found in other parts of statistics (see, for instance Tukey [7]). If the data has mean zero, the contamination could be of the form:

(i)   rank $|x_t|$ and reject top $\alpha\%$, or

(ii)   rank $|x_t - x_{t-1}|$ and reject top $\alpha\%$.

However, such rules are too arbitrary and, until the results of research currently being conducted become known, no worthwhile rule can be proposed.

11.6   Quality of Data and Effect of Errors

The quality of economic data has been considered both in general and for some particular series by Oskar Morgenstern in *On the Accuracy of Economic Observations* (Second Edition, Princeton University Press, 1963). As the problem of quality has there been dealt with more than adequately, we need only attempt to consider briefly and approximately the effects of the various possible errors on our analysis.

A. *Definition or Classification*

Although we may be attempting to discover facts about a general concept, it should always be remembered that the analysis deals with a particular series defined in a particular way. The actual series and the general concept (e.g., Standard-Poor Index of Stock Prices and the level of the New York Stock Exchange) will, of course, be closely related but the relationship will not be exact.

However, there are obvious problems of definition or classification when constructing any series. When aggregation occurs, it is possible that some participants have used one definition and others a slightly different one. Such problems of definition do not affect the statistical analysis but become important in interpretation of any results.

Of considerably more importance is the case when the series has a definition that changes with time. Such changes frequently occur, for instance, in government statistics. A similar problem arises when an index is used that attempts to represent a complex situation but the items included in the index do not remain constant. Examples are standard of living indices of certain countries, or the Dow-Jones Industrial Stock Price Index. Again, if the methods of collecting data have altered with time the effect will be similar to that of a changing definition.

All of the above cases induce non-stationarities of a complex kind into the data. As the data will frequently be the only ones available and so must be used, we need to consider the effect of such changes in the spectrum. Consider two series (x_t, y_t), each attempting to measure the same economic variable but using different definitions, definition A and definition B, respectively. The real data might be represented by

$$z_t = x_t, \qquad t = 1, \ldots, t_0 \qquad \text{(def. A)}$$

$$= y_t, \qquad t = t_0 + 1, \ldots, n \quad \text{(def. B)}.$$

If the transition from x_t to y_t involves no changes in scale, the effect on the estimated spectrum is likely to be slight, since unless definitions A and B differ considerably, the series $\{x_t, t = 1, \ldots, t_0\}, \{y_t, t_0 = t + 1, \ldots, n\}$ are likely to be very closely related, that is their coherence will be almost unity for all frequencies. Thus the (slight) change in definition will not be too important in the analysis, although it could make interpretation more difficult. If, however, the change of definition does mean that there are scale changes, then it will usually be better to transform either part of the data in a suitable way (by addition, multiplication or both) before analyzing the data. Clearly, no general rules can be formulated.

B. *Hiding of Information*

According to Morgenstern, "economic and social statistics are frequently based on *deliberate lies* of various types." It seems likely that the amount of lying will vary in some way with the overall level of the variable and so this phenomenon will affect both the mean and the variance of the series. However, such hiding of information is unlikely to introduce non-stationarities of a kind other than those considered in Chapter 9 and so are of no statistical consequence, although undoubtedly of economic significance.

C. *Errors Due to Printing, Copying, or Reading of Instruments*

It is virtually certain that any large amount of data will include at least one copying or printing error of a non-obvious nature. What is likely to be the effect of such spasmodic and unpredictable errors? Tukey and Hamming [6] suggest that such errors and also errors arising from the reading of instruments will have the same effect as white noise and so will add a small constant to the spectrum at each frequency. For a non-stationary series with increasing mean, say, the effect is likely to increase in proportion to the mean but will nevertheless be of little importance.

D. *Rounding-off Error*

If the real data is $\{x_t\}$, but we "round-off" the last few digits to get a series $\{y_t\}$, then the new series can be considered as $y_t = x_t - \eta_t$ where η_t will be white noise with x_t, η_t almost independent unless the rounding off has been carried out in a non-sensible manner. Thus, in general, the spectrum of the series $\{y_t\}$ will be the same as that of the original series with the addition of a constant, being the spectrum of the white noise η_t. (This result has been proved in a more sophisticated manner by Tukey and Hamming [6] and Grenander and Rosenblatt [5].)

By non-sensible rounding off one would mean that the variance of η_t approaches that of x_t, as, for instance, if x_t were a series of five digit numbers which were rounded off to one or two digit numbers. A second example is if $x_t = 10,000 + z_t$, where z_t is a normal process with variance 3, say. Rounding off to three figures in such a case would reduce the variance of x_t to zero.

The above theory indicates that, theoretically, the rounding off error is unlikely to be of importance if the rounding off is to three or four digits.

E. *Calculating Error*

It is clear that in a calculation involving a very large number of additions and multiplications, each one of which is automatically rounded off by the computer, the subsequent calculating error is of some real interest. It might seem possible that if an extremely large number of such calculations were involved the final calculating error might be of sufficient magnitude to swamp any real results. However, the larger computers now available deal in numbers with ten or more digits and invariably use floating point, and thus the economic series available will usually be of insufficient length for the problem to be a worrying one.

The problem of machine noise or calculating error usually only becomes of real consequence when near-singular matrices are inverted. For instance,

"the equations $\quad x - y = 1$
$\qquad\qquad\qquad x - 1.00001\, y = 0$
have solution $\quad x = 100001, y = 100000$, while the
equations $\qquad\quad x - y = 1$
$\qquad\qquad\qquad x - 0.99999\, y = 0$
have solution $\quad x = -99999, y = -100000$.

The coefficients in the two sets of equations differ at most by two units in the fifth decimal place, yet the solutions differ by 200,000." (Taken from W. E. Milne, *Numerical Calculus*, and quoted by Morgenstern.)

Although no inverting of matrices occurs in estimating the spectra or cross-spectra, the problem of calculating error can become important when model fitting is attempted or when testing for feedback.

The exact effect of rounding off and calculating errors on our methods has not been determined, and further research in this field would be desirable; although intuition and experience indicates that the effects are of little importance with data of less than several thousand pieces.

F. *General Considerations*

The basic inaccuracies inherent in economic data effectively limit the depth of analysis that can be contemplated by spectral or other methods of time series analysis. Whereas it may be possible to pick out a component contributing a few thousandths of the total variance in some physical series, such as ocean waves, it seems unlikely that such accuracy of analysis will ever be possible with economic series.

It would be desirable to be able to discuss fully the likely effects upon spectral analysis of inaccuracies in the data. One could, for instance, suppose that the observed data x_t obeyed a model of the kind $x_t = X_t + a_t$ where X_t is the "true" economic variable and $a_t = x_t - X_t$ is the "inaccuracy series." By allowing a_t to have various properties (e.g. white noise) and, by considering differing inter-correlations between X_t and a_t, the theoretical effects of inaccuracy can be studied. Such an approach, however, is likely to be of little practical use as we know too little about the spectral and other properties of the series a_t. One must, in fact, conclude that the present state of our knowledge of actual inaccuracies is insufficient for any very definite statements to be made.

It would, however, be both irresponsible and dishonest for a statistician to state that the problems of interpretation of the result of spectral analysis of an inaccurate series are not for him to solve, but rather for the economist. Admittedly, more specific remarks may be made by an economist who has studied the particular inaccuracies of the series being used, but it is felt that the following (purely personal) opinion may be of some value.

Intuitively, it appears reasonable to suggest that the serial correlation for the a_t series will be less than for the X_t series (i.e., a_t is nearer to white noise) and that the variance of a_t will be less (one hopes considerably less) than the variance of X_t. In such a case, the difference between the power spectrum of the observed series x_t and the power spectrum of the "true" series X_t will be greatest at the high frequencies. This could, in fact, give a misleading shape to the spectrum although the bands most affected are, generally, the least important.

If one can assume that the inaccuracies in two economic series are independent of one another, the suggested effect on cross-spectral analysis will be to lower the coherence for the high frequencies and thus to increase the sampling variance of the estimates of phase in the phase-diagram, at these frequencies.

It would thus seem that, if the above assumptions are correct, the effect of data being inaccurate will be unlikely to completely obscure such concepts as "business cycles" or relationships between series at the important high and middle frequencies, but subtle relationships at high frequencies might well be completely obscured. Thus, if we have a fairly low coherence between two series in a high frequency band, it will not be clear whether this is a true result or one merely due to the presence of inaccuracies.

It must be emphasized that these suggested effects are only intuitively indicated; a more complete analysis must await further investigation of the properties of the inaccuracy series.

11.7 Effect of Varying Month-length

Many economic series are recorded monthly but the length of a calendar month is not constant and the number of working days in a month varies quite considerably. The effects of such variations have been considered in detail elsewhere (Granger [4]) and so the results there obtained need only be outlined.

Clearly, the variations will affect instantaneously-recorded series and accumulated series[1] differently, and it was found that the effect on the former was so slight in practice that it can be ignored.

If it is assumed that any stationary accumulated series $\{Y_t\}$ can be approximated by

$$(11.7.1) \qquad\qquad Y_t = \frac{N_t}{N} X_t$$

[1] Defined in Section 2.1.

where N_t is the series of the number of working days in a month and $N = E[N_t]$, the process $\{X_t\}$ so defined may be called the undisturbed series. X_t approximates the accumulated series that would have occurred if all the months had contained an equal number of working days. Using obvious notation, the variance and power spectrum of $\{Y_t\}$ are given by

$$(11.7.2) \qquad \sigma_y^2 = \sigma_x^2 + \frac{m^2}{N^2}\sigma_N^2 + \sigma_x^2 \frac{\sigma_N^2}{N^2}$$

and

$$(11.7.3) \quad f_y(\omega) = \frac{1}{N^2} \int_{-\pi}^{\pi} f_x(\omega - \lambda) f_N(\lambda)\, d\lambda + f_x(\omega) + \frac{m^2}{N^2} f_N(\omega)$$

where $E[X_t] = m$ and the processes $\{N_t\}$ and $\{X_t\}$ are assumed to be independent.

The possible importance of the effect can be shown by considering these equations in some particular cases. If $X_t = k$, a constant for all t, then $\sigma_x^2 = 0$ but $\sigma_y^2 \neq 0$. If X_t is white noise with mean comparable in size with its variance, the spectrum of the process $\{Y_t\}$ will be

$$f_y(\omega) = a + \frac{m^2}{N^2} f_N(\omega)$$

which need not be at all like the spectrum of white noise.

The effect is even more important when cross-spectra are considered. If $\{Y_{1t}\}$, $\{Y_{2t}\}$ are two processes measured over the same months and the undisturbed series $\{X_{1t}\}$, $\{X_{2t}\}$ are defined by equations similar to (11.7.1) then the cross-spectrum between the Y's is given by

$$C^y(\omega) = C^x(\omega) + f_N(\omega)\frac{m_1 m_2}{N^2} + \frac{1}{N^2}\int_{-\pi}^{\pi} f_N(\lambda) C^x(\omega - \lambda)\, d\lambda$$

where $E[X_{1t}] = m_1$, $E[X_{2t}] = m_2$ and $C^x(\omega)$ is the cross-spectrum between the X processes. Generally, the convolution term will be negligible compared to the other terms and so, if $C^y(\omega) = c_0^y(\omega) + iq^y(\omega)$ we have

$$c_0^y(\omega) \cong c_0^x(\omega) + f_N(\omega)\frac{m_1 m_2}{N^2}$$
$$q^y(\omega) \cong q^x(\omega).$$

Thus, even if the undisturbed processes $\{X_{1t}\}$, $\{X_{2t}\}$ are independent, a spurious coherence will be found between the processes $\{Y_{1t}\}$, $\{Y_{2t}\}$, although no spurious phase-lag occurs. However, in the more general case when the undisturbed processes are correlated, both the coherence and the phase-diagrams will be disturbed by the effect being considered.

The power spectra for the series N_t were estimated for both five-day and five-and-a-half-day working weeks for the period 1933–1962 and in each case it was found that $f_N(\omega)$ could be fairly well represented by a curve $g(\omega)$ of the form

$$\log g(\omega) = a + b\omega$$

with a, b both positive, i.e., $\log g(\omega)$ increased with increasing ω.

When dealing with an accumulated series having mean comparable in size with variance, this effect may be worth removing. An approximate way of doing this, given data y_t, $t = 1, \ldots, n$ and assuming the series N_t is known, is, for a new series, to try

$$x_t = \frac{\overline{N}}{N_t} y_t.$$

However, if y_t is the aggregate of several series, each having different working-day rules, such a transformation will largely remove the effect, but not entirely.

REFERENCES

[1] Foster, F. B. and Stuart, A., "Distribution-free tests in time series based on the breaking of records," *J. Roy. Stat. Soc.* (B), vol. 16 (1954), p. 1.

[2] Granger, C. W. J., *Tests of Discrimination and Stationarity for Time Series*, unpublished Ph.D. Thesis, Nottingham, 1959.

[3] Granger, C. W. J., "First report of the Princeton economic time series project," *L'Industria* (1961), pp. 194–206.

[4] Granger, C. W. J., "The effect of varying month-length on the analysis of economic time series," *L'Industria* (1963) No. 1, pp. 41-53.

[5] Grenander, U. and Rosenblatt, H. M., *Statistical Analysis of Stationary Time Series*, New York, 1957.

[6] Tukey, J. W. and Hamming, R. W., *Measuring Noise Color*, unpublished memorandum.

[7] Tukey, J. W., "A survey of sampling from contaminated distributions," *Contributions to Probability and Statistics*, edited by I. Olkin *et al.*: Stanford, 1960, pp. 448–485.

CHAPTER 12

APPLICATION OF CROSS-SPECTRAL ANALYSIS AND COMPLEX DEMODULATION: BUSINESS CYCLE INDICATORS[1]

This chapter is a study of business cycle indicators using the techniques of cross-spectral analysis and complex demodulation. Business cycle indicators form a sample of important economic time series in various sectors of the economy. Thus, they provide an excellent object of study for the investigation of the filtering techniques which would be appropriate for the estimation of spectra and cross-spectra of economic time series. Furthermore, spectral analysis provides a technique for analyzing an important aspect of business cycle indicators that has not been analyzed well before, i.e., the lead-lag relationships in terms of *all* time points, rather than only in terms of peaks and troughs.

For readers with the background of mathematical statisticians rather than of economists, brief explanations of business cycle indicators are given in the first sections of the chapter. The problems which we wish to study are described from Section 12.2 on. In Section 12.7, the author's experiences with filtering are described. The filtering for the estimation of spectra and cross-spectra depends upon what one wants to study, but it is hoped that the author's results could be of use to those who wish to study business cycles in general. In Section 12.9, the results of cross-spectral analysis are summarized. The last two sections, 12.10 and 12.11, are an application of complex demodulation to the indicator series to see what are changes in the lead-lag relationship. The application is preliminary and unsatisfactory in some respects. A great deal more effort is needed in this particular area.

12.1 Business Cycle Indicators

The alternations of prosperity and depression in the economy have attracted the attention of economists since the middle of the nineteenth century. These alternations are called business cycles (or trade cycles in England). Business cycle indicators have been used to diagnose and predict these cycles.

[1] The author of this chapter is indebted to Geoffrey H. Moore, Associate Director of the National Bureau of Economic Research, who gave him important advice in the process of this study. The author is also grateful for comments made on the earlier draft by N. Baxter and C. W. J. Granger.

The history of business cycle indicators goes back to the 1920's when the Harvard Economic Service, under the leadership of Warren M. Persons, published what were called the Harvard indicators. Though they were popular in the 1920's, they had to be discontinued in the face of their failure after 1929.[2] In 1938, the National Bureau of Economic Research, under the direction of Wesley C. Mitchell and Arthur F. Burns, started to compile business cycle indicators. Compared with the Harvard indicators, those of the National Bureau have been based upon a more careful examination of a far greater number of economic time series.[3] Their indicators have been revised several times by Geoffrey H. Moore of the National Bureau. Further, Julius Shiskin of the Bureau of the Census has been working with Moore to develop a group of prediction techniques. Currently, the Bureau of the Census (of the U.S. Department of Commerce) is gathering and publishing indicators based upon the methodology and experience of the National Bureau.[4] These business cycle indicators appear frequently in newspapers and business magazines. The wide recognition of the National Bureau—Bureau of the Census indicators by the general public is mostly due to the fact that these indicators have been tested with fairly good success for many business cycles under widely different circumstances, such as the "roaring" 1920's, depressed 1930's, and prosperous 1950's.

Let us summarize that portion of the National Bureau methodology which is relevant to our study of business cycle indicators. The National Bureau has gathered so far no less than 1,000 economic time series data and has studied their cyclical components. A traditional definition of the cyclical component of a given economic time series is that part of the movement of the series which resembles a wave-like motion whose duration is between two and twelve years. (See Section 2.3.) Most economic time series reveal cyclical components, although usually trend and seasonal variations are superimposed on them. (Important exceptions are those of the agricultural sector, which has its own cycles unless these have been suppressed by government controls, and the service sector, which has no visible cycles.) One can easily visualize how cyclical components may be traced in the case of aggregate data such as gross national product or the index of total industrial production. In the case of disaggregated data, however, the tracing of cycles is often more difficult. After discarding those time series which do not have cyclical components,

---

[2] The best reference concerning the Harvard indicators, explaining both their success and failure, is Oskar Lange, *Introduction to Econometrics*, pp. 85–94.

[3] Among many publications by the National Bureau, the author recommends Arthur F. Burns, "New facts on business cycles," reprinted in Chapter 2 of Geoffrey H. Moore, ed., *Business Cycle Indicators*, pp. 13–44, as a source for a concise explanation of the methodology currently used, though it is not as authoritative as that in Burns and Mitchell, *Measuring Business Cycles*, Chapter 2.

[4] Bureau of the Census, *Business Cycle Developments*, monthly.

the National Bureau goes on to date the peaks and troughs of the cyclical components of each of the economic time series using seasonally adjusted data. When the contour of the cyclical component is clear, this dating is easy; otherwise, some arbitrary procedures are involved, but an explanation of these procedures is beyond the scope of the present chapter.[5]

When the National Bureau places on a calendar all the peaks and troughs of all the relevant economic time series, it finds that the peaks of most of the data cluster around certain months, and the troughs around certain other months. The clustering covers a fairly narrow interval of time, so that the cluster of peaks is clearly separated from that of the troughs. The National Bureau calls the months at the centers of these clusterings the *reference dates*. (Trueblood's recent study,[6] which is independent of the National Bureau, indicates that the arbitrariness involved in the selection of peaks and troughs of individual time series might result in a margin of error in the reference dates as large as 3–4 months.) The calendar can be split into segments marked by the peak reference dates and trough reference dates, as illustrated in Fig. 12.1. The unshaded portion between a trough and the next peak is the time during which most of the time series are expanding, and the shaded portion between one peak and the next trough is the time during which most of the series are declining.

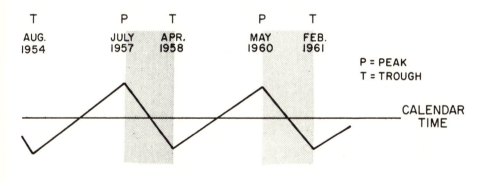

Figure 12.1

The usefulness of the concept of reference dates lies in some regularity (though not perfect) of the clustering of the peaks and troughs of many economic time series about the reference peaks and troughs. According

[5] See Burns and Mitchell, *op. cit.*, Chapter 4, Section 1.

[6] Lorman C. Trueblood, "The dating of postwar business cycles," 1961 *Proceedings of the American Statistical Association*, Business and Economic Statistics Section, pp. 16–26. The discrepancy between his results and those of the National Bureau is partly due to whether or not revised data are used.

to the findings of the National Bureau, cyclical components of certain economic time series almost always have their peaks before the peak reference dates and their troughs before the trough reference dates. For some other economic time series, the cyclical components have their peaks and troughs just about at the peak and trough reference dates. The cyclical components of yet other economic time series have their peaks after the peak reference dates and their troughs after the trough reference dates. Time series which fall into the first group are called *leading indicators,* the second group *coincident indicators,* and the last group *lagging indicators.*

The regularity mentioned above, if reliable, would be useful to diagnose and predict the movement of the business cycles of the economy. The downturn of leading indicators could predict the imminence of the downturn of all other economic time series; the upturn of the lagging indicators could confirm the end of a recession. Moore has developed many techniques for predicting the severity of a recession from the analysis of movements of leading and other indicators, but the explanation of these techniques is again beyond the scope of the present chapter.

We must admit that the above presentation represents an oversimplified picture of our economy. When one studies the history of business cycles in the United States, one cannot help but be impressed by the widely differing characteristics of expansions and, particularly, of recessions over time. The recession in 1926–1927 was so mild that it might have been avoided if the Ford Motor Company had not shut down its plants for a model change. Yet the recession which started just a few years later turned out to be one of the most severe in the entire history of capitalism. The varying natures of the recessions and expansions reflect the many ways in which different magnitudes of different factors are combined. Therefore, it should be obvious that we cannot possibly expect, for a given indicator, *constant* magnitudes of the leads or lags over all the reference dates for peaks and troughs. In fact, the National Bureau found that the dispersion of leads and lags over different reference dates is large. Even worse is the finding that many leading indicators lag occasionally behind the reference dates, and many lagging indicators lead occasionally. Furthermore, some indicators reveal something resembling a secular change in the magnitude of lead or lag. (Many leading indicators related to building construction have tended to show greater magnitude of lead over time.) These are some of the reasons why the National Bureau and the Bureau of the Census rely upon a large number of indicators rather than a few.

One point must be emphasized in order to avoid possible confusion about the lead-lag relationship. The National Bureau stresses the fact that there are different lead-lag relations depending on which one of the components in the decomposed time series is considered, i.e., lead-lag in terms of cyclical components would be different from that in terms of trend or in terms of seasonal variations. Throughout the above exposition we have been concerned with the lead-lag relations of cyclical components alone and *not* that of any other component.

12.2 Lead-lag in Terms of all Time Points

In the previous section we have explained that the National Bureau method is based upon peaks and troughs of cyclical components in different economic time series. In the process of translating the method of the National Bureau into the framework of spectral analysis, we make one important change. We intend to study business cycle indicators without using *peaks and troughs*; otherwise we stay essentially within the National Bureau's methodology. There are two motivations behind this approach.

First, many economists (e.g., Schumpeter[7]) think that the estimation errors of the data make the dating of peaks and troughs very difficult, and that exact dating is meaningless because of the possible influence of random disturbances. Anyone acquainted with the methodology of modern statistics is aware of the difficulty of working with extreme values, which are abnormal rather than normal phenomena. Further, even though the dating of peaks and troughs was originally proposed by Burns and Mitchell to define the expansion and contraction phases of the cyclical components and to study the lead-lag relationship *stage by stage* within these phases, it seems to the author that the peaks and troughs are now over-emphasized to the extent that the casual reader is distracted from the importance of the stage-by-stage relationship.

The second motivation is concerned with stabilization policies. The lead or lag of the National Bureau indicators is defined in terms of peaks and troughs only, ignoring all other phases of the cycles. Dates of peaks and troughs are most important in the timing of stabilization policies because many such policies must be executed once (or twice when one reverses them) in the duration of a cycle at the right moment (the change in the tax rate is an example), and it may be true that all we need to know is the lead-lag relationship in terms of peaks and troughs.

However, some important stabilization policies must be carried out constantly, or their possible use must be examined constantly. Suppose that the Federal Open Market Committee, which is in charge of open market operations in the United States, is afraid that a boom might get out of control and wishes to slow down the boom *without turning it into a depression*. (For readers unfamiliar with open market operations it may

---

[7] Schumpeter, *Business Cycles*, p. 151.

be mentioned that they consist of transactions of securities (mostly government securities) by the Federal Open Market Committee (a branch of the central bank of the United States) designed to influence directly deposits at banks in money markets where the transactions are made and indirectly the ability of all banks to lend; i.e., open market operations change the money supply and also credit conditions.) The Committee would like to know the length of time between any action it might take and its impact on the aggregate economy. This is a kind of lead-lag relation, but *not in terms of peaks or troughs* in economic activity. If we adopt a rigorous attitude, the findings by the National Bureau *cannot* be extended, without further confirmation, to leads or lags in terms of time points other than at peaks or troughs.

It seems obvious, therefore, that the ideal would be to study the lead-lag relation in terms of each different phase of the business cycle. To the best of the author's knowledge, there is presently no adequate statistical method for such a study. What we will present in this chapter then is a kind of preliminary study. A problem in the present chapter is: *Is there any consistent difference that prevails in most of the economic time series between the lead-lag in terms of peaks and troughs and the lead-lag in terms of all phases of the cycle?*

Further, in view of the finding (for some cycle indicators) that the magnitudes of lead-lag in terms of peak and trough reveal some persistent change over time, we should expect that the lead-lag in terms of all phases of cycles might also reveal some persistent change. Therefore, the second problem treated in this chapter is: *Is there any significant persistent change in the lead-lag in terms of all phases of cycles, and how does this change differ from the similar change in the lead-lag in terms of peaks and troughs?*

12.3 Frequency Band for the Major Component of the Cyclical Component

As stated above, by lead-lag we mean the lead-lag in terms of the cyclical component. In order to make spectral analyses of the cycle indicators, we must define the cyclical component by the use of the frequency band. In the present section we merely consider the frequency band for the major component, as compared with the harmonic component, of the cyclical component. As commented on earlier (Chapters 3 and 4), any component such as the cyclical component must be defined as a sort of weighted average of all the frequencies within a given band. In practice, the actual weights must be determined partly in view of the spectral window used. Therefore, at this point we merely determine the upper and lower bounds for the major component of the cyclical component.

Since most of the cycle indicators are monthly, we use a month as the time unit to represent frequency, and abbreviate cycles per month as c/m. As explained in Chapter 2, Burns and Mitchell's definition of business cycles has a duration between two years and twelve years. If we were to adopt this range of duration, then the corresponding frequency band would be between $\frac{1}{144}$ c/m and $\frac{1}{24}$ c/m. However, we are *not* going to adopt this definition.

On the one hand, Ruth Mack[8] found that many economic time series contain cyclical components whose duration is shorter than that of business cycles. The average duration of Mack's cycle is 24 months, compared with the average duration of about 50 months for National Bureau business cycles. The shortest possible duration of Mack's cycle may be put as 16 months. Since we plan to include Mack's cycle in our study, the upper bound of the frequency band becomes $\frac{1}{16}$ c/m.

On the other hand, the chronology of the National Bureau reference dates for the United States does not show any business cycles whose duration is as long as twelve years. The longest since 1854, 101 months, occurred in the 1870's, a severe depression period. Unfortunately, we cannot include $\frac{1}{101}$ c/m in our frequency band for most of our business cycle indicators because of the difficulty in treating low frequencies. As commented on earlier (see Section 4.2), what is considered a "low" frequency depends upon the length of data to be analyzed. In most cases the monthly time series of business cycle indicators contain 300–500 pieces of data, and for this length of data, $\frac{1}{101}$ c/m is really a low frequency. This may be seen in the following way: the frequency interval containing zero frequency does not provide any information as to the cross spectrum, and the first frequency interval, not containing zero, is strongly influenced by the zero frequency because of the spectral window. Suppose that we put $\frac{1}{101}$ c/m at the center of the second frequency interval, and ask ourselves what are the degrees of freedom in series with 300–500 pieces of data. Letting n be the number of data ($500 \geq n \geq 300$) and m the number of lags (using the Tukey-Hanning window), the center of the second frequency interval is $\frac{2}{2m}$, and we wish this to be equal to $\frac{1}{101}$ c/m. Therefore, $m = 101$. Since the degrees of freedom are $\frac{2n}{m}$, they lie between $\frac{1000}{101}$ and $\frac{600}{101}$, i.e., between 10 and 6.

[8] Ruth P. Mack, "Notes on subcycles in theory and practice," *American Economic Review*, May 1957, pp. 161–174.

We set $\frac{1}{96}$ c/m as the lower bound of the frequency band at which the weights reach zero. In other words, the frequencies for which the weights are significantly different from zero are substantially above $\frac{1}{96}$ c/m. The reason why $\frac{1}{96}$ c/m is chosen is that $\frac{1}{16}$ c/m, which is the upper bound, is six times $\frac{1}{96}$ c/m and because $\frac{1}{96}$ c/m is hopelessly low. This lower band, however, introduces a serious drawback forced upon us by limitations in length of available data. According to the National Bureau chronology of reference dates, the duration of the cycle containing the Great Depression as the recession phase is 93 months. In other words, the possible frequency of the business cycle can be nearly as low as $\frac{1}{96}$ c/m, and yet in our frequency representation of business cycles the weights attached to these low frequencies are nearly zero. We must say that our study of cycle indicators does not treat properly cycles containing a long depression or a long expansion.[9] Furthermore, we cannot treat the major cycles whose duration is about ten years.

So far we have determined only the upper and lower bounds where the weights used for the definition of cyclical components completely vanish. The actual distribution of weights is determined by the statistical techniques which we are going to use. Thus, in the use of the spectral and cross spectral analyses, the distribution of weights depends upon the number of lags used in their estimation. If the 96 lags are used in the Tukey-Hanning window, the unit frequency interval is $\frac{1}{192}$ c/m. The spectra and cross-spectra of the cyclical components, as defined above, are obtained as the estimates of these spectra over the frequencies from $\frac{4}{192}\left(=\frac{1}{48}\right)$ c/m to $\frac{10}{192}$ c/m. This is because the estimates of spectra and cross-spectra for the frequency interval centered at $\frac{1}{48}$ c/m include some portion of the spectra and cross-spectra for the frequency interval centered at $\frac{3}{192}$ c/m but practically none of the spectra and cross-spectra for the frequency interval centered at $\frac{2}{192}=\frac{1}{96}$ c/m. Similarly, a part of $\frac{11}{192}$ c/m but practically none of $\frac{12}{196}=\frac{1}{16}$ c/m is included in the estima-

---

[9] The cycle containing World War II also has a duration of 93 months. However, this can be ignored in our frequency representation of business cycles, because this particular cycle was due to abnormal circumstances.

tion of spectra and cross-spectra at $\frac{10}{192}$ c/m. In presenting the results of our cross-spectral analysis we use the notations for the frequency interval, $\left(\frac{1}{48} - \varepsilon\right)$ c/m to $\left(\frac{10}{196} + \varepsilon\right)$ c/m.

12.4 New Problems Brought Out by Cross-spectral Analysis

So far in this chapter we have been concerned with translating the traditional approach to the lead-lag relationship into frequency concepts, even though the lead-lag in terms of peaks and troughs was replaced by that in terms of all time points. But if we were to restrict our thinking only to the currently prevailing methodology in economics, we might not see new problems and other possible interpretations of economic events. As the present author sees it, spectral analysis represents not only a technical advance in statistics but also a whole new way of thinking. Thus we might overlook something important if we were to study only that frequency band, as defined above, corresponding to the cyclical component of traditional economics.

First of all, it is immediately apparent that Ruth Mack's cycle, which is centered at $\frac{1}{24}$ c/m, is really a harmonic component of the National Bureau business cycles, which can be centered at $\frac{1}{48}$ c/m. Thus it would be quite natural to study these two cycles simultaneously, and, further, to extend the study to the next harmonic component centered at $\frac{1}{16}$ c/m. This can be more easily seen if we first take an analogy from the seasonal variation. The seasonal variation can be considered to consist of 6 components (using a month as the time unit) represented by the frequencies $\frac{1}{12}$ c/m, $\frac{1}{6}$ c/m, $\frac{1}{4}$ c/m, $\frac{1}{3}$ c/m, $\frac{5}{12}$ c/m, and $\frac{1}{2}$ c/m. Even though the six components which result from the seasonal variation have different frequencies, there will be great similarity among them as to their influence upon economic time series. Therefore, it is important to study these six frequencies simultaneously. Coming back to the business cycle, the causes of business cycles might very well be considered as consisting of three components: one component represented by the frequency band centered at $\frac{1}{48}$ c/m, the second centered at $\frac{1}{24}$ c/m, and the third centered at $\frac{1}{16}$ c/m. These three frequency bands should be studied simultaneously.

However, it must be admitted that this study is greatly handicapped by the fact that what is meant by cycles in economics are not represented by a single frequency point but by a frequency band. (See Section 4.2.) This fact becomes extremely important when we deal with harmonic components. Let us consider a cycle which corresponds to the frequency band $\omega_0 - \varepsilon$ to $\omega_0 + \varepsilon'$. The first harmonic now corresponds to the band $2\omega_0 - 2\varepsilon$ to $2\omega_0 + 2\varepsilon'$. The next harmonic component has a frequency band whose width is three times as large as the original band. In the case of business cycles, if we define the original component as the band from $\frac{1}{48} - \frac{1}{96} = \frac{1}{96}$ c/m to $\frac{1}{48} + \frac{1}{96} = \frac{1}{32}$ c/m, then the band of the first harmonic is from $\frac{1}{24} - \frac{1}{48} = \frac{1}{48}$ c/m to $\frac{1}{24} + \frac{1}{48} = \frac{1}{16}$ c/m, and the band of the next harmonic is from $\frac{1}{16} - \frac{1}{32} = \frac{1}{32}$ c/m to $\frac{1}{16} + \frac{1}{32} = \frac{1}{10.1}$ c/m. Evidently, the three frequency bands overlap. Therefore, it is impossible to separate the three components.

In spite of this overlapping, it is still possible that the frequency band from $\frac{1}{96}$ c/m to $\frac{1}{12}$ c/m reflects basically the same phenomenon as $\frac{1}{12}, \frac{1}{6}, \cdots, \frac{1}{2}$ c/m reflect the phenomenon called "season." Therefore, we should extend our study from the frequency band defined in (12.3) at least up to $\frac{1}{12}$ c/m, the major seasonal component. A question which should be considered is: Is there any phenomenon which is common to all the frequencies from $\frac{1}{96}$ c/m to $\frac{1}{12}$ c/m? If we can find one, it may be a clue to further study of the true nature of business cycles.

At this point we have come to our first conclusion: *In the study of cyclical components one should study the whole frequency band from $\frac{1}{96}$ c/m to $\frac{1}{12}$ c/m.*

So far, we have discussed only the cyclical components, but as a sideline we can study another problem. As commented earlier in Chapter 6, the interpretation of a phase-diagram is simple when it reveals a fixed time lag or a fixed angle lag, although there is no a priori reason why we should expect such simple one-parameter lead-lag relations. It is worth while to point out that all the past econometric models have dealt with the fixed time-lag but never with the fixed angle lag. Therefore (apart from the complex relations which are neither fixed time-lag nor fixed angle lag), we would like to see which of the two simple one-parameter relations suggested by the cross-spectral analysis is more common. Logically, there can be a mixture of the two. Therefore, we must study all frequencies from zero to the Nyquist to look for a simple trend (including a flat trend) in the phase diagram. Further, the lead-lag in terms of the seasonal variation would be different from the lead-lag in terms of the cyclical component. As pointed out earlier, this is what the National Bureau emphasizes, but we can also see it in the cross-spectrum if we define the lead-lag in terms of all time points rather than in terms of lead and lag around the reference dates. Thus, in this related problem we would like to see *the entire frequency band from zero to the Nyquist and look for a simple trend in the phase-diagram as well as for any peculiarities in the seasonal frequencies.*

12.5   Selection of Cycle Indicators and Reference Time Series

The National Bureau expresses the lead-lag of every economic time series it analyzes in terms of the reference dates it has established. It would be convenient for our study to have some basic reference time series which could be taken as a standard in terms of which the leads and lags of all the other economic time series would be expressed.

Some of the business cycle indicators are quarterly and the data are available only since the 1930's. For these indicators, the natural choice of a basic reference series is gross national product in current dollars. However, most of the indicators are monthly, but any time series (except for personal income) in the framework of national income accounts are not available on a monthly basis. Therefore, the choice of a reference series for the monthly data became a serious problem.

After consultation with G. H. Moore, we decided to choose the Federal Reserve Board Index of Industrial Production as the reference series for the monthly indicators. This index is available for the period since 1919 and is classified as a coincident indicator by the National Bureau. Figure 12.2 indicates the estimates of spectra of the zigzag lines in Fig. 12.1 (the zigzag obtained by connecting the reference peaks and troughs) and the Federal Reserve Board Index of Industrial Production, both for the period since 1919. In order to conserve space, only the low frequency portions of the spectra are shown. Figure 12.3 shows the cross-spectrum between these two series. It appears that the zigzag line lags slightly behind the Index of Industrial Production. This will be discussed later. As the reference for the monthly series that start before 1919 we have chosen the bank clearing series.

The estimation of the cross-spectrum between each one of the business cycle indicators and the reference series is now our main subject matter. In *Business Cycle Indicators*, vol. II, G. H. Moore lists about 70 cycle

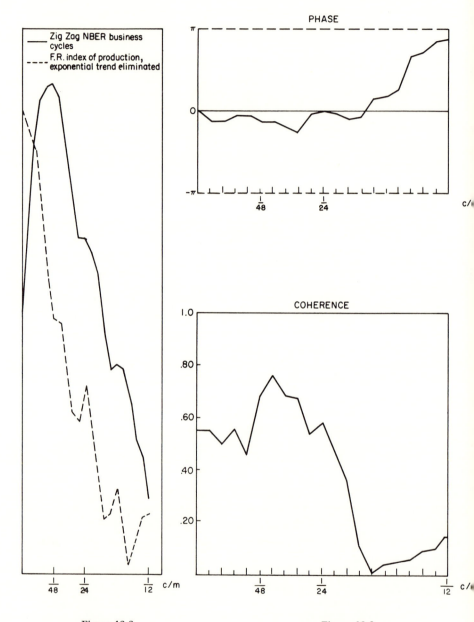

PHASE

COHERENCE

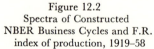

Figure 12.2
Spectra of Constructed
NBER Business Cycles and F.R.
index of production, 1919–58

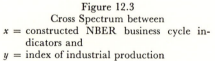

Figure 12.3
Cross Spectrum between
x = constructed NBER business cycle indicators and
y = index of industrial production

indicators (excluding the diffusion indices). With his advice, we selected 29 of them as the objects of our study. This selection was based on the following principles: (1) series that cover no more than 10–15 years are eliminated because they are too short for the purpose of studying the cyclical components; (2) series which have lost their significance due to the appearance of better series are included if they are sufficiently long, because the purpose of our study as described in section 12.2–12.5 is not to predict movements in the economy for a few months ahead of this writing; and (3) all the data used here are *not* seasonally adjusted. (Certain of the series are seasonally adjusted at the source, and unadjusted data are not available. These series are excluded from our study.) Some doubt has been expressed by econometricians as to how the currently-used seasonal adjustment methods (all of which are a version of Shiskin's method) affect each frequency. Until a large-scale study of the methods of seasonal adjustment is made,[10] it appears that the safest approach is to avoid the use of seasonally adjusted data.

All the cycle indicators used here can be classified according to the reference time series with which they are to be compared. Thus, we have the monthly series which start at or after 1919 (using the Federal Reserve Board Index of Industrial Production as the reference series), the monthly series which start before 1919 (using bank clearings as the reference series), and the quarterly series (using gross national product in current dollars as the reference series). The time series in each category are further subdivided according to the strength of the seasonal components because different methods of filtering must be applied to series having different strengths of seasonal components. The seasonal components are classified here as "minor" when the sharpest of the six peaks corresponding to the seasonals (i.e., $\frac{1}{12}$ c/m, $\frac{1}{6}$ c/m, $\frac{1}{4}$ c/m, $\frac{1}{3}$ c/m, $\frac{5}{12}$ c/m, $\frac{1}{2}$ c/m) has a spectrum not more than 6–10 times as great as the spectra in the adjacent frequencies; the seasonals are called "strong" when this ratio of the spectrum of the peak to the adjacent spectra is between 10 and 100; and the seasonals are called "very strong" when this ratio is over 100. This classification is only a rule of thumb. The numbers for the ratios given here are merely indicative because there is no simple way to estimate this ratio accurately on account of the leakage through the spectral window.

Thus, we have the following classification:

[10] The author is informed that Michael Godfrey, Herman Karreman, and Marc Nerlove have been engaged in studies of this kind. M. D. Godfrey and H. Karreman "Spectral Analysis Evaluation of Some Seasonal Adjustment Methods," *Essays in Mathematical Economics in Honor of Oskar Morgenstern,* edited by M. Shubik (forthcoming); M. Nerlove, "Spectral Analysis of Seasonal Adjustment Procedures," Report No. 6227, Econometric Institute, Rotterdam, The Netherlands.

Group I   (A) Monthly, starting at or after 1919, or can be so treated without loss of a large portion of the data; no or minor seasonals.

    I   (B) Monthly, starting at or after 1919, or can be so treated; strong seasonals.

    I   (C) Monthly, starting at or after 1919, or can be so treated; very strong seasonals.

   II   (A) Monthly, starting before 1919; no seasonals. (None of the series in this group has strong seasonals.)

 III   (B) Quarterly; strong seasonals. (All of the quarterly indicators used here have strong seasonals.)

The data for a few of the time series used in our study were obtained directly from the National Bureau which has extensively revised them after the publication of Moore's book (early 1961), and therefore these are different from the data given in the book, even though the title of the series is left unchanged. In addition, several indices are expressed in terms of new base years.

In Table 12.1 we give a brief description of each of the cycle indicators used in our study. A more complete description can be found in Moore's book (vol. II), cited above. The data are carried only up to June 1961 at the latest. Since the more recent data are often subject to revision, we do not feel that they should be included at this time (Spring of 1962). Most of the economic time series data have "breaks," i.e., some sort of discontinuity as to coverage, definition, estimation method, etc. Our calculations are made for the data during the longest period within which no serious "breaks" appear. Table 12.1 describes the period for each series. The only series for which a "piecing together" work was done by the author is the Retail Sales.

12.6 Experiences with Filtering for Monthly and Quarterly Data

Leakage through the spectral window from the frequencies with high power to those with low power was discussed in Chapter 8. It was pointed out that some sort of filter must be used before estimation of the spectrum, in order to eliminate or reduce the power of the frequencies which could be sources of leakage. In practice, this is very troublesome. Unless we know the true spectrum we cannot design the ideal filter, and, without an appropriate filter we cannot estimate the spectrum accurately. All we can do is the following: (1) make a rough estimation of the spectrum using a reasonable filter, and then (2) improve the estimation using other filters if the first, rough estimation reveals this improvement to be necessary. Various methods of filtering have various advantages and disadvantages.[10a] It is usually advisable to combine the results of different methods, relying upon one method for a frequency where it is superior to the others and using other methods for other frequencies where desirable. Further, it is usually advisable for beginners to try several lag values for the estimation of autocovariance and spectrum; e.g., if m is the maximum lag one can use for a given length of data, try $\frac{m}{2}$ or even $\frac{m}{4}$ in order to see which results are reliable and which are not. When experience has been accumulated, one can visually smooth the cross-spectra with lags m to obtain rough estimates of the cross-spectra with lags $\frac{m}{2}$, or $\frac{m}{4}$.

We have used throughout the present study the Tukey-Hanning window rather than the Parzen window. The reason is merely that we can probably study the leakage more easily by using the Tukey-Hanning window than the Parzen window because the former gives negative estimates of spectra when the leakage is significant. It is true that the leakage through the Parzen window is less significant than the leakage through the Tukey-Hanning window. If we merely concentrate on the negative estimates, we would miss the small leakage which takes place in either the Parzen or the Tukey-Hanning window. Nevertheless the negative estimates, especially in *the raw estimate* of spectrum, are useful for the study of leakage when the true spectrum and hence the extent of leakage is not known at all. When the present study was started, the author did not have any experiences with the estimation of spectrum, especially with the problem of leakage in the special case of economic time series. (In fact, after the present study has been completed, he still thinks that the estimation of spectrum is very difficult.)

As far as filtering is concerned, much depends upon the particular problems which one wants to solve. The problem posed in the present chapter is the study of (1) the frequency bands from $\frac{1}{96}$ c/m to $\frac{1}{12}$ c/m for the cyclical components, and (2) all frequencies in order to see the nature of the lead-lag relation by way of possible over-all trends in the phase diagram. For this problem, the sources of leakage for the estimations of spectrum (of every one of the cycles indicators) have turned out to be the very low frequencies and seasonals including the harmonics of

---

[10a] T. Wonnacott developed a pair of spectral windows, one of which is positive for all the frequencies and the other of which is negative for all but its main lobe. (By the main lobe we mean the central portion of the spectral window situated between the first cut-off points above and below zero frequency.) Thomas A. Wonnacott, "Spectral Analysis Combining a Bartlett Window with an Associated Inner Window," *Technometrics*, May, 1961, pp. 235–244. The author has no experience with the Wonnacott window, but the experiments using it might very well throw further light on the problem of leakage.

Group in our study, our code number	Title of Series	Period	NBER classification, their code number	Unit	Description
I(A) 00 (reference series)	Industrial Production Index	Jan. 1919–June 1961	Coincident 15.0	1957 = 100	Covering manufacturing, mining and utilities
I(A) 01	Average Work-Week in Manufacturing	Jan. 1932–June 1961	Leading 1.0	Hours/Week	
I(A) 02	Lay-Off Rate in Manufacturing	Jan. 1930–June 1961	Leading (after inversion) 3.0	No. per 100 employees	Job termination
I(A) 03	New Orders of Durable Goods	Jan. 1939–June 1961	Leading 4.0	Current Dollars	Net new orders placed with mfrs. of durable goods
I(A) 04	Business Failures	Jan. 1939–June 1961	Leading (after inversion) 8.0	Current Dollars	Liabilities, covering only industry and commerce
I(A) 05	Dow-Jones Industrial Stock Price	Jan. 1939–June 1961	Leading 10.1	Dollars per share	
I(A) 06	Industrial Raw Materials Spot Price Index	Jan. 1919–Dec. 1957	Leading 12.1	1947–49 = 100	
I(A) 07	Wholesale Price Index	Jan. 1919–June 1961	Coincident 21.0	1957–59 = 100	Excluding farm products and foods
I(A) 08	Bank Interest Rates on Business Loans	July 1939–June 1961	Lagging, basically 26.0	%	Interpolated from quarterly data
I(B) 00 (reference series)	Industrial Production Index	Jan. 1919–June 1961	Coincident 15.0	1957 = 100	Covering manufacturing, mining, and utilities
I(B) 01	Gross Accession Rate in Manufacturing	Jan. 1930–June 1961	Leading 2.0	No. per 100 employees	Additions to employment
I(B) 02	Housing Starts	Jan. 1939–Dec. 19..	Leading 1.0	No. of Structures	

		Series	Date Range	Timing	Units	Notes
		Contracts	1956	Leading 5.1	Square ft.	of the nation
I(B)	04	Commercial and Industrial Building Contracts	Jan. 1926–Dec. 1956	Leading 6.0	Square ft.	"
I(B)	05	Employment in Non-Agriculture	Jan. 1939–June 1961	Coincident 13.0	Number of Persons	
I(B)	06	Factory Employment Index	Jan. 1919–Dec. 1958	Coincident 13.1	1947–49 = 100	
I(B)	07	Bank Debits outside New York	Jan. 1919–Dec. 1942	Coincident 18.0	Dollars	*Checks and draft drawn against bank deposits
I(B)	08	Bank Debits outside New York	Jan. 1943–June 1961	Coincident 18.0	Dollars	" (no. of reporting centers and items reported changed in 1943)
I(B)	09	Wage Cost per Output of Manufacturing	Jan. 1919–Dec. 1958	Lagging 23.1		Including only straight pay for the production workers
I(B)	10	Manufacturers' Inventory	Jan. 1939–June 1961	Lagging 24.0	Book Values	Inventory holding not its change
I(B)	11	Consumer Installment Debt	Jan. 1929–June 1961	Lagging 25.0	Dollars	
I(C) (reference series)	00	Industrial Production Index	Jan. 1919–June 1961	Coincident 15.0	1957 = 100	Covering manufacturing, mining, and utilities
I(C)	01	Freight Car Loadings	Jan. 1919–June 1961	Coincident 15.2	No. of cars per week	
I(C)	02	Department Store Sales	Jan. 1919–June 1961	Coincident 20.1	1947–49 = 100	Based on dollar value
I(C)	03	Retail Sales	Jan. 1935–June 1961	Coincident 20.0	Current Dollars	
II(A) (reference series)	00	Bank Clearings	Jan. 1875–June 1961	Coincident 18.1	Current Dollars	Checks and draft cleared in the clearing house
II(A)	01	Business Failures	Jan. 1894–Dec. 1932	Leading (after inversion)	Current Dollars	Liabilities of all business failures except for railroads and banks

(continued)

TABLE 12.1 (continued)

Group in our study, our code number	Title of Series	Period	NBER classification, their code number	Unit	Description
II(A) 02	Standard and Poor Common Stock Prices	Jan. 1871–Dec. 1956	Leading 10.0	1935–39 = 100	
III(B) 00	GNP in current prices	1st qtr. 1939–2nd qtr. 1961	Coincident 16.0	Current Dollars	
III(B) 01	Corporate Profit after Taxes	1st qtr. 1939–2nd qtr. 1961	Leading 9.0	Current Dollars	Profits net of corporate tax *liability*
III(B) 02	Change in Business Inventory	1st qtr. 1939–2nd qtr. 1961	Leading 11.0	Current Book Value	

* Bank Debits inside New York are dominated by financial transactions and are thus excluded.

$\frac{1}{12}$ c/m. This is true as long as we use the spectral window whose side-lobes die down as one moves away from its center frequency, e.g., the Tukey-Hanning or Parzen windows (but not the Tukey-Hamming window). We have tried regression, moving average, and the type of filter discussed in Section 4.6, which might be called the trend-seasonal filter. Regression and moving average are used to reduce or eliminate the power at the very low frequencies, whereas the trend-seasonal filter is used to eliminate the low frequencies, maintain the power of cyclical components, and reduce the power of the seasonals.

We now summarize our experiences with different filters and trend-elimination methods as applied to our particular problems:

(a) *Regression.* When the general contour of trend of the time series is roughly linear, regression analysis for fitting the linear trend and calculating the residuals works well. The only possible drawback in this case is that when simple, unweighted regression is used, the residuals have trend in the variance. According to an unpublished study made by T. Wonnacott on *linear* regression, the variance of the residuals on either end of the time period is about twice the variance of the residuals in the middle of the time period. This extent of trend in the variance need not concern us in the estimation of cross-spectra.[11]

---

[11] This follows from a theorem on the pseudo spectrum. M. Hatanaka and M. Suzuki, "A theory of the pseudo spectrum and its applications to nonstationary dynamic econometric models" (especially the third section), to be contributed to *Essays in Mathematical Economics in Honor of Oskar Morgenstern* edited by Martin Shubik (forthcoming).

Pseudo spectrum is defined for a finite, discrete stochastic process x_t ($t = 1, 2, \ldots, N$) as

$$p_x(\omega) \equiv \frac{1}{N} E \left| \sum_{t=1}^{N} x_t e^{-i\omega t} \right|^2$$

(E should be dropped for the definition of pseudo spectrum of deterministic process) and, apart from complications due to the spectral windows, the pseudo spectrum is the mathematical expectation of the estimates of spectrum obtained with no regard to the stationarity of the process. If d_t is deterministic and x_t is stationary, the pseudo spectrum of $d_t x_t$ is the convolution of the spectrum of x_t and the pseudospectrum of d_t.

$$p_{dx}(\omega) = \int_{\omega-\pi}^{\omega+\pi} p_d(\omega') p_x(\omega - \omega') \, d\omega'$$

A rough sketch of d_t in the particular case mentioned in the text is shown here.

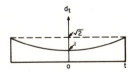

The pseudo spectrum of d_t would almost entirely concentrate in the frequencies very near zero. Thus the pseudo spectrum of $d_t x_t$ does not differ much from the spectrum of x_t, *unless the frequency unit is very narrow.*

When the time period under consideration includes the 1920's and 1930's as well as the postwar period, the general contours of trend in many economic time series are complicated, and the residuals, after fitting the linear trend, still maintain enormous power at the very low frequencies. Also, one must keep in mind that what corresponds to the very low frequencies depends upon the length of the data. Thus, in the case of Manufacturers' Inventories I(B), 10, we found that the data after the elimination of linear trend still maintain enormous power at the very low frequencies. The data cover mostly the intra and post war periods, and the strength of the National Bureau business cycle greatly outweighs the fluctuations of shorter duration during this period. For data of this length, the National Bureau business cycles are low frequencies, and they dominate the spectrum in the other frequencies after the elimination of trend. In order to study Mack's subcycles or any higher frequencies, the power of these low frequencies must somehow be reduced.

When the elimination of linear trend does not successfully reduce the power at the very low frequencies, and if the charts of these series after the elimination of linear trend reveal that the dominating low frequencies are *not* like the National Bureau business cycles (as in the case of Manufacturers' Inventories), then an obvious attempt for improvement is the successive application of regression analysis using higher orders of polynomials. As far as we know, no one has as yet worked on the extent of the trend in the variance of the residuals when a polynomial of order greater than one is fitted. Therefore, we have not used the polynomial regression method in our work.

(b) *Moving averages to reduce the power of the low frequencies.* Subtracting moving averages involves a very simple calculation and works well for the elimination of any complicated trend contour, thus successfully reducing the power at the very low frequencies for any time series. The great disadvantage of this method is that many pieces of data are lost in the process of calculating the moving average. A moving average of length m (an odd number) loses $\frac{m-1}{2}$ pieces of data at each end of the time period.

Unlike the regression method, the (simple or weighted) moving average is a black box, and its filter function can be easily estimated. In order to accomplish the desired filtering with a tolerable loss of data, we utilized this estimation of filter function extensively. Nevertheless, the difficulty in the selection of the proper moving average is great in our particular problem. This is because we would like to have the following two conditions satisfied by the filter function: (1) That the power at the very low frequencies after filtering should not be so strong as to become a source of leakage, and (2) that the power of the cyclical component after filtering should not be so weak as to be affected by leakage from the other frequencies. The difficulty arises from two facts: (1) The two conditions mentioned above are contradictory to each other unless the moving average is very long. This is because the very low frequency whose power must be eliminated or reduced by filtering is very close to the frequency of the cyclical component whose power must be maintained. With short moving averages the two conditions cannot be met simultaneously. (2) Whether or not the power of very low frequencies after filtering is going to be a source of leakage, and whether or not the power of the cyclical component is so weak as to be disturbed by leakage, depends not only upon the filtering method but also upon the concrete shape of the true spectrum of each time series. Evidently, only experiments with actual data would show whether a filtering method is good or bad.

In this kind of study, there are two kinds of moving average. One of them is intended to reduce or eliminate the power at the near-zero frequencies but to retain the *full power* at the frequency bands corresponding to the National Bureau business cycles and Mack's subcycles, or at least the latter. The other is intended to reduce or eliminate the power at the near-zero frequencies and retain *not the full power but some significant portion of the power* at the frequency bands corresponding to the National Bureau business cycle indicators and Mack's subcycles. For the former, we wish to have the filter function as in Fig. 12.4. For the latter, we wish to have the filter function as in Fig. 12.5.

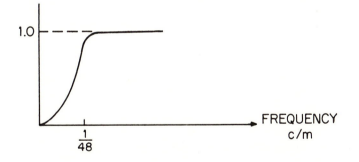

Figure 12.4

For the purpose of eliminating a possible source of leakage of power into the frequency band which we would like to study it is not necessary to eliminate *completely* the power at the source nor to retain the *full* power at the frequency which concerns us. However, it is desirable to accomplish both if it can be done easily. In fact, the filter function like Fig. 12.4 can be obtained only with the loss of a large number of data.

In order to retain the *full* power of the cyclical component, one needs a very long moving average—at least 80 months long—and thus the loss of data is enormous. Since the moving average covering an even number of data cannot be centered, and a non-centered moving average results

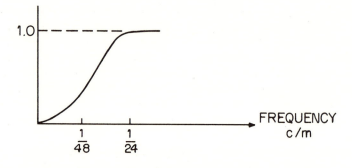

Figure 12.5

in a phase change (see Chapter 3), we might take a simple moving average of length 81 months. In fact, the filter function of an 81 month simple moving average is not exactly like Fig. 12.4, but has side-lobes which could be illustrated by Fig. 12.6. This is not a problem, however, as we

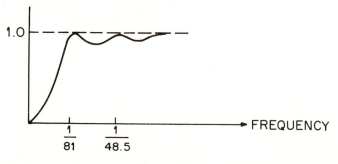

Figure 12.6

can calculate *exactly* the filter function of the 81 month simple moving average, and estimate these side-lobes exactly. If one wants to obtain an accurate estimate of the spectrum which is not distorted by side-lobes, one can calculate the recolored spectrum,

$$\frac{\text{spectrum of the data after the 81 month simple moving average}}{\text{the filter function of the 81 month simple moving average}}$$

in all frequency bands except near-zero frequencies. Further, the cross spectrum, as far as coherence and angle are concerned, is unaffected by the application of the simple moving average (which extends over an odd number of time points) to either one of the two series for which the cross-spectrum is to be calculated.

There have been many attempts in the past few years to derive more complicated filters than the simple moving averages in order to avoid the loss of data particularly in the last portion of the time period under study. At the time of this writing the author does not know the full implications of these filters.

In order to retain *not the full power* but a *significant portion* of the power of the cyclical components, we have tried a peculiar 31 month moving average with weights

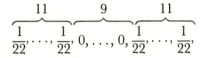

which we might call the *hollow 31 month moving average*. The filter function for the operation in which this moving average is subtracted from the original series is

$$\left(\frac{2}{22}\right)^2 (11 - \cos 5\omega - \cos 6\omega - \cdots - \cos 15\omega)^2.$$

Let us compare this with

$$\left(\frac{2}{31}\right)^2 (15 - \cos \omega - \cos 2\omega - \cdots - \cos 15\omega)^2,$$

which is the filter function for the operation in which the simple 31 month moving average is subtracted. Both of the above functions stay near zero in the very low frequencies. As far as the analysis of business cycle indicators is concerned, both filterings are effective in reducing the power of the very low frequencies to such an extent that they can never be a source of leakage. On the other hand, the first filter function misses five cosine terms which are present in the second, and, as a result, the rise of the first filter function from zero is sharper than the rise of the second. It is for this reason that we tried the hollow 31 month moving average. Yet, our attention must be directed further to the problem of whether the rise of the filter function for the subtraction of this moving average is sharp enough to retain a sufficient portion of the power of the cyclical component.

Actually, in one case, but only in one case, the frequencies about $\frac{1}{48}$ c/m and the lower frequencies are so weak after filtering that the estimates of spectra and cross-spectra are affected by leakage from the higher frequencies. This happens in the series Lay-off Rate, I(A), 02.

However, in this case, the spectrum of the raw data without trend elimination reveals that the power at the very low frequencies is not strong, and the trend-elimination was *not* necessary after all.

Except for this single case, the method worked fairly well. It is true that this drawback, which is so apparent in the case of the Lay-off Rate series, appears to a lesser extent in all the series. Thus we lose information as to the coherence and phase in the very low frequencies which are lower than the cyclical components. In judging the contours of the phase diagram, we frequently would like to have information as to these very low frequencies which are not exactly equal to but very near zero, even though the phase at zero frequency has no meaning. This information must come from the spectral estimate with the use of either a very long moving average or weighted regression.

The great advantage of the hollow 31 month moving average is the fact that it loses only 30 pieces of data, 15 at the beginning and 15 at the end of the period. If the dominating low frequencies are like cycles and cannot be fitted by a small order polynomial function of time, and if the data are not long enough for the application of a very long simple moving average, this method would probably be the only one available for reducing the power at the low frequencies. Needless to say, if one wants the estimate of the spectrum before filtering, one can recolor the estimate after filtering.

(c) *Trend-Seasonal Filter.* The trend-seasonal filter discussed in Section 4.6 was designed by the author to do three things simultaneously: (1) almost completely eliminate the very low frequencies which are lower than the cyclical components, (2) retain some significant portion of the power of the cyclical components, and (3) reduce the power of the seasonals. In many business cycle indicators the seasonal components are very strong. Frequently, the power at a harmonic of the seasonals is 100 times the power at the adjacent frequencies. In order to see the overall trend in the phase diagram, we must study the cross-spectrum for the frequencies located between two harmonic frequencies of the seasonals, which requires a reduction in the power of the seasonals. The trend-seasonal filter has a filter function

(12.1) for monthly data:

$$(6 + A - \cos \omega - \cos 2\omega - \cdots - \cos 6\omega - A \cos 12\omega)^2$$

(12.2) for quarterly data:

$$(B + C - B \cos \omega - C \cos 4\omega)^2;$$

the former is plotted in Fig. 12.7. The corresponding moving average in the case of monthly data involves the loss of 24 pieces of data, 12 at each end of the period.

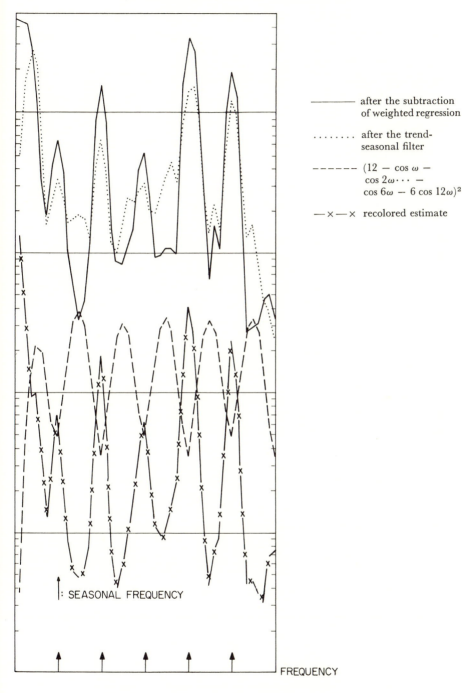

———— after the subtraction
       of weighted regression

· · · · · · · · after the trend-
       seasonal filter

– – – – – – $(12 - \cos \omega -$
       $\cos 2\omega \cdots -$
       $\cos 6\omega - 6 \cos 12\omega)^2$

—×—× recolored estimate

↑ : SEASONAL FREQUENCY

FREQUENCY

Figure 12.7.   Spectrum of Bank Debits outside New York

The major drawback of this filter is that when one wants to make a minute study of the spectrum and cross-spectrum using a narrow frequency unit, the dip in the filter function at the frequencies for the seasonals is too blunt compared with the sharpness of the peak of the spectrum at the seasonal frequencies. This results in leakage from the seasonal frequencies into the *directly adjacent* frequencies. When the lag used in the estimation of the spectrum is 48 or less, this does not seem to be serious. Since we would frequently like to use a lag of 120, this becomes a serious drawback. An obvious remedy is to take the fourth power (instead of the second power) in the above filter function so that the filter function will have a sharper dip at the seasonal frequencies. This could be achieved by using the same filter twice, but, the corresponding moving average in the case of monthly data involves the loss of 48 pieces of data rather than 24.

Another drawback of the trend-seasonal filter is that the filter reduces to an equal extent the power at *all six* harmonic frequencies of the seasonals, whereas the distribution of the power among the six harmonic frequencies is not usually even. However, this has never appeared to be a serious drawback. There is a great deal of freedom in the extent to which the power of the seasonals should be reduced. The purpose of this reduction is to reduce the leakage. One would be usually satisfied if, after filtering, the peaks of the spectrum at the seasonals were at most 10 times, and at least one-tenth, of the power at the frequencies between two harmonics of the seasonals.

Still another disadvantage of the trend-seasonal filter is the loss of information for the frequency bands not exactly equal to but very near the zero frequency. This loss, using the trend-seasonal filter, is less severe than the loss using the hollow 31 month moving average, but we must supply this information from the estimate using either regression or long moving averages.

So much for the explanation of the different filters that we tried. Since we have gone through a process of trial and error, our actual procedures were rather disorganized. We will indicate here what would have been done if the author had begun with the experience obtained only through trial and error. This procedure is *not* meant to be applicable to *any* economic problems, but only for the problems posed in the present chapter. (Furthermore, computer time was free to the author, and if it had not been, he would have chosen different procedures.)

The procedure is as follows: (1) Calculate the spectra of raw data without any filtering. From this calculation we can select those series for which trend removal is not necessary. (One might say that this selection can be made by visual inspection of the time series charts. In the author's experience, although the necessity of trend removal is obvious from the chart in many time series, there are a sufficient number of cases where this judgment is very difficult to make.) If one is dubious about the selection of the time series for which trend removal seems unnecessary, one should remove the trend. The rule of thumb that the author uses is to see whether or not the estimated spectrum at zero frequency is greater than 10 times the estimated spectrum at the frequencies corresponding to the cyclical components. Incidentally, it is frequently not possible to select those series for which the reduction of power of the seasonals is necessary. This is because the leakage from the very low frequencies partly or wholly submerges the peaks at the seasonals. (2) Calculate the spectra and cross-spectra of the time series after removing the trend by using linear regression or the hollow 31 month moving average and a long simple moving average. The moving average should be used only when linear regression fails to reduce the power at the very low frequencies success-fully. The reason why both the 31 month moving average and a very long simple moving average are used is that the former tends to lose information in the very low frequencies. After this calculation, we can see whether or not the power of the seasonals should be reduced by estimating the ratio of the spectrum at the highest peak to the spectra at the adjacent frequencies. From these procedures we obtained the classification of the business cycle indicators according to the strength of the seasonals, as given in the previous section (12.5). This classification should not be taken as a fixed one because of the following two reasons: (a) there is a great deal of freedom in the extent to which the power of the seasonals should be reduced; (b) the ratio mentioned above may *not* reveal the ratio between the peak of the *true* spectrum and the *true* power at the adjacent frequencies. (3) For those series for which reduction of the power of the seasonals *appears* to be desirable, apply the trend-seasonal filter to the original data, using, in the case of the monthly series (see the filter function numbered as (12.1) previously),

$$A = 6 \text{ for Group I(B)}$$

$$A = 18 \text{ or more for Group I(C)}$$

(In the case of the series for Department Store Sales, I(C), 02, we had to use $A = 100$.) In the case of quarterly data (see the filter function numbered as (12.2) previously) use,

$$\begin{matrix} B = 3 \\ C = 3 \end{matrix} \text{ for Group III(B)}$$

In the particular case of our study, the industrial production index, used as our reference time series, has a minor seasonal, and as I(B), 00, and I(C), 00 the filter function used is

$$(8 - \cos \omega - \cdots - \cos 6\omega - 2 \cos 12\omega)^2.$$

However, for this same series as I(A), 00 the filter function used is

$$(15 - \cos 5\omega - \cos 6\omega - \cdots - \cos 11\omega - 5\cos 12\omega$$

$$- \cos 13\omega - \cos 14\omega$$

$$- \cos 15\omega)^2,$$

which is a sort of combination of the hollow 31 month moving average and the trend-seasonal filter. (This is done in order to facilitate the processing of data cards since the loss of data caused by the use of this filter is the same as that caused by the hollow moving average which is to be applied to the series in the Class I(A).)

In interpreting the results of spectra and cross-spectra, we use the estimates of the spectra and cross-spectra obtained by the trend-seasonal filter (in case the seasonals appear to be strong) or by the 31 month moving average (in case the seasonals do not appear to be strong) for all frequency bands except for the very low frequencies, and we use the estimates obtained by regression or by the very long simple moving average (say 81 months) for the very low frequencies.

Figure 12.7 is an illustration of some of the procedures described above. The data used are bank debits outside New York, I(B), 08. Since there is a break in the data in 1942, the period used is 1943–1961. The data are too short for the application of a very long simple moving average. Using semi-logarithmic paper, Fig. 12.7 shows (1) the estimate of the spectrum after the linear trend is removed by weighted regression, (2) the estimate of the spectrum after the trend-seasonal filter with $A = 6$ is applied, (3) the filter function of this filter, and (4) the recolored estimate of the spectrum. In order to put all four curves in a single diagram, different scales are used for different curves, but this should not be confusing because one can add or subtract visually the different curves on the semi-logarithmic paper.

Figure 12.8 shows two different estimates of the cross-spectrum between bank debits outside New York, I(B), 08, and the Federal Reserve Board Index of Industrial Production, I(B), 00. One estimate uses bank debits after subtraction of the weighted linear regression, and the other, bank debits after filtering with the trend-seasonal filter. (Between two estimates of the cross-spectrum the same filtering is used for the industrial production index.) The comparison between the two estimates shows that the coherence obtained with the use of the linear regression is lower than the coherence obtained with the use of the trend-seasonal filter in the frequencies located between two harmonics of the seasonal frequencies. This probably indicates that the trend-seasonal filter reduced the extent of leakage out of these seasonal frequencies. Probably the leakage is not too significant even with the use of linear regression because the two estimates of the phase of the

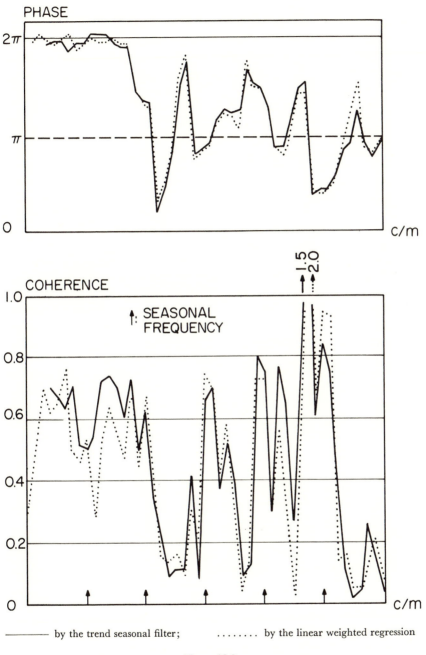

by the trend seasonal filter; .... by the linear weighted regression

Figure 12.8
Cross-spectrum between x = bank debits outside New York
and y = index of industrial production
1943–1961

cross-spectrum coincide so well. Further, in the frequencies between $\frac{32}{96}$ and $\frac{40}{96}$ c/m the leakage still takes place even when the trend-seasonal filter is used, because the estimate of coherence is greater than 1 at $\frac{36}{96}$ c/m. We should have taken a greater value for A than 6. This shows the difficulty of filtering.

12.7 Strength of Cyclical Components; a Digression

The present chapter is primarily about the application of cross-spectral analysis and complex demodulation to business cycle indicators. In the present section, however, we digress from the main outline of the chapter in order to discuss the spectra of business cycle indicators.

The power spectrum shows the decomposition of the total variance of the time series in terms of various frequencies. An important problem is concerned with the variance of cyclical components as a representation of their strength relative to the other components. As judged from the power spectra of the business cycle indicators, the frequencies lower than those for the cyclical components are far more powerful than those for the cyclical components, but the frequencies higher than those for the cyclical components are less powerful than the cyclical components.

Another interesting problem is whether or not the frequencies corresponding to the cyclical components form a well-defined region in the spectrum characterized by the peaks (see Fig. 12.9 and Fig. 12.10).

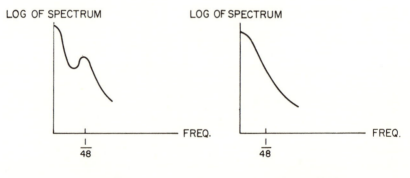

Figure 12.9   Figure 12.10

If there is a gap in the spectrum between the frequencies for the cyclical component and the lower frequencies, as illustrated in Fig. 12.9, then the cyclical component can be considered meaningful on this basis. If there is no such gap, as in Fig. 12.10, the cyclical component is not meaningful on the basis of power spectrum alone. (Of course, there is a possibility that it can be well defined on the basis of the cross-spectrum.)

We have commented earlier (see Section 4.3) on the difficulty of dealing with low frequencies. We have also explained that low frequency depends upon the length of the data. For most of the business cycle indicators which we have studied, the data are not long enough for studying the possible gap between zero frequency and the frequencies corresponding to the cyclical components. General indications are that the decline of the spectrum starting from zero frequency stops just about at the frequencies corresponding to the cyclical components, and the decline is resumed beyond the frequencies corresponding to the cyclical components. In the case of some cycle indicators, the spectra even show a very small hump about the frequencies of the cyclical components, as illustrated in Fig. 12.11. Further, the raw estimate of the spectrum (using

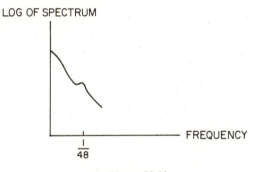

LOG OF SPECTRUM

FREQUENCY

$\frac{1}{48}$

Figure 12.11

the Tukey-Hanning window) does reveal a fairly sharp peak about the frequencies corresponding to the cyclical components.[11a]

In the case of two cycle indicators, the Standard and Poor Common Stock Price Index and bank clearings, the available data covering the period from the 1870's to the 1950's are long enough to study the possible gap in the spectrum. We have estimated the spectra of *logarithms* of these series. In such a minute study of spectra as the present one, the trend in the variance makes a significant difference in the spectra. The trend in the variance in these time series expressed in logarithms is much less visible than the trend in the variance in the original time series, and, therefore, the spectra of the logarithmic series indicate the peaks more clearly, if there are any, than do the spectra of raw data.[12] We can now summarize the results of our estimation. The spectra of both

[11a] In the case of the spectrum of Federal Reserve production index shown in Fig. 12.2 the significance of the small hump at $\frac{1}{48}$ c/m is strengthened by the peaks about $\frac{1}{24}$ c/m and $\frac{1}{16}$ c/m.

[12] See footnote 11 of this chapter and Section III of M. Hatanaka and M. Suzuki, *op. cit.*

stock prices and bank clearings over the entire period for which data are available indicate a fairly significant peak about $\frac{11}{480} - \frac{12}{480}$ c/m (minor cycle) (using 240 lags in the Tukey-Hanning window). Further, a brief stop in the decline of the spectrum appears at about $\frac{4}{480}$ c/m (major cycle), and the raw spectrum of bank clearings has a sharp peak about this frequency.[13] Some economists in the 1920's and the 1930's argued that the business cycle ceased to exist after World War I. We have split the available data into two portions: one before June, 1914, and the other after 1919. Consequently, the data are too short to make any comments about $\frac{4}{480}$ c/m. We can, however, make some comments about $\frac{11}{480} - \frac{12}{480}$ c/m. The spectrum for each of the two series, for each portion of the period, shows a small jump about $\frac{7}{320} - \frac{8}{320}$ c/m (using 160 lags). It might be noted, however, that this hump for bank clearings after 1919 is so insignificant that it could be described as a "brief stop in the decline of the spectrum." In short, we can say that the significance of approximately 40 months is greatly reduced after 1919 in the case of bank clearings. As for the stock prices, the significance of the peaks about $\frac{7}{320} - \frac{8}{320}$ c/m before and after World War I are just about equal. But in all cases the peaks are so insignificant that the spectra of raw data rather than of logarithms do not indicate any peaks.

In short, the cyclical component, whether in the form of National Bureau business cycles, minor cycles, or major cycles, is not significant on the spectrum alone.

12.8 Examples of Cross-spectra and their Interpretations

We now show four examples of cross-spectra in terms of coherence and phase. The first is the cross-spectrum between factory employment index, I(B), 06, and industrial production index, I(B), 00. Both series cover mostly manufacturing. In fact, the relation between output and employment is dictated by technological conditions, apart from the aggregation bias inherent in both of the two series. Therefore, we should expect a very high coherence in all frequency bands. Figure 12.12 indicates that this is generally so. It is true that the coherence is low in

---

[13] An unpublished study by M. Suzuki and M. Hatanaka on the rate of growth of national income indicates a little more clearly the significance of major cycles (about 10 years) and minor cycles (about 4 years).

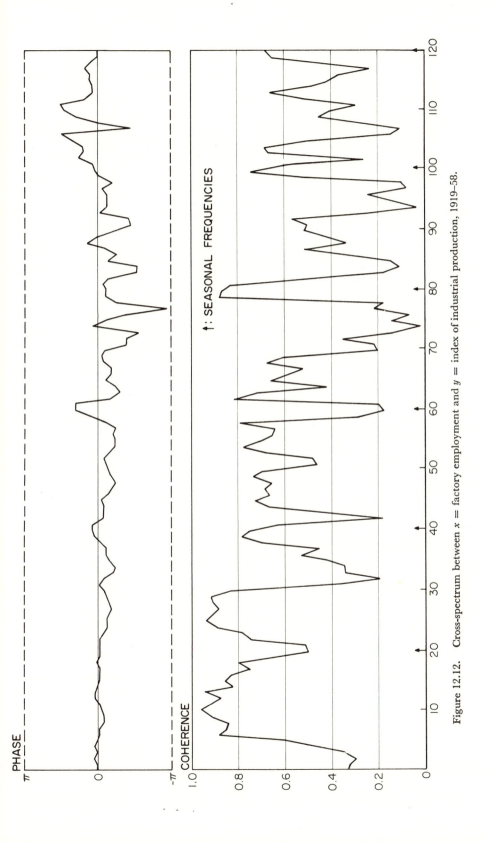

Figure 12.12. Cross-spectrum between x = factory employment and y = index of industrial production, 1919–58.

certain frequency bands, but there are not many cross-spectra which have coherence as high as this in most of the frequencies. Concerning the phase, one should expect a slight lag of the production index behind employment, by possibly a few months. This is not borne out in the phase diagram. If there is any trend in the phase diagram, it is a downward trend between 0 and $\frac{5}{12}$ c/m. This means that employment is lagging behind production, which is the opposite of what we would expect. The slope of this downward trend is very small and indicates a lag of about one-half month. This is one of many cases where the resulting cross-spectrum does not correspond with expectations before this calculation. However, we can resolve this dilemma at least partially. It is well known that a substantial portion of the estimate of output in the Federal Reserve Board production index is estimated indirectly using man-hours data of labor input, and this may explain why we do not observe employment leading production. However, this does not explain the lead of employment over production which we obtained in the cross-spectrum. A possible explanation is that the factory employment index is computed from the *number* of workers rather than from man-hours. It is generally true that management prefers adjustment of the work-week to adjustment of the labor force whenever and wherever the former is possible. The lag in the adjustment of the number of workers in the face of the change in the labor input in terms of man-hours might explain the seemingly strange result in the cross-spectrum.[14]

Next, we show a cross-spectrum involving two of the National Bureau's leading indicators. Figure 12.13 indicates the cross-spectrum between the lay-off rate, I(A), 02, and the industrial production index, I(A), 00. (The data for the lay-off rate are revised data supplied by the National Bureau.) In treating this series as a leading indicator, the National Bureau inverts the lay-off rate series (i.e., treats the peaks as troughs and the troughs as peaks), because lay-offs increase as production declines and vice versa. It is interesting to see how this procedure is related to our cross-spectrum. The phase diagram reveals fairly clearly that the nature of the lead-lag is roughly a fixed-time lead or lag in the frequency bands between 0 and $\frac{1}{12}$ c/m. Even though the phase at zero frequency means nothing, the general trend of the phase diagram in this frequency band clearly suggests that the phase at the frequency very near zero is about π. Therefore, a natural way to think about the lead-lag relation in our cross-spectrum is (1) to make up an artificial series

---

[14] This problem and some others that arise in the following examples of cross-spectra presented in this section are all concerned with the labor market, and a fuller treatment of these problems is presented in M. Hatanaka, "A spectral analysis of business cycle indicators; lead-lag in terms of all time points," a Research Memorandum of the Econometric Research Program, Princeton University.

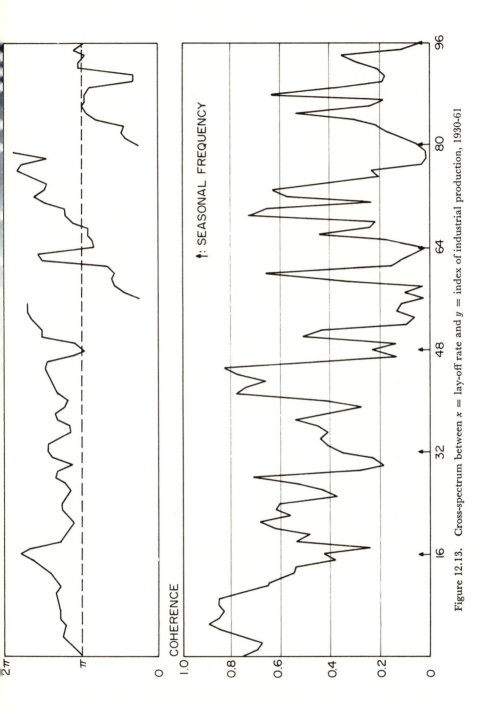

Figure 12.13. Cross-spectrum between x = lay-off rate and y = index of industrial production, 1930-61.

from the lay-off rate by shifting each frequency of the latter by 180°
and then (2) to study the lead-lag relation between this artificial series
and the industrial production index. Let us call this artificial series the
inverted series. Then, the phase diagram of Fig. 12.13 indicates that the
inverted lay-off rate leads the production index by about 3–4 months
(a sort of fixed time lead model) in the frequency band between 0 and
$\frac{1}{12}$ c/m. The coherence is also very high in the same frequency band.
In other words, the (inverted) lay-off rate is a very good leading indicator
of the cyclical component. (It is true that the degree of freedom in Fig.
12.13 is small. However, when the estimate of coherence is high *over
all the contiguous frequencies* within a range such as $\frac{3}{192} - \frac{11}{192}$ c/m in
Fig. 12.13, this high coherence is maintained even when the lags are
reduced and the degree of freedom is raised. This is because the estimate
of cross-spectrum with less lags is obtained by smoothing the estimate of
cross-spectrum with more lags.)

When we turn to the frequency band between $\frac{1}{12}$ c/m and $\frac{1}{4}$ c/m,
we see a very flat phase diagram (apart from the oscillations possibly due
to sampling fluctuations), i.e., fixed angle lead. The inverted lay-off
rate leads the industrial production index by about 45°, i.e., one-eighth
of the cycle. Considering the frequency band beyond $\frac{1}{4}$ c/m, we do not
see any well-defined pattern in the phase diagram, and further, the
coherence becomes small. Thus, the entire cross-spectrum is a mixture
of fixed time lag, fixed angle lag, and no relationship.

The lead of the inverted lay-off rate must be related to the lead of
$x_t - x_{t-1}$ over x_t in general. In our particular case, if we ignore the
quits and discharges, gross accession rate minus lay-off rate is equal to the
changes in employment. This investigation will be made elsewhere.[15]

At the time of this writing, the ability of the stock price indices
to predict movements in the general economy is being questioned. Figure
12.14 shows the cross-spectrum between the Dow-Jones industrial stock
prices, I(A), 05, and the industrial production index, I(A), 00. Since the
estimate of coherence and phase *with lags 120* (after application of
hollow 31 month moving average to the stock prices) reveal quite
irregular oscillations, we also show in Fig. 12.14 the estimate of coherence
and phase *with lags 60*. One can see that the high coherence observed
at *scattered* points of frequency when lags 120 are used really represents
sampling fluctuations because, when the lag are reduced and the degree

---

[15] See M. Hatanaka, "A spectral analysis of business cycle indicators: lead-lag in
terms of all time points," *op. cit.*

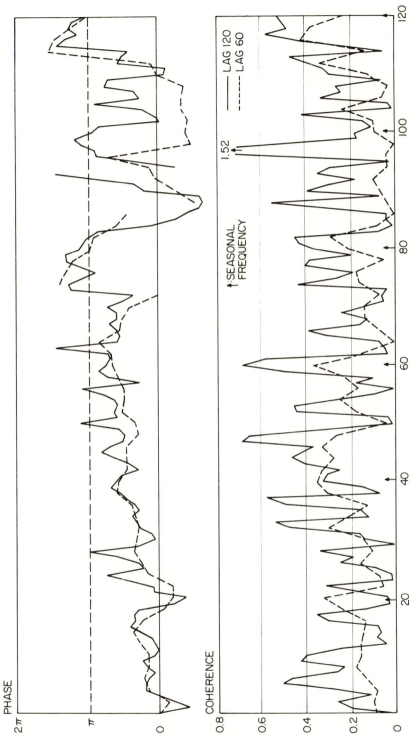

Figure 12.14. Cross-spectrum between x = Dow Jones Stock Prices and y = index of industrial production, 1919–61

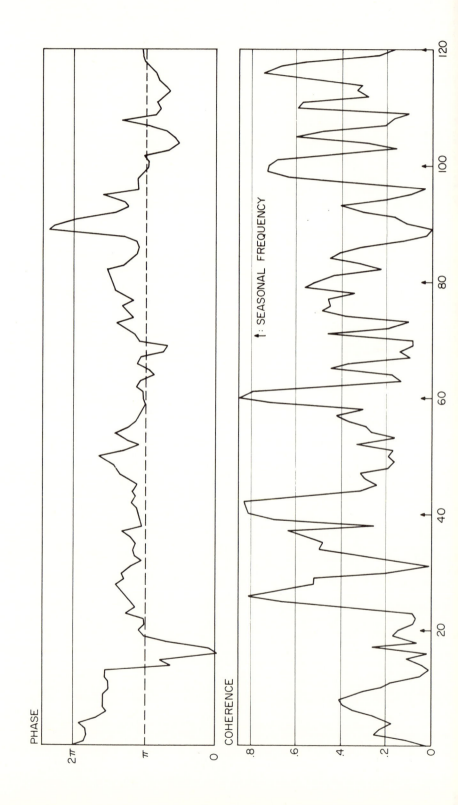

of freedom is increased, the high coherence totally disappears. Thus, the Dow-Jones industrial stock price series cannot be a good indicator. The phase diagram indicates some evidence that this series leads production, but the magnitude of the lead is only about one month.

Finally, we turn to a lagging indicator. Figure 12.15 indicates the cross-spectrum between wage cost per unit of output in manufacturing, I(B), 09, and the industrial production index, I(B), 00. The National Bureau treats the series, wage cost per unit of output, as a lagging indicator. A study by Hultgren[16] indicates that the behavior of this series is based upon a precarious balancing of the wage rate and the efficiency of labor input, and, further, that the finding using the National Bureau method is seriously affected by the trend factor within the time period equal to one business cycle. Looking at Fig. 12.15, we see in the frequency band corresponding to the cyclical component that the coherence is low and the phase diagram does not reveal any clear-cut simple pattern. Between $\frac{1}{40}$ c/m and $\frac{1}{24}$ c/m we see a fixed angle lag of about $80°$, whereas between 0 and $\frac{1}{24}$ c/m we see a sort of fixed time lag of about six months. We must admit, however, that as to the latter fitting a straight line is not good, and hence the first interpretation would be more reasonable. In the frequency band beyond $\frac{1}{24}$ c/m, the coherence is high mostly at the seasonal frequencies. The angle is fairly steady in this band. It would be interpreted as a fixed angle lag of about $160°$. Another way to look at the phase diagram in the frequencies beyond $\frac{1}{24}$ c/m is that the inverted wage cost per output series is leading production by about $20°$. Thus, this cross-spectrum again reveals a very complicated type of lead-lag relationship. In terms of the cyclical component, wage cost per unit of output is a poor lagging indicator. In the higher frequencies, the series, when inverted, is a somewhat better leading indicator. Presumably in these frequencies, the wage cost per unit of output is mostly dominated by man-hours per unit of output (i.e., the inverse of the efficiency of labor input), and, the latter is inversely related to the output. Why this relationship is fixed angle lead is not known.

12.9 Conclusions from the Cross-spectra

The result of the estimation of the cross-spectra are summarized in Table 12.2.

[16] Thor Hultgren, *Changes in Labor Cost during Cycles in Production and Business*, Occasional Paper 74, National Bureau of Economic Research. Edwin Kuh has also made a similar study. Edwin Kuh, "Profits, profit markups, and productivity," Study Paper 15 for *Employment Growth and Price Levels*, Joint Economic Committee, 86th Congress.

Let us first compare our results as to the frequency bands of cyclical components and the results of the National Bureau. (The National Bureau estimates in Table 12.2 are for the period described in Table 12.1.) The National Bureau measures leads and lags in terms of peaks and troughs, whereas our cross-spectral analysis measures leads or lags using all time points in regard to the particular frequency band corresponding to the cyclical component.

Table 12.2 indicates that in most cases the direction of lead-lag in our result is the same as classification of indicators among leading, coincident, and lagging by the National Bureau. There are three exceptions, however. One is the industrial raw materials spot price index, I(A), 06, which is treated as a leading indicator by the National Bureau, whereas in our results the phase is zero on the average over the frequency band of the cyclical component; i.e., coincident. However, the phase diagram is very complicated, and it might be worth while to describe its details in regard to the frequency band under consideration. At about $\frac{1}{48}$ c/m. i.e., the average business cycle duration, the industrial materials spot price series is *leading* the reference series by about 35°, i.e., 48 months $\times \frac{35}{360} = 5$ months. At about $\frac{1}{24}$ c/m, where the coherence is higher than in the previous frequency, the series is *lagging* by about 50°, i.e., 24 months $\times \frac{30}{360} = 3$ months.

Another discrepancy is retail sales, I(C), 03. This series is treated as a coincident indicator by the National Bureau, although the author understands that many people have questioned the performance of this series as a coincident indicator. According to our cross-spectral analysis, this series is leading in all frequencies corresponding to the cyclical components, including both $\frac{1}{48}$ c/m and $\frac{1}{24}$ c/m. Yet another discrepancy is department store sales, I(C), 02, which is treated as a coincident indicator by the National Bureau. According to the cross-spectral analysis, the series is roughly coincident about $\frac{1}{48}$ c/m and leading about $\frac{1}{24}$ c/m.

However, these discrepancies are of minor importance, and what is to be emphasized is that the *direction* of lead-lag in our results corresponds well to the National Bureau results. It also must be emphasized that *about half of cycle indicators have very low coherence* in the frequency band corresponding to the cyclical components. Among the series considered leading indicators by the National Bureau, only the lay-off rate, I(A), 02, housing starts I(B), 02, residential building contracts, I(B), 03, and corporate profit after tax, III(B), 02, have any reasonably larger values of coherence. Many of the coincident indicators do have high coherence, but we cannot find any lagging indicators having high coherence. The best is probably manufacturers' inventory, I(B), 10.

As to the magnitude of the lead-lag, one would not possibly expect to get the same results from using the National Bureau method and the cross-spectrum because of their conceptual difference as to lead-lag. Table 12.2 indicates that this is indeed so. It seems, however, that the magnitude of leads as obtained from the cross-spectral analysis tends to be less than the lead obtained by the National Bureau method, and that the magnitude of lag as obtained from the cross-spectral analysis tends to be greater than the lag obtained from the National Bureau method. One possible reason for this is that the National Bureau works entirely with peaks and troughs. The basic reference series can be put in their framework as an artificial series which is drawn in Fig. 12.1 as a zigzag line. The cross-spectrum between our reference series (industrial production index) and their reference series is shown in Fig. 12.3. We find that the two are perfectly coincident in regard to the frequency interval about $\frac{1}{24}$ c/m, but the National Bureau reference series lags behind ours by 3 months in the frequency band about $\frac{1}{48}$ c/m, and furthermore, in the frequency bands between these two, their reference series lags behind ours by as much as 3.5 months. (However, in the frequency bands lower than $\frac{1}{48}$ c/m, the two reference series are perfectly coincident.) This can explain discrepancies between their and our results in regard to the magnitude of lead-lag. Of course, it does *not* explain the discrepancy in any specific cycle indicator.[16a]

We have raised the question as to the characteristics of lead-lag in terms of the over-all trend in the phase diagram. The attempt to indicate the pattern of the phase diagram is generally unsuccessful. For many cycle indicators the coherence is low, and therefore the phase diagram does not show any clear trend. For many other indicators, the coherence is significant only in terms of the harmonics of the seasonal components, and the phase diagram does not reveal systematic patterns. There are some indicators, however, for which the phase diagram reveals a consistent pattern (some of which were discussed in the previous section). Some show a fixed time lead or lag while others show fixed angle (lead or lag). Since the sample is so small, we cannot say which is more common.

[16a] Since the above was written, G. H. Moore suggested that we compare the magnitudes of lead-lag between the cycle indicators and our reference series (rather than the NBER reference dates) as obtained by the National Bureau method and by the cross-spectral analysis. This comparison is certainly more meaningful than the one in the above text. Since the author was not able to estimate the lead-lag by the National Bureau method, Moore kindly supplied the results of this estimation. The estimates by the cross-spectral analysis and the National Bureau method were very close. See M. Hatanaka, "A Spectral Analysis of Business Cycle Indicators," *op. cit.*

TABLE 12.2

Code number	Series title abbreviated	Used filter	For the cyclical component $\frac{1}{96}$ c/m − $\frac{1}{12}$ c/m			All other frequency bands			NBER classification & estimate of lead-lag (median of −lead+lag) for both reference peak & trough dates
			Frequency band where coherence fairly high	Average coherence in that band	Phase	Frequency band where coherence fairly high	Average coherence in that band	Phase	
I(A),	01 Average Work Week	Hollow 31 mos. mov. aver. *and* none	$0 - \left(\frac{1}{16}+\varepsilon\right)$ c/m*	0.55	Fixed time *lead* 1 mo.	(a) $\frac{1}{12} - \frac{1}{24}$ c/m	0.45	Fixed angle lead appr. 30°	− 5 mos.
						(b) $\frac{1}{3.3} - \frac{1}{2.8}$ c/m	0.55	Complicated, some lag	Leading
I(A),	02 Lay-off Rate	None	$0 - \left(\frac{1}{24}+\varepsilon\right)$ c/m	0.85	Fixed time lead 3 mos. after inversion	(a) $\frac{1}{12} - \frac{1}{6.7}$ c/m	0.7	Inverted series with fixed angle lead 45°	− 7 mos.
			$\left(\frac{1}{24}-\varepsilon\right) - \left(\frac{1}{13}+\varepsilon\right)$ c/m	0.50		(b) $\frac{1}{5.5} - \frac{1}{4.3}$ c/m	0.7	,, ,,	Leading (after inversion)
I(A),	03 New Orders	Linear regression	$0 - \left(\frac{1}{24}+\varepsilon\right)$ c/m	0.55	Complicated angle *lead*, about 25°; e.g., 48 mos. × $\frac{25}{360}$ = 3 mos.	(a) about $\frac{1}{3}$ c/m	0.7	Complicated angle lag, appr. 90°	− 5.5 mos.
						(b) about $\frac{5}{12}$ c/m	0.7	,, ,,	Leading

Series	Filtering	Main frequency band (c/m)	Phase in band	Secondary coherence bands	Coherence	Phase	Time lead	Conclusion
Failures	regression and hollow 31 mos. aver.	$\left[\ldots \left(\tfrac{1}{48}\right) \ldots \left(\tfrac{1}{24}\right) \right]$ c/m**	inverted series *lead* by about 40° in this frequency band; e.g., 48 mos. × 40/360 = 10 mos.					Leading
I(A), 05 D.-J. Stock prices since 1919	81 mos. and hollow 31 mos. mov. aver.	$\left[\left(\tfrac{1}{48} - \varepsilon\right) - \left(\tfrac{1}{24} + \varepsilon\right)\ 0.40\right]$ c/m	Angle *lead* appr. 25° in this frequency band, e.g., 48 mos. × 25/360 = 4 mos.	None		Fixed time lead: 1 mo.	−4 mos.	Leading
I(A), 06 Raw Materials Price	81 mos. and hollow 31 mos. mov. average	$\left[\left(\tfrac{1}{48} - \varepsilon\right) - \left(\tfrac{2}{24} + \varepsilon\right)\ 0.55\right]$ c/m	Complicated; aver. angle in this freq. band is *zero*	None		Messy	−1.5 mos.	Leading
I(A), 07 Wholesale Prices	81 mos. and hollow 31 mos. mov. average	$\left[\left(\tfrac{1}{60} - \varepsilon\right) - \left(\tfrac{1}{30} + \varepsilon\right)\ 0.3\right]$ c/m	Complicated; aver. angle in this freq. band is *zero*	None		Messy	+1 mo.	Coincident
I(A), 08 Bank Interest	81 mos. and hollow 31 mos. mov. average	$\left[0 - \left(\tfrac{1}{36} - \varepsilon\right)\ 0.45\right]$ c/m	Fixed time *lag* 7 mos.	None		Messy	+5 mos.	Lagging
I(B), 01 Gross Accession Rate	None and trend seasonal	$\left[\left(\tfrac{1}{96} - \varepsilon\right) - \left(\tfrac{1}{24} + \varepsilon\right)\ 0.35\right]$ c/m	Complicated; aver. angle *lead* in this freq. band is appr. 70°, e.g., 48 mos. × 70/360 = 9 mos.	(a) $\tfrac{1}{10} - \tfrac{1}{8}$ c/m	0.7	Fixed angle lead appr. 60°	−6 mos.	Leading
				(b) $\tfrac{1}{6} - \tfrac{1}{5}$ c/m	0.65	,, ,,		
				(c) about $\tfrac{1}{4}$ c/m	0.5	Slight lead		
				(d) about $\tfrac{5}{12}$ c/m	0.6	About zero		

(continued)

⟨ 249 ⟩

TABLE 12.2 (continued)

Code number	Series title abbreviated	Used filter	For the cyclical component $\frac{1}{96}$ c/m − $\frac{1}{12}$ c/m			All other frequency bands			NBER classification & estimate of lead-lag (median of −lead+lag) for both reference peak & trough dates
			Frequency band where coherence fairly high	Average coherence in that band	Phase	Frequency band where coherence fairly high	Average coherence in that band	Phase	
I(B),	02 Housing Starts	None and trend seasonal	$\left(\frac{1}{72}-\varepsilon\right)-\left(\frac{1}{36}+\varepsilon\right)$ c/m $\left[\left(\frac{1}{30}-\varepsilon\right)-\left(\frac{1}{12}+\varepsilon\right)\right]$ c/m	0.7 0.45	Complicated; aver. angle *lead* in this band is 85°; e.g., 24 mos. × 85/360 = 6 mos.	(a) about $\frac{1}{6}$ c/m (b) about $\frac{5}{12}$ c/m	0.8 0.8	Angle lag 20° Angle lead 40°	−10.5 mos. Leading
I(B),	03 Residential Building Contracts	Linear regression and trend seasonal	$\left(\frac{1}{48}-\varepsilon\right)-\left(\frac{1}{19}+\varepsilon\right)$ c/m	0.7	Complicated; aver. angle *lead* is 90°; 48 mos. × 90/360 = 12 mos.	(a) about $\frac{1}{6}$ c/m (b) about $\frac{1}{4}$ c/m (c) about $\frac{5}{12}$ c/m	0.9 0.65 0.8	Angle lag 25° 180° Angle lead appr. 120°	−7.5 mos. Leading
I(B),	04 Com'l and Industrial Building Contracts	Linear regression and trend seasonal	$\left[\left(\frac{1}{86}-\varepsilon\right)-\left(\frac{1}{32}-\varepsilon\right)\right]$ c/m	0.3	Fixed time *lead* appr. 30 mos.(?)	None		Messy	−3.5 mos. Leading

Series	Method	Band	Coherence	Angle (zero degrees)	Lag
Non-Agriculture	and trend seasonal	(b) about $\frac{1}{3}$ c/m	0.85	Coincident	
		(c) about $\frac{5}{12}$ c/m	0.8	Coincident	
I(B), 06 Factory Employment	Linear regression and trend seasonal	$\left(\frac{1}{80} - \varepsilon\right) - \left(\frac{1}{13} + \varepsilon\right)$ c/m	0.85	Angle is zero	
		(a) $\frac{1}{10} - \frac{1}{8}$ c/m	0.85	Fixed time lag 0.5 mos.	0 mos.
		(b) $\frac{1}{5.4} - \frac{1}{4.1}$ c/m	0.65		
		(c) about $\frac{1}{3}$ c/m	0.85	Coincident	
		(d) about $\frac{5}{12}$ c/m	0.7		
I(B), 07 Bank Debits outside New York before 1943	Linear regression and trend seasonal	$0 - \left(\frac{1}{18} + \varepsilon\right)$ c/m	0.75	Angle is zero	
		About $\frac{1}{6}$ c/m	0.9	Complicated; aver. angle lag is 90°	0 mos.
		Other		Messy	Coincident
I(B), 08 Bank Debits outside New York after 1943	Linear regression and trend seasonal	$0 - \left(\frac{1}{18} + \varepsilon\right)$ c/m	0.65	Angle is zero	
		$\frac{1}{12} - \frac{1}{6}$ c/m	0.65	Angle zero	−2 mos.
		Other		Messy	Coincident
I(B), 09 Wage Cost per Unit of Output	81 mos. and trend seasonal	$\left[\left(\frac{1}{40} - \varepsilon\right) - \left(\frac{1}{24} + \varepsilon\right)\right]$ c/m	0.3	Complicated; aver. angle *lag* is 80° in this freq. band, e.g., 40 mos. × 80/360 = 7 mos.	
		(a) $\frac{1}{9.6} - \frac{1}{8.9}$ c/m	0.7	Fixed angle, inverted series *lead* by 20°	+8 mos.
		(b) about $\frac{1}{6}$ c/m	0.75	Lagging	
		(c) about $\frac{1}{4}$ c/m	0.7		
		(d) about $\frac{5}{12}$ c/m	0.7		

(continued)

TABLE 12.2 (continued)

Code number	Series title abbreviated	Used filter	For the cyclical component $\frac{1}{96}$ c/m $-$ $\frac{1}{12}$ c/m			All other frequency bands			NBER classification & estimate of lead-lag (median of $-$lead$+$lag) for both reference peak & trough date
			Frequency band where coherence fairly high	Average coherence in that band	Phase	Frequency band where coherence fairly high	Average coherence in that band	Phase	
I(B), 10	Manufacturers' Inventory	trend seasonal	81 mos. and $\left(\frac{1}{36} - \varepsilon\right) - \left(\frac{1}{18} + \varepsilon\right)$	0.6	Complicated; aver. angle lag is 70°, e.g., 24 mos. × 70/360 = 5 mos.	(a) $\frac{1}{12} - \frac{1}{8}$ c/m	0.5	Fixed angle lag 60°	+2 mos.
						(b) about $\frac{1}{6}$ c/m	0.9	180°	Lagging
						(c) about $\frac{1}{4}$ c/m	0.95	complicated; aver. is zero	
						(d) about $\frac{1}{3}$ c/m	0.7	complicated	
I(B), 11	Consumer Install-ment debt	trend seasonal	81 mos. and $\left[\left(\frac{1}{48} - \varepsilon\right) - \left(\frac{1}{24} + \varepsilon\right) \; 0.45\right]$ c/m	0.8	Complicated; aver. angle lag is 45°, e.g., 48 mos. × 45/360 = 6 mos.	(a) $\frac{1}{6}$ c/m	0.9	The angle at the seasonal frequencies line up well to give about 2.5 mos. fixed time lag	+4 mos.
						(b) $\frac{1}{4}$ c/m	0.8		Lagging
						(c) $\frac{1}{3}$ c/m	0.95		
						(d) $\frac{5}{12}$ c/m	0.9		
I(C), 01	Freight Car Loadings	Linear regression and trend	$\left(\frac{1}{40} - \varepsilon\right) - \left(\frac{1}{20} + \varepsilon\right)$ c/m	0.8	Angle is zero	(a) $\frac{1}{9.6} - \frac{1}{6}$ c/m	0.8	Fixed time (angle) lag	0 mos. Coincident

				Phase conclusion	Frequency band	Coherence	Conclusion	Lead/Lag
I(C), 02	Department Store sales	regression and trend seasonal ($A = 100$)	$\left(\frac{1}{40} - \varepsilon\right) - \left(\frac{1}{21} + \varepsilon\right)$ c/m		aver. angle *lead* is 17°; e.g., 40 mos. × 17/370 = 2 mos.	(a) $\frac{1}{6}$ c/m			Coincident
						(b) $\frac{1}{4}$ c/m	0.8	the seasonal frequencies line up well to give about 2.5 mos. fixed time lag	Coincident
						(c) $\frac{1}{3}$ c/m	0.8		
						(d) $\frac{5}{12}$ c/m	0.9		
I(C), 03	Retail Sales	81 mos. mov. aver. and trend seasonal	$\left(\frac{1}{48} - \varepsilon\right) - \left(\frac{1}{24} + \varepsilon\right)$ c/m	0.6	Complicated, angle *lead* is appr. 18° in this band, e.g., 48 mos. × 18/360 = 2 mos.	(a) $\frac{1}{6}$ c/m	0.5	Messy	Coincident
						(b) $\frac{1}{4}$ c/m	0.6		− 1 mos.
						(c) $\frac{1}{3}$ c/m	0.6		
						(d) $\frac{5}{12}$ c/m	0.6		
II(A), 01	Business Failures before 1932	81 mos. mov. aver. and trend seasonal	$0 - \left(\frac{1}{24} + \varepsilon\right)$ c/m	0.8	Inverted series leads, fixed time lead of 2.2 mos.	(a) $\frac{1}{15} - \frac{1}{12}$ c/m	0.7	Inverted series has angle lead of 135°	− 7 mos.
						(b) about $\frac{1}{4}$ c/m		Inverted series has angle lead of 18°	Leading (after inversion)
						(c) Other		Messy	
II(A), 02	Standard and Poor Stock Prices (1875–1956)	81 mos. mov. aver. and trend seasonal	$\left(\frac{1}{240} - \varepsilon\right) - \left(\frac{1}{80} + \varepsilon\right)$ c/m	0.6	Nothing definite can be said about the phase in this freq. band	$\frac{1}{10} - \frac{1}{7}$ c/m	0.6	Fixed time *lead* appro. 2 mos. between 0 and 1/4 cm; beyond this the angle is messy	− 4 mos. Lagging

(continued)

TABLE 12.2 (continued)

Code number	Series title abbreviated	Used filter	For the cyclical component $\frac{1}{96}$ c/m $-$ $\frac{1}{12}$ c/m			All other frequency bands			NBER classification & estimate of lead-lag (median of $-$lead$+$lag) for both reference peak & trough date
			Frequency band where coherence fairly high	Average coherence in that band	Phase	Frequency band where coherence fairly high	Average coherence in that band	Phase	
III(B), 01	Corporate Profits	Trend seasonal	$\left(\frac{1}{48} - \varepsilon\right) - \left(\frac{1}{8} + \varepsilon\right)$ c/q****	0.85	Average lead is appr. 40°, e.g., 12 qrt. × 40/360 = 1.3 qrt.	(a) $\frac{1}{3.4} - \frac{1}{2.9}$ c/q	0.85	Lagging	-5.5 mos.
			$\left(\frac{1}{8} - \varepsilon\right) - \left(\frac{1}{48} + \varepsilon\right)$ c/q	0.70	Average angle is zero	(b) $\frac{1}{2.4} - \frac{1}{2}$ c/q	0.85	Lagging	Leading
III(B), 02	Changes in Business Inventory	Trend seasonal	$\left(\frac{1}{24} - \varepsilon\right) - \left(\frac{1}{48} + \varepsilon\right)$ c/q	0.5	Average lead is appr. 36°, e.g., 12 qrt. × 36/260 = 1.2 qrt.	$\frac{1}{3.4} - \frac{1}{2.6}$ c/q	0.85	About zero	-10 mos.
									Leading

* The reading of frequency 1/16 c/m is the center of the last frequency unit to which the description applies according to the *estimates* of cross-spectra. Because of the spectral window the cross-spectra at this center frequency actually contain a part of the information as to the frequencies beyond 1/16 c/m and this fact is indicated by $+\varepsilon$.

** The estimates of cross-spectrum at 1/48 c/m contain some information as to the frequencies lower than this frequency. This is indicated by $-\varepsilon$.

*** [ ] is used to indicate the case in which even the highest coherence within the frequency band is low.

**** Abbreviation of cycles per quarter.

In Section 12.7 we found that the cyclical component is not meaning-ful as far as the spectrum is concerned. When we turn to the cross-spectrum, Table 12.2 shows that many cycle indicators reveal higher coherence about the frequency of the cyclical component than for any other frequencies (apart from the seasonals). In other words, we can say possibly that different economic time series are interrelated in terms of their cyclical components more closely than in terms of other components. In this sense, the cyclical component is a meaningful concept.

12.10 Complex Demodulation to Study the Changes in Lead-lag

It would be important to note that the magnitudes of lead-lag as obtained from the estimates of cross-spectra are a sort of average of the lead-lag over the entire period for which the data are used for the estimation.[17] A problem which has been set forth in the present chapter is how the magnitudes of lead-lag of the business cycle indicators are changing over time.

We have tried to use the complex demodulation method for the esti-mation of the change in lead-lag. The "instantaneous cross-spectrum" is explained in Section 10.2. Let $\varphi_{\omega_x}(t)$ be the phase angle of x series at time t and at the frequency ω and let $\varphi_{\omega_y}(t)$ be likewise the phase angle of y series. Theoretically, the instantaneous phase difference, $\varphi_{\omega_x}(t) - \varphi_{\omega_y}(t)$, should indicate the change in the lead-lag between each one of the cycle indicators (x series) and the reference time series (y series). In practice, however, we have faced an enormous difficulty.

This difficulty is concerned with the meaning of the phase angle as obtained from the complex demodulation. The relationship between x series and y series has nothing to do with this difficulty, and we may consider only one series, say x series. As explained in Section 10.3, we *cannot* investigate what change is taking place at a frequency *point* ω_0. What we observe from the complex demodulation method is a sort of weighted average over a certain frequency band about ω_0, more specif-ically, the change over time of some weighted averages of amplitude and phase over a frequency band, $[\omega_0 - \delta, \omega_0 + \delta]$.

---

[17] This follows from a theorem on cross-pseudospectrum, which is a mathematical expectation of the estimates of cross-spectrum obtained by ignoring the problem of non-stationarity. The average of angles θ_1 and θ_2 should be defined as

$$\tan^{-1} \frac{\sin \theta_1 + \sin \theta_2}{\cos \theta_1 + \cos \theta_2}$$

When the changes over time are uniform over all frequencies, the theorem takes a neat form: when the changes over time are uniform over narrow frequency bands, the theorem is a little more complicated and takes a form of double averages. M. Hatanaka and M. Suzuki, "A Theory of the Pseudospectrum and its Application to Nonstationary Dynamic Econometric Models," in Essays in Mathematical Economics, M. Shubik, ed.

We are concerned here with the phase rather than the amplitude. Let us first assume that the amplitude of every frequency is constant over time. Our difficulty in the application of complex demodulation to the study of the changes in lead-lag arises from the fact mentioned above, namely that the method deals with a band of frequency rather than a point of frequency. We can illustrate this difficulty by comparing two simple examples.

(1) Suppose that the time series x_t contains only one frequency ω_0, where the phase angle changes over time. Let $\Phi(t)$ be the time function to represent this phase change. Suppose that we demodulate at ω_0.

$$x_t = a \cos (\omega_0 t + \Phi(t))$$

$$x_t \cos \omega_0 t = \frac{a}{2} [\cos \Phi(t) + \cos (2\omega_0 t + \Phi(t))]$$

$$x_t \sin \omega_0 t = -\frac{a}{2} [\sin \Phi(t) - \sin (2\omega_0 + \Phi(t))]$$

$$F(x_t \cos \omega_0 t) = \frac{a}{2} F(\cos \Phi(t)) \approx \frac{a}{2} \cos \Phi(t), \quad \begin{array}{l} \text{if } \Phi(t) \text{ is a slowly chang-} \\ \text{ing function of time} \end{array}$$

$$F(x_t \sin \omega_0 t) = -\frac{a}{2} F(\sin \Phi(t)) \approx -\frac{a}{2} \sin \Phi(t), \quad \begin{array}{l} \text{if } \Phi(t) \text{ is a slowly} \\ \text{changing function of} \\ \text{time.} \end{array}$$

Thus the phase obtained from the complex demodulation is

$$-\tan^{-1} \frac{F(x_t \sin \omega_0 t)}{F(x_t \cos \omega_0 t)} \approx \Phi(t).$$

(2) Next, suppose that the time series x_t contains two frequencies $\omega_0 - \varepsilon$ and $\omega_0 + \varepsilon$ in each of which *the phase angles are constant*. Also suppose that the amplitudes of the two frequencies are not equal. Let us demodulate at ω_0.

$$x_t = a \cos ((\omega_0 - \varepsilon)t + \theta_1) + b \cos ((\omega_0 + \varepsilon)t + \theta_2)$$

$$x_t \cos \omega_0 t = \frac{a}{2} [\cos (-\varepsilon t + \theta_1) + \cos ((2\omega_0 - \varepsilon)t + \theta_1)]$$

$$+ \frac{b}{2} [\cos (\varepsilon t + \theta_2) + \cos ((2\omega_0 + \varepsilon)t + \theta_2)]$$

$$x_t \sin \omega_0 t = -\frac{a}{2} [\sin (-\varepsilon t + \theta_1) - \sin ((2\omega_0 - \varepsilon)t + \theta_1)]$$

$$- \frac{b}{2} [\sin (\varepsilon t + \theta_2) - \sin ((2\omega_0 + \varepsilon)t + \theta_2)]$$

$$F(x_t \cos \omega_0 t) = \frac{a}{2} F(\cos(-\varepsilon t + \theta_1)) + \frac{b}{2} F(\cos(\varepsilon t + \theta_2))$$

$$F(x_t \sin \omega_0 t) = -\frac{a}{2} F(\sin(-\varepsilon t + \theta_1)) - \frac{b}{2} F(\sin(\varepsilon t + \theta_2)).$$

Thus, the phase obtained from the complex demodulation is

$$-\tan^{-1} \frac{F(x_t \sin \omega_0 t)}{F(x_t \cos \omega_0 t)} = -\tan^{-1} \frac{A \sin(\varepsilon t + \Phi_1)}{B \cos(\varepsilon t + \Phi_2)} \quad \text{if } \varepsilon \text{ is small}$$

where

$$A = \sqrt{\left(\frac{a}{2} \sin \theta_1 + \frac{b}{2} \sin \theta_2\right)^2 + \left(\frac{a}{2} \cos \theta_1 - \frac{b}{2} \operatorname{cso} \theta_2\right)^2}$$

$$B = \sqrt{\left(\frac{a}{2} \sin \theta_1 - \frac{b}{2} \sin \theta_2\right)^2 + \left(\frac{a}{2} \cos \theta_1 + \frac{b}{2} \cos \theta_2\right)^2}$$

$$\Phi_1 = -\tan^{-1} \left(\frac{\frac{a}{2} \sin \theta_1 + \frac{b}{2} \sin \theta_2}{\frac{a}{2} \cos \theta_1 - \frac{b}{2} \cos \theta_2} \right)$$

$$\Phi_2 = -\tan^{-1} \left(\frac{\frac{a}{2} \sin \theta_1 - \frac{b}{2} \sin \theta_2}{\frac{a}{2} \cos \theta_1 + \frac{b}{2} \cos \theta_2} \right).$$

Unless we introduce some special conditions, the phase obtained from the complex demodulation, $-\tan^{-1} \dfrac{F(x_t \sin \omega_0 t)}{F(x_t \cos \omega_0 t)}$, is a function of time. The only simple case where this becomes a constant is when $a = b$. If $\theta_1 + \theta_2 \neq n\pi$ (n: any integer) and $a = b$, then $\Phi_1 - \Phi_2 = \dfrac{\pi}{2} \pm n\pi$ and hence

$$-\tan^{-1} \frac{F(x_t \sin \omega_0 t)}{F(x_t \cos \omega_0 t)} = \frac{\sin(\varepsilon t + \Phi_1)}{\cos(\varepsilon t + \Phi_2)} = \pm 1$$

for all t. It is important to point out that even if $\theta_1 = \theta_2$, the phase is not necessarily a constant unless $a = b$.

This explains the difficulty in attempting to interpret the *apparent* change in the phase obtained from the complex demodulation as an *actual* change in the phase angle. In practice we treat the time series which have some power in every infinitesimal interval of frequency, and we must consider some sort of average of phase angle over a continuous interval of frequency. Yet the above two examples suggest the point which we are trying to make. As the first example indicates, the phase as obtained from the complex demodulation could really be the change in the phase angle. However, as the second example indicates, the phase of the complex demodulation could change even if the phase angle of each frequency is constant over time. Such change could be due to the fact that the spectrum of the time series is not symmetric about ω_0 at which the demodulation is made.

Now the next problem is to eliminate the possibilities of the phase of the complex demodulation being influenced by the factors other than the real changes in the phase angle. Obviously we *cannot* eliminate these possibilities entirely, because if we can, this means that the spectrum of the time series must be perfectly symmetric. Therefore, let us ascertain the effect of small asymmetry of spectrum.

Let us suppose that $a \neq b$ but $\theta_1 = \theta_2 = \theta$ in the second case used above. If a does not differ greatly from b so that $(a + b)^2 \gg (a - b)^2$ but not necessarily $(a + b) \gg (a - b)$,

$$-\tan^{-1}\frac{F(x_t \sin \omega_0 t)}{F(x_t \cos \omega_0 t)} \approx -\tan^{-1}\left(\tan \theta \frac{\sin (\varepsilon t + \Phi_1)}{\cos (\varepsilon t + \Phi_2)}\right)$$

$$\Phi_1 = -\tan^{-1}\frac{(a + b) \sin \theta}{(a - b) \cos \theta}, \qquad \Phi_2 = -\tan^{-1}\frac{(a - b) \sin \theta}{(a + b) \cos \theta}.$$

Thus, the phase as obtained from the complex demodulation depends upon time. Therefore it seems that we must eliminate the asymmetry of the spectrum as much as we can, in order to identify the change in the phase of complex demodulation as the actual change in the phase angle.

Throughout the entire presentation above we have assumed that the power of every frequency does not change. Once we drop this assumption, there can be no unique interpretation of the change in the phase as obtained from the complex demodulation. This is because the change in the distribution of power about a frequency ω_0, assuming that the average of power over time is equal among all the frequencies about ω_0 so that the spectrum is flat about ω_0, is exactly identical to the change in the phase angle at the frequency ω_0. Even though we use the words "change in the phase" we must be aware of the fact that these words can also mean a change (over time) in the relative distribution of power among different frequencies.

12.11 Examples of Complex Demodulation to Study the Changes in Lead-lag

In order to perform the study of the changes in the lead-lag on such a large scale as in the present study of business cycle indicators, it is necessary to have some sort of mechanical methods of filtering to make the spectrum symmetric about any given frequency point. Possibly we should try to flatten the spectrum in the frequency band $\frac{1}{96}$ c/m $- \frac{1}{12}$ c/m. Since the filtering method must be determined for each specific form of spectrum, we wish to have some sort of iterative method, checking after each run to see whether the spectrum is flat enough. We have not been able to develop such a method. In the present section, we present only a few examples of the changes in the lead-lag obtained by an extremely clumsy method of filtering to make the spectrum symmetric.

The estimates of spectra of the business cycle indicators after the trend-seasonal filter or the hollow 31 months moving average indicate the peaks centered at certain frequencies between $\frac{1}{24}$ c/m and $\frac{1}{40}$ c/m. In the case of Lay-off Rate I(A), 02 and Industrial Production Index I(A), 00 the peaks are located at $\frac{1}{24}$ c/m. It is hoped that the complex demodulation at $\frac{1}{24}$ c/m tells us about the change in the lead-lag about this frequency. We would like to see this change about some other frequencies included in the cyclical component. We have tried to apply the simple moving averages of appropriate lengths to the data which are already the output of trend-seasonal filter or hollow 31 months moving average, in order to shift the center of symmetry from $\frac{1}{24}$ c/m to $\frac{1}{32}$ c/m. It has turned out that the 9 months simple moving average for Industrial Production Index and the 15 months simple moving average for Lay-off Rate transform the spectra in such a way that the transformed spectra are roughly symmetric about $\frac{1}{32}$ c/m.

Figures 12.16 and 12.17 show the phases of Lay-off Rate and Industrial Production Index obtained from the complex demodulation at $\frac{1}{24}$ c/m and $\frac{1}{32}$ c/m. The lengths of two moving averages used within the complex demodulation are 32 and 18 in all cases. The figures mainly indicate the difficulties in the interpretation of the results of complex demodulation. Keeping in mind the fact that the phase angle as obtained by complex demodulation at ω for the time series $\cos(\omega t + \theta)$ is actually $-\theta$, we note that Figure 12.17 indicates the persistent lead of the inverted lay-off rate over the industrial production index except for the war period. However, the magnitude of the lead is substantially greater than the lead indicated by the cross-spectrum. Further, Figure 12.16 indicates the persistent *lag* of the inverted lay-off rate, and this contradicts the evidence obtained from the cross-spectrum. The sudden change in the phase angle of the production index during the World War II is clearly observed about 1/32 c/m but it is not about 1/24 c/m. This further poses

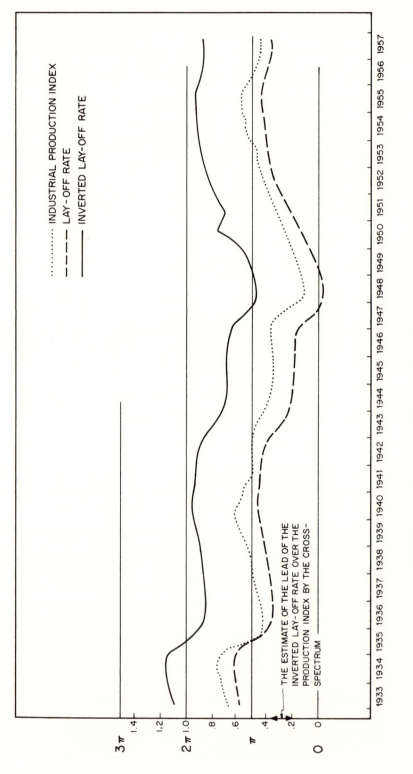

Figure 12.16.   Phase Angle Estimated by Complex Demodulation 1/24 c/m

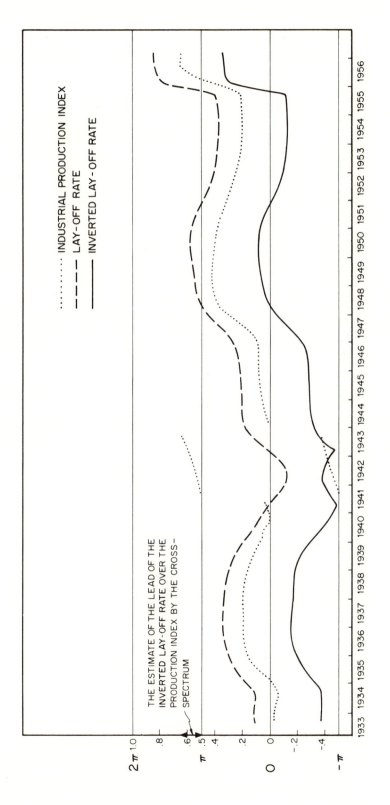

Figure 12.17. Phase Angle Estimated by Complex Demodulation 1/32 c/m

difficulties of interpretation, as does the sudden change in 1956 observed for 1/32 c/m.

12.12 Suggestions for Future Study

In spite of the fact that the data used are extended up to June 1961, the charts in Figures 12.16–12.17 all end in 1957. This is certainly a serious drawback of the method used here. The reason for this is that we have lost data twice, once when the trend-seasonal filter (and the simple moving average) is used in order to make the spectrum symmetric, and the second time, when two simple moving averages are used in the complex demodulation. We have made some experiments to see the effect of one-sided moving averages in the complex demodulation, in order not to lose the last portion of the data. An apparent cause of the difficulty with the use of one-sided moving averages is that it changes the phase angles. It appears, however, that if we demodulate the time series whose spectrum is symmetric about the frequency at which the demodulation is made, then we can correct the changes in the phase angle. Thus, the essential problem boils down to how we can make the spectrum symmetric, without losing many data in the last portion of the time period.[18]

[18] Since the above text was written, David Brillinger and John Tukey have suggested to the author a method, not the complex demodulation, by which we can study the changes in the lead-lag relationships. The method has been further extended to obtain the moving spectrum and the moving cross-spectrum. See D. Brillinger and M. Hatanaka, "An Harmonic Analysis of Nonstationary Multivariate Stochastic Processes: I Theoretical Basis for Moving Spectrum and Moving Cross-spectrum, II Cyclical Components in the U.S. Macro-Economic Structures since 1890's," a forthcoming Research Memorandum of Econometric Research Program, Princeton University.

CHAPTER 13

APPLICATION OF PARTIAL CROSS-SPECTRAL ANALYSIS: TESTS OF THE ACCELERATION PRINCIPLE FOR INVENTORY CYCLES[1]

Partial cross-spectral analysis, described in Section 5.8, is a very useful technique for studying economic relationships. In the present chapter we use this technique to study the inventory cycle. An elementary explanation of the significance of the inventory cycle is given in Section 13.1. There, it will be shown that economic theory suggests the existence of a feedback relation between inventory investment and GNP. As explained in Chapter 7, cross-spectral analysis, in its present stage, is not applicable when different *feed-back* relations might hold among different frequencies. We shall study one of the relations involved in these feed-back relations by taking a small sector of the economy, department stores, because the possibility of feed-back within such a small sector is very slight. The relation to be studied is the effect of sales on inventory holdings. Thus, in Sections 13.2–13.5 we shall formulate a simple form of the acceleration principle and test it against two alternative hypotheses, one now called the square root principle, and the other one suggested by members of the National Bureau of Economic Research. In Sections 13.6–13.7 we shall show the tests of a more sophisticated version of the acceleration principle. In all these tests we are concerned with the cyclical components of sales and inventory. The changes in the inventory holdings in the very long run are presumably the results of the improvements in the inventory control method, the distribution method etc., and we are studying the changes in the inventory holdings over the business cycles and subcycles which do not involve such long-run effects. However, since we use sales, inventory and other data for department stores, the results of the tests are applicable only to this special category of the inventory cycle.

[1] The author is grateful to Samuel Flannel of the National Retail Merchants Association, who supplied the information as to management practices used by department stores, and to Mr. David R. Hull, Jr., of the Board of Governors of the Federal Reserve System, who supplied the statistical data used in Section 13.7. The author also appreciates the comments made by John Cragg on an earlier draft. Ruth P. Mack gave important advice for possible revisions and further extension of the present study after the manuscript was sent to the press. Unfortunately, only a minor portion of her advice has been incorporated.

13.1 Inventory Cycles

If we consider the entire economy of our nation as a network of pipelines and joints through which are allocated different kinds of goods to different economic units, such as consumers and producers, we will find, at any moment of time, a certain amount of goods in the pipeline. These goods are called inventories and may be classified into three groups: finished goods, goods in process (of production), and raw materials, from the standpoint of the economic units which hold them. (Of course, exactly the same type of commodity can be held as an inventory of raw material by one form and as an inventory of finished goods by another firm.) In the case of retailers and wholesalers, goods in process may be a meaningless concept, and the other two categories, finished goods and raw materials, can be reduced to one category. Inventory in the hands of consumers is usually ignored.

Inventory is held for various purposes. Perhaps the best way to review the motivations and other possible causes for inventory holding is to consider it from the viewpoints of different departments of a firm: (a) The sales department wants to carry an inventory of finished goods as a buffer stock for unexpected demand, because the time between the issue of an order to the production department (or to the purchasing department) and the actual receipt of the commodity is not usually zero. This time period is usually called the lead-time or the replenishment period,[2] but here we shall call it the procurement lag in order to convey the meaning more directly. Furthermore, the sales department wants to facilitate the technicalities (e.g., transportation, etc.) involved in moving commodities from the production department (in the case of wholesalers and retailers, purchasing from the producers or other stores) to the point at which sales are made. Even if future sales could be forecast perfectly, some inventories would be in the hands of the sales department for the latter reason. In addition there are unwanted inventories, e.g., due to delivery from the production department earlier than expected or to overestimates of sales. (b) The production department wants to operate as smoothly as possible despite the fluctuations in sales of finished goods or in purchases of material, because too frequent changes in production scheduling are costly. Therefore, the sales and purchasing departments have to carry inventories to meet expected or unexpected fluctuations in the demand and supply. Further, inventory in the form of goods in process arises mostly for technological reasons in the production department. (c) The purchasing department wants to exploit the economies of large-lot purchasing (quantity discounts, lower book-keeping costs, etc.), which means purchasing only once in a certain

---

[2] The phase "replenishment period" is used mostly when a system such as two-bin system is used.

period despite continuous production. This automatically results in holding inventories of raw materials. Sometimes the purchase of raw materials is prompted by an expected price rise or an anticipated shortage. Further, if the production schedule may be subjected to some unexpected change, the purchasing department wants to hold some inventory for the same reason as the sales department does. (d) The finance department prefers not to have too much capital tied up in inventory. Further, attempts are made to minimize losses due to obsolescence, storage costs, and interest payments which are involved in the holding of inventory. Actual inventory holding is a result of (1) these different motivations concerning the management plans of a firm, (2) the discrepancies between the expectations on which the plans are based and the realization of the expectations, and (3) the natural consequences of technology.

In the present chapter *inventory investment* is defined as the change in the holdings of all inventories in the aggregate economy. Thus, if I_t represents the inventory held at the end of period t, $I_t - I_{t-1}$ is the inventory investment during the period t. The *inventory cycle* is the cyclical component of the time series of inventory investment. To study inventory cycles, we can concentrate on the inventory investment in the business sector. Inventory holding by the government sector is considered to be very smooth over time (although we do not have sufficient statistical evidence to support this assumption), and hence the change in this inventory holding has a very small cyclical component.

The reason why the inventory cycle in the business sector is important in a study of business cycles is that a causal relationship exists between inventory investment and gross national product, i.e., between the inventory cycle and the business cycle.[3] In fact, economic theory tells

[3] The literature on the inventory cycle is very limited, and we can easily list the important studies, including both the theoretical and empirical ones. (We have excluded those which have lost their significance because of the appearance of later studies.) Paul G. Darling, "Inventory fluctuations and economic instability," *Inventory Fluctuations and Economic Stabilization*, Joint Economic Committee, 87th Congress, 1st Session, 1961; L. R. Klein and J. Popkin, "An econometric analysis of the postwar relationship between inventory fluctuations and changes in aggregate economic activity," *ibid.*; Charles C. Holt and Franco Modigliani, "Firm cost structures and the dynamic responses of inventories, production, work force, and orders to sales fluctuations," *ibid.*; Michael C. Lovell, "Manufacturers' inventories, sales expectations, and the acceleration principle," *Econometrica*, July 1961; Michael C. Lovell, "Buffer stocks, sales expectations, and stability: A multi-sector analysis of the inventory cycle," *Econometrica*, April 1962; Ruth P. Mack and Victor Zarnowitz, "Causes and consequences of changes in retailers' buying," *American Economic Review*, March 1959; Ruth P. Mack, *Consumption and Business Fluctuations* 1956; L. A. Metzler, "The nature and stability of inventory cycles," *Review of Economic Statistics*, August 1941; Ragnar Nurkse, "Period analysis and inventory cycle," *Oxford Economic Papers*, September 1954; N. Y. Robinson, "The acceleration principle: inventories." *American Economic Review*, June 1959; Jacob T. Schwartz, *Lectures on the Mathematical Method in Analytical Economics*, 1961, chaps. 5, 6, and 7; Thomas M. Stanback, *Post War Cycles in Manufacturing Inventories*, 1962; Thomson M. Whitin, *The Theory of Inventory Investment*, 2nd ed., 1957. Further, Edwin S. Mills, *Price, Output, and Inventory Policy*, 1962, discusses many problems that are relevant to inventory cycle.

us that there exists a two-way causality: 1) from gross national product to inventory investment, and 2) from inventory investment to gross national product. In order to study this causality we can concentrate on the non-farm business sector. Fluctuations in farm inventory in the private sector presumably have characteristics and causes different from those of business cycle fluctuations. Also, the lags are substantially longer for the effects of farm inventory investment on the general economy —assuming there are any significant effects, which is doubtful—than for the effects of average non-farm business inventory investment on the general economy.

Let us consider first the latter of the two causalities mentioned above, i.e., from inventory investment to GNP. In the national income accounts, which are a sort of income statement for the entire nation, inventory investment (not inventory holding) of the business sector appears as one of the three categories of private investment. (Price investment is defined as the increase of private real capital stock in the nation, and therefore inventory investment is considered to be one kind of private investment.) The other two categories of private investment are construction and investment in durable equipment. According to Keynesian economics, a change in investment causes a change in GNP. In fact, this is an oversimplification, particularly in the treatment of the impact of inventory investment upon GNP (because of unintended inventory investment, which will be explained later). Nevertheless, Table 13.1 indicates that the amplitude of the cyclical component of non-farm business inventory investment is great compared with the amplitudes of the cyclical components of other parts of investment. Thus, the inventory cycle deserves careful study as a possible cause of business cycles.

TABLE 13.1

CHANGES FROM PEAKS TO TROUGHS[4] IN THE DIFFERENT COMPONENTS OF INVESTMENT

	1948–49 recession	1953–54 recession	1957–58 recession	1960–61 recession
Non-farm Business Inventory Investment	−8.6	−9.0	−10.7	−15.3
Investment in Durable Equipment	−4.4	−2.7	−6.6	−5.5
New Construction	−1.9	increase	−1.8	−1.2

[4] Unit: billions of dollars on a quarterly basis at the annual rate. The peak quarters and trough quarters vary among the three components of investment listed here. The peaks and troughs here are not necessarily the National Bureau specific peaks and troughs, but are the highs and lows within the time period that is obtained by extending in both directions by three quarters the time period between the National Bureau reference peak and trough quarters.

The reason why inventory investment, and not inventory itself, should be associated with GNP may be seen by a few examples. Suppose that the entire business sector maintains a constant amount of inventory, i.e., zero inventory investment. Other things (especially the sales) remaining constant, the rate of production per unit of time would be constant at a certain level. Suppose that the business sector decides to *keep increasing* its inventory holdings by one billion dollars every year, i.e., a *constant amount*, one billion dollars, of inventory investment. Other things remaining unchanged, the production necessary to maintain this situation is higher (by exactly one billion dollars if the sales do not change) than for the condition of zero inventory investment. Yet, apart from the short period of adjustment, production will be constant at this higher level. In other words, a constant level of production is associated with a constant level of *inventory investment*.

As to the other causality, i.e., from GNP to inventory investment, the relationship called the acceleration principle has been discussed widely. There are different versions of this principle, as will be explained in the next section, but its basic form is

desired inventory investment in t = a function of the change in expected sales over certain periods around t.

This theory is frequently applied to all three categories of investment, and has been subject to severe criticism. However, as long as the theory is confined to inventory investment, most of the criticisms become irrelevant.

In connection with the testing of the acceleration principle, a few important points must be mentioned. First, the inventory holdings have been generally declining in the long run in relation to the sales. Presumably this is due to the improvement of inventory control and distribution. Since our main concern is about the relationship between the inventory cycles and business cycles, we would like to study the relation between the inventory investment and sales changes in *regard to their cyclical component* only, excluding any other time series components such as the trend or the seasonals. This is one of the basic points throughout the present chapter.

Second, for the study of movements of inventory holdings by the non-farm business sector it is important to distinguish *desired* inventory holdings and unintended holdings. Businessmen try to adjust inventory levels according to a certain objective and some rules that follow from it—however crude the rules may be. Thus, at least a portion of the actual inventory holding is deliberate, and this portion of inventory holdings is called *desired*. On the other hand, businessmen's decisions concerning inventory holdings are based partly on expectation of future sales, and this expectation is not perfect. Thus, the *actual* inventory holdings either contain more than they want to hold in the light of actual sales or run short of what they want to hold. The difference between the actual and the desired inventory holdings is called *unintended* inventory holding.

From the standpoint of hypotheses-testing, we first define the hypotheses as to the desired inventory holdings and the formation of expected future sales, and then we proceed to test whether or not the observed movement of actual inventory holdings is consistent with these hypotheses. Actually the acceleration principle should be considered as a hypothesis of desired inventory holdings. It does not specify any hypothesis as to the formation of expected future sales. Therefore, there can be as many forms of the inventory hypotheses associated with the acceleration principle as the different hypotheses of the formation of expectation with which the acceleration principle should be combined.

Third, although our main concern is the effect of sales upon inventory holding, the obvious existence of the feed-back relationship between inventory investment and sales in the aggregate economy and the inadequacy of the cross-spectral analysis (in its present stage) to treat such feed-back relationships compel us to study a number of small sectors in our economy in regard to any hypotheses as to the effect of sales upon inventory holding. It is hoped that the feed-back effect of inventory investment in such a small sector upon its own sales is insignificant. Although this needs an empirical substantiation, we might support this hope on an a priori ground in the following way. Let us consider that the economy consists of a number of small sectors, each of which holds some inventory and is engaged in sales. Since the effect of inventory investment by a small sector is dissipated into many channels of sales, the *direct* feed-back effect upon its own sales should not be significant. Still there is a possibility of *spurious* feed-back effect due to the possible resemblance of this direct effect to the aggregate causal relation from inventory investment to sales by way of income. Against this possibility one might argue that the relative positions of these small sectors in the entire network of the relationship in the economy are substantially different. For example, the feed-back effect of the inventory investment in a sub-sector of retail trade upon its sales would not be identical to the feed-back effects of the inventory investment in a sub-sector of manufacturing upon its own sales. Even though the aggregate feed-back effect might be significant, this must be a consequence of aggregation of substantially different relationships, none of which is quite like this aggregate feed-back relationship.

Actually we have selected the sector of department stores[4a] The

---

[4a] Ruth P. Mack suggested to the author a consideration of spurious feed-back in the study of department stores. The coherence between the aggregate inventory investment and the departmentstores inventory investment is .3 about frequency 1/16 cycle per quarter and .4 about 1/8 cycle per quarter. However, the coherence between the aggregate consumption expenditure and the department store sales is .9 about frequency 1/16 cycle per quarter and 1.0 about frequency 1/8 cycle per quarter.

reasons why we use this particular example of inventory investment are as follows: (1) The Board of Governors of the Federal Reserve System has accumulated a very long time series of the indices of department store sales and department store stocks on a monthly basis since 1919[5]. A series of this length is necessary for the satisfactory study of cyclical components, although we must frequently use shorter series because of the limited availability of data. (2) Where goods made to order (rather than made to stock) are involved, a study of the inventory cycle must be combined with a study of unfilled orders (the purchase orders that have been received by the producers but have not yet been worked on by them). Unfilled orders as well as inventory play an important role in cushioning the fluctuation of new orders against production. Since department stores have no production, this complication does not arise. Because of this simplification, their problems are suitable for the purpose of illustrating our statistical techniques. Here we need consider only the positions of the sales and purchasing departments. (3) However, for some commodities, the problems of department store inventory investment are not so simple as to be trivial. The procurement lag can be as long as six months, and outstanding orders (the purchase orders that have been issued by the department stores and have not yet been fulfilled by the delivery of the goods) are usually about one-half of the inventory holding. Thus, some consideration must be given to the complicated relations among sales forecast, procurement lag, inventory holding, and outstanding orders.

The use of the data for department sales and stocks involves a disadvantage as well. Department stores are really an aggregation of various stores which may have different inventory control policies and thus aggregation may present a serious problem. However, it does not seem to be any more serious than in any other parts of the business sector, such as manufacturing.

The study of the tests of the acceleration principle as applied to department store inventory investment will be divided into two parts. In the first part, we assume that the aggregate forecast errors of aggregate sales by department stores are random, and because of this assumption the acceleration principle tested in this part is very simple. In the second part, we remove this assumption and introduce some standard formulae to represent sales expectation. Further, we give some consideration to

---

[5] These appear to be the only data of sales and inventories which extend for more than 20 years. The data necessary for the study of inventory cycles in the other sectors have been prepared specifically for this purpose only recently. Probably the longest series are those which were prepared by Bratt for different industries within manufacturing, and they begin in 1947 or 1948. (Elmer C. Bratt, "Availability and reliability of inventory data needed to study economic change", Joint Economic Committee, 87th Congress, 1st Session, 1961. His data include not only sales and inventories, but also new and unfilled orders, which make them a superb object of study.)

outstanding orders and new orders in order to study the relationship among sales forecasts, orders, and inventory holding. Therefore, the acceleration principle in this second part of our study becomes more complicated.

13.2 A Simple Version of the Acceleration Principle

Let $\tilde{I}_r(t_1, t_2)$ be the real quantity (as compared to monetary value) of the *desired* inventory holding of a certain commodity (or some aggregated "commodity") for the end of period t_1 as desired as of period t_2, $\tilde{S}_r(t_1, t_2)$ be the real quantity of *expected* sales of the same commodity for the period t_1, as expected as of period t_2, and ω_i be certain non-negative constant weights. Both $\tilde{I}_r(t_1, t_2)$ and $\tilde{S}_r(t_1, t_2)$ are stochastic variables in the sense that our economy is a stochastic process involving random disturbances, but especially they are subjective stochastic variables representing anticipation. The inventory-sales ratio of the commodity in period t is defined as

$$\tilde{\alpha}_r(t) \equiv \frac{\tilde{I}_r(t, t)}{\sum_{i \geq 0} \omega_i \tilde{S}(t + i, t)}.$$

The reason we study this ratio is that the inventory holding at the end of period t is a preparation for future expected sales. The weights ω_i reflect partly what portion of the expected sales in the period $(t + i)$ must be prepared for in the inventory holding in the present period t. This proportion depends partly upon the procurement lag, which, in turn, varies with the supply conditions of the markets in which the department stores purchase. However, we must assume in this test of a simple version of the acceleration principle that these weights ω_i are constant over time. The concept of the inventory-sales ratio chiefly reflects the viewpoint of the sales department in the case of departmental stores, which looks upon inventory as a preparation for future sales. However, the value of $\tilde{\alpha}_r(t)$ would also depend upon the lot-size of a single purchase order determined by the purchasing department.

If $\tilde{\alpha}_r(t)$ is roughly constant, then, by taking the difference between two consecutive periods, we can obtain desired inventory investment in period $t + 1$ as

$$\tilde{\alpha} \times \left[\sum_{i \geq 0} \omega_i \tilde{S}_r(t + i + 1, t + 1) - \sum_{i \geq 0} \omega_i \tilde{S}_r(t + i, t) \right],$$

which is a version of the acceleration principle. Therefore, we would like to test the constancy of $\tilde{\alpha}_r(t)$, the inventory-sales ratio.

However, there are many problems which must first be discussed. These problems arise primarily because the time series data which we are using represent the *aggregate* of all commodities *actually* sold by all the department stores or the *aggregate* of all inventories *actually* held.

First, we must establish that the result of our test cannot be derived definitely from any information other than the results of statistical tests. The alternative to our statistical tests is obviously information as to the inventory control method used by the department stores. It is true that they compile the data of the inventory-sales ratio using figures for "such and such months' (or weeks') supply" which exists in the form of inventory. Therefore, if they aim at a specific target for the inventory-sales ratio, and if they seldom change this target, then the acceleration principle must be true apart from the forecast errors of the sales and the errors in purchases resulting from the forecast errors. The inventory control actually used seems to be as follows: On the one hand, department stores do *not* have any specific targets for their inventory-sales ratio except that they have some vague ideas as to the appropriate upper and lower bounds within which they think the ratio should always stay. Therefore, there is no reason to believe that the acceleration principle must be true. On the other hand, the managers of department stores *do* study the inventory-sales ratio constantly, even though this ratio is but one of many factors which they consider. Therefore, there is also no reason to believe a priori that the acceleration principle is a meaningless hypothesis that does not explain any significant part of inventory investment.

Further, it is important to point out that in the study of inventory cycles we are concerned with the aggregate behavior of many economic units rather than with the micro-economic aspect of the behavior of a single unit. In general, there is no obvious relationship between the macro- and micro-aspects of behavior. Frequently, a variable that plays an important role in a micro-relationship loses its significance in a macro-relationship, and vice versa. Since we are testing the acceleration principle as applied to the aggregate of all department stores, the validity of this theory cannot simply be guessed from the analysis of one department store. Different departments of department stores as well as different department stores have differing patterns of purchasing and inventory policies. Thus conclusions based on an aggregation of all department stores cannot be made without the use of some statistical tests.

Second, the sales in the inventory-sales ratio are the *expected* sales. Department stores are in a fairly fortunate position in regard to the forecasting of aggregate sales (the sales of all kinds of commodities, rather than of a specific brand or design). This is because department store sales are subject to a very strong, well-defined, seasonal variation. Our preliminary estimates of the spectrum of department store sales indicates that a large part of the variance of this time series is accounted for by the seasonal component. Since the seasonal variation maintains essentially the same pattern every year except for the moving date of Easter which is known in advance, the error in the prediction of the aggregate sales of all kinds of commodities is fairly small.

The time series data which we use are those representing the aggregate sales of all commodities for all department stores in the United States. Therefore, it may not be a bad strategy to assume that the forecast errors of the aggregate sales are random. Let $\tilde{S}$ represent the expected sales and S the actual sales (again both $\tilde{S}$ and S are stochastic variables, but particularly the former, which is a subjective stochastic variable representing anticipation). Then our assumption is that $\varepsilon(t)$ defined by

$$\varepsilon(t) \; = \; \frac{\sum_i \omega_i \tilde{S}_r(t+i, t)}{\sum_i \omega_i S_r(t+i)}$$

is a random noise that is independent of sales. (However, as mentioned above, this assumption will be removed later.)

The above assumption results in a seemingly strange causality relationship, i.e., the future appears to influence the present. Actually, the *expected* sales *determined at the present* influence the present holding of inventory, thus,

$$\tilde{S}_r(t+i, t) \; \Rightarrow \; I(t), \qquad i \geqq 0.$$

But, because of the assumption made about forecast errors, we obtain

$$S_r(t+i) \; \Rightarrow \; I(t), \qquad i \geqq 0.$$

However strange this may be, *sales are treated as independent variables, and inventories as dependent variables in our test.* Further, the feed-back relation will be simply assumed away.

Third, the inventory in the inventory-sales ratio represents desired inventory. The discrepancy between desired and actual inventory holdings depends upon two factors: (1) mistakes in predicting the parameters of the (subjective) probability distribution of expected sales, whose parameters are taken into consideration in order to determine the desired inventory level, and (2) the length of the procurement lag. The latter is important because, given the mistakes mentioned in (1), the procurement lag is a factor in determining how quickly the mistakes can be remedied. (Another factor is the price premium on filling orders with immediate delivery.) In the case of department stores, we have already commented that the prediction of sales is fairly easy. However, the procurement lag for some commodities can be as long as six months.

The discrepancy between the actual and desired inventory can result in a series that is far more complicated than the forecast errors of the sales. This is because the procurement lag is not constant but varies with supply conditions. When supply conditions are tight, the procurement lag is lengthened, and therefore it is more difficult to raise the actual inventory to the desired level.

In our tests of the simple version of the acceleration principle we will assume that, if a proper length of time unit is chosen, the relation between desired inventory $\tilde{I}_r(t)$ and actual inventory $I_r(t)$ can be represented as

$$\frac{\tilde{I}_r(t, t)}{I_r(t + \tau)} = \text{a noise that is independent of sales} \qquad (\tau \geqq 0)$$

for all integral values of t and some appropriate (possibly rational) numbers for τ. Thus, if one adjusts for the unknown lag, τ, due to the lag in decision-making, the procurement lag, etc., and if we ignore all the frequencies except a low frequency band F, then the discrepancy between the desired and actual inventories is random and independent of sales. Since the proper length of time unit is not known, the testing procedures must be designed in such a way that this information does not have to be used.

We can make a casual check of the above assumption because of the definitional identity that *actual inventory investment equals actual purchases minus actual sales*. Suppose that an unexpected increase in sales takes place. Then the actual purchases, which are a result of decisions made earlier, cannot respond to these unexpected sales. Therefore, this would tend to move the actual inventory investment in the opposite direction; this is a symptom of the discrepancy between the actual and desired inventory. Therefore, if this discrepancy dominates in any frequency band—and the chances are that it might dominate more strongly in the high frequencies than in the low frequencies—we would see it as 180° phase difference between the time series of actual sales and inventory investment. The results of such a test will be described below.

Fourth, the inventory-sales ratio $\tilde{\alpha}_r(t)$, as defined above, deals with the real quantity of inventory and sales, whereas the data which we are using represent the dollar values of inventory and sales (in fact, the index with base period 1947–1949) covering all different types of commodities.

To adjust for this discrepancy we must have the price indexes of sales and inventories. It seems that nearly all department stores use practically the same inventory evaluation method. According to this method, they use the mark-down of the current sales price, but whenever the marked-down sales price is below the actual purchase price, the latter is used. In short, the price used for the evaluation of inventory by department stores is extremely complicated. Yet, a casual inspection of the prices of several categories of commodities indicates that the fluctuation in prices can be quantitatively a significant factor. Therefore, we must design our test in such a way that we can take into account price changes without using explicitly the price indices of sales and inventory. This can be done, as will be seen later, by working with the logarithms of sales and inventory, if the price indices for sales and inventories move roughly in proportion.

13.3 The Acceleration Principle Compared with the Square Root Principle and the "Supply Conditions" Hypothesis

Let

$$\tilde{\alpha}_r(t) \equiv \frac{\tilde{I}_r(t, t)}{\sum_{i \geq 0} \omega_i \tilde{S}_r(t+i, t)}$$

be the (desired) real inventory-sales ratio of the aggregates of all commodities sold by the departmental stores. Let us make an assumption, which is *not* a part of the hypothesis to be tested,

$$\log \sum_{i \geq 0} \omega_i \tilde{S}_r(t, ti, t) = \log \sum_{i \geq 0} \omega_i S_r(t, ti) + \text{a noise that is independent}$$
$$\text{of sales}$$

$$(13.3.1) \quad \log \tilde{I}_r(t, t) = \log I_r(t+\tau) + \text{a noise that is independent of}$$
$$\text{sales}$$

$$(\tau \geq 0) \text{ if a proper time unit is chosen,}$$

i.e., as explained in the previous section, the error of sales forecast and the discrepancy between the desired and actual inventory are random and independent of sales when a proper time unit is chosen. The assumption of (13.3.1) is a link between the expected or desired quantities designated by $\sim$ on top and the actual quantities. Let us now define the *actual* inventory-sales ratio in monetary value with lag τ as

$$\alpha_m(t, \tau) = \frac{I_m(t+\tau)}{\sum_{i \geq 0} \omega_i S_m(t+i)}$$

where both I_m and S_m are *actual monetary* values of inventory and sales, respectively. Let us also define the price index of inventory as

$$P_i(t) \equiv \frac{I_m(t)}{I_r(t)},$$

and the price index of sales as

$$P_s(t) \equiv \frac{\sum_{i \geq 0} \omega_i S_m(t+i)}{\sum_{i \geq 0} \omega_i S_r(t+i)}.$$

Then we obtain from (13.3.1)

$$\log \alpha_m(t, \tau) = \log I_r(t+\tau) - \log \sum_{i \geq 0} \omega_i S_r(t+i) + \log P_i(t+\tau)$$
$$- \log P_s(t)$$
$$= \log \tilde{I}_r(t, t) - \log \sum_{i \geq 0} \omega_i \tilde{S}_r(t+i, t) + \log P_i(t+\tau)$$
$$- \log P_s(t) + \text{a noise}$$
$$= \log \tilde{\alpha}_r(t) + \log P_i(t + \tau) - \log P_s(t)$$
$$+ \text{a noise.}$$

We make a further assumption, which is *not* a part of the hypothesis to be tested,

(13.3.2) $\log P_i(t + \tau) - \log P_s(t)$ = a constant + a noise.

This means that the price indices of sales and inventory move roughly in proportion, if one adjusts for the lag in the prices for inventories. Equation (13.3.2) eliminates the need for the use of price indices.

Now, the acceleration principle, the hypothesis to be tested, is that $\tilde{\alpha}_r(t)$ *be constant over time except for a random disturbance*. In the present framework, the hypothesis to be tested becomes

$\log \tilde{\alpha}_r(t)$ = a constant + a noise that is independent of sales.

Under assumptions (13.3.1) and (13.3.2), the hypothesis to be tested is transformed into

(13.3.3) $\log I_m(t+\tau) = \log \sum_{i \geq 0} \omega_i S_m(t+i)$ + a constant + a noise

that is independent of sales, $S_m(t)$.

It is true that mathematically (13.3.3) is *not* equivalent to the constancy of $\tilde{\alpha}_r(t)$, although (13.3.3) follows from the constancy of $\tilde{\alpha}_r(t)$. However, for the purpose of the test, (13.3.3) *is* equivalent to the constancy of $\alpha_r(t)$ in the sense that if $\tilde{\alpha}_r(t)$ depends upon a certain variable, so does (13.3.3), and vice versa.

Summarizing the above for the acceleration principle, we have

Assumption 1: (13.3.1)
Assumption 2: (13.3.2) } if a proper time unit is chosen,

Acceleration   holding in the frequency band F where the
Principle to   (13.3.3)   discrepancy between the actual and desired
be tested: inventory can be considered as random.

An important aspect of Assumptions 1 and 2 is that the noise is independent of sales so that $\log \sum_{i \geq 0} \omega_i S_m(t+i)$ *can be treated as the independent* and $\log I_m(t+\tau)$ *as the dependent variable in* (13.3.3).

In order to test this form of the acceleration principle, it is advisable to set forth the alternative hypotheses and compare them to the acceleration principle. As mentioned earlier, the acceleration principle is a hypothesis about desired inventory holding. It can be combined with any hypotheses about the formation of expectation. The alternative hypotheses considered here are also concerned with desired inventory holding and they too can be combined with any hypotheses about the formation of expectation. In this section and the two following, these three hypotheses of desired inventory holding will be combined with the same hypothesis of the formation of expectation and adjustment for the errors in expectation, namely (13.3.1).

The first of the two hypotheses alternative to the acceleration principle is called the square root principle. It was formulated by Whitin in the process of his research for scientific inventory control. Obviously, department stores had not been aware of sophisticated inventory control methods (until recently); also, much of the goods sold at department stores is style goods and no one, to the best of the author's knowledge, has ever claimed that the square root principle was valid for such goods. Nevertheless, according to Whitin, his method has some relevance to the deviation of the actual movement of inventory investment from the acceleration principle.[6] Under this hypothesis, the ratio

$$\frac{\tilde{I}_r(t, t)}{\sqrt{\sum_{i \geq 0} \omega_i \tilde{S}_r(t+i, t)}}$$

is constant. Let us first observe that the only difference between Whitin's hypothesis and the acceleration principle is that square root is applied to sales in his method. One can easily repeat the explanation made earlier for the acceleration principle to transform the test of Whitin's hypothesis into the following:

Assumption 3: (13.3.1)

Assumption 4: $\log P_i(t) - \frac{1}{2} \log P_s(t) =$ a constant + a noise that is independent of sales.

(13.3.4) The square root principle to be tested:

$$\log I_m(t+\tau) - \frac{1}{2} \log \left(\sum_{i \geq 0} \omega_i S_m(t+i) \right) =$$

a constant + a noise that is independent of sales (holding in the frequency band F where the discrepancy between the actual and desired inventory can be considered as random).

Since the square root sign might be rather shocking to readers who are not familiar with scientific inventory control methods, it would be worth while to indicate one of the many inventory control problems for which Whitin developed the square root principle. Using his notations, let Y designate the expected yearly sales (in physical quantities), let

[6] Thomson M. Whitin, *The Theory of Inventory Management*, pp. 94–98.

Q be the purchase quantity in a single placement of order, which is to be optimized in our problem, let C be the unit carrying cost, which is assumed to be a constant, and let S be the cost involved in the process of a single procurement, which is assumed to be a constant. The problem is, what is the optimum value of Q, given Y, C, and S, if we purchase an equal amount in every procurement? The sum of the total carrying cost and total procurement cost is

$$\frac{QC}{2} + \frac{SY}{Q}.$$

Setting the derivative of this with respect to Q equal to zero, we obtain

$$Q = \sqrt{\frac{2YS}{C}} = \text{a constant} \times \sqrt{Y}.$$

Since the average inventory holding is $\frac{Q}{2}$ (if the purchase is made exactly when the inventory is exhausted), the inventory holding is in proportion to the square root of expected sales.

The second alternative hypothesis is the one presented in the empirical studies of inventory cycles by Mack, Stanback, and Zarnowitz. The hypothesis states that the (desired) inventory-sales ratio $\tilde{\alpha}_r(t)$ is *not* constant, but depends upon the supply conditions of the commodities. This is from the standpoint of the purchasing departments. When supply is easy, the procurement lag is short, the chance of orders being cancelled is small, prices are stable or might have a chance of future decline, careful selection among different qualities of commodities is feasible, etc. All these conditions tend to reduce the holding of desired inventory relative to sales. On the other hand, when supply is tight, the procurement lag is lengthened, every buyer is eager, as a result of which prices tend to rise; rising prices induce the purchasing departments to place advance orders to cover far future sales, and so on. All these conditions tend to increase the desired inventory relative to sales.

It is not easy to find a good indicator for supply conditions. In the present test we use the change in the wholesale price index for other than food and farm products as the index of supply conditions. It is true that this index includes the prices of raw materials which are not sold in department stores. However, when supply conditions are tight in the expansion phase of business cycles, these conditions appear most clearly in the prices of raw materials. Since, as mentioned above, we do not have a satisfactory price index for department store sales or purchases, the wholesale price index for other than food and farm products is one of the best available indicators of supply conditions.[6a]

[6a] Ruth P. Mack suggested a recalculation of the present test by using other indicators of supply conditions.

The reason why the *change* in the wholesale price rather than the *level* of the price is used is that according to a dynamic economic theory the rate of change in the price is roughly in proportion to the magnitude of excess demand (the difference between the quantities demanded and the quantities supplied at a given price level). We must be careful about the lead-lag relationship involved in the effect of the change in wholesale price upon inventory holdings. The change in wholesale price is used as a proxy for the abstract concept, "supply conditions," but the change in this price might lag behind "supply conditions." On the other hand, "supply conditions" can influence inventory holdings only after they are realized by businessmen, and their *realization* of "supply conditions" might also lag behind "supply conditions." We cannot tell on a priori grounds which of the two lags would be greater. Thus we must accept the Mack-Stanback-Zernowitz hypothesis as long as the change in wholesale price is closely related to inventory holdings, even though the former lags behind the latter.

It is true that the assumption of the constant distribution of the weights in

$$\sum_{i \geq 0} \omega_i S_m(t+i)$$

is contradictory to the spirit of the "supply conditions" hypothesis, but if we drop this assumption, we can go no further. Therefore, let us keep it. It is quite easy to see how the "supply conditions" hypothesis can be transformed:

Assumption 5: $(13.3.1)$
Assumption 6: $(13.3.2)$ if a proper time unit is chosen

The "supply conditions" hypothesis to be tested

$(13.3.5)$ $\log I_m(t+\tau) - \log \sum_{i \geq 0} S_m(t+i)$

$= \beta[P(t+h+1) - P(t+h)] +$ a constant $+$ a noise that is independent of sales

$(\tau \geq 0)$
(h can have any signs)

(holding in the frequency band F where the discrepancy between the actual and desired inventory can be considered as random).

Here β is a constant parameter.

13.4 Testing Procedures with the Use of Cross-spectra and Partial Cross-spectra

Now we consider the implications of the three hypotheses in terms of the cross-spectra and partial cross-spectra in order to develop the testing procedures. We are concerned with the frequency band corresponding to the cyclical components, including both Mack's subcycles and business cycles. As explained in Chapter 12, this frequency band corresponds to $\frac{1}{96}$ c/m to $\frac{1}{16}$ c/m. In fact, if the frequency band F, mentioned above, does not contain this band, our tests must be abandoned.

All the hypotheses which we are going to test assert that there is a relationship among $\log I_m(t+\tau)$, $\log \sum_i \omega_i S_m(t+i)$, and $P(t+h) - P(t+h-1)$. The acceleration principle asserts that, if a proper time unit is chosen, the coherence between $\log I_m(t+\tau)$ and $\log \sum_i \omega_i S_m(t+i)$ is high, and more pointedly, that the gain of $\log I_m(t+\tau)$ over $\log \sum_i \omega_i S_m(t+i)$ is 1 (see (13.3.3)). On the other hand, the square root principle asserts high coherence between $\log I_m(t+\tau)$ and $\log \sum \omega_i S_m(t+i)$, if a proper time unit is chosen, but, more pointedly, that the gain of $\log I_m(t+\tau)$ over $\log \sum_i \omega_i S_m(t+i)$ is $\frac{1}{2}$ (see (13.3.4)). The "supply conditions" hypothesis asserts that, if a proper time unit is chosen, the multiple correlation (in regard to the frequencies corresponding to the cyclical component) between $\log I_m(t+\tau)$ on the one hand and $\log \sum \omega_i S_m(t+i)$ and $P(t+h) - P(t+h-1)$ on the other is high, and more pointedly, that the coherence in the partial cross-spectrum between $\log I_m(t+\tau)$ and $P(t+h) - P(t+h-1)$ must be high.

These implications of the three hypotheses contain many unknowns, and our first task is to see how we can test these hypotheses despite the lack of information. First, the problem of proper time unit can be disposed of, if we can agree on the statement that the proper time unit is shorter than the shortest period included in the cyclical component, i.e., shorter than 16 months, e.g., less than or equal to 8 months. The changes in the time unit do not affect the coherence, gain, and multiple correlation in regard to the frequency bands $\frac{1}{96} - \frac{1}{16}$ c/m, as long as the changes in the time unit are applied to all the time series, and as long as these changes do not reduce to zero the theoretical values of the spectra of these series in the frequencies with which we are concerned.[7]

The unknown parameters τ and h do not present any problem. The coherence and gain between $\log I_m(t+\tau)$ and $\log \sum \omega_i S_m(t+i)$ are equal to the coherence and gain between $\log I_m(t)$ and $\log \sum \omega_i S_m(t+i)$. Further, the coherence in the partial cross-spectrum among $\log I_m(t+\tau)$, $\log \sum \omega_i S_m(t+i)$ and $P(t+h) - P(t+h-1)$ is equal to the coherence among $\log I_m(t)$, $\log \sum \omega_i S_m(t+i)$ and $P(t) - P(t-1)$. Similarly the multiple correlation among the former set of three series is identical to the multiple correlation among the latter.

---

[7] The changes in the time unit involve first, some sort of moving average, and second shifting the Nyquist frequency.

So far, we have not considered exactly what sort of weighting, ω_i, should be used in

$$\sum_{i \geq 0} \omega_i S_m(t+i).$$

The maximum procurement lag for department stores seems to be about six months. Therefore, it is highly unlikely that the stores would keep an inventory for future sales beyond six months. Therefore, the non-zero weights ω_i must extend over at most six months. Further, all the weights must be non-negative. The sum of the weights $\sum \omega_i$ is immaterial for the purpose of our tests, and we can assume $\sum \omega_i = 1$. (If $\sum \omega_i = \bar{\omega}$, then

$$\log \left(\sum_i \omega_i S_m(t+i) \right) = \log \bar{\omega} + \log \left(\sum_i \frac{\omega_i}{\bar{\omega}} S_m(t+i) \right),$$

$$\sum_i \frac{\omega_i}{\bar{\omega}} = 1,$$

where $\log \bar{\omega}$ is a constant.)

We do not know the exact, relative distribution of ω_i's over six months. (It is probably skewed, as the mean is closer to zero than to six months.) Thus, the main problem in developing the testing procedure is how to test the three hypotheses without knowing the exact, relative distribution of ω_i's. In order to test the acceleration principle against the square root principle, we need to know the gain of $\log I_m(t)$ over $\log (\sum_{i \geq 0} \omega_i S_m(t+i))$ in the frequency band of cyclical components. *If this gain turns out to be nearer 1 than $\frac{1}{2}$, the acceleration principle is preferred to the square root principle and vice versa.* We can calculate the gain of $\log I_m(t)$ over $\log S_m(t)$ by using the available data. Therefore, if we can form some ideas as to the gain of $\log S_m(t)$ over $\log \sum_{i \geq 0} \omega_i S_m(t+i)$, then we can obtain some information as to the gain of $\log I_m(t)$ over $\log (\sum_i \omega_i S_m(t+i))$. It is hoped that the (skewed) moving average $\sum \omega_i$ would be roughly equal to a *simple* moving average of either 2, 3, or 4 months in regard to its effect upon the spectrum. We can calculate the gain of $\log S_m(t)$ over the logarithm of the *simple* moving average of $S_m(t)$ with length of either 2, 3, or 4 months, and use the result to ascertain the gain of $\log S_m(t)$ over $\log \sum_i \omega_i S_m(t+i)$. The result would be a plausible *band* (rather than the points) for this gain. Hence we obtain only a plausible band for the gain of $\log I_m(t)$ over $\log \sum \omega_i S_m(t+i)$, which is the ultimate goal of our calculation. If the band is too wide for our test, we must abandon the test.

This problem of unknown ω_i's does not arise in the comparison between the acceleration principle and the "supply conditions" hypothesis. This is because the coherence of the multiple correlation or partial correlation in regard to $\log I_m(t)$, $\log \sum \omega_i S_m(t+i)$ and $P(t) - P(t-1)$, is the same as the coherence of the multiple correlation or partial correlation in regard to log $I_m(t)$, log $S_m(t)$, and $P(t) - P(t-1)$ if log $\sum_i \omega_i S_m(t+i)$ can be represented approximately by a linear function of log $S_m(t+i)$ which seems to be true.

The data used for the present test are (1) the monthly, seasonally *unadjusted* series of department store sales and stocks as published in Federal Reserve Bulletin for the period from 1919 to 1961, and (2) the monthly, seasonally unadjusted series, for the same period, of the index of the wholesale prices of commodities other than the farm products and food (1957–59 = 100) collected by the Bureau of Labor Statistics and supplied by the National Bureau of Economic Research. It might be worth pointing out that although the trend-seasonal filter described in Section 12.6 is applied to all the time series used here, this does not affect the coherence and gain with which we are concerned.

13.5 Results of the Tests

First of all we must mention the results of two preliminary tests: (1) the cross-spectrum between actual sales and inventory investment which shows the significance of unintended investment in the frequency band corresponding to the cyclical component, and (2) the gain of log $S_m(t)$ over the logarithm of the simple moving average of $S_m(t)$ of length 2–4 months. As for the first test, the phase of the cross-spectrum is between $-\frac{1}{3}\pi$ and $\frac{1}{3}\pi$ in the frequency band between $\frac{2}{240}$ c/m and $\frac{15}{240}$ c/m; thus, there is no indication that unintended investment is quantitatively significant in the frequency band. As for the second test, the gain is nearly 1 in the frequency band between $\frac{1}{120}$ and $\frac{2}{120}$ c/m, and between 1 and 1.1 in the frequency band between $\frac{3}{120}$ c/m and $\frac{8}{120}$ c/m.

The coherence between log $I_m(t)$ and log $S_m(t)$ is very high. It is about 0.7 at $\frac{1}{48}$ c/m. However, the coherence in the higher frequencies within the cyclical component band is much lower. The multiple correlation coefficient between log $I_m(t)$ on the one hand and log $S_m(t)$ and $P(t)$ on the other is about 0.8 around $\frac{1}{48}$ c/m.

As for the test of the acceleration principle against the square root principle, the gain of log $I_m(t)$ over log $\sum \omega_i S_m(t + i)$ is greater than 1 in most of the frequencies corresponding to the cyclical component. Thus, the acceleration principle is preferred to the square root principle. Table 13.2 indicates the estimate of this gain of log $I_m(t)$ over log $S_m(t)$. Since the gain of log $S_m(t)$ over log $\sum_i \omega_i S_m(t + i)$ should be at least 1, (no matter what the distribution of ω_i's), and since the figures in Table 13.2 are greater than 1 in most of the frequencies listed there, there is no ambiguity affecting the decision leading to acceptance of the acceleration principle over the square root principle.[8] It turns out that the band estimate for the gain of $\log S_m(t)$ over $\log \sum_i \omega_i S_m(t + i)$ is not needed for this judgment.

TABLE 13.2
THE GAINS OF $\log I_m(t)$ OVER $\log S_m(t)$

Frequency	Estimates with Maximum Lag 120	Estimates with Maximum Lag 60
$\frac{3}{240}$ c/m	1.2	—
$\frac{4}{240}$ c/m	1.4	1.3
$\frac{5}{240}$ c/m	1.4	—
$\frac{6}{240}$ c/m	1.1	1.2
$\frac{7}{240}$ c/m	1.1	—
$\frac{8}{240}$ c/m	1.2	1.1
$\frac{9}{240}$ c/m	1.5	—
$\frac{10}{240}$ c/m	1.0	1.0
$\frac{11}{240}$ c/m	0.3	—
$\frac{12}{240}$ c/m	0.6	0.5
$\frac{13}{240}$ c/m	2.0	—
$\frac{14}{240}$ c/m	2.3	1.5

[8] The data used for $I_m(t)$ and $S_m(t)$ are indexes with 1947–1949 as the base period. When the logarithms of these data are taken, the units become immaterial for the comparisons among the three hypotheses.

As for the test of the acceleration principle against the "supply conditions" hypothesis, Table 13.3 indicates the coherence in the partial and multiple correlations. Comparing the partial correlation between the sales and the inventory on the one hand and the partial correlation between the "supply conditions" and the inventory, we observe in Table 13.3 that the explanatory power of the "supply conditions" is only slightly less than that of the sales. We also observe that the addition of the "supply conditions" to the sales significantly improves the multiple correlation. Thus, we must conclude that the "supply conditions" hypotheses is useful.

TABLE 13.3

COHERENCE IN THE PARTIAL AND MULTIPLE CORRELATIONS

Frequency	Estimates of Coherence in the Partial Correlation between $\log S_m(t)$ and $\log I_m(t)$	Estimates of Coherence in the Partial Correlation between $P(t) - P(t-1)$ and $\log I_m(t)$	Estimates of Coherence in the Multiple Correlation between $\log S_m(t)$ and $P(t) - P(t-1)$ on the one hand and $\log I_m(t)$ on the other
$\frac{2}{120}$ c/m	0.5	0.4	0.8
$\frac{3}{120}$ c/m	0.4	0.4	0.7
$\frac{4}{120}$ c/m	0.5	0.4	0.7
$\frac{5}{120}$ c/m	0.3	0.3	0.6
$\frac{6}{120}$ c/m	0.1	0.4	0.5

13.6 Different Assumptions as to Sales Expectations and Their Effect upon the Results of the Tests

In the previous sections we have assumed that the expectation of sales is formed in such a way that the forecast error is a random noise that is independent of sales. In the present section we shall analyze what difference appears in the results of the tests if we adopt different assumptions about the sales expectation. In neither the previous sections nor in the present section, are the assumptions as to the sales expectation a part of the hypotheses to be tested.

In the kind of business where seasonal variation is important—and department stores are such businesses—one frequently compares the sales in the current month with the sales in the *same* month in the previous year. Let us suppose that this ratio plays a vital role in sales expectation.

It would simplify our analysis tremendously if we reformulate the acceleration principle and the other two hypotheses, as hypotheses on $I_m(t)$ and $S_m(t)$ rather than on $I_r(t)$ and $S_r(t)$. To be more concrete, we formulate the acceleration principle as the assertion that

$$\tilde{\alpha}_m(t) \equiv \frac{\tilde{I}_m(t, t)}{\sum_{i \geq 0} \omega_i \tilde{S}_m(t+i, t)}$$

is a constant, apart from its random fluctuation. The square root principle is reformulated similarly as the assertion of the relationship between $\tilde{I}_m(t, t)$ and the square root of $\sum_{i \geq 0} \omega_i \tilde{S}_m(t+i, t)$. Obviously, the formulation in terms of real quantities, as in Section 13.2, is desirable, but, once we introduce a sophisticated assumption as to sales expectation, this formulation becomes too cumbersome.

From this point on, sales and inventory are always monetary values, and therefore, we use the symbols S_t and I_t (rather than $S_m(t)$ and $I_m(t)$ used before) to represent the sales and inventory in monetary values in period t. We still use $\sim$ to represent the expected value or desired value.

Following the practice of comparing adjacent years, we first assume that a certain ratio, R_t, is used to project the *actual* sales in the last (current) year into the *expected* sales in the current (or next) year, no matter what months they refer to. Thus,

(13.6.1) $$\frac{\tilde{S}_{t+i, t}}{S_{t+i-12}} = R_t \quad \text{for all relevant } i\text{'s}$$

where $\tilde{S}_{t+i, t}$ is the expected sales for period $t+i$, as of the present time, t.

Thus the formation of sales expectation is transformed into the formation of the expectation for R_t. We can introduce a now well known hypothesis as to the formation of expectation, i.e., expected value is a weighted moving average of past actual values. A special case of this hypothesis can be derived from an intuitively meaningful hypothesis, called adaptive expectation by Marc Nerlove and others, that expected value $\tilde{x}_{t+1, t}$ of any variable x is obtained by taking into account the past error of expectation, i.e.,

$$\tilde{x}_{t+1, t} = \tilde{x}_{t, t-1} + r(x_t - \tilde{x}_{t, t-1}).$$

This latter hypothesis implies

$$\tilde{x}_{t+1,t} = r \sum_{j \geq 0} (1-r)^j x_{t-j}$$

which is a special case of the hypothesis that expected value is a weighted average of past actual values.[8a] R_t can now be considered as being generated by a sort of moving average of the time series $\dfrac{S_{t-1}}{S_{t-13}}, \dfrac{S_{t-2}}{S_{t-14}}, \ldots$

For the purpose of combining the sales expectation with the hypotheses with which we are concerned, it would be more convenient if we use a geometric mean in this moving average, i.e.,

$$(13.6.2) \qquad \log R_t = \sum_{j=1}^{\infty} \mu_{-j}(\log S_{t-j} - \log S_{t-12-j})$$

We shall make one modification of (13.6.2) before we combine it with (13.6.1). It is possible that S_{t+i-12} reflects some abnormal situations that are peculiar to the period $t+i-12$. In case of department stores the peculiarities might be due to consumers behaviors but could very well be due to the department stores themselves; e.g., an attempt to eliminate unintended inventory holding by price reduction or abnormal increase of selling costs, which is apparently done occasionally but not persistently. To the extent to which such peculiarities should be taken into account in the formation of the expectation of R_t, (13.6.2) needs a modification.[8b] We shall assume that the effects of such peculiarities can be considered as a noise that is independent of sales, if a sufficiently long time unit is chosen. (A similar procedure has been adopted for the treatment of the discrepancy between desired and actual inventory holding.) Thus, for a proper time unit,

$$(13.6.2) \qquad \log R_t = \sum_{-j} (\log S_{t-j} - \log S_{t-12-j}) + \text{a noise that is inde-}$$
$$\text{pendent of sales}$$

We can now make the following representation of sales expectation:

$$(13.6.3) \qquad \log \sum_{i \geq 0} \omega_i \tilde{S}_{t+i} = \log \sum_{1} \omega_i S_{t+i-12}$$
$$+ \sum_{j=1}^{\infty} \mu_{-j}(\log S_{t-j} - \log S_{t-12-j})$$
$$+ \text{a noise}$$

[8a] This hypothesis has been successfully used in many different applications, agriculture, inflation, demand for cash balances, consumption function, etc. Further it is interesting to note that this hypothesis is consistent with a well known observation as to the formation of expectation, underestimation of changes. For this underestimation and also a test of other hypotheses on the formation of expectation, see H. Theil, *Economic Forecast and Policy*, chapters 4, 5, and 6.

[8b] This was pointed out to the author by Michael D. Godfrey and Ruth P. Mack.

When we make an assumption as to the unintended investment that, for a properly chosen length of time unit,

$$\log \tilde{I}_t = \log I_{t+\tau} + \text{a noise}$$

(the same assumption was made in the previous test), then the acceleration principle becomes

$$\log I_{t+\tau} = \log \sum_{i \geq 0} \omega_i S_{t+i-12} + \sum_{j=1}^{\infty} \mu_{-j}(\log S_{t-j} - \log S_{t-12-j})$$
$$+ \text{a noise};$$

the square root principle becomes

$$\log I_{t+\tau} = \tfrac{1}{2} \log \sum_{i \geq 0} \omega_i S_{t+i-12} + \tfrac{1}{2} \sum \mu_{-j}(\log S_{t-j} - \log S_{t-12-j})$$
$$+ \text{a noise};$$

and finally, the "supply conditions" hypothesis becomes

$$\log I_{t+\tau} = \log \sum_{i \geq 0} \omega_i S_{t+i-12} + \sum_{j=1}^{\infty} \mu_{-j}(\log S_{t-j} - \log S_{t-12-j})$$
$$+ \beta[P(t+h+1) - P(t+h)] + \text{a noise}.$$

For the test of the "supply conditions" hypothesis and the acceleration principle we have used in the previous sections, the partial coherence between $\log I_t$ and $P(t-1) - P(t)$ after eliminating the effect of $\log S_t$. Since the coherence between $\log S_t$ and $\log \sum_i \omega_i S_{t+i-12} + \sum_j \mu_{-j}$ $(\log S_{t-j} - \log S_{t-12-j})$ must be nearly unity[9] in frequency band of the cyclical component, the partial coherence mentioned above is practically equivalent to the partial coherence between $\log I_t$ and $P(t-1) - P(t)$ after eliminating $\log \sum_i \omega_i S_{t+i-12} + \sum \mu_{-j}(\log S_{t-j} - \log S_{t-12-j})$, which we need for testing the "supply conditions" hypothesis in the present section. Therefore, *the result of the test of the acceleration principle against the "supply conditions" hypothesis is not different from the one which we obtained in the previous section.*

The result of the test of the acceleration principle against the square root principle undergoes only one change, which, however, is an important one. In the previous test we estimated the gain of $\log S_t$ over $\log \sum_i \omega_i S_{t+i}$. In the present test we must estimate the gain of $\log S_t$ over $\log \sum \omega_i S_{t+i-12} + \sum_{j=1}^{\infty} \mu_{-j}(\log S_{t-j} - \log S_{t-12-j})$. Since the values of ω_i's and μ_{-j}'s are not known, all we can do is to set reasonable upper and lower bounds of this gain by using a reasonable class of possible values of ω_i's and μ_{-j}'s.

---

[9] The coherence *must be* unity, if there exist some weights γ_i's such that $\log \sum_i \omega_i S_{t+i-12} = \sum_i \gamma_i \log S_{t+i-12}$, so that $\log \sum_i \omega_i S_{t+i-12} + \sum_j \mu_{-j}(\log S_{t-j} - \log S_{t-12-j})$ is a *linear* transformation of $\log S_t$.

Let us assume that the following conditions (1), (2), and (3) set forth a reasonable class of possible values of ω_i's and μ_{-j}'s. (1) The moving average $\sum \omega_i$ in $\log \sum_i \omega_i S_{t+i-12}$ is equivalent to a simple one-sided moving average of $\log S_{t+i-12}$ with a length of 2 or 3 months, as far as the relationship of the results of these moving averages to $\log S_t$ (in terms of gain and phase) is concerned in the frequency band between $\frac{1}{48}$ c/m and $\frac{1}{24}$ c/m. (In Section 13.4 we commented on $\sum \omega_i = 1$.) (2) When we put $\mu = \sum_{j=1}^{\infty} \mu_{-j}$, then $1 \geq \mu \geq \frac{1}{2}$. For the expectation of a variable that should fluctuate around 1 (R_t is such a variable) $\mu \leq 1$ reflects a widely observed phenomenon, under estimation of changes. (3) The moving average of $\log S_t - \log S_{t-12}$ in (13.7) is equivalent to a simple one-sided moving average of $\mu(\log S_t - \log S_{t-12})$ with some length between 3 and 9 months, in so far as the relationship of the results of these moving averages to $\log S_t - \log S_{t-12}$ (in terms of gain and phase) is concerned in the frequency band between $\frac{1}{48}$ c/m and $\frac{1}{24}$ c/m.

Let us put

$$S_1(\omega) = \text{spectrum of } \log \sum_i \omega_i S_{t+i-12}$$

$$S_2(\omega) = \text{spectrum of } \sum_j \mu_{-j}(\log S_{t-j} - S_{t-12-j})$$

$$S_3(\omega) = \text{spectrum of } \log \sum_i \omega_i S_{t+i-12} + \sum_j \mu_{-j}(\log S_{t-j} - \log S_{t-12-j}).$$

Then,

(13.6.4) $\quad S_3(\omega) \approx S_1(\omega) + S_2(\omega) + 2\sqrt{S_1(\omega)S_2(\omega)} \cos \theta(\omega)$

where $\cos(\omega)$ is the phase difference between $\log \sum \omega_i S_{t+i-12}$ and $\sum_j \mu_{-j}(\log S_{t-j} - \log S_{t-12-j})$. This is because the coherence between $\log \sum \omega_i S_{t+i-12}$ and $\sum_j \mu_{-j}(\log S_{t-j} - \log S_{t-12-j})$ must be almost unity in the frequency band of the cyclical component. (In general, when (i) the coherence between x_t and y_t is unity, (ii) $z_t = x_t + y_t$, (iii) Sx, Sy, Sz, and Cxy are respectively the spectrum of x_t, of y_t, of z_t, and the cross-spectrum between x_t and y_t, then

$$Sz = Sx + Sy + 2Re(Cxy)$$

$$= Sx + Sy + 2\sqrt{SxSy} \cos \theta(\omega)$$

where Re means the real part and $\theta(\omega)$ is the phase of the cross-spectrum Cxy.)

If we accept (1), (2), and (3), we can evaluate the upper and lower bounds of $S_1(\omega)$, $S_2(\omega)$ and $\theta(\omega)$, and, from these upper and lower bounds and (13.6.4), we can obtain the upper and lower bounds of $S_3(\omega)$.

Then the gain for which we are trying to set the upper and lower bounds, i.e., the gain of $\log S_t$ over $\log \sum_i \omega_i S_{t+i-12} + \sum_j \mu_{-j}(\log S_{t-j} - \log S_{t-12-j})$ is roughly equal to the ratio of the spectrum of $\log S_t$ over $S_3(\omega)$, because the coherence between the two must be nearly unity in the frequency of the cyclical component. Therefore, we shall set the upper and lower bounds to $S_1(\omega)$, $S_2(\omega)$, and $S_3(\omega)$ *using the spectrum of $\log S_t$ as the unit of measuring these spectra.*

First, at $\omega = \dfrac{2\pi}{24}$ c/m

$$S_1(\omega) = 0.99^a \leftrightarrow 0.95^b$$

$$S_2(\omega) = 4 \times 1 \times 0.95^c \leftrightarrow 4 \times \tfrac{1}{4} \times 0.60^d$$

$\left(\text{The filter function for } y = \log S_t - \log S_{t-12} \text{ and }\right.$

$x = \log S_t \text{ is 4 at } \omega = \dfrac{2\pi}{24}.\Big)$

$$\theta(\omega) = \frac{2\pi}{24}(12 - 1^b - 4^d) \leftrightarrow \frac{2\pi}{24}(12 - 0.5^a - 1^c)$$

$\left(\text{The transfer function for } y = \log S_t - \log S_{t-12} \text{ and }\right.$

$x = \log S_t \text{ has zero angle at } \omega = \dfrac{2\pi}{24}.\Big)$

In obtaining the upper and lower bounds we must remember that between $S_1(\omega)$ and $S_2(\omega)$ on the one hand, and $\theta(\omega)$ on the other, numbers having the same superscripts a, b, c, d, must be combined to calculate (13.6.4). Then we obtain 2.7 as the upper bound and 0.2 as the lower bound for $S_3(\omega)$. This range is so large that we *cannot* test between the acceleration principle and the square root principle about the frequency $\dfrac{1}{24}$ c/m.

Second, at $\omega = \dfrac{2\pi}{48}$ c/m

$$S_1(\omega) = 1.0$$

$$S_2(\omega) = 2 \times 1 \times 1.0^c \leftrightarrow 2 \times \tfrac{1}{4} \times 0.9^d$$

$\left(\text{The filter function for } y = \log S_t - \log S_{t-12} \text{ and } x = \log S_t\right.$

$\text{is 2 at } \omega = \dfrac{2\pi}{48}.\Big)$

$$\theta(\omega) = \frac{2\pi}{48}(12 - 1 + 6 - 4^d) \leftrightarrow \frac{2\pi}{48}(12 - 0.5 + 6 - 1^c).$$

$\left(\text{The transfer function for } y = \log S_t - \log S_{t-12} \text{ and }\right.$

$\left. x = \log S_t \text{ has the angle } \dfrac{\pi}{4} \text{ at } \dfrac{2\pi}{48}.\right)$

The upper and lower bounds to $S_3(\omega)$ are, respectively, 2.3 and 0.7. Again this range is so large that we *cannot* test between the acceleration principle and the square root principle.

One possible set of values of μ_{-j}'s is not included in the conditions (2) and (3) mentioned on the previous page. This is the case where

$$R_t = \frac{S_{t-1}}{S_{t-13}} + \text{a white noise,}$$

i.e., R_t is obtained by a simple projection of $\dfrac{S_{t-1}}{S_{t-13}}$. In this case $\mu = 1$, $\mu_{-1} = 1$, $\mu_{-j} = 0$ for all j not equal to 1. When $\omega = \dfrac{2\pi}{24}$ c/m, the value of $S_3(\omega)$ is nearly 1, and at $\omega = \dfrac{2\pi}{48}$ c/m it is about 3, both in terms of the spectrum of $\log S_t$. Therefore, the gain of $\log S_t$ over $\log \sum \omega_i S_{t+i-12}$ $+ (\log S_{t-1} - \log S_{t-13})$ is about 1 at $\dfrac{1}{24}$ c/m and about 0.3 at $\dfrac{1}{48}$ c/m. Using the figures in Table 13.2 we conclude that the square root principle is preferred to the acceleration principle at $\dfrac{1}{48}$ c/m but the acceleration principle is preferred to the square root principle at $\dfrac{1}{24}$ c/m.

In short, we must conclude that *preference as between the acceleration principle and the square root principle depends upon the sales expectation very sensitively*, and, without further research on the sales expectation, no significant conclusion can be derived.[10]

13.7 Treatment of Outstanding Orders
Some Problems to be Solved

Each of the three hypotheses, as treated in the previous sections, ignores the fact that outstanding orders and inventory can play a somewhat similar role.[11] As mentioned earlier, the acceleration principle is considered mostly from the position of sales department. When we consider the purchasing department, we immediately realize that, under ordinary supply conditions, the purchasing department can rely upon the goods

---

[10] The available anticipations data are too short for study of the cyclical component by cross-spectral analysis.

[11] Ruth P. Mack first pointed this out. See footnote 3.

on outstanding orders to meet future demand, just as it can upon the inventory. In the case of department stores, the aggregate value of outstanding orders amounts to about half of the aggregate value of inventory. It is true, of course, that outstanding orders are normally inferior substitutes for inventory holding because the goods on outstanding orders may not arrive on time to serve as a buffer for unexpected demand. We shall study outstanding orders in the present section.

Let us first reformulate the three hypotheses in order to treat outstanding orders. Suppose that the managers of department stores are examining their inventory and outstanding orders as of the end of period $t - 1$. They must compare (1) the sales expectation for the period from t to $t + T$, (T is left unspecified) with (2) the inventory which they now have as of the end of period $t - 1$, and the goods on outstanding orders which are expected to arrive during the period from t to $t + T$. If they think that the (2) is not enough, then they would issue new orders in the coming period. If they think that the (2) is excessive, they can gradually deplete the inventory and outstanding orders by not issuing new orders or cancelling some orders until the proper balance is regained between the sales expectation on the one hand and the inventory and outstanding orders on the other.

We must make two assumptions which are not a part of the hypotheses to be tested. Once we treat explicitly outstanding orders, it is obvious that we should consider not only the aggregate value of outstanding orders but also its structure in regard to the expected arrival time. But no data are available for the structure of outstanding orders and, therefore, in our reformulation of the three hypotheses we must ignore the structure of outstanding orders. Thus the first assumption we make is that the changes in the structure of outstanding orders, as they have taken place in the period for which the data are used for our study, have nothing to do with the relationship between sales expectation on the one hand, and inventory and outstanding orders on the other.

The unintended holding of inventory and outstanding orders poses the same difficulty as in the previous sections. The second assumption which we make is that when a proper length of time unit is chosen, the unintended holding is random and independent of sales; and further, that this proper length of time unit is less than 16 months, the shortest cycle within the cyclical component. As we have described in previous sections, the change in time unit does not affect the derivation of our conclusions concerning the frequency band of cyclical components.

Let I_{t-1} and 0_{t-1} be the inventory and outstanding orders as of the end of period $t - 1$, let N_t be the new orders which will be issued during the next period, t, and let $\tilde{S}_{t+i}$ be the expected sales for period $t + i$. When the two assumptions above are made, all the three hypotheses can be represented as a special case of

(13.7.1) $\log \left[I_{t-1} + \beta_{t-1}(O_{t-1} + N_t) \right]$
$$= \alpha \log \left[\sum_{i \geqq 0} \omega_i \tilde{S}_{t+i} \right] + \text{a constant} +$$

a noise that is independent of sales.

If $\alpha = 1$ and β_t is a constant, then we obtain the acceleration principle. If $\alpha = \frac{1}{2}$ and β_t is a constant, then we obtain the square root principle. We can have an essence of the "supply conditions" hypothesis when β_t is not a constant because the extent to which the outstanding orders can be relied upon as a substitute for inventory holding depends upon the supply conditions. Thus, if β_{t-1} is a function of the change in the price, $P_{t-1} - P_{t-2}$, then we obtain the "supply conditions" hypothesis. We can also obtain the hybrid of the acceleration principle and the "supply condition" hypothesis in the case where $\alpha = 1$ and β_t is a function of $P_{t-1} - P_{t-2}$, and also the hybrid of the square root principle and the "supply conditions" hypothesis in the case where $\alpha = \frac{1}{2}$ and β_t is a function of $P_{t-1} - P_{t-2}$.

In order to specify the "supply conditions" hypothesis in a testable form, we linearize the dependence of β_t upon the price changes, i.e.,

$$\beta_{t-1} = a - b(P_{t-1} - P_{t-2})$$

where P_t is the wholesale price index (excluding food and farm products) for a month t. There are three conditions which a and b must satisfy on a priori grounds. According to (13.7.1) β_t dollars of outstanding orders plus newly issued orders are equivalent to 1 dollar of inventory holding. (1) Since outstanding orders are normally inferior substitutes for inventory holding, $1 > \beta_{t-1} \geqq 0$ for all t's. Given the data for P_t, this sets a certain restriction to the values of a and b. (2) When the price P_t increases, "supply conditions" worsen and hence the extent to which one can rely upon the outstanding orders declines. Hence $b \geqq 0$. For a given amount of expected sales in (13.7.1), this means that the worse the "supply conditions", the greater the total dollar value of inventory and outstanding orders. (3) Since $\beta_{t-1} = a$ when $P_{t-1} = P_{t-2}$, condition (1) implies $1 > a \geqq 0$.

Our testing procedure essentially consists of the estimation of the coherence and gain between the time series

(13.7.2) $\log \left[I_{t-1} + \{a - b(P_{t-1} - P_{t-2})\}(O_{t-1} + N_t) \right]$

and the time series

(13.7.3) $\log \sum_{i \geqq 0} \omega_i \tilde{S}_{t+i}$

The first time series (13.7.2) can be generated by using the available monthly, seasonally unadjusted data for I_t, 0_t, and N_t and the possible, alternative values of a and b. We have chosen the following values of a and b, all of which satisfy the three conditions mentioned above.

$$
\begin{array}{ll}
a = 0.8 & b = 0 \\
a = 0.8 & b = 1 \\
a = 0.8 & b = 2 \\
a = 0.8 & b = 3 \\
a = 0.5 & b = 0 \\
a = 0.5 & b = 1 \\
a = 0.5 & b = 2 \\
\end{array}
$$

(The scale of b depends upon the scale of P_t. In the above list, the ordinary scale for index member with base 100 is used for P_t.) Given the value of a, this table contains both the minimum and maximum values of b, that satisfy conditions 1, 2, and 3.

In the previous section we have shown that the gain of (13.7.3) upon log S_t depends very sensitively upon the specific formulae by which sales expectation is formed. In the present section we will go back to the assumption that forecast errors are random, the assumption used in Sections 13.2–13.4.

The data used for the test cover the period from January 1947, to June 1961. Actually data are available for the period since February, 1941, but the data prior to 1947 were eliminated because under price control the price index obviously does not reflect "supply conditions." The testing procedures used in the present section are so similar to those described in Section 13.4 that we shall not repeat their explanation.

The results of the tests turned out to be roughly the same as in Section 13.5. For all the value of a and b presented above, the acceleration principle is better than the square root principle both around $\frac{1}{48}$ c/m and $\frac{1}{24}$ c/m. (It must be admitted, however, that the data used are not long enough to analyze $\frac{1}{48}$ c/m properly.) The "supply conditions" hypothesis does not fare well in the present test. Both around $\frac{1}{48}$ c/m and $\frac{1}{24}$ c/m the coherence between (13.7.2) and (13.7.3) goes down when the value of b increases, and thus the acceleration principle is clearly better than the "supply conditions" hypothesis.[12]

---

[12] The coherence is low in the frequency band beyond 1/24 c/m, but in this band the greater the value of b, the higher the coherence.

13.8 Conclusions

We have failed to derive any clear-cut conclusions as to the choice among the acceleration principle, the square root principle, and the "supply conditions" hypothesis. The reason for this failure, however, is not in the partial cross-spectral analysis but in the lack of adequate data, especially the lack of the data necessary to test the hypotheses on sales expectation. The availability of statistical techniques is but one of many conditions that determine what kind of empirical studies can be done. Without great advancements in other conditions the improvement of statistical techniques alone cannot produce a great result. Yet the development of spectral analysis is definitely a great contribution to the study of business fluctuations. In fact, the comparative tests among the three hypotheses on the inventory holdings *in regard to the cyclical components* cannot be done without the use of the cross-spectral analysis.

It is hoped that the present chapter has illustrated what we might be able to do in this field.

CHAPTER 14

PROBLEMS REMAINING

14.1   Some Problems to be Solved

New results invariably raise new problems. In this chapter the important gaps in the current theory and the obvious fields of generalization are pointed out in the hope that research workers will take up some of these problems. The problems are not presented in any particular order, although those clearly most important will be mentioned first.

(1) *Theory of Non-stationary Time Series*

Although a few papers have appeared which attempt to generalize spectral methods to certain non-stationary cases or which attempt general results for time series with no stationarity condition, the field is still virtually untouched. It is felt that the useful interpretations connected with the spectral approach may be available for certain classes of non-stationary series, but the boundaries and properties of these classes are required together with information as to whether or not economic series fall within these classes.

(2) *Generalization of Feedback Theory*

The method of determining how causality and feedback vary with frequency introduced in Chapter 7 is practical but crude. A more direct approach based on sounder theory is required. The importance of the normality assumption in Whittle's test needs to be determined, together with the robustness of the method when dealing with non-stationary series.

If it were possible to determine the direction of causality or feedback when the causality lag is less than the time interval used for recording the series, many currently important economic problems could be tackled with the data now available. It seems likely that the simultaneous equation approach may provide a method, although estimation procedures capable of dealing with time-trending coefficients need to be devised.

(3) *Time Series Data and Cross-sectional Data*

For certain economic problems both time series and cross-sectional data are available. The new techniques for analyzing time series need to be incorporated with cross-sectional methods to help derive the required relationships. Doubtless new methods of interpreting the results will arise.

(4) *Robustness of Spectral Methods*

Various problems of robustness arise, in particular the confidence bands on the estimated spectra assume near-normality and near-stationarity and it would be interesting to discover how important are these assumptions. The sampling theory for the estimated coherence, phase-angle, partial coherence, etc. also needs strengthening. Some of the various ways that economic series can be "disturbed" have been briefly considered in Chapter 11 but a more rigorous approach is needed.

(5) *Removal of Seasonal Component*

Many methods of removing a seasonal component from data have been suggested, but none are fully satisfactory as they do not obey the following two requirements: (i) if the data does not include any seasonal component, then the method should not alter the series, and (ii) removal should be carried up to the present moment of time.

As virtually any time series will not have zero power at the frequency bands corresponding to the seasonal, the current methods will be inclined to remove or reduce this power. However, this is not what is required. A satisfactory method would need to determine if the power at these bands was extraordinarily large compared to the power in neighboring bands; if it is the power should be reduced; if not, the method should remove nothing from the data.

The second requirement is particularly important in policy-making and a one-sided or non-symmetric filter may provide a method satisfying this requirement.

(6) *Economic Interpretation*

Throughout this work, we have attempted to interpret the statistical results in terms of familiar economic concepts. Such interpretations need further study and many of the laws, hypotheses, and assumptions of economics can perhaps be sharpened by the use of the concepts introduced in earlier chapters.

14.2 Conclusions

In this book, a number of techniques have been introduced along with a number of applications. It should be clear by now that no general, mechanical method of "analyzing" a time series or group of series is possible. Every group is likely to present particular problems of investigation or interpretation. What is required is a good grounding in the available techniques plus a large amount of experience in their use.

The future development of the analysis of economic series, and possibly of economics as a subject, will depend upon the experience gained in the use of the available methods. There is a continual feedback between the problems thrown up by actual investigation, and those advanced in methodology. For instance, if more information were available regarding the types of non-stationarity most commonly occurring in economics, the subsequent theory could be directed at this class. The current spectral theory is by no means complete, but should certainly provide a more powerful method of analysis and interpretation than has been hitherto available.

INDEX